ETHICAL STUDIES

ETHICAL STUDIES

BY

F. H. BRADLEY

SECOND EDITION
REVISED, WITH ADDITIONAL NOTES
BY THE AUTHOR

WITH AN INTRODUCTION BY

RICHARD WOLLHEIM

Die Philosophie soll nicht erst die substantielle Wahrheit geben, noch hat die
Menschheit erst auf die Philosophie zu warten gehabt, um das Bewusstseyn der
Wahrheit zu empfangen.—HEGEL.

THE CLARENDON PRESS · OXFORD

Oxford University Press, Walton Street, Oxford OX2 6DP

Oxford New York Toronto
Delhi Bombay Calcutta Madras Karachi
Petaling Jaya Singapore Hong Kong Tokyo
Nairobi Dar es Salaam Cape Town
Melbourne Auckland

and associated companies in
Berlin Ibadan

Oxford is a trade mark of Oxford University Press

Published in the United States by
Oxford University Press, New York

First published 1876
Second edition 1927
First published in paperback 1962
Reissued 1988
Reprinted 1989

ISBN 0–19–824110–0
ISBN 0–19–881039–3 (Pbk)

Printed in Great Britain by Biddles Ltd
Guildford and King's Lynn

PREFACE

TO THE SECOND EDITION

ETHICAL STUDIES appeared in 1876, was soon out of print, and has never been re-published. For many years stray copies of the book have been eagerly sought for, but for students and the general public it has remained practically unobtainable.

Written at a time when philosophical thought in England, with some striking exceptions, was stagnant under the domination of the Utilitarian school, the volume included a brilliant and incisive criticism of what the author held to be false in the reasoning and conclusions of the prevailing English philosophy. How far the book contributed to the advance of philosophic thought in England must be left to conjecture, but that it contains matter of permanent value can hardly be doubted. In the opinion of a contemporary it 'suffered from the excess of thought and experience which it contained . . . a page of it would dilute into a hundred of any other'.[1]

The reasons which for over forty years held the author firm in his refusal to reprint this, his first, book may be of interest.

In 1893 he referred to it as follows: 'a book which, in the main, still expresses my opinions . . . ⟨and⟩ would have been reprinted had I not desired to re-write it. But I feel that the appearance of other books, as well as the decay of those superstitions against which largely it was directed, has left me free to consult my own pleasure in the matter'.[2]

---

[1] *Life and Philosophy*, by Bernard Bosanquet, in *Contemporary British Philosophy*, 1924, p. 59.

[2] *Appearance and Reality*, p. 402, note.

His 'own pleasure' was 'to be in earnest with meta-physics' and 'give himself up to it',[1] and the reader of *Ethical Studies* will recognize (p. 247) that he was already chafing at the restrictions imposed by his subject.

Again, the book was highly polemical, and, as life advanced, polemics became increasingly distasteful to him. There is reason to believe that, had he been able to carry out his first intention of re-writing the book, much would have been softened or omitted. Destructive criticism was for him only one form of the quest for truth, and, formidable as it was in his hands, he never hesitated to turn the point against himself (see, for instance, p. 337, note).

Another, and perhaps still more characteristic, reason was his intense dislike of even appearing to assume the role of a moral teacher. A caustic and amusing expression of this will be found on p. 450 of *Appearance and Reality*.

But towards the end of his life a change came to his feeling on the matter. In 1920 he wrote: 'I have often regretted that this early work of mine has been so long out of print. I hope at some time to re-issue it with additional matter, but, so far as I can see, without re-writing it. For with the removal of some of its defects it would lose its connection with a certain date, and what I hope I may call its interest might otherwise be lessened.'

In the early summer of 1924 he began, in an interval of leisure, to make rough notes for that additional matter which he contemplated. But they were never completed, and the pages between 50 and 89 were left untouched at his death.

These rough notes, only a few of which he had in any degree re-written or revised, are incorporated in the present volume, practically as he left them, together with those changes of the text which he had intended. The new notes will easily be recognized by the square brackets in

[1] *Appearance and Reality*, p. 452.

which they are enclosed. They were obviously meant solely for his own further use, certainly not for publication in their present form. But, while this cannot be too strongly insisted on, and while some ambiguities remain, it is believed that they form a valuable addition for the student, both from the light they throw upon the writer's thought in its maturity, and as an example of that untiring search for truth which was his chief characteristic.

In publishing this edition of *Ethical Studies* the sister and brother of the author desire to offer their warm thanks to Professor H. H. Joachim for his invaluable advice on many points, and especially for his help in the editing of the new notes.

AUTHOR'S PREFACE

TO THE FIRST EDITION

THE object of this volume is not the construction of a system of Moral Philosophy. It is very far from attempting either an exhaustive or a systematic treatment of ethical questions. Nor is the Author so much as prepared to define the sphere of Moral Philosophy, to say what does fall within it and what does not.

The writer's object in this work has been mainly critical. He sees that ethical theories rest in the end on preconceptions metaphysical and psychological. He believes that many of the fundamental ideas now current, especially in England, are confused or even false; and he has endeavoured, by the correction of some of these, at least to remove what seem obstacles to the apprehension of moral facts. These Essays are a critical discussion of some leading questions in Ethics, and are so far connected that, for the most part, they must be read in the order in which they stand.

The writer knows how much is demanded by his task. It demands an acquaintance with the facts of the world which he does not possess; and it demands that clearness of view on the main conceptions which govern our thoughts, which comes, if at all, to the finished student of metaphysic. The reader must not expect this either.

These Essays may be dogmatic and one-sided. They were produced and are published because the writer knows no English moral philosophy which does not, rightly or wrongly, seem to him to be at least as one-sided and even more dogmatic. Whatever they may be, if they bring any fresh element to the chaos of our philosophical literature they will be of use to the student.

But the ideas brought forward in these pages are not new. The source of every argument might in most cases have been given, and the reader referred to the works of one or two great men; and it is because the substance of the whole is not original that the writer has made scarcely any acknowledgements in detail. He has come forward not because what he has to say is new, but because our literature compels the belief that to the larger part of our philosophical public, and even of our philosophers, a great deal of it must be both novel and necessary.

This must be his excuse if the polemical part of his work (and too much is polemical) appears anywhere wanting in respect towards authors of repute and merit. But he thinks that he has nowhere overstepped the fair limits of controversy, a controversy into which he never would have ventured, were it not too much the fashion to take no account of views which are now more than half a century old, and the neglect of which he is convinced has done much to preclude the possibility of a solution.

1876

CONTENTS

ESSAY I

THE VULGAR NOTION OF RESPONSIBILITY IN CONNEXION WITH THE THEORIES OF FREE-WILL AND NECESSITY   I

ESSAY II

WHY SHOULD I BE MORAL? 58

ESSAY III

PLEASURE FOR PLEASURE'S SAKE . . . 85

ESSAY IV

ESSAY V

ESSAY VI

ESSAY VII

INTRODUCTION

BRADLEY'S *Ethical Studies* first appeared in 1876, when its author, who had been elected to a fellowship at Merton College, Oxford, six years earlier, was 30. The reception it received was far from enthusiastic. Henry Sidgwick, reviewing it in the first volume of *Mind*, described it as 'rhetorical' and 'vehemently propagandist': he found it deficient in 'lucid exposition', the product of an 'uncritical dogmatism': and in his opinion the awareness it displayed of opposing views was 'always rather superficial and sometimes even unintelligent'. But it is the concluding sentence of Sidgwick's Critical Notice that is really revealing: 'On the whole his [Bradley's] book, though crude and immature, is certainly interesting and suggestive: perhaps all the more from its marked antagonism to current philosophical opinion.'

For it is important to realize that Bradley's *Ethical Studies* was in its day a highly heterodox book. So apt are we to identify nineteenth-century Oxford with its own peculiar variant of Idealist metaphysics, that it comes as something of a shock when we realize how late—and for that matter how short-lived—was the triumph of this particular tradition. When Bradley wrote, in ethics, in logic, in political thought, in the philosophy of mind Utilitarianism was still the dominant mode of thought. And in all these different fields Bradley thought it to be wrong, and viciously wrong. In its conception of knowledge as the accumulation of singular facts, in its attachment to the individual and in the equation of his ultimate good with the attainment of pleasure, in its commitment to democracy and to generalized humanitarian sentiment, and in its contented optimistic belief in the forces of Progress and of secular advance,

Bradley regarded it as dedicated to the cult of empty 'abstractions', the mere ghosts of human thinking. And as an intellectual force, quite apart from the actual ideas it professed, he saw it as a giant upas-tree suffocating all forms of free speculation.

It is the unorthodox nature of Bradley's point of view that accounts for the blazing invective of his style, for those excesses of irony and rhetoric which sweep his thought along, only too often into obscurity. And it is all part of the same fact that when in 1893 Bradley came to reconsider *Ethical Studies* and saw that many of the 'superstitions' against which he had written were now in decay, he felt that either the book would have to be rewritten or else it had better remain out of print.

On this last point, however, we need not and should not accept Bradley's own assessment of the matter. For undoubtedly the interest of *Ethical Studies* is not exclusively, nor even predominantly, historical. In matters of detail this has already received recognition. The criticism of Hedonism, as this is developed in Essay III, has long been considered a *locus classicus* for arguments against Utilitarianism, at least in its more traditional form. And the discussion of 'the vulgar notion of Responsibility' in Essay I must make a special appeal to the modern reader: endeavouring, as it does, to show that what is wrong or unacceptable in the two great classical theories on this subject, Free-Will and Necessity, is that they both pick upon, and exaggerate to the detriment of the whole, some one element in 'the ordinary view'.

But perhaps students of philosophy will increasingly go back to *Ethical Studies* not just for these isolated critical arguments, which can be detached from their context and independently utilized, but for the positive theory of morality that Bradley tries to develop across the length of the book. But if this is to happen, then it is extremely important that the principle upon which the various essays

have been put together should be properly appreciated.
For *Ethical Studies* is essentially *dialectical* in its structure.
Hegelian in many of its ideas, it is to an even greater extent
Hegelian in its method, in the way in which it works its
way forwards through different and conflicting theories. It
is Bradley's technique to start with one particular view of
morality, to examine its merits and its defects, and this
leads him on to another view of morality which, while
retaining as far as possible the merits of the original view,
will be free of its defects: this view in turn shows itself not
to be without error, and so the process of correction and
refinement goes on indefinitely. That this is the principle
upon which *Ethical Studies* is written has sometimes been
overlooked by critics, perhaps because of the assertiveness
with which at the time Bradley puts forward a view that
turns out ultimately to be merely provisional. In particular,
the theory of 'My Station and its Duties', considered in
Essay V, has—indeed from Sidgwick's review onwards—
often, and quite falsely, been identified with Bradley's own
ultimate position.

The unity of *Ethical Studies* lies in the attempt to give
a satisfactory interpretation to the thesis—which Bradley
regards as self-evidently true—that morality is 'self-
realization'. The first interpretation of this thesis that
Bradley considers is that provided by Hedonism, which,
as we have seen, was the prevailing orthodoxy of the day.
From this Bradley moves on to a kind of Kantian theory,
which would identify the realization of the self with the
exercise of a purely formal will. However, the lack of
content involved in this particular notion of the self leads
Bradley next to equate the self with the self of the social
organism: this is the doctrine of 'My Station and its Duties',
which Bradley goes some way to summarizing in the
notorious epigram 'To wish to be better than the world is
to be already on the threshold of immorality'. Ultimately
Bradley allows force to the obvious objections—as well as

a few more, which are rather less obvious—that can be brought against this moral theory, and so comes to postulate the theory of Ideal Morality. *Ethical Studies* concludes with a lengthy discussion of why it is that the realization of the good, as opposed to the bad, self is true self-realization.

One of the most interesting aspects of Bradley's ethical philosophy is the way in which he constantly endeavours to relate morality and its leading ideas to the study and analysis of the mind. In this respect Bradley may have a special significance for our day. For it is a very marked feature of the moral philosophy of the recent past that it has sedulously separated questions of philosophy from questions of psychology. This has been a very important thing to do, and has resulted in the careful distinction of differences traditionally obscured. But now that the differences have been firmly noted, it may well be the task of the moral philosophy of the immediate future no longer to hold apart the two aspects of human behaviour so distinguished. Moral philosophy, in other words, may revert from the tradition of Kant to that of Aristotle and Hume: if such a change is ever effected, *Ethical Studies* could be a benign and salutary influence upon its course.

RICHARD WOLLHEIM

July, 1961

ETHICAL STUDIES

ESSAY I

THE VULGAR NOTION OF RESPONSIBILITY IN CONNEXION WITH THE THEORIES OF FREE-WILL AND NECESSITY

WHAT is *not* the scope of this essay? We must begin with that, for round the phrases which appear in our title there exist 'perverse associations', which may lead our readers to expect, some this, and others that. And, because we think that some of these expectations will be disappointed, we will start with saying what it is that we do not propose to treat of.

The scope of this essay might have been the solution of one, or both, of two difficult problems. We might have asked what responsibility at bottom is; whether it implies necessity or freedom, and what these mean; and then we should have come to questions of abstract metaphysic. Or again, our task might have been the limitation of our accountability with reference to legal imputation, and here we should have had a juridical inquiry. But our object is not the solution of either one or the other of these questions.

What then is the end which we do set before us? It is a threefold undertaking: to ascertain first, if possible, what it is that, roughly and in general, the vulgar mean when they talk of being responsible; to ask, in the second place, whether either of the doctrines of Freedom and Necessity (as current among ourselves) agrees with their notions; and, in case they do not agree, lastly to inquire in what points or respects they are incompatible with them.

And, at first sight, this undertaking may seem to the reader both easy and worthless; easy, because what every one thinks must be known by all men; and worthless, because the theories of philosophers do not stand and fall with the opinions of the people. To a more thoughtful consideration, however, it will appear to be neither.

It is not so easy to say what the people mean by their ordinary words, for this reason, that the question is not answered until it is asked ; that asking is reflection, and that we reflect in general not to find the facts, but to prove our theories at the expense of them. The ready-made doctrines we bring to the work colour whatever we touch with them ; and the apprehension of the vulgar mind, at first sight so easy, now seems, because *we* are not vulgar, to present a difficulty. And to know the signification of popular phrases is, in the second place, not worthless. Not all our philosophy professes its readiness to come into collision with ordinary morality. On the subject of responsibility this is certainly the case ; the expounders of 'Free-Will' believe their teaching to be thoroughly at one with popular ideas, and even to be the sole expression and interpretation of them. So much does this weigh with many men, that their belief in vulgar moral accountability is the only obstacle to their full reception of Necessitarianism. And not to all of the disciples of Necessity has been given that strength of mind, which still survives in our Westminster Reviewers, and for which 'responsibility or moral desert in the vulgar sense' are terms which stand for 'horrid figments of the imagination' (*West. Rev.*, Oct. 1873, p. 311). But, if to any philosophy what we call responsibility is not yet a figment, then it can not be without interest to know, on the one side, the conclusions of that philosophy ; on the other side, the beliefs of the vulgar ; and whether the two can be reconciled with one another. This is the limit of our present essay. Beyond us lie the fields of metaphysic, which the reader must remember we are, so far as possible, not to enter but merely to indicate.

So much by way of preface ; what we have now to do is, first, to enter on a question of fact. What is the popular notion of responsibility? The popular notion is certainly to be found in the ordinary consciousness, in the mind of

the plain or non-theoretical man, the man who lives without having or wishing for opinions of his own, as to what
living is or ought to be.   And, to find this plain man, where
are we to go?   For nowadays, when all have opinions, and
too many also practice of their own; when every man
knows better, and does worse, than his father before him;
when to be enlightened is to be possessed by some wretched
theory, which is our own just so far as it separates us from
others; and to be cultivated is to be aware that doctrine
means narrowness, that all truths are so true that any truth
must be false; when 'young pilgrims', at their outset, are
'spoiled by the sophistry' of shallow moralities, and the
fruit of life rots as it ripens—amid all this 'progress of the
species' the plain man is by no means so common as he
once was, or at least is said to have been.   And so, if we
want a moral sense that has not yet been adulterated, we
must not be afraid to leave enlightenment behind us.   We
must go to the vulgar for vulgar morality, and there what
we lose in refinement we perhaps are likely to gain in
integrity.

Betaking ourselves, therefore, to the uneducated man, let
us find from him, if we can, what lies at the bottom of his
notion of moral responsibility.

What in his mind is to be morally responsible?   We see
in it at once the idea of a man's appearing to answer.   He
answers for what he has done, or (which we need not
separately consider) has neglected and left undone.   And
the tribunal is a moral tribunal; it is the court of conscience,
imagined as a judge, divine or human, external or internal.
It is not necessarily implied that the man does answer for
all or any of his acts; but it is implied that he might have
to answer, that he is liable to be called upon—in one word
(the meaning of which, we must remember, we perhaps do
not know), it is *right* that he should be subject to the
moral tribunal; or the moral tribunal has a *right* over him,
to call him before it, with reference to all or any of his
deeds.

He must answer, if called on, for *all* his deeds.   There

is no question of lying here; and, without lying, he can
disown none of his acts—nothing which in his heart or his
will has ever been suffered to come into being. They are all
his, they are part of his substance; he can not put them
on one side, and himself on the other, and say, 'It is not
mine; I never did it.' What he ever at any time has done,
that he *is* now; and, when his name is called, nothing
which has ever been his can be absent from that which
answers to the name. In this (real or supposed) juridical
sphere the familiar saying of Agathon,

μόνου γὰρ αὐτοῦ καὶ θεὸς στερίσκεται,
ἀγένητα ποιεῖν ἅσσ' ἂν ᾖ πεπραγμένα

is as inexorably true, as it is false when we pass into
a higher region, where imputation of guilt is as meaningless
as even the *Westminster Review* would have it be.

And he must account for all. But to give an account
to a tribunal means to have one's reckoning settled. It
implies that, when the tribunal has done with us, we do not
remain, if we were so before, either debtors or creditors.
We pay what we owe; or we have that paid to us which is
our due, which is owed to us (what we deserve). Further,
because the court is no civil court between man and man,
that which is owed to us is what *we pay* (alas for the figments of the unenlightened mind). In short, there is but
one way to settle accounts; and that way is punishment,
which is due to us, and therefore is assigned to us.

Hence, when the late Mr. Mill said, 'Responsibility
means punishment,' what he had in his mind was the
vulgar notion, though he expressed it incorrectly, unless on
the supposition that all must necessarily transgress. What
is really true for the ordinary consciousness; what it clings
to, and will not let go; what marks unmistakably, by its
absence, a 'philosophical' or a 'debauched' morality, is
the necessary connexion between responsibility and liability
to punishment, between punishment and desert, or the
finding of guiltiness before the law of the moral tribunal.
For practical purposes we need make no distinction between
responsibility, or accountability, and liability to punishment.

Where you have the one, there (in the mind of the vulgar) you have the other; and where you have not the one, there you can not have the other. And, we may add, the theory which will explain the one, in its ordinary sense, will also explain the other; and the theory which fails in the one, fails also in the other; and the doctrine which conflicts with popular belief as to one, does so also with regard to the other.

So far we have seen that subjection to a moral tribunal lies at the bottom of our answering for our deeds. The vulgar understand that *we* answer; that we answer not for everything, but only for what is ours; or, in other words, for what can be imputed to us. If now we can say what is commonly presupposed by *imputability*, we shall have accomplished the first part of our undertaking, by the discovery of what responsibility means for the people. And at this point again we must repeat our caution to the reader, not to expect from us either law or systematic metaphysics; and further to leave out of sight the slow historical evolution of the idea in question. We have one thing to do, and one only, at present—to find what lies in the mind of the ordinary man.

Now the first condition of the possibility of my guiltiness, or of my becoming a subject for moral imputation, is my self-sameness; I must be throughout one identical person. We do say, 'He is not the same man that he was,' but always in another sense, to signify that the character or disposition of the person is altered. We never mean by it, 'He is not the same *person*,' strictly; and, if that were our meaning, then we (the non-theoretical) should also believe, as a consequence, that the present person could not rightly be made to answer for what (not his self, but) another self had done. If, when we say, 'I did it,' the I is not to be the one I, distinct from all other I's; or if the one I, now here, is not the same I with the I whose act the deed was, then there can be no question whatever but that the ordinary notion of responsibility disappears.

In the first place, then, I must be the very same person

to whom the deed belonged ; and, in the second place, it must have belonged to me—it must have been *mine*. What then is it which makes a deed mine ? The question has been often discussed, and it is not easy to answer it with scientific accuracy ; but here we are concerned simply with the leading features of the ordinary notion. And the first of these is, that we must have an act, and not something which can not be called by that name. The deed must issue from my will; in Aristotle's language, the ἀρχή must be in myself. Where I am forced, there I do nothing. I am not an agent at all, or in any way responsible. Where compulsion exists, there my will, and with it accountability, do not exist. So far the ordinary consciousness is clear, and on this point we must not press it further. To fix the limits of compulsion ; to say where force ends, and where will begins ; to find the conditions, under which we may say, 'There was no possibility of volition, and there could have been none'[1]— is no easy matter, and fortunately one which does not concern us. [See more, Note A.]

Not only must the deed be an act, and come from the man without compulsion, but, in the second place, the doer must be supposed intelligent ; he must know the particular circumstances of the case. (Τὸ ἑκούσιον δόξειεν ἂν εἶναι οὗ ἡ ἀρχὴ ἐν αὐτῷ εἰδότι τὰ καθ᾽ ἕκαστα ἐν οἷς ἡ πρᾶξις.) If the man is ignorant, and if it was not his duty to know (for, supposing that to be his duty, the act, done in ignorance, is imputed to the will through the ignorance itself, which is criminally imputable), then the deed is not his act. A certain amount of intelligence, or 'sense', is thus a condition of responsibility. No one who does not possess a certain minimum of general intelligence can be considered a responsible being; and under this head come imbecile persons, and, to a certain extent, young children. Further, the

---

[1] If, through my bad habits, it is my fault that what presumably would not have been compulsion amounted to it in my case, then I am responsible for what I do under such compulsion. The degree is of course another matter.

person whose intellect is eclipsed for a time—such eclipse being not attributable to himself—can not be made accountable for anything. He can say, and say truly, 'I was not myself'; for he means by his self an intelligent will.

Thirdly, responsibility implies a *moral*[1] agent. No one is accountable, who is not capable of knowing (not, who *does* not know) the moral quality of his acts. Wherever we can not presume upon a capacity for apprehending (not, an actual apprehension of) moral distinctions, in such cases, for example, as those of young children and some madmen, there is, and there can be, no responsibility, because there exists no moral will. Incapacity, however, must not be imputable to act or wilful omission.

No more than the above is, I believe, contained in the popular creed. There are points which that creed has never encountered, and others again where historical development has, to some extent, been the cause of divergences.

If we asked the plain man, What is an act? he could not possibly tell us what he meant by it. The problem, In what does an act consist? has never come home to his mind. To some extent we shall see the opinions of that mind, when we see (as we shall) what are *not* its opinions. For the present we may say, that what seems to lie at the bottom of its notion is this, that an act translates mere thoughts into corresponding external existence; that, by the mediation of the body, it carries what was only in the mind into the world outside the mind, in such a way that the changes thereby produced in the outer world are, on the other side, alterations in itself; and that in that quality

---

[1] *If* there are in fact any adult sane persons, of whom it can be said that (capacity or no capacity) they not only are without any notions of good and bad, but have never had any the smallest chance of having them, and so are incapable, and whose fault it therefore in no sense is that they are what they are, *then* such persons must be considered as out of the moral sphere, and therefore, in the court of conscience, irresponsible and lunatic (whatever they have to be in law). But what standard a man is to be *morally* judged by, is quite another question, which we do not discuss.

they all form part of, and are all for ever preserved in, the self.[1]

And there are points again, where ordinary morality shows divergences of opinion. In the absence of intelligence and moral capacity responsibility can not exist. A beast or an idiot is not accountable. But the vulgar could not tell us beforehand the amount of sense which is required, and, even in particular cases, would often be found to disagree amongst themselves. If we asked again about the relation of act to intent, we should find little more than confusion. What consequences are, and what are not, contained in the act itself, and how far are they contained? What, in such cases, is the degree of moral responsibility? Does a criminal state (e.g. drunkenness) make a man accountable for what he does in that state, and, if so, to what degree? How far, again, does a wrong act, done for an object innocent in itself, make the doer responsible for consequences issuing contrary to his intention? With regard to such points we should find a sterner and a softer view. One section would emphasize the act, and the other the (actual or possible) intention. The one sees crime committed, and is prone to neglect the mind of the doer; while the other is always ready to narrow the field of criminality, to see incapacity rather than guilt, and to make absence of crime in the intent carry its quality into the act.

[1] If we act 'without thinking', are we responsible? I am not concerned to decide whether we ever do so; but, given a case where thinking in no sense was, yet responsibility may be even there. The act may come from presence or absence of habits of mind, for the creation, or non-creation, or non-suppression of which we certainly are responsible. Our self means thought, and the act is the outcome and issue of our self. Let us take an instance: a man of violent disposition, accustomed to handle weapons, is insulted at table by another man. A knife is in his hand, with which he at once stabs. Is he responsible? Yes; the deed came not merely from his disposition—a man is more than his disposition; it came from his character, the habits which his acts have formed. These acts have issued from the thinking self, and the thinking self is therefore responsible for the outcome of the habits. Hence for our dreams, and for what may seem to be merely physical, we *may* be accountable. The description in the text, let me remark, applies only to an *overt* act.

To resume then: according to vulgar notions, a man must act himself, be now the same man who acted, have been himself at the time of the act, have had sense enough to know what he was doing, and to know good from bad. In addition, where ignorance is wrong, not to have known does not remove accountability, though the degree of it may be doubtful. And everything said of commission applies equally well to omission or negligence.

We have found roughly what the ordinary man means by responsibility; and this was the first task we undertook. We pass to the second, to see whether, and how far, the current theories of Freedom and Necessity (better, Indeterminism and Determinism) are consistent with his beliefs.

Let us first take the theory which goes by the name of the Free-will doctrine, and which exists apparently for the purpose of saving moral accountability. We have to ask, Is it compatible with the ordinary notions on the subject?

This doctrine, we are told, is the only one which asserts Freedom, and without liberty responsibility can not exist. And this sounds well: if we are not free to do as we will, then (on this point the plain man is clear) we can not be responsible. 'We must have liberty to act according to our choice': is this the theory? 'No, more than that; for that', we shall be told, 'is not near enough. Not only must you be free to *do* what you will, but also you must have liberty to *choose* what you will to do. It must be your doing, that you will to do this thing, and not rather that thing; and, if it is not your doing, then you are not responsible.'

So far, I believe, most persons would agree that the doctrine has not gone beyond a fair interpretation of common consciousness. On the whole I think this is so, if we except perhaps a class of acts we have mentioned above, sudden so-called 'instinctive' actions. For *if* responsibility must imply choice, and *if* it can be maintained that no alternatives, in these cases, came before the mind at all, that all reflection, and therefore all choice, was absent— *then*, on that showing, we should not in these cases be accountable; and hence, as a consequence, the free-will doctrine would come into collision with the vulgar mind, which holds that a man can act freely without exercising choice.

Let us pass by this, however, as a point which we need not discuss, and, on the whole, we are still at one with ordinary notions. To proceed—we are free to choose, but what does that mean? 'It means', will be the answer, 'that our choice is not necessitated by motives; that to will and to desire are different in kind; that there is a gap between them, and that no desire, or complication of desires, carries with it a forcing or compelling power over our volitions. My will is myself, and myself is superior to my desires, and exercises over them an independent faculty of choice, wherein lies freedom and with it responsibility.' And all this again, in the main, does not appear contrary to ordinary beliefs, unless it implies that we are able to act altogether in the absence of, and independent of, desire; and that seems certainly a curious idea, though we need not stop to consider it here.

But it is not right that we should learn the teaching of Free-will, as the opposite (real or supposed) of Necessitarianism, because as yet we do not know what the latter is. We must therefore ask, not what the Free-will theory is *not*, but what it is. What *is* then liberty of choice? 'Self-determination. I determine myself to this or that course.' Does that mean that I make myself do the act, or merely that my acts all issue from my will? 'Making is not the word, and very much more is implied than the latter. You are the uncaused cause of your particular volitions.' But does not what I am come from my disposition, my education, my habits? 'In this case certainly not. The ego in volition is not a result, and is not an effect, but a cause simply; and of this fact we have a certain and intuitive knowledge.' Or, if we express the answer in a different metaphysical language, it amounts to this: 'The I is a universal, which has the power to abstract from all its particulars, and to suspend itself over them, before in choice it takes any one

of them into itself, so as to realize that one, and itself
thereby. This I, in the act of " I will ", is the self, as pure I,
which is superior to all its contents, desires, &c., and
descends into them only by its own *libertas arbitrii*.'

We have stated the doctrine in its clearest form, without
troubling ourselves to keep too closely to our English
expositors. That to a large extent it rightly expresses
indubitable facts, the thoughtful reader will perceive. But
we are not to ask, Is it true, and if so, how far true? but to
find, if we can, how far it agrees with responsibility as
commonly accepted. And so, reflecting on the theory, we
see that, in the main, it is only the denial of the opposite
theory. It is positive, so far as it asserts the self to be
more than a collection of particulars, desires, &c., and to
be necessarily concerned in the actions which are imputed
to it. And so far the doctrine agrees well enough with
common ideas. But the chief bearing of its conclusion is
merely negative; and here, as we shall see, it comes into
sharp collision with vulgar notions of responsibility.

In this bearing, Free-will means Non-determinism. The
will is not determined to act by anything *else*; and, further,
it is not determined to act by anything *at all*. Self-determination means that the self, the universal, *may* realize
itself by and in this, that, and the other particular; but it
also implies that there is no reason why it should identify
itself with this one, rather than with that one; there is no
rational connexion between the two sides; there is nothing
in the self which brings this, and not that, act out of it.
Turn it as we will, the *libertas arbitrii* is no more at last
than *contingentia arbitrii*. Freedom means *chance*; you
are free, because there is no reason which will account for
your particular acts, because no one in the world, not even
yourself, can possibly say what you will, or will not, do
next. You are 'accountable', in short, because you are a
wholly 'unaccountable' creature.

We can not escape this conclusion. If we always can do
anything, or nothing, under any circumstances, or merely
if, of given alternatives, we can always choose either, then it

is always possible that any act should come from any man. If there is no real, no rational connexion between the character and the actions (as the upholder of 'Freedom' does not deny there is between the actions and the character), then, use any phrases we please, what it comes to is this, that volitions are contingent. In short, the irrational connexion, which the Free-will doctrine fled from in the shape of external necessity, it has succeeded only in reasserting in the shape of chance.

The theory was to save responsibility. It saves it thus. A man is responsible, *because* there was no reason why he should have done one thing, rather than another thing. And that man, and *only* that man, is responsible, concerning whom it is impossible for any one, even himself, to know what in the world he will be doing next; possible only to know what his actions are, when once they are done, and to know that they might have been the diametrical opposite. So far is such an account from saving responsibility (as we commonly understand it), that it annihilates the very conditions of it. It is the description of a person who is *not* responsible, who (if he is anything) is idiotic.

The doctrine of Indeterminism asserts that the actions are in no case the result of a given character, in a given position. The self, or the will, of Indeterminism is not the man, not the character at all, but the mere characterless abstraction, which is 'free', because it is indifferent. It has been well called 'a will which wills *nothing*'.[1]

But here we have not to investigate the doctrine, but to bring it into contact with ordinary life. Let us suppose a man of good character, innocent of theoretical reflections. Our apostle of Freedom would assure him of his responsibility, and our plain man would welcome and emphasize the statement. Our apostle would inform him that the secret of man's accountability was in his possession. He would

---

[1] 'The doctrine of Determinism is a will which *wills* nothing, which lacks the form of will; the doctrine of Indeterminism is a will which wills *nothing*, a will with no content.'—Erdmann, *Psychologie*, sec. 160, note. We shall come to the first part of this statement lower down.

be received with attention, though perhaps not belief. He might go on to say that a man was responsible, because he always had liberty of choice; and so far he might be followed. But, when he advanced, and began to explain that such freedom of choice must mean, that before a man acted, it was never certain how he would act, then, I think, he might get for an answer, 'that depends on what sort of man he is'. Perhaps at this point he might appeal to his hearer's consciousness, and put it to him, whether he was not aware that, on opportunities rising for the foulest crimes, he could not only do these acts if he would, but also that it was quite possible, in every case, that he should do them. Such a question, if asked, would be answered, I doubt not, by an indignant negative; and should a similar suggestion be made with respect to a friend or relation, the reply might not confine itself to words. What sayings in life are more common than, 'You might have known me better. I never could have done such a thing,' or 'It was impossible for me to act so, and you ought to have known that nothing could have made me'?

We have seen that responsibility (on the usual understanding of it) can only exist in a moral agent. And, if it be true of any man, that his actions are matters of chance, and his will in a state of equilibrium disturbed by contingency, then I think that the question whether such a being is a moral agent, is a question answered as soon as raised. And, if this is so, then, with the best of intentions (such good intentions are the ruin of thinking), the saviours of accountability have failed to save it. They may have held their own against the enemy, and borne in triumph their ark from the contest. But what is brought out of the battle is a very different thing from that which went in, or, perhaps, which never was there at all.

Having first seen what responsibility was for the vulgar mind, we have now also seen what it is (or ought to be) for the one of 'our two great schools'; and we have seen that the creed of the philosophical, so far, seems seriously different from that which the people hold by. In saying thus much we feel ourselves safe; but we are far indeed from suggesting that the belief of the philosopher is not every whit as superior in theory, as it doubtless, so far as we can conceive it realized, might in some respects prove convenient in practice.

But, be that as it may, the doctrine of Free-will does not square with popular views; and, bearing in mind that, of 'two great philosophies', when one is taken, but one remains, it is natural to think that Necessity, as the opposite of Free-will, may succeed in doing what its rival has left undone. The enemy, perhaps, after all will be our friend, and the saviour of the reality, and not of an Idolon.

The strict interpretation of the doctrine of Freedom is that *no* actions can be predicted; the plain man believes that at least *some* actions can be predicted with tolerable certainty; while the necessitarian affirms that, given the data, *all* our actions could be foretold beforehand.

But, at this point, the upholder of Liberty may threaten summarily to destroy us. 'Let my theory be as false', he may say, 'as I, on the other hand, am sure that it is true, yet about one thing there is no disputing. *If* human actions can be predicted, then responsibility is unmeaning; and the ordinary man, confused as he may be on other points, sees this well enough, and will tell you so if you ask him.'

If this were so, it would be waste of time to inquire any further, but I think it is not so; and, before we embarrass ourselves with exposition or criticism of necessitarian doctrine, it is necessary to get what light we can on the matter.

Is it a fact that the plain man objects to the prediction of his actions; and, if it is a fact, does the objection apply to all, or only to some? If he objects in some cases only, where does he not object, and where does he? And further, why does he object? What is the ground that underlies his objection? These questions must be answered, and they are not easy. It is hard to get the facts, and hard to interpret them; but I hope to suggest to the thoughtful reader what, if new to him, may be worth his consideration.

We have seen already that in certain cases the man who is not a philosopher has no objection to the mere prediction of his actions. On the contrary, he demands it. We saw that his notion of responsibility implied, together with rationality, a capacity for acting rationally; and further that this means to act with some regularity, to act so that your actions can be counted on, and, if counted on, then with more or less certainty predicted.

Nothing is clearer than that the plain man does not consider himself any less responsible, because it can be foretold of him that, in a given position, he is sure to do this, and will certainly not do that; that he will not insult helplessness, but respect it; not rob his employer, but protect his interests. And, if this be admitted, as I think it must be, then it will follow that it can not be *all* his actions, to the prediction of which he entertains an objection.

So much being settled, we must ask, Is there *no* prediction then which he does find objectionable? I think there is. I believe that if, at forty, our supposed plain man could be shown the calculation, made by another before his birth, of every event in his life, rationally deduced from the elements of his being, from his original natural endowment, and the complication of circumstances which in any way bore on him—if such a thing were possible in fact, as it is conceivable in certain systems, then, I will not go so far as to say that our man would begin to doubt his responsibility; I do not say his notions of right and wrong would be unsettled (on this head I give no opinion); but I believe that he would be most seriously perplexed, and in a manner outraged.

Let us take these two points for granted then, that some prediction is not objectionable, while some, on the other hand, is; and let us now proceed, if we can, to distinguish the cases, and find, in the first place, what is not, and in the second, what is objected to.

Subject to the correction of the reader, I say that, when we confine ourselves to *mere* prediction (as we must, because the attendant circumstances *may* always annoy), the man of healthy mind has no objection to the prediction of *any* actions, which he looks on as issuing from his *character*.[1] A formed man, if healthy, feels himself to be what he is; he is ' made'; he has certain principles, certain habits, certain ways. He has, in a word, a certain self. He knows what that self is; he is not ashamed of it, and he has no objection whatever to the world knowing what it is: he likes it to be known. He is aware what he would do, under given conditions; and why in the world, then, should other people *not* be able to tell beforehand, how he would act, and what he would do under those conditions? He sets no great store by ideal moralities; there he is, pretty much what he ought to be, with peculiarities of his own, as he sees that his fellows have all their own points, which belong to them, all of them ' bound' to do this or that, as their friends could tell you beforehand. He may not be what other men are, but he is quite as good, and he has his own ways; right or wrong, he is not very likely to alter them now. Will he answer for them? Why, for what else should he answer? They are *his*, they are *himself*.

Let us take an instance. After a certain action, he is told that his friend said of him, ' I know him, and he will do this.' Is he disturbed? In no way. Rather he is pleased to be understood. And when to his face his friend tells him, 'I knew that you would say that,' he smiles in silence, or as he inquires, ' Why, how did you know it?'

The strongest proof that no connexion whatever exists between belief in accountability and the mere idea of knowledge beforehand, is the fact that, for the faults we were sure beforehand we should commit, and which we know for certain we should commit again, we never for one moment doubt we are responsible.

Our result at present is this: the prediction which is not objected to, is mere simple prediction founded on knowledge

---

[1] We can not use, as an instance, the prediction of bad actions, i.e. such actions as the man himself considers bad. This is painful, not because it is a prediction, but because here the man is forced to see that he is bad, that another knows it for certain, and also has said it.

of character. There may be extraneous conditions which, in some cases, make such prediction offensive; but these do not affect our conclusion.

We now have to ask, what is the prediction which *is* objectionable? Would it be going too far, if we said that the ordinary man would not like the foretelling of any one of his conscious acts, unless so far as they issued from his character? I do not think it would be. Let us take a trivial illustration, and if it border on the ludicrous, so much the better. Suppose that on several occasions our man finds that another has said beforehand what fruit he would choose from a large variety, and on no two occasions the same. He would be much surprised; but if told by the other, 'I knew you would do it, because I have noticed you, and you always have done it,' I believe he would be satisfied at once. But failing this, and failing a conclusion to his choice from any of his habits or ways, I think he would be most uncomfortable. His feeling would be, that the other man knew something he had no right, and which was not his, to know. And we might see the same thing in a number of instances, as the reader will find by considering the matter.

At present we have only to discover the facts, and no doubt so far they appear irrational; but the next illustration will, I hope, begin to enlighten us. As we have already remarked, the ordinary man would probably be little short of horrified to find that the whole of his history, everything which has gone to settle his character, every element in the evolution which has made him what he is, had been foretold in detail before his birth. If I am right, he would be inclined to say, 'The growth of my character has been predicted when I was not; and how then can I have had anything to do with it?'

We are certain, unless we are careful, to miss the important point here. It is *not* the mere fact of his present character being beforehand an object of knowledge, which troubles him so much. For his notions are not clear, as they well may not be. He is his self, and his self is his character; and he being born, his character, when he so considers it, is likewise born. And thus, sinking the fact of the process of his development, he is what he is; he is such, and may be known as such, and the sooner or later are unimportant considerations, which may be dropped out of sight. And hence the prediction is the prediction of his character with its actions, which in no way troubles him. But what he was horrified at was to find the qualities of his being deduced from that which is not himself. He can not bear to see the genesis of himself, or his self in becoming. And so, if I see the facts rightly, when we put out of view the results of his character, it is not the *irrational* prediction of his doings which disquiets him, but rather, and very much more, the *rational*.[1]

This seems at first sight a surprising result, but nevertheless it is far from inexplicable.

We must consider, first, that irrational prevision need not imply (among ourselves it does not imply) the belief in Fate, as a negative power that stands over, sways, and crushes individuals. And, this being so, the individual stands and is left to himself; he is not interfered with by a foreign element; his deeds are his own doing—they come from himself. It is a mere question of knowing them sooner or later; and the plain man never dreams of reasoning that, because they are foreknown, therefore they preexist, and therefore they are not his. But if they are his, then he is responsible for them; and, if he is troubled, he

---

[1] By 'rational' prediction I mean the calculation beforehand, by certain laws and from given data, of a definite result. This gives an answer to the question How? or the question Why? in one of its applications. By 'irrational' prediction is meant the foretelling without a ground or a reason why. Thus (real or supposed) supernatural or magical predictions are always irrational; the fortune is told through (or without) certain means or signs; but the means or signs are not the reason of the fortune, for which there may exist (in most cases there does exist) no reason at all. The prevision gives the future, it does not explain it; it takes and it leaves the individual in its own un-rationalized individuality; it sees an object of sight, and the 'now' and the 'then' are distnctions which make no difference. The reader will understand that I express no opinion on the obscure subject of irrational prediction.

is troubled so far as the doctrine of Fate is suggested, and because Fate means a non-moral, inhuman order of the world. So far, then, as irrational prevision implies a non-moral order of the world, and so far as such order is incompatible with accountability; so far, and no further, does irrational prevision conflict with ordinary morality. But we must not linger here, for much still lies before us.

We have now done with the question of fact, and we come to the question 'Why'. What is the ground of objection to rational prevision (always apart from knowledge of character)? And the first point to remark is, that when a man is disquieted by that, there does seem no reason at all to suppose that what comes before him is, directly and primarily, his accountability.

What really does lie and does work in his mind would appear to be this. He is sure that he exists. A man, as we know, may doubt of many things, of anything *else*; but he never can doubt of his own being. And he is sure that he is nothing but himself. His notions on the matter are entirely hazy. It would be idle and absurd to ask him questions; but he cannot think of himself and not-himself, and bring the two ideas together. He can think (and it is a delusion to say he can *not* think) of the world, apart from and without himself. The stage is there, and he can come on or go off. He can appear or not appear, be or not be; can come in and go out, like a candle, which must be alight or not alight—a fire, which must be 'in' or 'out'; but by no possibility can he conceive of himself as in becoming. How can *he* (there already) *become* himself? And how can he (there still) be ceasing to be himself? It is impossible that this should come before his mind.

What he means by his self, we have already remarked, he knows not; and indeed his views are much confused; for at times, as we said, he identifies his character with his self (anything but his character would not be *his* self), and carries it back to the beginning of his life; and, at times again, he will tell you that without his bringing-up and education, and without his own resolution and self-denial, he never would have been the sort of man he is now; and here the self, which is there from the first, is *not* the character. You may tell him his character was born with him, that is one of his views; or you may tell him it has been developed, that is another; but then you must add (fairly ᴣo represent him) that *he* has developed it.

Suppose that all this is lying in his mind, and one sees directly the ground of our man's dislike for rational prediction; for such prediction is, in a word, the construction of himself out of what is not himself; and that, as we saw, he can not understand. If, from given data and from universal rules, another man can work out the generation of him like a sum in arithmetic, where is his self gone to? It is invaded by another, broken up into selfless elements, put together again, mastered and handled, just as a poor dead thing is mastered by man. And this being so, our man feels dimly that, if another can thus unmake and remake him, he himself might just as well have been anybody else from the first, since nothing remains which is specially his. The sanctum of his individuality is outraged and profaned; and with that profanation ends the existence that once seemed impenetrably sure. To explain the origin of a man is utterly to annihilate him.

Even when the character is formed, and the knowledge of it by others is not objected to, every one knows it is the grossest rudeness to affect to understand a man, or to know him, as well as or better than he knows himself, unless the parties are on intimate terms. And one ground of this is no doubt the feeling just mentioned, that a man can not be worked like a sum, but repels the intrusion of an external mind.

That a man feels no pain at the thought that God knows his inmost being, and the elements of it; or that he feels such pain only when irreligiously he thinks of himself and of God as two finite persons, is a confirmation of the above account. In that religious relation the relation ceases; the self loses sight of its private selfness, and gives itself up, to find itself and more than itself.

The objection to the rational development of the character

is founded, I believe, on the above ideas. But, if we come now to belief in responsibility, and ask how far, in the mind of our man, it stands connected with these notions, the answer must be, that immediately, and in the mind of the practical man, it is not so connected at all. He is responsible for that which he is, no matter what he is, and no matter how he became so; provided only that the conditions of imputation are present. But what the ordinary man would think is one thing; what he ought to think, if he saw more clearly, is another thing. And if we state the question differently, and ask whether rational prevision is consistent with all that is *implied* in accountability, can coexist with the *conditions* of imputation, a different reply must, I think, be given. We saw that a man was accountable, because he himself, and no other, has acted; and now, so far as I am able to see, the possibility of the explanation of his self means that his self does not exist at all, and therefore, of course, can not act.

The matter in hand has important bearings, and I do not think that, in general, our ideas are very clear concerning it. It is common to find some such belief as this. Either the human world is subject to law, or it is not; and if it is subject, then there is no reason in the nature of things, why you should not so understand the characters of men and the principles of historical development, as to be able to say beforehand what a man or a stage in history is to be. As a matter of fact, you can not go beyond 'tendencies'; but that is only because you never have a sufficiency of particular data ; and, given these, it would be possible rationally to foresee the future man or stage in history. Such a notion, I think, is altogether erroneous; and, if we ask what the proposal comes to in plain language, it is this—*a priori* to construe an individual man (or state of society) out of his elements, such individual being unknown, and not yet in existence. Let us see what there is to be said against that.

I am far from suggesting that the human world is not 'under law'; partly, because I am not sure that I know what that means. And, though I consider the word 'result' inaccurate and here misleading, I do not deny that the character of a man does follow, as a result, from his natural endowment together with his environment. If his self is the negation of all its particulars, that does not mean that it is *not* determined by them. But I do say that, given the knowledge of a man's innate disposition, and given the knowledge of his outward world (in the fullest possible sense), yet you *can not*, from these data, deduce his character. I do say that, given historical materials, and given any knowledge of laws which you please, it *does not follow* that you can construe from them a future state of society; and, if society is organic (and a better theory tells us it is *more* than organic), and if history is progressive, then you may guess and foresee many things by a practical insight; but, give you what knowledge of 'laws' and what particular existing data you please, you *can not calculate* the future. You can predict the result, only so far as your experience goes, i. e. so far as you know the result; and as long as history does not repeat itself, and while no two men are ever born the same, so long will the individual result you want be lacking to you.

Even if we suppose, what is very hard to suppose, that the character is inborn, yet even then it is knowable only so far as manifested, and, therefore, not till later in life. Or suppose, again, that the character is known, and the environment the same as others of which we have had experience, yet even here the question arises, Are you able to generalize laws of the action and reaction of character and circumstances, when character does not mean disposition or temperament (the man is more than these)? If you can not *class* characters, so as to deduce particulars from them, then even the premises we have supposed you to possess are useless to you.

But if, turning from suppositions, which we can not here discuss, but which we believe to be at the mercy of criticism, we hold, as the only conclusion possible, that the character of the man is not what is made, but what makes itself, out of and from the disposition and environment; and if, again, we suppose that everything which exists outside the self must, to make that definite self which we know, be fused together in the self, in such manner as to be one thing or another thing, or well-nigh anything, according to the quality of the whole individuality; if every part is in the whole, and determines that whole—if the whole is in every part, and informs each part with the nature of the whole— then it does seem mere thoughtlessness to imagine that by 'compounding' and 'deducing' we are likely to do much. The whole question lies in a nutshell. *If* the man is made by what answers to your theoretical deduction, *then* you can deduce him in anticipation; but if he is not, then you can not. And so with society. *If* a stage in history is the result of what corresponds to your intellectual putting to- gether of conclusions from premises, *then* you may calculate it; but if it is not, then you can not. *If* the individual self and society are 'compositions' of that order that a knowledge of their elements gives you, *apart from experience*, a know- ledge of the individuals, *then* you can 'compound' them, and construe them *a priori*; but if they are not, you can not.

To 'understand' (the word is used in the loosest sense) a result when you have it before you or in you, is one thing; to construe it by the intellect beforehand, altogether and absolutely another thing. I do not say, that is never done; everybody knows that, in certain spheres, you can and do deduce from laws and data: but I do say that the fact that, in respect of one subject-matter, you can do it here, gives you no right to say that, in respect of another subject- matter, you can do it there. And as to 'science of tenden- cies', what has science to do with such loose phrases? If 'tendencies' mean *abstractions*, there is no objection to that in itself. The question to be answered is, 'Are the abstrac- tions possible?'; and we have answered that in the negative, so far as the science of character is concerned. Its 'laws' are 'empty opinions';[1] there is not one sphere in which

---

[1] The reader will be enlightened here by Hegel, *Phänom. d. G. Werke*, ii. 218–24 (1841), but Hegel must not be considered responsible for everything I say.

they hold good. If they are not, they ought to be, false *outside* the character, because they profess to be specially laws *of* the character; and inside the character they are false, because they abstract from the character; and where they happen to be right, it is only because they happen not to be wrong. And what applies to the individual man, applies *mutatis mutandis* to a stage in historical progress.

If the above be in any way correct, then the rational prediction of human character is a sheer impossibility; and to maintain it to be possible may not be to jar with the plain man's feelings and beliefs, but it is to collide with his notion of accountability; because, as we saw, that notion contains the idea of an individual self, and because, unless that idea be *not* real, rational prediction is out of the question. So much for rational prediction: but how far, and whether, irrational prediction strikes at the root of individuality, is a question we can not enter into here.

At the cost of a somewhat lengthy digression, we are now, I hope, in a better position to ask how far responsibility, as it exists for the vulgar, agrees with the teaching of the expounders of Necessity. We saw that the plain man did not think himself *accountable* for the reason that he *never could be counted on*; and if necessity meant no more than the regularity of his volitions, the possibility of telling, from his character, his action in a given position, then, I believe, no objection would be made to it. But we saw as well that, if necessity means the theoretical development of the characterized self, then necessity collides with popular morality.

But this last point need not at present engage us; let us confine our attention to the full-grown man. When he hears of necessity, he is sure to object to it. 'But that', says the believer, 'is only because he does not understand our terms; by "cause" we mean one thing, and he means another; and so with "necessity".' In that case, we may answer, speaking in the place, though not with the words, of our vulgar objector, you really should not go on using these terms, since you must be aware that you generate confusion; and

also, in the writings of our necessitarians, we can not see
that these terms do signify what they do not signify for the
non-philosophical.   Where we see that words go on standing
for the same matters, it is hard to believe that their meaning
is so different.   You take phrases, which we apply to the
natural world, and you apply them to what we think the
non-natural world ; you break down our distinction between
the physical and the mental.   You say, indeed, that this
matters not, since your view of the physical world also is
different from ours ; but we say, in answer, that we are not
philosophers, and do not know what they think of it ; but
when you speak to us of stones, and sticks, and what we
understand ; and talk of a blow from a stick causing bruises,
and the necessity of a stone breaking panes in a window,
then your view of nature seems at bottom to be ours, and
we believe that you take that common view and transfer it
to the human world ; and there, so far as we understand you,
we do not believe in you.   Your theoretical definition of
cause and necessity may be different from anything in our
minds, but your practical application we see to be, everywhere else, much the same, and we do not trust you when
you tell us that here it is different.

When you speak to us plainly, you have to say that you
really understand a man to be free, and free in no other
sense than a falling stone, or than running water.   In the
one case there is as little necessity as in the other, and
just as much freedom.   And we believe that this is your
meaning.   But we know that, if these things are so, a man
has no more of what we call freedom than a candle or
a coprolite, and of that you will never succeed in convincing
us.   You must persuade us either that the coprolite is
responsible, or that we are *not* responsible ; and, with all
due respect to you, we are going to believe neither.

And this, no doubt, is what lies at the bottom of the
objection entertained against ordinary determinism.   The
vulgar are convinced that a gulf divides them from the
material world ; they believe their being to lie beyond the
sphere of mere physical laws ; their character, or their will,

is to them their thinking and rational self; and they feel
quite sure that it is not a thing in space, to be pushed here
and there by other things outside of it.   And so, when you
treat their will as a something physical, and interpret its
action by mechanical metaphors, they believe that you do
not treat it or interpret it at all, but rather something quite
other than it.   It is not that you say about it what you
should not say, but that you never say anything about
it at all; that you ignore the centre of their moral being,
that which for them means freedom, and *is* freedom; and
this is what is signified, when it is said of determinism, that
'it holds by a will which *wills* nothing', just as we saw
that indeterminism did indeed hold by a will, but 'a will
that willed *nothing*'.

But we must not allow our client, or ourselves, too great
a liberty in what may be considered the assertion of
a theory; for we have not to assert, but to understand and
criticize.   We must see for ourselves, in what the consistent
determinist can not endorse the plain man's notion of moral
accountability.

We saw above that responsibility and liability to punishment might be taken as convertible, and that, hence, the
theory which would justify punishment would account for
responsibility; and that, where the former (in its ordinary
sense) was meaningless, there the latter must also be
wanting.

Let us see, then, what punishment means first for the
vulgar, and, next, for the believer in Necessity.   Let us see
for ourselves[1] if the two ideas are compatible; and then inquire wherein they are incompatible, in case they are so.

If there is any opinion to which the man of uncultivated
morals is attached, it is the belief in the necessary connexion
of punishment and guilt.   Punishment is punishment, only
where it is deserved.   We pay the penalty, because we owe
it, and for no other reason; and if punishment is inflicted

---

[1] The reader must not consider me anxious to prove against a theory
what it is ready to admit; but if we do not see the facts for ourselves,
we shall not find the reasons.

for any other reason whatever than because it is merited by wrong, it is a gross immorality, a crying injustice, an abominable crime, and not what it pretends to be. We may have regard for whatever considerations we please— our own convenience, the good of society, the benefit of the offender; we are fools, and worse, if we fail to do so. Having once the right to punish, we may modify the punishment according to the useful and the pleasant; but these are external to the matter, they can not give us a right to punish, and nothing can do that but criminal desert. This is not a subject to waste words over: if the fact of the vulgar view is not palpable to the reader, we have no hope, and no wish, to make it so.

I am not to be punished, on the ordinary view, unless I deserve it. Why then (let us repeat) on this view do I merit punishment? It is because I have been guilty. I have done 'wrong'. I have taken into my will, made a part of myself, have realized my being in something which is the negation of 'right', the assertion of not-right. Wrong can be imputed to me. I *am* the realization and the standing assertion of wrong. Now the plain man may not know what he means by 'wrong', but he is sure that, whatever it is, it 'ought' not to exist, that it calls and cries for obliteration; that, if he can remove it, it is his business to do so; that, if he does not remove it, it rests also upon him, and that the destruction of guilt, whatever be the consequences, and even if there be no consequences at all, is still a good in itself; and this, not because a mere negation is a good, but because the denial of wrong is the assertion of right (whatever 'right' means); and the assertion of right is an end in itself.

Punishment is the denial of wrong by the assertion of right, and the wrong exists in the self, or will, of the criminal; his self is a wrongful self, and is realized in his person and possessions; he has asserted in them his wrongful will, the incarnate denial of right; and in denying that assertion, and annihilating, whether wholly or partially, that incarnation by fine, or imprisonment, or even by death, we annihilate the wrong and manifest the right; and since this, as we saw, was an end in itself, so punishment is also an end in itself.

Yes, in despite of sophistry, and in the face of sentimentalism, with well-nigh the whole body of our self-styled enlightenment against them, our people believe to this day that *punishment is inflicted for the sake of punishment*; though they know no more than our philosophers themselves do, that there stand on the side of the unthinking people the two best-known names of modern philosophy.[1]

---

[1] The following passages from Kant will perhaps surprise those persons among us who think nothing 'philosophical' but immoral Humanitarianism. Kant's *Werke*, vi, pp. 331-2 and p. 333. ⟨See p. 57.⟩

'*Judicial* punishment (*poena forensis*) is not the same as *natural* (*poena naturalis*). By means of this latter, guilt brings a penalty on itself; but the legislator has not to consider it in any way. Judicial punishment can never be inflicted simply and solely as a means to forward a good, other than itself, whether that good be the benefit of the criminal, or of civil society ; but it must at all times be inflicted on him, for no other reason than *because he has acted criminally*. A man can never be treated simply as a means for realizing the views of another man, and so confused with the objects of the law of Property. Against that his inborn personality defends him, although he can be quite properly condemned to forfeit his civil personality. He must first of all be found to be *punishable*, before there is even a thought of deriving from the punishment any advantage for himself or his fellow-citizens. The penal law is a categorical imperative ; and woe to that man who crawls through the serpentine turnings of the happiness-doctrine, to find out some consideration, which, by its promise of advantage, should free the criminal from his penalty, or even from any degree thereof. That is the maxim of the Pharisees, "it is expedient that one man should die for the people, and that the whole nation perish not"; but if justice perishes, then it is no more worth while that man should live upon the earth.'

'Even if a civil society were to dissolve itself by the vote of all its members (e. g. if a people, inhabiting an island, were to resolve to separate from one another, and scatter themselves over the surface of the globe), nevertheless, before they go, the last murderer in prison must be executed. And this, that every man may receive what is the due of his deeds, and the guilt of blood may not rest upon a people which has failed to exact the penalty; for, in that case, the people may be considered as participators in this public violation of justice.' I am not to be considered as endorsing wholly Kant's views. Cf. Hegel, *Phil. d. Rechts*, §§ 97-104, and Trendelenburg, *Naturrecht*, p. 136, foll.

But, even were we able, it is not our task here to expound to the reader, what this, or again what the other metaphysician understands by punishment. The above is no more than the theoretical expression of the popular view, viz. that punishment is justice; that justice implies the giving what is due; that suppression of its existence, in one form or other, is due to guilt, and so to the guilty person; and that, against his will, to give or take from a man what is not due, is, on the other hand, injustice. We have now to see what punishment is for the believer in Necessity.

And here the Necessitarian does not leave us in doubt. For him, it is true, 'responsibility' may 'mean punishment', or rather the liability thereto; and perhaps he would not mind saying that guilt deserves punishment. But when we ask him, what is to be understood by the term 'desert', then we are answered at once, that its meaning is something quite other than the 'horrid figment' which we believe in; or, lost in phrases, we perceive thus much, that the world we are in is certainly not that of the vulgar mind.

We must be careful here not to suffer ourselves to be led astray. The empirical origin in history, or in the individual, of the notions of justice and desert is for us altogether beside the point. For we are concerned with the 'What', and not here at all with the question, 'How comes it to be?' And though often (I do not say, always) for a complete result we must consider both, yet to run them into one, and confuse them together, is an error as common as it is utterly ruinous. We have to answer no more than the question 'what', and that in the sense of, what *is* the vulgar notion? And secondly, we must not wander to a discussion on the right to punish. We need not ask how it is that, if 99 men are of opinion that it is more convenient, for both the 99 and the 100th, or for the 100th without the 99, or the 99 without the 100th, that he, the 100th, should cease to exist—that *therefore* it is right for their opinion to be conveyed to him by the hanging of him, whatever may be his opinion on the subject. The discussion of this question we leave to utilitarian philosophers.

We must keep to facts, and fortunately they are plain. For our vulgar, once more, punishment is the complement of criminal desert; is justifiable only so far as deserved; and further is an end in itself. For our Necessitarian, punishment is avowedly *never* an end in itself; it is *never* justifiable, except as a means to an external end.

'There are two ends,' says the late Mr. Mill (*Hamilton*, p. 592), and he means there are *only* two ends, 'which, on the Necessitarian theory, are sufficient to justify punishment: the benefit of the offender himself, and the protection of others.'[1]

And (p. 597), 'If indeed punishment is inflicted for any other reason than in order to operate on the will; if its purpose be other than that of improving the culprit himself, or securing the just rights of others against unjust violation '[justice', the reader must remember, may be for him and Mr. Mill two different things], then, I admit, the case is totally altered. If any one thinks that there is justice in the infliction of purposeless suffering; that there is a natural affinity between the two ideas of guilt and punishment, which makes it intrinsically fitting that wherever there has been guilt, pain should be inflicted by way of retribution [the reader will not forget that for him, beside that of justice, there may also be other spheres, and possibly higher: what is *merely* just need not be intrinsically fitting]; I acknowledge that I can find no argument to justify punishment inflicted on this principle. As a legitimate satisfaction to feelings of indignation and resentment which are on the whole salutary and worthy of cultivation [the figments are not 'horrid' to Mr. Mill; he seems willing even to encourage them], I can in certain cases admit it; but here it

---

[1] Although it is not connected with the subject, I must continue the quotation as a specimen of our English philosophizing. 'The first justifies it, because to benefit a person cannot be to do him an injury.' If 'injury' is the opposite of 'benefit', the 'because' disappears; if of 'justice', we have the *unproved assertion* of a controverted proposition; one which I, for instance, consider not merely false, but monstrous. The proviso of 'a proper title' in the following sentence makes matters no better.

is still a means to an end.   The merely retributive ['merely'
is misleading] view of punishment derives no justification
from the doctrine I support.'

Punishment to Mr. Mill is 'medicine'; and, turn himself
aside as he might from the issue (pp. 593-4), he could not
avoid the conclusion forced on him by the 'Inquirer', that
if rewards carried with them the benefits of punishment, then
I should deserve rewards, when, and because, I am wicked.

Now against this theory of punishment I have nothing
here to say.   The great and ancient names, which in
punishment saw nothing but a means to the good of the
State or the individual, demand that we treat that view
with respect; and hence I will not even say that the old
Hellenic doctrine is not also the latest and best to be had.[1]
But what we must say, what nearly every one will admit,
what we must take for granted without further discussion,
is this, that whatever else it may be it is at least *not* the
opinion of the vulgar.

We need not dwell on the point.   If, on the one side,
punishment is always an end in itself, whatever else it may
be, and if, on the other, whatever else it is, it *never* can be
an end in itself, we may take it for granted that between
the two there is no agreement.[2]

---

[1] Still it is not the *only* doctrine; and Mr. Bain, in his *Manual of
Mental and Moral Science* (p. 404), really should not talk to the
student as if it were.   For Mr. Bain's solid work in psychology I have
a great respect, but still I (or any one else) have a right to protest
against this.   Still more right have I to protest against the statement
in his preface, 'Part Second—the Ethical Systems—is a full detail of
all the systems, ancient and modern'; when, by his own admission
(p. 725), this is not the case.

[2] There are two points we can not pass over—(1) Punishment of
children; (2) Correction of animals.   (1) We must distinguish punishment and discipline, or correction; the former is inflicted because of
wrong-doing, as desert, the latter is applied as means of improvement.
It is right to inflict the former only in the case of a being either
wholly or partially accountable.   The application of the latter (which
is not punishment) is a practical question for parents or tutors, both
in respect of the occasion and amount.   Pedagogic punishment (proper)
differs from judicial in admitting greater latitude of particular considerations in the individual case.   (2) If many persons meant what

But if, as we saw, to understand punishment is to understand responsibility, and not to know the one is to be ignorant of the other, and to hold an opposite theory on the one is to hold, as a consequence, an opposite theory on the other; if 'responsibility means punishment', and punishability is the same as accountability; and if, further, the teaching of the Necessitarian with respect to punishment is in flagrant contradiction with vulgar opinion—how, if he were so minded, is he to assert that his teaching on responsibility is not so also? How is he to deny that accountability is a 'figment'; and that his moral world is, in everything but names and phrases, *not* the moral world of the vulgar? If, to repeat, on the theory of Necessity I am not punishable in the ordinary sense, then (for we saw that the two went together) I am not responsible either.

Our result so far then is this: we have seen what punishment is for the vulgar and for the Determinist respectively; and to see that is to see that the two are altogether incompatible; and so in like manner the responsibilities, which correspond

---

they said, animals are moral and responsible, and animals are punished. And a time would seem coming, when we shall hear of the 'rights of the beast'. Why *not*, in Heaven's name? Why is the beast not a subject of right, civil at least, if not political? But this is for our emancipators of the future. We are content to hold the vulgar creed that a beast is no moral agent, actual or possible; is not responsible, nor the subject of rights, however much the object of duties. According to vulgar notions, a beast ought not to be punished because he deserves it, but only to make him better; and though practice is bad on this head, yet I think most persons would say that a man, who habitually punished a dog for a fault, in respect of which he was ὅλως ἀνίατος, was not fit to keep a dog at all; but the ὅλως ἀνίατοι among men, the hardened habituals, are the men whom *we* consider *most* punishable. On the other hand, though the beast can not be punished, yet he can be corrected as often as is convenient and to any extent. I was once told of a west-country sportsman who, on starting for the field before the day's work was begun, used regularly to tie up his dogs to a gate and thrash them, and at intervals during the day's sport repeat the νουθέτησις. Whether it was wise to correct for no fault is a question for the dog-breaker; but surely no man in his senses would call it punishment. And yet it was good utilitarian punishment. And that is what is meant, when it is said that such punishment is the treating a man like a dog.

to them, are not the same. And our conclusion must be, that neither the one nor the other of our 'two great philosophical modes of thought', however excellent they may (or may not) be as philosophies, each by itself and the one against the other, does in any way theoretically express the moral notions of the vulgar mind, or fail in some points to contradict them utterly.

But to perceive the fact is not enough for us. It has not been a discovery, but has been admitted and professed by teachers of Determinism. Our interest is mainly to see *wherein* it is that Necessitarianism fails to interpret the popular belief. It fails in this, that it altogether ignores the rational self in the form of will; it ignores it in the act of volition, and it ignores it in the abiding personality, which is the same throughout all its acts, and *by which alone* imputation gets a meaning.

A man, to express what the people believe, is only responsible for what (mediately or immediately) issues from the act of volition; and in that act his will is present, his will being himself, and neither a part of himself nor a certain disposition of elements not *in* a self, but the whole self expressing itself in a particular way, manifesting itself as will *in* this or that utterance, and, in and by such manifestation, qualifying the will which manifests itself. The will must be in the act, and the act in the will; and as the will is the self which remains the same self, therefore the act, which was part of the self, is now part of the self, since the self is that which it has done. We say 'I will', and we mean something by it. We distinguish 'I' and 'will'. 'I' is what we always say, when we speak of thinking or doing at all, and 'will' means now some particular act which we will. And again in 'I will' we unite 'I' and 'will' in such a way that the notion of dividing them is absurd; when of each it can be said that the one is in the other, partition is out of the question. 'I' was there, as a solid individual; then, when a particular act was before it, 'I' became to us that which included and was wider than this, that, or the other possible particulars; and lastly, in 'I will' there is no particular nor universal apart, but an inseparable whole. The vulgar, as we know, are the prey of delusions, which we think our 'inductive' psychology, and our anti-metaphysical metaphysic, and our all too metaphysical 'Baconian' science make impossible for ourselves ; and the sole possible expression of the one most widely spread amongst all these rooted beliefs is this, that a universal is real, and that that universal is conscious of itself.

We said that our Necessitarians ignored the self, both as willing self and as self-same will. Let us begin with the first. We saw (to repeat it) that 'the will must be in the act, and the act in the will'; and phrases of this sort, which express the beliefs of the vulgar mind, should warn us that either we are living in a universe of 'figments', or else that, in the world we have entered, no physical theories which apply to things outside of each other in space are likely to avail us. And so when we hear such phrases as 'the mechanism of the human mind', we feel at a loss, if at least we believe that the sphere of mere mechanism has ceased, before that of the mind has even begun; and when, further, we learn the avowed intention to bring nothing but physical methods to bear on the interpretation of mind, what confidence we had altogether vanishes. And proceeding to inquire into the determination of the will by 'motives', we find every term and phrase has a meaning not until we import into the consideration of ourselves the coarsest and crassest mechanical metaphors of pulls and pushes, drawings and thrustings, which we believed to exist not anywhere except in the lowest phenomena of the natural world. Just as, in reading Locke and so many of the friends of Locke, we have nothing before our understanding, until, as it were, we call up before our eyes solid things in space, denting, and punching, and printing another thing called a mind, and this other thing in like manner (how, heaven knows) making marks and prints on *itself* also—so, in reading our determinists, the one chance of their terms bringing anything at all before the intellect is for us to keep in sight a thing called a will, pushed and pulled by things called motives ; or else certain 'forces' called motives, acting within a given space called self, and, by their 'composition', resulting in no movement at all or a movement called ' will'; uncertain whether such movement is a movement of the whole 'collection' in the space called self, or a movement only of part of that collection.

If now we can bring these objects before our minds, and know that the will is a thing 'in a bag' called self, and is moved by other things out of or in the bag; or (more refinedly) that states of mind, called motives, stand to the mind, of which they are the states, as forces stand to the space they meet in—then Determinism is intelligible enough, and considered as an intellectual amusement is perhaps a pleasing theory. But when such a theory is brought into relation with the actions of ourselves, then, speaking not merely for ourselves alone, we can say little more than that we really can see no connexion between the theory and the facts we know. The phrases of one sphere lose all their meaning when applied to the other sphere. That the self in desire should have gone beyond itself, and yet not be beside itself; that the many desires should all be the desires of the self; that the self should be divided against itself in desire; that the self should from all its desires distinguish itself; that it should confront them and, taking some one of them into itself, should free itself so from all other attractions, and spend its whole being in that *one* direction; that the realized desire is the utterance of the self, and that the act which is that utterance should remain in the self, even as the self went out in the act—all and every one of these sayings become senseless, when translated into the language of mechanism, into motives, and tractions, and compositions of forces. You may name them as you please, if you do not prefer to ignore them altogether; you may call them the ghosts of the delusions of the vulgar, shamelessly walking in the daylight and shrouded in the phrases of a mystical jargon; but you can not get rid of one simple fact, that they represent what to the unphilosophical mind is reality palpable as the noonday sun, and that your philosophy is impotent to explain them.

But not only in the act of 'I will' does Determinism entirely lose sight of the 'I', and hence fail to recognize the characteristic of the will; not only does it hold by a will that *wills* nothing, and misses thereby an element involved in responsibility; but, also, it ignores or denies the identity of the self in all the acts of the self, and without self-sameness we saw there was no possibility of imputation.

On this important point it is simply impossible to state the vulgar belief too strongly. If I am not now the same man, the identical self that I was; if the acts that I did are not the acts of the one and individual I which exists at this moment, then I can not deserve to be punished for that which myself has not done. For imputation it is required that the acts, which were mine, now also are mine; and this is possible only on the supposition that the will, which is now, is the will which was then, so that the contents of the will, which were then, are the contents of the self-same will which is now existing. On this point again repetitions are wearisome, and words are wasted; without personal identity responsibility is sheer nonsense; and to the psychology of our Determinists personal identity (with identity in general) is a word without a vestige of meaning.

And I am far from saying that in the regions of philosophy their doctrines are not right. For on these matters I advance no opinion at present; and, for anything I have to say here, their conclusions may be the correct ones. We are right, it may be, here again to apply to the self the methods, or what are said to be the methods, of all physical inquiry, to view through the glass of an accurate introspection this nebula of the ordinary vision, till it breaks into points, which laws, not their own, move hither and thither in the limited space which once seemed to be fullness. I do not assert that the self is not 'resolvable' into coexistence and sequence of states of the mind. I am far from denying that the I or the self is no more than 'collective', than a collection of sensations, and ideas, and emotions, and volitions swept together with one another and after one another by 'the laws of association'; though I confess that to a mind which is but little 'inductive', and which can not view the world wholly *à posteriori*, these things are very difficult even to picture, and altogether impossible in any way to understand. We can bring before the mind certain atoms in space; we can call them feelings, or ideas, or what we will; and we can say that we mean by the mind a given collection of these pictured atoms: and so far we do well enough. But then comes our first trouble. We have imaged to ourselves a collection of points in space, and that means we see the collection itself, as covering a given area, with other spaces and collections outside of it. Are we to say that the mind is in space? 'Oh, no!' we shall be told; 'for that is to talk about things in themselves: our knowledge is relative, which means that we must confine ourselves to our given collection; the question is unanswerable, because unintelligible.' And so, by talking ourselves about 'things in themselves', we change, so to speak, a subject of conversation which was beginning to be slightly improper, and continue, as before, to picture the mind as a collection in space of material points; or if time be spoken of, we have but, as it were, to give a turn to our kaleidoscope. And so far still we are doing pretty well.

But still we must not be too confident. We forgot for the moment that the units of the collection are, each one separately, a state of the collection (they are 'states of mind', and the mind is 'collective'), and we can see well enough that in a bag of marbles or a bunch of grapes the state of the marbles affects the state of the bag, and the state of the grapes is the state of the bunch; but it is very hard to see why each marble is to be called a state of the bag of marbles, and each grape a state of the bunch of grapes, unless we suppose an 'entity' inside the bag irresolvable into marbles, or an 'entity' in the grapes of the bunch irresolvable into grapes. And that, as we know, has been exploded long ago. We feel that there are, and must be, some questions it is useless to ask; and if we use self-control, and abstain from asking them, we still, as before, can see things very well.

But here, unfortunately, our troubles are not over: this collection is aware of itself; it talks about itself as if it were simple. And this it is impossible to picture at all; and we here (I speak for myself, so far as I have tried) are reduced to despair; for we want to keep the collection steadily before us, and yet, as often as we have to imagine it aware of itself, our picture is at once in confusion, and we do not know what we have before us at all: all we are sure of is that it is *not* a collection, while we know all the time that it really is so; and we must comfort ourselves, I suppose, by saying that, so long as we remain 'scientific', such difficulties as these must not be made too much of. But when we hear collections affirming that they really are not collections, and saying that what is many is really at the same time one, and that what is complex is really at the same time simple, and that what is different is none the less identical, and declaring that all this is contained in that which they call themselves, and which they say it is impossible for them to doubt of, because existence, for them, implies the thinking so—then we know with whom we have to do. These collections are trying to be 'entities' and 'things in themselves' or perhaps even the Absolute; and that is the only reason they have for saying these things, which can not be true, because, if they were, what we say would be false. This matter Hume—whom we have our reasons for not talking about, but keep, as it were, in reserve—has settled, and settled for ever. Such beliefs are nothing but fictions of the mind, and the mind itself is a fiction of the mind.

Let us take an illustration. We have all seen onions on a rope. Now each of these onions is not any other onion— it may be taken by itself, as a separate individual; and yet each of these onions is a state of the rope of onions. And further, this rope of onions is aware of itself—it talks about itself and generally comports itself as if it were inseparable, and, no doubt, it really is what it calls self-conscious. But here is the beginning of delusion; for, talking about

' self', we (i.e. the onions) fall into the belief that there is something there under the onions and the rope, and on looking we see there is nothing of the kind. But on looking we see even more than this; for the rope of the onions is a rope of straw, and that is, being interpreted, no rope at all, but the fiction of a rope. The onions keep together because of the laws of association of onions; and because of these laws it is, that the mutual juxtaposition of the onions engenders in them the belief in a rope, and the consequent foolish ideas of a self, which we see in all their foolishness when we perceive, first, that there is nothing but a rope, and then that the rope is nothing at all. The only thing which after all is hard to see is this, that we ourselves, who apprehend the illusion, are ourselves the illusion which is apprehended by us;[1] and perhaps, on the theory of ' relativity', in order to know a fiction you yourself must *be* the fiction you know; but it all is hard to understand, especially to a mind which is little 'analytical' and, I begin to fear, not at all 'inductive'.

We can see that a stream is a flux, and that the wisp which plays on it has really no more of permanence than the stream; but how that wisp is ever to think about these things, and to delude itself into the belief, and to publish the theory, that it can not help thinking of itself as one being, and that yet after all it is nothing but a wisp—to see how this is seems really impossible. The only way to represent it is to picture a delusion, which is nothing but a delusion, and which, after belief that it is *not* a delusion, has at length found out that really it *is* a delusion. And since this, to the non-philosophical mind, appears meaningless nonsense; and since this is the conclusion to which ' inductive' psychology, if we carry it out, seems necessarily to lead,[2]

---

[1] Mr. Bain collects that the mind is a collection. Has he ever thought who collects Mr. Bain?

[2] I am perfectly aware that it is possible to inherit both premisses and conclusions, and then, while holding to the premisses, to ignore or refuse to accept the conclusions, so far as they are found to be inconvenient. When a fact stopped the way of Hume's conclusions,

I do not see much reason to think that the premisses of that psychology would not to the vulgar seem similar nonsense, if they only were aware what those premisses did really stand for and signify.

We have dwelt too long on this matter. If the self is ignored in the psychology of our Determinists, or recognized in a sense which is not the vulgar sense, then responsibility and punishment and all the beliefs intellectual and moral, which hang from (as we have seen) and involve in their being the reality of the vulgar sense, with the non-reality thereof fall and are destroyed; or survive, at most, in a form and in a shape which, whatever and however much better it may be, is absolutely irreconcilable with the notions of the people. A criminal is as 'responsible' for his acts of last year as the Thames at London is responsible for an accident on the Isis at Oxford, and he is no more responsible. And to punish that criminal, in the vulgar sense, is to repeat the story of Xerxes and the Hellespont. It may be true that, by operating on a stream in one place, you may make that stream much better in all places lower down, and possibly also may influence other streams; but if you think that, because of this, the stream is punishable and the water responsible in anything like the way in which we use the words, then you do most grossly deceive yourselves. And our conclusion must be this, that of 'the two great schools' which divide our philosophy, as the one, so the other stands out of relation to vulgar morality; that for both alike responsibility (as we believe in it) is

he banished it as a fiction. The late Mr. Mill's was a mind of a different order. Starting from premisses the same, with the same fact before him, which gave the lie to his whole psychological theory, he could not ignore it, he could not recognize it, he would not call it a fiction; so he put it aside as a 'final inexplicability', and thought, I suppose, that by covering it with a phrase he got rid of its existence. But against his adversary (p. 561) he expressed himself otherwise. 'He' (the theorist) 'is not entitled to frame a theory from one class of phænomena, extend it to another class which it does not fit, and excuse himself by saying that if we cannot make it fit, it is because ultimate facts are inexplicable.' (Mill, on Hamilton.)

a word altogether devoid of signification and impossible of explanation.

Now, if this conclusion be the true one, and, it not being mine in particular, I may say that I do not doubt that it is true; and further, if the drawing of morals be not out of the fashion, it would seem that there are several morals which here might well be drawn. And the first is the vulgar one, that seeing all we have of philosophy looks away (to a higher sphere doubtless) from the facts of our unenlightened beliefs and our vulgar moralities, and since these moralities are what we most care about, that therefore we also should leave these philosophers to themselves, nor concern ourselves at all with their lofty proceedings. This moral I think, on the whole, to be the best; though in our days perhaps it also is the hardest for all of us to practise. And the moral which comes next is, of course, the philosophical one, that, seeing the vulgar are after all the vulgar, we should not be at pains to agree with their superstitions, but, since philosophy is the opposite of no philosophy, we rather should esteem ourselves, according as our creed is different from, and hence is higher than theirs. And this moral, as for some persons it is the only one possible, so also I recommend it to them as their certain road to an unmixed happiness. But there remains still left a third moral, which, as I am informed, has been drawn by others; that if we are not able to rest with the vulgar, nor to shout in the battle of our two great schools, it might then be perhaps worth our while to remember that we live in an island, and that our national mind, if we do not enlarge it, may also grow insular; that not far from us there lies (they say so) a world of thought, which, with all its variety, is neither one nor the other of our two philosophies, but whose battle is the battle of philosophy itself against two undying and opposite one-sidednesses; a philosophy which *thinks* what the vulgar *believe*; a philosophy, lastly, which we all have refuted, and, having so cleared our consciences, some of us at least might take steps to understand.

NOTES TO ESSAY I

A.—COMPULSION AND RESPONSIBILITY

ON this difficult point I will venture a few remarks, though my want of acquaintance with what juridical and other literature there may be on the subject, as well as my own very partial insight, prevent my attempting to deal with the matter fully.

Ignorance, as a plea for non-responsibility, is easier to discuss. It seems that ignorance either of particular facts, or of moral distinctions generally, or of the moral quality of this or that act, removes, so far, moral responsibility,[1] provided only that the ignorance itself be not imputable to us as a fault.

What is compulsion? The word is no doubt used loosely, but we see at once that it is applicable strictly to nothing which has not will.[2] We do not talk of the inanimate being 'compelled'. This raises the question, 'unless I am compelled to *do* something, am I compelled?' But this we shall not trouble ourselves to answer, as at any rate we may be able to say, 'I am forced'; and in relation to the will we had better take force and compulsion to be the same, even if the words are not quite synonymous.

To proceed then, when I am forced there is some state (in the widest sense) of my body or mind, which is referred to me without being referred to my will (properly speaking). And so compulsion will be the production, in the body or mind of an animate being, of a result which is not related as a consequence to its will, in the highest sense of the term will. And to that we must add that the result must be contrary to the actual desire of the person forced, or, given knowledge, would have been contrary;[3] e. g. if a man is

---

[1] [*Not* legal, cf. l. 2.]

[2] [e. g. 'cloud-compelling' in poetry.]

[3] [I don't think this will hold. Even if you believe that the person probably *would* have given way, yet, if the will is put in abeyance, the result actually is force. See the definition above.

To some extent 'force', and to a greater extent 'compulsion', imply not merely abeyance of will, but some kind of opposition to will—more than mere externality thereto. The will in absolute compulsion must, I think, be taken as contrary. But that will may be actual, or presumable, or (*thirdly*) possible in the sense that its absence (given the knowledge) cannot be assumed. The *onus* here

first drugged and then robbed, it is compulsion. This is why, where compulsion is doubtful, present repentance has been used as a test; because, given present grief for a past event, from that we infer in the past a presumable will contrary to the event (Arist. *Eth*. III. i. 13). But (to say nothing of ' repentance ') grief need not follow compulsion, and is not always a sign of it. I must be forced, or not, at the time; I can not by subsequent sorrow make myself to have been forced, and it is possible I may now be glad to have been really forced.

This we may call *absolute* compulsion ; and ordinary examples are any forcible action on my body, direct or by creation of physical circumstances ; and, again, the production of any psychical state not under the control of my will.

Here there is little difficulty, since, properly speaking, I neither do nor abstain. The only thing which in any degree can make me accountable here, is that it is my fault that I was able to be compelled. Then all is, to some extent, the issue of my action or omission ; in either case, of my will.

The real problem is what follows. When I have to say anywhere, ' *I did it*,' can I then escape imputation by pleading compulsion ? Can my *will* be forced ?

This has been denied. It has been said that compulsion of the will is hypothetical and 'relative' only, not absolute ; that all it means is, *if* I will to have or be without this or that, *then* something else must follow, as a consequence which I can not escape. Choose to defy consequences on one side, and to renounce them on the other, and there can be no compulsion. ' No one can be compelled to anything, unless he wills to let himself be compelled.' (See Hegel, *Propädeutik*, xviii. 35 ; *Ph. d. Rechts*, viii. 128 (1840).)

I do not think this will hold. We see at once that, in a given case, there may be only one or two courses for me (my not-acting may be a course of action) ; and all of these

falls on the person using external force. If he can assume that the other person (given knowledge) would *not* have objected (e. g. in a swoon), then it is *not* compulsion, but otherwise it must, I think, be called so in principle.

Of course if the will is put in abeyance, then, unless you can assume that not only the abeyance, but the abeyance for a certain further consequence, was in accordance with an actual will (e. g. in hypnotism), or not against a presumable or even (given knowledge) a possible will, then it is compulsion. Of course you cannot (with a sane person) exclude the possibility of resistance, however improbable you may think it, given knowledge, unless you do so from positive knowledge of what the person's *general* will is.]

I may dislike and disapprove. But one course I *must* accept. In short, I may be compelled to an alternative; and here whether what I do is morally imputable, depends on whether it is my fault that I am in the position I am in.

But let us pass by this, since the far more serious question awaits us, 'Apart from alternatives, can I not be made to do this or that? Can not the will be forced to this or that result?'

It all depends on the way in which we use 'will'. If by 'will' we mean 'choice', 'volition', the conscious realizing of myself in the object of one desire (in the widest sense), which has been separated from and put before the mind, as a possibility not yet real—then the will can not be forced. For, supposing you could produce a state of mind, which certainly would issue in such and such a volition, yet the result, when produced, comes from the self. There is no saying, 'I did not will it'; or, 'If I could have willed, I would have willed otherwise'.[1]

But if will be used (as it often must be) in a lower sense, then I am afraid we can not deny that the will may be, and often is, forced, and forced not relatively but absolutely.

How is this? To put it shortly, it is because, by the application of compulsion, the psychical conditions of volition can be suppressed, so that it becomes impossible for me to decide myself for this and not for that.

Let us explain. (1) What are called (by a metaphor, and no more than a metaphor) 'automatic' acts may be produced by compulsion. I need not illustrate. Where my conscious will has no control, or has not had time to exert that control, there what must be called the 'uncon-

---

[1] Hence what issues from volition can not issue from compulsion. But the question arises, 'Can a volition be compelled into existence?' This we must answer in the negative. Force and compulsion are terms not here applicable. For *directly* to produce a volition in another is absolutely impossible; and supposing that, by compulsion, you can produce a state of mind, on which the volition follows, yet you have not compelled the volition. That is not the *effect* of the state you have produced. It is the reassertion of the self, which has been drawn back from the whole content of the self; and the whole self asserts itself in the act. Compulsion may *lead to* volition, it can not *cause* it.*

---

* [This is not satisfactory. An act may be technically, and formally, a volition in the proper sense; and yet, if it is the result of an abnormal state into which a person has been forced, or again led by a false pretence or ignorantly (e.g. hypnotism), the volition is *not* (as such) imputable, and the other person *has* used what *may be called* 'force'.]

scious will' can be stimulated to react. Here, obviously, I am not accountable, unless the state of my will, or the circumstances, are imputable to me as a fault. Strictly speaking, I do not know what I am doing, and there is no act proper.

The difficulty is to limit this class. If a pistol is suddenly presented at my head, what I do, before I have time to collect myself, may not be imputable to me at all. The problem is, if I have time enough, may the deed still be 'automatic', in the sense of not proceeding from the conscious will? I possess no private experience in these matters, but I suppose that, given extreme terror or great bodily weakness or some abnormal state of mind, a deed may be done on compulsion, not only without conscious will, but also without the possibility of it. Here, of course, we are not responsible, except so far as it is our own fault that we are in the above condition.

(2) But by far the most awkward question is, ' Given the knowledge of what we are doing, can we then plead compulsion as a ground of irresponsibility ? '

If we know what we do, so far as to know we do this thing, but not so far as to perceive it in relation to other things, the question is easier to answer. There we can not collect ourselves ; and when the deed is being done, we do not know it in its specific character. For instance, if a woman is to sign some document which may be a gross wrong upon her children, she, I suppose, may be so frightened by violence, that she signs, knowing that she is signing, but not at the moment knowing anything but that she is signing. Here we do not know what we do to be wrong, when we are doing it, and here there may be no accountability.

But when I know[1] what I am doing, and also know the quality of it, know the relation in which it stands to the rest of my life, and know that it is wrong, can I then be forced to do it ? It is with some diffidence that I express an opinion, but I think we must say, yes.

Whenever I *can* not collect myself, so as by conscious volition to decide one way or the other, there (provided that it is not my fault that I am unable), it seems to me,

---

[1] [But see note on p. 44. In this whole discussion clearly too much weight is given to the possibility of collecting oneself, drawing a hard-and-fast line. And, clearly, below this, the matter becomes so much one of degree that no *formal* definition is possible. And in the end (p. 47) the question of ' why ' raises hopeless difficulties ; for how much is ' natural ' and how much not ?]

we must say I am not accountable, I did not do the act; there was force put upon me; whether proceeding simply from an uncontrollable element of my nature, or, in addition, from a will outside me, makes no difference. Where volition is a psychical impossibility, and where it is not my fault that it is so impossible, there I am not responsible.

Do such cases exist in fact? I believe they do. There seems no doubt that insanity supplies them; and apart from that, and with regard only to sane persons, such cases are possible. Violent physical pain, with great weakness, may destroy the conditions of volition, by destroying energy; or, further, violent emotion may make it impossible for the person to keep two courses before him and decide—impossible to separate himself from the strain put on him, so as either to resist it or to identify himself with it. In such cases the agents can not collect themselves so as to will, and though with knowledge, yet with pain and feeling of guiltiness, as in a dream, they perform some act which is abhorrent to them, and which they impute to themselves as guilt, but which (provided always their fault has not led to it) the sober onlooker may be unable to impute to them, in their character of a moral agent. I can not doubt, for instance, that in *some* cases a woman is seduced really against her will; and though morally accountable for what has preceded, is not so for anything else. With the practical bearing of this we are not concerned; but I must be allowed to remark that there are dangers besides those of moral laxity. There is a false self-condemnation which takes on the will more than belongs to it, and hopelessness and self-desertion, which lets itself become really what it is not yet, because it thinks it is so already. In morality the past is real because it is present in the will; and conversely, what is not present in the will is only past.

Where the act was only voluntary, where there was no conscious volition, and where volition was psychically impossible, there we are responsible only so far as we ourselves have made the impossibility. If this is not so, we can plead compulsion.

But we foresee the objection that will at once be made. 'This doctrine', it will be said, 'excuses well-nigh everything. For when we go wrong, we do not always say, "I will," and so act. We often intend nothing beforehand, and suddenly, being tempted, we find that we are in the fault before we know what we are doing. And here volition does not take place. Do you say, "But it was possible"?

What do you mean? Are you not deluding yourself with phrases? We say, of course it was possible; of course all might have been otherwise, if it had not been what it was. But then it *was* so, and not otherwise. What you say about possibility here might be said everywhere else and about everything else.'

We must explain. We admit that in a given case it may fairly be said to be psychically impossible that a man, being tempted, should exercise volition one way or the other. But we add that he need not, therefore, be any the less accountable.

The point is this. The impossibility being admitted, *why* is it there? From what comes it? Is it because solicitation to bad is so strong, or because desire of good is so weak? And if it be answered, 'That makes no difference, for it all is relative', we say that, in this sense, it is not 'all relative' at all. The question is, can the man say, 'It is not my doing that my will for good is not stronger. It is not my doing that solicitation to bad is not weaker?' Can he say, 'What energy was in me has, so far as my power went, been made one with good and withdrawn from bad. My standing will, for which volition was not possible, was in this respect not of my own making'? If a man can truly say this, then he may also say, 'I did not have a volition because I could not; and therefore I am not responsible for the act, because not responsible for the will.'

No man can be tempted except by his own will; and the point is, Is it his fault that his will is not otherwise? If that is not his fault, then we admit that he was overborne— that volition was really impossible; and we think that to him, as a moral agent, the deed is not imputable.

But now in our turn we ask, How many bad acts will this account of the matter excuse? Not many, we think.

To repeat, wherever a man can truly say, 'It was not that through my act or neglect my will is generally weak, nor that what will I have is too little made one with the good and turned away from the bad, but my finite strength was overborne;' there we say there is no moral imputation, because it did not lie with the man's will, nor was it in his power, that volition should have taken place.

But where we collect ourselves and volition does take place, I think we must say that, given knowledge, there is always imputation. The *degree* of guilt is of course another matter, which we do not enter on.

The doctrine that our will can be forced to voluntary

acts should not, I think, alarm or distress us. It seems to me by no means an immoral doctrine; and that charge holds good far more against the teaching that there is always a possibility of resistance to evil and performance of good at any moment, and under any previous and present conditions. Possibility of compulsion should make us see more clearly the need of so strengthening our will for good as to make that compulsion impossible for us, except in theory. It should also make us afraid of circumstances, of which most people seem to me not enough afraid, being encouraged in some cases by the doctrine of *libertas arbitrii*. But what we, who reject that doctrine, should encourage ourselves with, is the clear fact that again and again, and by the weak, what we should have said beforehand it was impossible to resist has been resisted, and simply because they had made their will one with the good.

This is all I have to say on compulsion in relation to responsibility, and I know I have not done justice to it. The compulsion which makes irresponsible is absolute compulsion.[1] Relative compulsion, no one would say, relieves us from responsibility; for this means not an unconditional ' must ', but a ' must ' only in case I make up my mind to have this, or decide that I can not face that. Here we can collect ourselves to take which course we choose.

And at this point we should stop; but I should like to wander beyond the subject so far as to call attention to a matter on which there seems to be a great want of light. Everybody sees that any and every sort of influence does not amount to compulsion; but if I may judge from Mr. Stephen's interesting book on Liberty, &c., and the few reviews of it which I saw, there is a general inability to draw the line between them. This is somewhat surprising, and as, from wrong views on this point, wrong conclusions

---

[1] The above doctrine, I think, will cover all maniacal phenomena. In connexion with these let me remark against Dr. Maudsley that not all metaphysicians have denied, or ignored, insane irresistible impulses, coexisting with knowledge of the moral quality of the act. See, for instance, Hegel, *Phil. d. G.*, vii. (2), 222 (1845). Dr. Maudsley's book on ' Responsibility in mental disease ', which I read with much interest and I hope some profit, seems to me to proceed in a somewhat unscientific fashion. How in the world is it possible to say what relieves a madman of responsibility, until you know what makes a sane man responsible? But that Dr. M. does not tell us. And until we know whether a writer is one with us in our main beliefs as to a sane man's responsibility, how can we (unless we are most foolish) receive his evidence as to any one's non-responsibility, when, so far as we can see, on *his* showing *no* one (sane or mad) would be what we call responsible?

follow on most important matters, I will venture to say something. Absolute compulsion, we saw above, is the production in a man of a state of mind or body, without his actual will and against his actual or presumable will (pp. 42–3); and I compel, when with intent I produce this state in another. Relative compulsion rests on the belief in conditional absolute compulsion. In this sense I try to compel, when I cause another to believe that in the case of a certain event taking (or not taking) place, a certain state, against his will, will be produced in him through my agency. Relative compulsion is influence by holding forth of absolute compulsion. It is not mere warning, nor again mere command, but it is a threat; *for the compulsion is, directly or indirectly, to issue from my will.* This last point is of the essence of the matter; and it is here that we think Mr. Stephen went quite wrong (p. 125, ed. ii), and, not keeping in mind the distinction between 'warning' and 'threat', so failed further to distinguish 'persuasion' from 'force'. Of course, in one sense of the word 'force', persuasion is 'force', but not in the sense of 'compulsion'. If I say, 'Cross the stream now, or the rising water will break the bridge, and you will be forced to remain', that is warning; and if, further, I try to convince the man's intellect that the fact is as I state it, with a view perhaps so to influence his conduct, that is persuasion. But if I say, 'Cross now, or I will have the bridge broken', that is threat. It is an attempt at relative compulsion, because it is the holding forth of conditional absolute compulsion, which is to be the result of my will. So if a priest (see Mr. Stephen) says, 'If you do this, it is my conviction or my fear that you will be lost', that is warning. It is holding forth of painful consequences *not* to be the result of the will of the warner (in fact, you may 'warn' of what certainly and unconditionally will be; e. g. if an imaginary priest thought you were one of the *massa damnata*, he might conceivably tell you so). And if the priest by reasoning tried to bring the fact of these consequences home to you, that would be persuasion. But if the priest says, 'If you do this, I, or what I represent, will take such order that you will or may be lost: what we do will, or may, depend on what you do; and what we do will, or may, make a difference in your future prospects', then that is a threat and an attempt at relative compulsion. Persuasion is the bringing about a change in the beliefs or opinions of a man (with or without a view to an answering change in his conduct), by con-

siderations addressed to his understanding; such considerations to put before his mind (as facts) actual or possible
facts, existing or to exist.[1] This, I think, will be clear to
the reader on reflection. The *argumentum baculinum* and
the 'persuaders' of the horseman are jokes; the joke lying
in the incongruity of such things with persuasion. In persuasion consequences to come from the persuader *may* be
the fact we are to be persuaded of; but all that that means
is that persuasion may be *used* in threat. Mere persuasion
is the mere bringing home the fact as a fact, and in
abstraction from *what* the fact is, and from the relation of
it to the *will* of the party persuading and the party persuaded. Further, in persuasion there must be reflection
and reasoning of some kind. Jacob did not *persuade* Esau
with the mess of pottage; he might have done so if he had
argued the point. I should be glad, did space permit me,
to develop this against possible objections; but as it is,
I must ask the reader to pardon the digression, on the
ground that want of clearness here must mean want of clearness in some of the first principles of politics.

B.—CHARACTER, HOW FAR FIXED

Thoroughly to understand what character means is to
know what individuality in general means, and in what
sense a man's self is individual. And to understand this
(need we say it?) is to be clear on some of the most difficult
questions. This we do not for a moment pretend to be;
and all that we are going to say must be looked on as more
or less superficial remark.

'Given such a character and such a stimulus, such an act
must follow.' This is the view which certainly is making
its way. To prove it by particular experiences is from the
very nature of the case impossible; nevertheless, when we
understand it so—'Supposing you have the self-same
character and the self-same stimulus, and nothing else,
must not what follows be also the same?'—it seems quite
impossible to refuse our assent to it, or possible only if we
are prepared to question the truth of any and every general
proposition. But before we assent, we should see that the,
statement is not true except in the abstract. It is true
only *if* you have *nothing but* the same character and
stimulus.

---

[1] [This is 'persuasion' in the strict sense. It is, I think, sometimes
used so as to include, *also and in addition*, personal influence. This
seems a loose use.]

This suggests the inquiry, Is the abstraction any more than idle? The whole statement stands and falls with the '*given*'. No doubt, hypothetical conclusions from a fiction may be useful, but it is not well to forget the fictitious character of the starting-point. So we must ask, Do we ever have such a supposed 'given'? (1) Is there such a thing as a character which remains the same? and (2) In all action are we not forced to recognize something besides character and stimulus?

There is a view which supposes character to be inborn and unalterable. Here we may say that what solicits the character to react alters, but the character does not alter; and further, nothing falls outside the character; it includes the whole individual. And this being so, we might have a stimulus, if not perfectly indistinguishable, yet so much the same that we can say, what has solicited once may solicit again; and, if so, what has been willed once must be willed again. I do not deny that there are some facts on the side of this view, but we must reject it; since, apart from the metaphysical and psychological objections to which it lies open, it is impossible to reconcile it with the palpable fact that characters at least sometimes do alter.[1]

On the above view our abstract statement was as near fact as general statements need be. But let us suppose the opposite view to be true. If character is *not* fixed at all, if it alters perpetually, then if you have what would have been the same stimulus you may always have a different reaction. Here the doctrine, 'same character, same stimulus, same act', is not positively incorrect, but is quite idle, and tells you nothing worth knowing. But this second view, again, is in collision with plain facts, since more or less you can count on human action. Indeed on this view there would be no such thing as character at all.

What facts point to is, however, a third view; and that we may express by saying 'Character is *relatively* fixed'. Having once been formed from the disposition and circumstances, it may alter so little, and so unessentially, that we have a right to say it remained the same. Facts tell us that with many men there is a system of principles, conscious or unconscious, from which most of their acts

[1] This view has been not originated but most clearly and recklessly developed by Schopenhauer. It is interesting to see how with him one one-sidedness leads to the other. Having first supposed intellect to have nothing to do with character, he is then forced by facts to admit the 'acquired character', which, as I understand him, is nothing *but* intellect.

proceed, and which we can presume upon. Again, others alter so much that, as to the man you counted on some years ago, you know not what he will do in such or such a case. And then there are persons who undergo 'conversions', and we have to say, 'Since such a time he is quite another man.'

On this view, 'Same character and stimulus, same act' is again more than not positively incorrect. It stands for something more or less real, and holds good more or less as characters are more or less fixed. But it never loses its hypothetical nature.

Nay more, unless regarded as standing for the abstraction of an element which really is inseparable from other elements, it is positively false. Here we come back to the second question we asked. Are we not forced to recognize something besides character and stimulus? If so, if the act issues from anything *beside* the character, then it is downright false to say, 'Same character, same act'; unless all you mean is, 'Supposing that to take place which perhaps does not ever take place, supposing that you never had anything *but* character, *then* you would have the same act.'

Thus, really to appreciate the truth of 'same character, same act', we have to keep in view, (1) That characters are alterable; (2) That acts do, or may, proceed from something beside the character. And these two qualifications, which are closely connected, we must try to understand more fully.

Character is fixed, but only relatively fixed. When we see how the first comes about, we see that the latter is true. The material of the character is disposition in relation to circumstances. The character is what I have made myself into from these elements, and the reason it remains fixed is that the conditions have, so to speak, been used up and realized into the individuality. What I am I have made myself, out of, in relation to, and against my raw material with its external conditions. The external conditions are more or less permanent, and the raw material is more or less systematized. Hence well-nigh everything is now subsumed under, and takes its quality from, my character. The self is more and more determined and realized, and so excludes possibilities, fixes and closes itself; in short, gets hardened.

Hence, knowing a man to be a certain system (conscious or unconscious), we can tell how things will present themselves to him, and how he will manifest himself against particular stimuli. And we say the man is settled and made, and we know what he is and have a practical certainty that he will always keep so, because we are sure that nothing will happen to him which he has not had before in some form, and which has not some principle in his character under which it will be brought. This is what we mean by the character being fixed.

But the fixedness is not more than relative. There is always a theoretical possibility of change, and sometimes a good deal more than this. The reason is twofold. (1) We cannot exhaust all possible external conditions; (2) We can never systematize the whole self.

(1) You never can say, a man has withstood all sorts of temptations and all combinations of them; and thus there remains the theoretical possibility of some unknown and fatal kind. And (2) the man's self and his character never quite coincide. The character is always the narrower; and moreover, its materials shift, or may shift. This must be, because a man's body changes through change of climate, disease, or age, and so too desires change their force and their nature; and the character to the last, though made, is always in making, and hence there is a possibility of change in it. And to the former consideration, that a man's character does not exhaust his self, it is quite as necessary to keep our eyes open. Character is the 'second nature'; but, besides that, there is something of the first nature left. The *raw* material of the disposition is not *all* systematized in the character, but some element or elements probably remain beside, or rather beneath, the conscious self which affirms itself in the world. Hence, given some new external condition, some strange psychical combination, and the, so to speak, underground self comes to light as a felt want or known desire; and the result of the volition is uncertain. The self is now the abstraction, not from what has been brought under the character, but from that plus a new desire; and what emerges can not be predicted with theoretical certainty. Everybody must feel that he has unrealized possibilities; and what would he do if there was a chance of realizing them, if, so to speak, they could be let loose?

Now so far as the habitual self is both well systematized, and wide enough to cover possibilities, we are pretty safe. But, as we have seen, no man can order his whole self with all its underground longings. Hence something might always come up, if not kept down by the habituated self. Suppose now that this takes place, and there ensues a collision between desire and principle; then, as the conclusion is not through habit a foregone one (there is only a general habit of acting on principle, not on principle against *this* desire), the strength of the temptation can not be calculated, and so also not the issue. Take for example an elderly man, who never has had temptation in the way of sexual love, and now, through some accident, is in love where the passion ought to remain unsatisfied. Here *such* a temptation has not been resisted by the character. The volition results not merely from the habituated or principled self, but from that plus a new force; and if the volition were a 'resultant' only, the result *must* be different. As it is, all we can say is that it *may* be.

If there is thus no theoretical certainty of the future with a systematic principled character, how will it be when the habituated self involves contradictions? Here we must guess by analogy, but we can do no more than guess. The act depends on the whole conscious and unconscious self;[1] and if that is more or less chaotic, it must be variable and subject to mere accident; nor, given a fresh combination of the elements, so far as I can see, is it possible theoretically to deduce the result. The result is *not* a mere 'resultant'.

It has been remarked that before the time comes it is not possible to have an absolutely certain knowledge, how we shall act. The reason partly, no doubt, is that particular knowledge of details is wanting to us; but this is not all the reason. The act does not answer to the mere theoretical application of a principle. The desire in the presence of the object can not be excluded from the calculation, nor can that desire always be fore-realized by the presentation of the object before the understanding and imagination. In the act the will is the reaction of the whole self against the presented object, and we can know how that will be determined, only so far as the self, which we have not habituated and do not know, can be excluded.

Thus the self we have habituated ourselves into is the only self to be counted on, and so none of us is quite safe. Many of us show selves to ourselves and the world, which are not the realization of another element which we take about with us, and which quietly, or it may be longingly, remains below the 'floor of consciousness', perhaps never to

---

[1] Let me observe that this consideration destroys the last refuge of the 'freedom' which rests on abstract possibility or mere chance. Where the act can not be accounted for by what is *before* the mind, we have still to consider what is *in* the mind.

appear, perhaps to burst out in we know not what, in light and love, or in 'dirt and fire'. But this should be a mere theoretical possibility; and if it really comes about, yet the self that we know should be strong enough to make the best of it.

This consideration (though in most cases there is little need for it) will help to explain mysterious conversions and changes; but we must bring this note to an end.

Our result is that we may have practical certainty that a man will not change; and hence, knowing his ways, we may be pretty sure what he will do. But since the conditions he will meet with can not be theoretically exhausted, and his habituated self does not cover his whole nature, therefore theoretical possibility of fresh act and change of character remains;[1] and this is important; for we see, on the whole, that it is only a part of the facts which is covered by 'same character and stimulus, same act'.

C.—FREEDOM

I am not going to try to treat such a subject as this by the way, but a very few words may be of use to the beginner. If we put it in as ordinary language as we can, the main difficulty is this—*If* there is a 'because' to my acts, responsibility seems to go; and yet we have an irresistible impulse to find a 'because' everywhere. But is it not the *sort* of 'because' which gives all the trouble?

(1) We may say there is one kind of 'because', and one only. Then I am put on a level with nature; and whether you take your 'because' from mechanism, or start from will and put nature on a level with me, makes no practical difference, since in neither case do you distinguish.

(2) We may say there is *no* 'because' for us, and may say,

    (*a*) We know will, and it is beyond the 'because'. It = chance. Or,

    (*b*) Will is unknowable. 'Because' is for thought only, and for intelligible objects.

Neither of these assertions can hold; for, apart from metaphysical difficulties, we actually do predict volitions to a large extent.

---

[1] This bears on a practical difficulty. Often we feel tolerably sure that this or that old reprobate is hopelessly hardened, but we can not say there is *no* chance of his turning again. Hence the theoretical justification of the practical religious maxim not to give up any man as lost.

(3) We may admit the 'because' (or rather, since our will is rational, we may demand it), but may say, there is more than one sort of 'because'. There is mechanical 'because', but that is not adequate to the lowest life, still less to mind. And if we take this line, we may find that the 'because' which excludes accountability is only the 'because' which does *not* apply to the mind, but to something else.

If 'must' always means the 'must' of the falling stone, then 'must' is irreconcilable with 'ought' or 'can'. Freedom will be a bare 'not-must', and will be purely negative.

But how if the 'must' is a higher 'must'? And how if freedom is also positive—if a merely negative freedom is no freedom at all? We may find then that in true freedom the 'can' is not only reconcilable with, but inseparable from, the 'ought'; and both not only reconcilable with, but inseparable from, the 'must'. Is not freedom something positive? And can we give a positive meaning to freedom except by introducing a will which not only 'can', but also 'ought to' and 'must', fulfil a law of its nature, which is *not* the nature of the physical world?

There is a view, which says to the necessitarian, 'Are you not neglecting distinctions?'; to the believer in 'liberty', 'Are you sure you *are* distinguishing? Is there the smallest practical difference between external necessity and chance? Can you even define them theoretically, and keep them distinct? Is the opposite of a false view always true? Is it not much rather often (and always in some spheres) just *as* false?'; and to both, 'So long as you refuse to read metaphysic, so long will metaphysical abstractions prey upon you.'

Or, to put the same thing in a slightly different way, we all want freedom. Well then, what is freedom? 'It means not being made to do or be anything. "Free" means "free *from*".' And are we to be quite free? 'Yes, if freedom is good, we can not have too much of it.' Then, if 'free'='free *from*', to be quite free is to be free from everything—free from other men, free from law, from morality, from thought, from sense, from—Is there anything we are *not* to be free from? To be free from everything is to be—nothing. Only nothing is quite free, and freedom is abstract nothingness. If in death we cease to be anything, then there first we are free, because there first we are—not.

Every one sees this is not the freedom we want. '" Free" is " free from", but then *I* am to be free. It is absurd to think that I am to be free from myself. I am to be free to exist and to assert myself.' Well and good ; but this is not what we began with. Freedom now means the self-assertion which is nothing *but* self-assertion. It is not merely negative—it is also positive, and negative only so far as, and because, it is positive.

'I am to assert myself and nothing else, and this is freedom.' So far as this goes we quite agree; but it tells us scarcely anything. I am to assert myself, but then what action *does* assert myself; or rather, what action does *not* assert myself? And if I am to assert nothing *but* myself, what can I do, so as to do this and nothing but this ? What, in short, *is* this self, the assertion of which is freedom?

'*My* self', we shall hear, 'is what is *mine*; and mine is what is *not* yours, or what does not belong to any one else. I am free when I assert my private will, the will peculiar to me.' Can this hold? Apart from any other objection, is it freedom? Suppose I am a glutton and a drunkard; in these vices I assert my private will; am I then free so far as a glutton and drunkard, or am I a slave—the slave of my appetites ? The answer must be, 'The slave of his lusts is, so far, not a free man. The man is free who realizes his *true* self.' Then the whole question is, What is this true self, and can it be found apart from something like law ? Is there any 'perfect freedom' which does not mean 'service'?

Reflection shows us that what we call freedom is both positive and negative. There are then two questions— *What* am I to be free to assert ? *What* am I to be free from ? And these are answered by the answer to one question—*What* is my true self?

---

[1] The references on p. 28 are to the Royal Prussian Academy of the Sciences' edition of Kant's *Werke*. They are from *Die Metaphysik der Sitten*, in *Allgemeine Anmerkung* to § 49, under (*É*) *Vom Straf- und Begnadigungsrecht.*

ESSAY II

WHY SHOULD I BE MORAL?[1]

WHY should I be moral? The question is natural, and yet seems strange. It appears to be one we ought to ask, and yet we feel, when we ask it, that we are wholly removed from the moral point of view.

To ask the question Why? is rational; for reason teaches us to do nothing blindly, nothing without end or aim. She teaches us that what is good must be good for something, and that what is good for nothing is not good at all. And so we take it as certain that there is an end on one side, means on the other; and that only if the end is good, and the means conduce to it, have we a right to say the means are good. It is rational, then, always to inquire, Why should I do it?

But here the question seems strange. For morality (and she too is reason) teaches us that, if we look on her only as good for something else, we never in that case have seen her at all. She says that she is an end to be desired for her own sake, and not as a means to something beyond. Degrade her, and she disappears; and, to keep her, we must love and not merely use her. And so at the question Why? we are in trouble, for that does assume, and does take for granted, that virtue in this sense is unreal, and what we believe is false. Both virtue and the asking Why? seem rational, and yet incompatible one with the other; and the

[1] Let me observe here that the word 'moral' has three meanings, which must be throughout these pages distinguished by the context. (1) Moral is opposed to *non*-moral. The moral world, or world of morality, is opposed to the natural world, where morality can not exist. (2) Within the moral world of moral agents, 'moral' is opposed to *im*moral. (3) Again, within the moral world, and the moral part of the moral world, 'moral' is further restricted to the *personal* side of the moral life and the moral institutions. It stands for the *inner* relation of this or that will to the universal, not to the whole, outer and inner, realization of morality.

better course will be, not forthwith to reject virtue in favour
of the question, but rather to inquire concerning the nature
of the Why?

Why should I be virtuous? Why should I? Could anything be more modest? Could anything be less assuming?
It is not a dogma; it is only a question. And yet a question may contain (perhaps must contain) an assumption
more or less hidden; or, in other words, a dogma. Let us
see what is assumed in the asking of our question.

In 'Why should I be moral?' the 'Why should I?' was
another way of saying, What good is virtue? or rather,
For what is it good? and we saw that in asking, Is virtue
good as a means, and how so? we do assume that virtue is
not good, except as a means. The dogma at the root of
the question is hence clearly either (1) the general statement
that only means are good, or (2) the particular assertion
of this in the case of virtue.

To explain; the question For what? Whereto? is either
universally applicable, or not so. It holds everywhere, or
we mean it to hold only here. Let us suppose, in the first
place, that it is meant to hold everywhere.

Then (1) we are taking for granted that nothing is good
in itself; that only the means to something else are good;
that 'good', in a word, = 'good for', and good for something
else. Such is the general canon by which virtue would have
to be measured.

No one perhaps would explicitly put forward such a canon,
and yet it may not be waste of time to examine it.

The good is a means: a means is a means to something
else, and this is an end. Is the end good? No; if we hold
to our general canon, it is not good as an end: the good
was always good for something else, and was a means. To
be good, the end must be a means, and so on for ever in
a process which has no limit. If we ask now What is good?
we must answer, There is nothing which is *not* good, for
there is nothing which may not be regarded as conducing
to something outside itself. Everything is relative to something else. And the essence of the good is to exist by

virtue of something else and something else for ever. Everything *is* something else, is the result which at last we are brought to, if we insist on pressing our canon as universally applicable.

But the above is not needed perhaps; for those who introduced the question Why? did not think of things in general. The good for them was not an infinite process of idle distinction. Their interest is practical, and they do and must understand by the good (which they call a means) some means to an end in itself; which latter they assume, and unconsciously fix in whatever is agreeable to themselves. If we said to them, for example, 'Virtue is a means, and so is everything besides, and a means to everything else besides. Virtue is a means to pleasure, pain, health, disease, wealth, poverty, and is a good, because a means; and so also with pain, poverty, &c. They are all good, because all means. Is this what you mean by the question Why?', they would answer No. And they would answer No, because something has been taken as an end, and therefore good; and has been assumed dogmatically.

The universal application of the question For what? or Whereto? is, we see, repudiated. The question does not hold good everywhere, and we must now consider, secondly, its particular application to virtue.

(2) Something is here assumed to be the end; and further, this is assumed *not* to be virtue; and thus the question is founded, 'Is virtue a means to a given end, which end is the good? Is virtue good? and why? i.e. as conducing to what good is it good?' The dogma, A or B or C is a good in itself, justifies the inquiry, Is D a means to A, B, or C? And it is the dogmatic character of the question that we wished to point out. Its rationality, put as if universal, is tacitly assumed to end with a certain province; and our answer must be this: *If* your formula will not (on your own admission) apply to everything, what ground have you for supposing it to apply to virtue? 'Be virtuous that you may be happy (i. e. pleased)'; then why be happy, and not rather virtuous? 'The pleasure of all is an end.'

Why all? 'Mine.' *Why* mine? Your reply must be, that you take it to be so, and are prepared to argue on the thesis that something not virtue is the end in itself. And so are we; and we shall try to show that this is erroneous. But even if we fail in that, we have, I hope, made it clear that the question, Why should I be moral? rests on the assertion of an end in itself which is not morality;[1] and a point of this importance must not be taken for granted.

It is quite true that to ask Why should I be moral? is *ipso facto* to take one view of morality, is to assume that virtue is a means to something not itself. But it is a mistake to suppose that the general asking of Why? affords any presumption in favour of, or against, any one theory. If any theory could stand upon the What for? as a rational formula, which must always hold good and be satisfied, then, to that extent, no doubt it would have an advantage. But we have seen that all doctrines alike must reject the What for? and agree in this rejection, if they agree in nothing else; since they all must have an end which is not a mere means. And if so, is it not foolish to suppose that its giving a reason for virtue is any argument in favour of Hedonism, when for its own end it can give no reason at all? Is it not clear that, if you have any Ethics, you must have an end which is above the Why? in the sense of What for?; and that, if this is so, the question is now, as it was two thousand years ago, Granted that there is an end, *what* is this end? And the asking that question, as reason and history both tell us, is not in itself the presupposing of a Hedonistic answer, or any other answer.

The claim of pleasure to be the end we are to discuss in another paper. But what is clear at first sight is, that to take virtue as a mere means to an ulterior end is in direct antagonism to the voice of the moral consciousness.

---

[1] 'The question itself [Why should I do right?] can not be put, except in a form which assumes that the Utilitarian answer is the only one which can possibly be given. ... The words "Why should I" mean "What shall I get by", "What motive have I for" this or that course of conduct?'—Stephen, *Liberty*, &c., p. 361, ed. ii.

That consciousness, when unwarped by selfishness and not blinded by sophistry, is convinced that to ask for the Why? is simple immorality; to do good for its own sake is virtue, to do it for some ulterior end or object, not itself good, is never virtue; and never to act but for the sake of an end, other than doing well and right, is the mark of vice. And the theory which sees in virtue, as in money-getting, a means which is mistaken for an end, contradicts the voice which proclaims that virtue not only does seem to be, but is, an end in itself.[1]

---

[1] There are two points which we may notice here. (1) There is a view which says, 'Pleasure (or pain) is what moves you to act; therefore pleasure (or pain) is your motive, and is always the Why? of your actions. You think otherwise by virtue of a psychological illusion.' For a consideration of this view we must refer to Essay VII. We may, however, remark in passing, that this view confuses the motive, which is an object before the mind, with the psychical stimulus, which is not an object before the mind and therefore is not a motive nor a Why?, in the sense of an end proposed.

(2) There is a view which tries to found moral philosophy on theology, a theology of a somewhat coarse type, consisting mainly in the doctrine of a criminal judge, of superhuman knowledge and power, who has promulgated and administers a criminal code. This may be called the 'do it or be d——d' theory of morals, and is advocated or timidly suggested by writers nowadays, not so much (it seems probable) because in most cases they have a strong, or even a weak, belief in it; but because it stops holes in theories which they feel, without some help of the kind, will not hold water. We are not concerned with this opinion as a theological doctrine, and will merely remark that, as such, it appears to us to contain the essence of irreligion; but with respect to morals, we say that, let it be never so true, it contributes nothing to moral philosophy, unless that has to do with the means whereby we are simply to get pleasure or avoid pain. The theory not only confuses morality and religion, but reduces them both to deliberate selfishness. Fear of criminal proceedings in the other world does not tell us what is morally right in this world. It merely gives a selfish motive for obedience to those who believe, and leaves those who do not believe, in all cases with less motive, in some cases with none. I can not forbear remarking that, so far as my experience goes, where future punishments are firmly believed in, the fear of them has, in most cases, but little influence on the mind. And the facts do not allow us to consider the fear of punishment in this world as the main motive to morality. In most cases there is, properly speaking, *no* ulterior motive. A man is moral because he likes being moral; and

Taking our stand then, as we hope, on this common consciousness, what answer can we give when the question Why should I be moral?, in the sense of What will it advantage me?, is put to us? Here we shall do well, I think, to avoid all praises of the pleasantness of virtue. We may believe that it transcends all possible delights of vice, but it would be well to remember that we desert a moral point of view, that we degrade and prostitute virtue, when to those who do not love her for herself we bring ourselves to recommend her for the sake of her pleasures. Against the base mechanical βαναυσία which meets us on all sides, with its 'what is the use' of goodness, or beauty, or truth, there is but one fitting answer from the friends of science, or art, or religion and virtue, 'We do not know, and we do not care.'

As a direct answer to the question we should not say more: but, putting ourselves at our questioner's point of view, we may ask in return, Why should I be immoral? Is it not disadvantageous to be so? We can ask, is your view consistent? Does it satisfy you, and give you what you want? And if you are satisfied, and so far as you are satisfied, do see whether it is not because, and so far as, you are false to your theory; so far as you are living not directly with a view to the pleasant, but with a view to something else, or with no view at all, but, as you would call it, without any 'reason'. We believe that, in your heart, your end is what ours is, but that about this end you not only are sorely mistaken, but in your heart you feel and know it, or at least would do so, if you would only reflect. And more than this I think we ought not to say.

What more are we to say? If a man asserts total scepticism, you can not argue with him. You can show that he

he likes it, partly because he has been brought up to the habit of liking it, and partly because he finds it gives him what he wants, while its opposite does not do so. He is not as a rule kept 'straight' by the contemplation of evils to be inflicted on him from the outside; and the shame he feels at the bad opinion of others is not a mere external evil, and is not feared simply as such. In short, a man is a human being, something larger than the abstraction of an actual or possible criminal.

contradicts himself; but if he says, 'I do not care'—there is an end of it. So, too, if a man says, 'I shall do what I like, because I happen to like it; and as for ends, I recognize none'—you may indeed show him that his conduct is in fact otherwise; and if he will assert anything as an end, if he will but say, 'I have no end but myself', then you may argue with him, and try to prove that he is making a mistake as to the nature of the end he alleges. But if he says, 'I care not whether I am moral or rational, nor how much I contradict myself', then argument ceases. We, who have the power, believe that what is rational (if it is not yet) at least is to be real, and decline to recognize anything else. For standing on reason we can give, of course, no further reason; but we push our reason against what seems to oppose it, and soon force all to see that moral obligations do not vanish where they cease to be felt or are denied.

Has the question, Why should I be moral? no sense then, and is no positive answer possible? No, the question has no sense at all; it is simply unmeaning, unless it is equivalent to, *Is* morality an end in itself; and, if so, how and in what way is it an end? Is morality the same as the end for man, so that the two are convertible; or is morality one side, or aspect, or element of some end which is larger than itself? Is it the whole end from all points of view, or is it one view of the whole? Is the artist moral, so far as he is a good artist, or the philosopher moral, so far as he is a good philosopher? Are their art or science, and their virtue, one thing from one and the same point of view, or two different things, or one thing from two points of view?

These are not easy questions to answer, and we can not discuss them yet. We have taken the reader now so far as he need go, before proceeding to the following essays. What remains is to point out the most general expression for the end in itself, the ultimate practical 'why'; and that we find in the word *self-realization*. But what follows is an anticipation of the sequel, which we can not promise to make intelligible as yet; and the reader who finds difficulties had better go on at once to Essay III.

How can it be proved that self-realization is the end? There is only one way to do that. This is to know what we mean, when we say 'self', and 'real', and 'realize', and 'end'; and to know that is to have something like a system of metaphysic, and to say it would be to exhibit that system. Instead of remarking, then, that we lack space to develop our views, let us frankly confess that, properly speaking, we have no such views to develop, and therefore we can not *prove* our thesis. All that we can do is partially to explain it, and try to render it plausible. It is a formula, which our succeeding Essays will in some way fill up, and which here we shall attempt to recommend to the reader beforehand.

An objection will occur at once. 'There surely are ends', it will be said, 'which are not myself, which fall outside my activity, and which, nevertheless, I do realize, and think I ought to realize.' We must try to show that the objection rests upon a misunderstanding, and, as a statement of fact, brings with it insuperable difficulties.

Let us first go to the moral consciousness, and see what that tells us about its end.

Morality implies an end in itself: we take that for granted. Something is to be done, a good is to be realized. But that result is, by itself, not morality: morality differs from art, in that it can not make the act a *mere* means to the result. Yet there is a means. There is not only something to be done, but something to be done by me—*I* must do the act, must realize the end. Morality implies both the something to be done, and the doing of it by me; and if you consider them as end and means, you can not separate the end and the means. If you chose to change the position of end and means, and say my doing is the end, and the 'to be done' is the means, you would not violate the moral consciousness; for the truth is that means and end are not applicable here. The act for me means my act, and there is no end beyond the act. This we see in the belief that failure may be equivalent morally to success— in the saying, that there is nothing good except a good will. In short, for morality the end implies the act, and the act implies self-realization. This, if it were doubtful, would be shown (we may remark in passing) by the feeling of pleasure which attends the putting forth of the act. For if pleasure be the feeling of self, and accompany the act, this indicates that the putting forth of the act is also the putting forth of the self.

But we must not lay too much stress on the moral consciousness, for we shall be reminded, perhaps, that not only can it be, but, like the miser's consciousness, it frequently has been explained, and that both states of mind are illusions generated on one and the same principle.

Let us then dismiss the moral consciousness, and not trouble ourselves about what we think we ought to do; let us try to show that what we do do, is, perfectly or imperfectly, to realize ourselves, and that we can not possibly do anything else; that all we can realize is (accident apart) our ends, or the objects we desire; and that all we can desire is, in a word, self.

This, we think, will be readily admitted by our main psychological party. What we wish to avoid is that it should be admitted in a form which makes it unmeaning; and of this there is perhaps some danger. We do not want the reader to say, 'Oh yes, of course, relativity of knowledge—everything is a state of consciousness', and so dismiss the question. If the reader believes that a steam-engine, after it is made, is nothing[1] but a state of the mind

---

[1] We may remark that the ordinary 'philosophical' person, who talks about 'relativity', really does not seem to know what he is saying. He will tell you that 'all' (or 'all we know and can know'—there is no practical difference between that and 'all') is relative to consciousness—not giving you to understand that he means thereby any consciousness beside his own, and ready, I should imagine, with his grin at the notion of a mind which is anything more than the mind of this or that man; and then, it may be a few pages further on or further back, will talk to you of the state of the earth before man existed on it. But we wish to know what in the world it all means; and would suggest, as a method of clearing the matter, the two questions—(1) Is my consciousness something that goes and is beyond myself; and if so, in what sense? and (2) Had I a father? What do I mean by that, and how do I reconcile my assertion of it with my answer to question (1)?

of the person or persons who have made it, or who are looking at it, we do not hold what we feel tempted to call such a silly doctrine; and would point out to those who do hold it that, at all events, the engine is a very different state of mind, after it is made, from what it was before.

Again, we do not want the reader to say, 'Certainly, every object or end which I propose to myself is, as such, a mere state of my mind—it is a thought in my head, or a state of me, and so, when it becomes real, I become real'; because, though it is very true that my thought, as my thought, can not exist apart from me thinking it, and therefore my proposed end must, as such, be a state of me;[1] yet this is not what we are driving at. All my ends are my thoughts, but all my thoughts are not my ends; and if what we meant by self-realization was, that I have in my head the idea of any future external event, then I should realize myself practically when I see that the engine is going to run off the line, and it does so.

A desired object (as desired) is a thought, and my thought; but it is something more, and that something more is, in short, that it is desired by me. And we ought by right, before we go further, to exhibit a theory of desire; but, if we could do that, we could not stop to do it. However, we say with confidence that, in desire, what is desired must in all cases be self.

If we could accept the theory that the end or motive is always the idea of a pleasure (or pain) of our own, which is associated with the object presented, and which is that in the object which moves us, and the only thing which does move us, then from such a view it would follow at once that all we can aim at is a state of ourselves.

We can not, however, accept the theory, since we believe it both to ignore and to be contrary to facts (see Essay VII), but, though we do not admit that the motive is always, or in most cases, the idea of a state of our feeling self, yet we think it is clear that nothing moves unless it be desired,

---

[1] Let me remark in passing that it does not follow from this that it is nothing but a state of me, as this or that man.

and that what is desired is ourself. For all objects or ends have been associated with our satisfaction, or (more correctly) have been felt in and as ourselves, or we have felt ourselves therein; and the only reason why they move us now is that, when they are presented to our minds as motives, we do now feel ourselves asserted or affirmed in them. The essence of desire for an object would thus be the feeling of our affirmation in the idea of something not ourself, felt against the feeling of ourself as, without the object, void and negated; and it is the tension of this relation which produces motion. If so, then nothing is desired except that which is identified with ourselves, and we can aim at nothing, except so far as we aim at ourselves in it.

But passing by the above, which we can not here expound and which we lay no stress on, we think that the reader will probably go with us so far as this, that in desire what we want, so far as we want it, is ourselves in some form, or is some state of ourselves; and that our wanting anything else would be psychologically inexplicable.

Let us take this for granted then; but is this what we mean by self-realization? Is the conclusion that, in trying to realize we try to realize some state of ourself, all that we are driving at? No, the self we try to realize is for us a whole, it is not a mere collection of states. (See more in Essay III.)

If we may presuppose in the reader a belief in the doctrine that what is wanted is a state of self, we wish, standing upon that, to urge further that the whole self is present in its states, and that therefore the whole self is the object aimed at; and this is what we mean by self-realization. If a state of self is what is desired, can you, we wish to ask, have states of self which are states of nothing (compare Essay I); can you possibly succeed in regarding the self as a collection, or stream, or train, or series, or aggregate? If you can not think of it as a mere one, can you on the other hand think of it as a mere many, as mere ones; or are you not driven, whether you wish it or not, to regard it as a one in many, or a many in one? Are we not forced to look on the self as a whole, which is not merely the sum of its parts, nor yet some other particular beside them? And must we not say that to realize self is always to realize a whole, and that the question in morals is to find the true whole, realizing which will practically realize the true self?

This is the question which to the end of this volume we shall find ourselves engaged on. For the present, turning our attention away from it in this form, and contenting ourselves with the proposition that to realize is to realize self, let us now, apart from questions of psychology or metaphysics, see what ends they are, in fact, which living men do propose to themselves, and whether these do not take the form of a whole.

Upon this point there is no need, I think, to dwell at any length; for it seems clear that, if we ask ourselves what it is we should most wish for, we find some general wish which would include and imply our particular wishes. And, if we turn to life, we see that no man has disconnected particular ends; he looks beyond the moment, beyond this or that circumstance or position; his ends are subordinated to wider ends; each situation is seen (consciously or unconsciously) as part of a broader situation, and in this or that act he is aiming at and realizing some larger whole, which is not real in any particular act as such, and yet is realized in the body of acts which carry it out. We need not stop here, because the existence of larger ends, which embrace smaller ends, can not be doubted; and so far we may say that the self we realize is identified with wholes, or that the ideas of the states of self we realize are associated with ideas that stand for wholes.

But is it also true that these larger wholes are included in one whole? I think that it is. I am not forgetting that we act, as a rule, not *from* principle or with the principle before us, and I wish the reader not to forget that the principle may be there and may be our basis or our goal, without our knowing anything about it. And here, of course, I am not saying that it has occurred to every one to ask himself whether he aims at a whole, and what that is; because considerable reflection is required for this, and the amount need not have been reached. Nor again am I saying that every man's actions are consistent, that he does not wander from his end, and that he has not particular ends which will not come under his main end. Nor further do I assert that the life of every man does form a whole; that in some men there are not co-ordinated ends, which are incompatible and incapable of subordination into a system.[1] What I am saying is that, if the life of the normal man be inspected, and the ends he has in view (as exhibited in his acts) be considered, they will, roughly speaking, be embraced in one main end or whole of ends. It has been said that 'every man has a different notion of happiness', but this is scarcely correct, unless mere detail be referred to. Certainly, however, every man has *a* notion of happiness, and *his* notion, though he may not quite know what it is. Most men have a life which they live, and with which they are tolerably satisfied, and that life, when examined, is seen to be fairly systematic; it is seen to be a sphere including spheres, the lower spheres subordinating to themselves and qualifying particular actions, and themselves subordinated to and qualified by the whole. And most men have more or less of an ideal of life—a notion of perfect happiness, which is never quite attained in real life; and if you take (not of course any one, but) the normal decent and serious man, when he has been long enough in the world to know what he wants, you will find that his notion of perfect happiness, or ideal life, is not something straggling, as it were, and discontinuous, but is brought before the mind as a unity, and, if imagined more in detail, is a system where particulars subserve one whole.

Without further dwelling on this, I will ask the reader to

[1] The unhappiness of such lives in general, however, points to the fact that the real end is a whole. Dissatisfaction rises from the knowing or feeling that the self is not realized, and not realized because not realized as a system.

reflect whether the ends, proposed to themselves by ordinary persons, are not wholes, and are not in the end members in a larger whole; and, if that be so, whether, since it is so, and since all we can want must (as before stated) be ourselves, we must not now say that we aim not only at the realization of self, but of self as a whole; seeing that there is a general object of desire with which self is identified, or (on another view) with the idea of which the idea of our pleasure is associated.

Up to the present we have been trying to point out that what we aim at is self, and self as a whole; in other words, that self as a whole is, in the end, the content of our wills. It will still further, perhaps, tend to clear the matter, if we refer to the form of the will—not, of course, suggesting that the form is anything real apart from the content.

On this head we are obliged to restrict ourselves to the assertion of what we believe to be fact. We remarked in our last Essay that, in saying 'I will this or that', we really mean something. In saying it we do not mean (at least, not as a rule) to distinguish a self that wills from a self that does not will; but what we do mean is to distinguish the self, as will in general, from this or that object of desire, and, at the same time, to identify the two; to say, this or that is willed, or the will has uttered itself in this or that. The will is looked on as a whole, and there are two sides or factors to that whole. Let us consider an act of will, and, that we may see more clearly, let us take a deliberate volitional choice. We have conflicting desires, say A and B; we feel two tensions, two drawings (so to speak), but we can not actually affirm ourselves in both. Action does not follow, and we reflect on the two objects of desire, and we are aware that we are reflecting on them, or (if our language allowed us to say it) over them. But we do not merely stand looking on till, so to speak, we find we are gone in one direction, have closed with A or B. For we are aware besides of ourselves, not simply as something theoretically above A and B, but as something also practically above them, as a concentra-

tion which is not one or the other, but which is the
possibility of either; which is the inner side indifferently of
an act which should realize A, or one which should realize
B; and hence, which is neither, and yet is superior to both.
In short, we do not simply feel ourselves in A and B, but
have distinguished ourselves from both, as what is above
both. This is one factor in volition, and it is hard to find
any name better for it than that of the universal factor, or
side, or moment.[1] We need say much less about the second
factor. In order to will, we must will something; the
universal side by itself is not will at all. To will we must
identify ourselves with this, that, or the other; and here we
have the particular side, and the second factor in volition.
Thirdly, the volition as a whole (and first, as a whole, is it
volition) is the identity of both these factors, and the
projection or carrying of it out into external existence; the
realization both of the particular side, the this or that to be
done, and the realization of the inner side of self in the
doing of it, with a realization of self in both, as is proclaimed
by the feeling of pleasure. This unity of the two factors
we may call the individual whole, or again the concrete
universal; and, although we are seldom conscious of the
distinct factors, yet every act of will will be seen, when

---

[1] As we saw in our last Essay, there are two dangers to avoid here,
in the shape of two one-sided views, Scylla and Charybdis. The first
is the ignoring of the universal side altogether, even as an element;
the second is the assertion of it as more than an element, as by itself
will. Against this second it is necessary to insist that the will is what
it wills, that to will you must will something, and that you can not
will the mere form of the will; further, that the mere formal freedom
of choice not only, if it were real, would *not* be true freedom, but that,
in addition, it is a metaphysical fiction; that the universal is real only
as one side of the whole, and takes its character from the whole; and
that, in the most deliberate and would-be formal volition, the self that
is abstracted and stands above the particulars, is the abstraction
not only from the particular desire or desires before the mind,
but also from the whole self, the self which embodies all past acts,
and that *the abstraction is determined by that from which it is
abstracted*, no less than itself is a moment in the determination of the
concrete act.

analysed, to be a whole of this kind, and so to realize what is always the nature of the will.

But to what end have we made this statement? Our object has been to draw the attention of the reader to the fact that not only what is willed by men, the end they set before themselves, is a whole, but also that the will itself, looked at apart from any particular object or content, is a similar whole: or, to put it in its proper order, the self is realized in a whole of ends because it is a whole, and because it is not satisfied till it has found itself, till content be adequate to form, and that content be realized; and this is what we mean by practical self-realization.

'Realize yourself', 'realize yourself as a whole', is the result of the foregoing. The reader, I fear, may be wearied already by these prefatory remarks, but it will be better in the end if we delay yet longer. All we know at present is that we are to realize self as *a* whole; but as to *what* whole it is, we know nothing, and must further consider.

The end we desire (to repeat it) is the finding and possessing ourselves as a whole. We aim at this both in theory and practice. What we want in theory is to understand the object; we want neither to remove nor alter the world of sensuous fact, but we want to get at the truth of it. The whole of science takes it for granted that the 'not-ourself' is really intelligible; it stands and falls with this assumption. So long as our theory strikes on the mind as strange and alien, so long do we say we have not found truth; we feel the impulse to go beyond and beyond, we alter and alter our views, till we see them as a consistent whole. There we rest, because then we have found the nature of our own mind and the truth of facts in one. And in practice again, with a difference, we have the same want. Here our aim is not, leaving the given as it is, to find the truth of it; but here we want to force the sensuous fact to correspond to the truth of ourselves. We say, ' My sensuous existence is thus, but I truly am not thus; I am different.' On the one hand, as a matter of fact, I and my existing world are discrepant; on the other hand, the instinct of my nature tells me that the world is mine. On that impulse I act, I alter and alter the sensuous facts, till I find in them nothing but myself carried out. Then I possess my world, and I do not possess it until I find my will in it; and I do not find that, until what I have is a harmony or a whole in system.

Both in theory and practice my end is to realize myself as a whole. But is this all? Is a *consistent* view all that we want in theory? Is an *harmonious* life all that we want in practice? Certainly not. A doctrine must not only hold together, but it must hold the facts together as well. We can not rest in it simply because it does not contradict itself. The theory must take in the facts, and an ultimate theory must take in all the facts. So again in practice. It is no human ideal to lead 'the life of an oyster'. We have no right first to find out just what we happen to be and to have, and then to contract our wants to that limit. We can not do it if we would, and morality calls to us that, if we try to do it, we are false to ourselves. Against the sensuous facts around us and within us, we must for ever attempt to widen our empire; we must at least try to go forward, or we shall certainly be driven back.

So self-realization means more than the mere assertion of the self as a whole.[1] And here we may refer to two principles, which Kant put forward under the names of 'Homogeneity' and 'Specification'. Not troubling ourselves with our relation to Kant, we may say that the ideal is neither to be perfectly homogeneous, nor simply to be specified to the last degree, but rather to combine both these elements. Our true being is not the extreme of unity, nor of diversity, but the perfect identity of both. And 'Realize yourself' does not mean merely 'Be a whole', but 'Be an *infinite* whole'.

At this word, I am afraid, the reader who has not yet despaired of us will come to a stop, and refuse to enter into

---

[1] I leave out of sight the important question whether any partial whole *can* be self-consistent. If (which seems the better view) this can not be, we shall not need to say 'Systematize *and* widen', but the second will be implied in the first.

the region of nonsense.   But why should it be nonsense?
When the poet and the preacher tell us the mind is infinite,
most of us feel that it is so; and has our science really
come to this, that the beliefs which answer to our highest
feelings must be theoretical absurdities?   Should not the
philosophy which tells us such a thing be very sure of the
ground it goes upon?   But if the reader will follow me,
I think I can show him that the mere finitude of the mind
is a more difficult thesis to support than its infinity.

It would be well if I could ask the reader to tell me
what he means by 'finite'.   As that can not be, I must
say that finite is limited or ended.   To be finite is to be
some one among others, some one which is *not* others.
One finite ends where the other finite begins; it is bounded
from the outside, and can not go beyond itself without
becoming something else, and thereby perishing.[1]

'The mind', we are told, 'is finite; and the reason why
we say it is finite is that we know it is finite.   The mind
knows that itself is finite.'   This is the doctrine we have
to oppose.

We answer, The mind is *not* finite, just because it knows
it *is* finite.   'The knowledge of the limit suppresses the
limit.'   It is a flagrant self-contradiction that the finite
should know its own finitude; and it is not hard to make
this plain.

Finite means limited from the outside and by the outside.
The finite is to know itself as this, or not as finite.   If its
knowledge ceases to fall wholly within itself, then so far it
is not finite.   It knows that it is limited from the outside
and by the outside, and that means it knows the outside.
But if so, then it is so far not finite.   If its whole being fell
within itself, then, in knowing itself, it could not know that
there was anything outside itself.   It does do the latter;
hence the former supposition is false.

Imagine a man shut up in a room, who said to us, 'My

---

[1] We have not to dwell on the inherent contradiction of the finite.
Its being is to fall wholly within itself; and yet, so far as it is finite, so
far is it determined wholly by the outside.

faculties are entirely confined to the *inside* of this room. The limit of the room is the limit of my mind, and so I can have no knowledge whatever of the outside.' Should we not answer, 'My dear sir, you contradict yourself. If it were as you say, you could not know of an outside, and so, by consequence, not of an inside, as such.' You should be in earnest and go through with your doctrine of "relativity"'?

To the above simple argument I fear we may not have done justice. However that be, I know of no answer to it; and until we find one we must say that it is not true that the mind is finite.

If I am to realize myself, it must be as infinite; and now the question is, What does infinite mean? and it will be better to say first what it does not mean. There are two wrong views on the subject, which we will take one at a time.

(1) Infinite is not-finite, and that means 'end-less'. What does endless mean? Not the mere negation of end, because a mere negation is nothing at all, and infinite would thus = O. The endless is something positive; it means a positive quantity which has no end. Any given number of units is finite; but a series of units, which is produced indefinitely, is infinite. This is the sense of infinite which is in most common use, and which, we shall see, is what Hedonism believes in. It is, however, clear that this infinite is a perpetual self-contradiction, and, so far as it is real, is only finite. Any real quantity has ends, beyond which it does not go. 'Increase the quantity' merely says 'Put the end further off'; but in saying that, it does say 'Put the end'. 'Increase the quantity for ever' means 'Have for ever a finite quantity, and for ever say that it is not finite'. In other words, 'Remove the end' does imply, by that very removal and the production of the series, the making of a fresh end; so that we still have a finite quantity. Here, so far as the infinite exists, it is finite; so far as it is told to exist, it is told again to be nothing but finite.

(2) Or, secondly, the infinite is *not* the finite, no longer in the sense of being more in quantity, but in the sense of being something else, which is different in quality. The infinite is not in the world of limited things; it exists in a sphere of its own. The mind (e. g.) is something *beside* the aggregate of its states. God is something beside the things of this world. This is the infinite believed in by abstract Duty. But here once more, against its will, infinite comes to mean merely finite. The infinite is a something over against, beside, and outside the finite; and hence is itself also finite, because limited by something else.

In neither of these two senses is the mind infinite. What then is the true sense of infinite? As before, it is the negation of the finite; it is not-finite. But, unlike both the false infinites, it does not leave the finite as it is. It neither, with (1), says 'the finite *is to be* not-finite, nor, with (2), tries to get rid of it by doubling it. It does really negate the finite, so that the finite disappears, not by having a negative set over against it, but by being taken up into a higher unity, in which, becoming an element, it ceases to have its original character, and is both suppressed and preserved. The infinite is thus 'the unity of the finite and infinite'. The finite was determined from the outside, so that everywhere to characterize and distinguish it was in fact to divide it. Wherever you defined anything you were at once carried beyond to something else and something else, and this because the negative, required for distinction, was an outside other. In the infinite you can distinguish without dividing; for this is a unity holding within itself subordinate factors which are negative of, and so distinguishable from, each other; while at the same time the whole is so present in each, that each has its own being in its opposite, and depends on that relation for its own life. The negative is also its affirmation. Thus the infinite has a distinction, and so a negation, in itself, but is distinct from and negated by nothing but itself. Far from being one something which is *not* another something, it is a whole in which both one and the other are mere elements. This whole is hence 'relative' utterly and through and through, but the relation does not fall outside it; the relatives are moments in which it is the relation of itself to itself, and so is above the relation, and is absolute reality. The finite is relative to something *else*; the infinite is *self*-related. It is this sort of infinite which the mind is. The simplest symbol of it is the circle, the line which returns into itself, not the straight line produced indefinitely; and the readiest way to find it is to consider the satisfaction of desire. There we have myself and its opposite, and the return from the opposite, the finding in the other nothing but self. And here it would be well to recall what we said above on the form of the will.

If the reader to whom this account of the infinite is new has found it in any way intelligible, I think he will see that there is some sense in it, when we say, 'Realize yourself as an infinite whole'; or, in other words, 'Be specified in yourself, but not specified by anything foreign to yourself'.

But the objection comes: 'Morality tells us to progress; it tells us we are not concluded in ourselves nor perfect, but that there exists a not-ourself, which never does wholly become ourself. And, apart from morality, it is obvious that I and you, this man and the other man, are finite beings. We are not one another; more or less we must limit each other's sphere; I am what I am more or less by external relations, and I do not fall wholly within myself. Thus I am to be infinite, to have no limit from the outside; and yet I am one among others, and therefore am finite. It is all very well to tell me that in me there is infinity, the perfect identity of subject and object: that I may be willing perhaps to believe, but none the less I am finite.'

We admit the full force of the objection. I *am* finite; I am both infinite *and* finite, and that is why my moral life is a perpetual progress. I must progress, because I have an other which is to be, and yet never quite is, myself; and so, as I am, am in a state of contradiction.

It is not that I wish to increase the mere quantity of my true self. It is that I wish to be nothing *but* my true self, to be rid of all external relations, to bring them all within me, and so to fall wholly within myself.

I am to be perfectly homogeneous; but that I can not be unless fully specified, and the question is, How can I be extended so as to take in my external relations? Goethe[1] has said, 'Be a whole *or* join a whole', but to that we must answer, 'You can not be a whole, *unless* you join a whole'.

The difficulty is: being limited and so not a whole, how extend myself so as to be a whole? The answer is, be a member in a whole. Here your private self, your finitude, ceases as such to exist; it becomes the function of an organism. You must be, not a mere piece of, but a member in, a whole; and as this must know and will yourself.

The whole, to which you belong, specifies itself in the detail of its functions, and yet remains homogeneous. It lives not many lives but one life, and yet can not live except in its many members. Just so, each one of the members is alive, but not apart from the whole which lives in it. The organism is homogeneous because it is specified, and specified because it is homogeneous.

'But', it will be said, 'what is that to me? I remain one member, and I am not other members. The more perfect the organism, the more is it specified, and so much the intenser becomes its homogeneity. But its "more" means my "less". The unity falls in the whole, and so outside me; and the greater specification of the whole means the making me more special, more narrowed, and limited, and less developed within myself.'

We answer that this leaves out of sight a fact quite palpable and of enormous significance, viz. that in the moral organism the members are aware of themselves, and aware

---

[1] 'Immer strebe zum Ganzen, und kannst du selber kein Ganzes
Werden, als dienendes Glied schliess' an ein Ganzes dich an.'
—*Vier Jahreszeiten*, 45.

of themselves as members. I do not know myself as mere this, against something else which is not myself. The relations of the others to me are not mere external relations. I know myself as a member; that means I am aware of my own function; but it means also that I am aware of the whole as specifying itself in me. The will of the whole knowingly wills itself in me; the will of the whole is the will of the members, and so, in willing my own function, I do know that the others will themselves in me. I do know again that I will myself in the others, and in them find my will once more as not mine, and yet as mine. It is false that the homogeneity falls outside me; it is not only in me, but for me too; and apart from my life in it, my knowledge of it, and devotion to it, I am not myself. When it goes out my heart goes out with it, where it triumphs I rejoice, where it is maimed I suffer; separate me from the love of it, and I perish. [See further, Essay V.]

No doubt the distinction of separate selves remains, but the point is this. In morality the existence of my mere private self, as such, is something which ought not to be, and which, so far as I am moral, has already ceased. I am morally realized, not until my personal self has utterly ceased to be my exclusive self, is no more a will which is outside others' wills, but finds in the world of others nothing but self.

'Realize yourself as an infinite whole' means, 'Realize yourself as the self-conscious member of an infinite whole, by realizing that whole in yourself'. When that whole is truly infinite, and when your personal will is wholly made one with it, then you also have reached the extreme of homogeneity and specification in one, and have attained a perfect self-realization.

The foregoing will, we hope, become clear to the reader of this volume. He must consider what has been said so far as the text, which the sequel is to illustrate and work out in detail. Meanwhile, our aim has been to put forward the formula of self-realization, and in some measure to explain it. The following Essays will furnish, we hope, something like a commentary and justification. We shall see that the self to be realized is not the self as a collection of particulars, is not the universal as all the states of a certain feeling; and that it is not again an abstract universal, as the form of duty; that neither are in harmony with life, with the moral consciousness, or with themselves; that when the self is identified with, and wills, and realizes a concrete universal, a real totality, then first does it find itself, is satisfied, self-determined, and free, 'the free will that wills itself as the free will'.

Let us resume, then, the results of the present Essay. We have attempted to show (1) That the formula of 'what for?' must be rejected by every ethical doctrine as not universally valid; and that hence no one theory can gain the smallest advantage (except over the foolish) by putting it forward: that now for us (as it was for Hellas) the main question is: There being some end, what is that end? And (2), with which second part, if it fall, the first need not fall, we have endeavoured briefly to point out that the final end, with which morality is identified, or under which it is included, can be expressed not otherwise than by self-realization.

NOTE TO ESSAY II

PERHAPS the following remarks, though partly repetition of the above, may be of service.

There being an end, that end is realization, at all events; it is something to be reached, otherwise not an end.

And it implies self-realization, because it is to be reached by me. By my action I am to carry it out; in making it real my will is realized, and my will is myself. Hence there is self-realization in all action; witness the feeling of pleasure.

'Yes,' it will be said, 'but that does not show there is nothing but self-realization. The content of the act is not the self, but may be something else, and this something else may be the end. The content is the end.'

This is very easy to say, but it overlooks the psychological difficulties. How is it possible to will what is not one's self, how can one desire a foreign object? What we desire must be in our minds; we must think of it; and besides, we must be related to it in a particular way. If it is to be the end, we must feel ourselves one with it, and in it; and how can we do that, if it does not belong to us, and has not been made part of us? To say, 'thoughts of what is and is to be exist in you, are in your head, and then you carry them out, and that is action', is futile; because these thoughts, if desired, are not merely *in* me, they are felt to be mine, ideally to be myself, and, when they are carried out, that therefore is self-realization.

Or shall we be told that 'to talk of carrying out is nonsense. In action we produce changes in things and in ourselves, answering to thoughts: things resemble thoughts, but, strictly speaking, thought is not realized, because that is unmeaning'? If we hold to this, however, we are met by the impossibility then of accounting for thought and action, as ordinarily viewed; we should know not the real, but something like the real, and should do not what we mean, intend, have in our minds, but only something like it. But this, unfortunately, is not action. If I do not what I will, but only something like it, then, strictly speaking, so far it is not my act, and would not be imputed to me. An act supposes the content on each side to be the same, with a difference, or, under a difference, to be the same. It does suppose that what was in the mind is carried out; and, unless you think that something can be in the self and carried out by the self, without being of the nature of the self (and you would find the difficulties of such a view insuperable), you must say that volition is self-realization.

But doubtless there are many persons who, not raising metaphysical or psychological questions, but standing merely on facts, would say, 'Theory apart, surely when I act I do realize more than myself. I quite see that I may not do so; but when I devote myself to a cause, and at my own expense help to carry it out, how then am I realizing only myself?'

The difficulty no doubt is very serious, and we can not pretend here to go to the bottom of it. But we may point out that it arises from a preconception as to the self (i. e. the identification of it with the particular self), which can not be defended. It is clear that, on the one side, selves do exclude one another. I am not you, you are not he; and, resting on this notion of exclusiveness, we go on to look at the self as a repellent point, or, as we call it, a mere individual. But, apart from metaphysics, facts soon compel us to see that this is not a reality, but an abstraction of our minds. For, without troubling ourselves about the relation of one person to others, as soon as we imagine this mere 'individual' acting, we see he must bring forth something, and, to do that, must have something in him, must have a content, and, if so, is not any longer a bare point, which we now perceive to be a mere form. Hence we now try to give him a content which falls wholly within himself, and is not common to him with others, and, finding it impossible to account for facts on this supposition, suddenly we turn round and fly to the other extreme, and now suppose him to realize the sheer suppression of himself; not seeing that now we have abjured our premises without having refuted them, and are face to face with the psychological difficulty of how a man is to bring out of himself what was not in himself and part of himself, and with the facts which testify that action without interest is a fiction.

But if from a better metaphysic, or attention to facts, we are willing to give up those metaphysical preconceptions we took for fact, and now see to be futile, then we may also see that, though certainly one person can not be 'like Cerberus, three gentlemen at once', yet that, beside being thus exclusive, none the less in respect of their content (and that makes them what they are) persons are not thus exclusive; that I am what I will and will what I am, that the content qualifies me, and that there is no reason in the world why that content should be confined to the 'this me'. In the case of a social being, this is impossible; and to point out any human being, in whom his exclusive self is the whole content of his will, is out of the question. But if so, where is the difficulty of my object being one and the same with the object of other people; so that, having filled the form of my personality with a life not merely mine, I have at heart, and have identified with and made one with myself, objective interests, things that are to be, and in and with the existence of which I am not to satisfy my mere private self; so that, as I neither will nor can separate myself from what makes me myself, in realizing them I realize myself, and can do so only by realizing them? (We shall come on this again—see especially Essay VII.)

Well then, just as we must accept the teaching that 'all is relative to self', but supplement and correct it with the teaching that 'myself also is relative', so we must accept the teaching of the selfish theory that I can will myself only, but correct it by the addition 'and yet the self which is myself, which is mine, is not merely me'. Hence that all willing is self-realization is seen not to be in collision with morality.

To conclude—If I am asked why I am to be moral, I can say no more than this, that what I can not doubt is my own being now, and that, since in that being is involved a self, which is to be here and now, and yet in this here and now is not, I therefore can not doubt that there is an end which I am to make real; and morality, if not equivalent to, is at all events included in this making real of myself.

If it is absurd to ask for the further reason of my knowing and willing my own existence, then it is equally absurd to ask for the further reason of what is involved therein. The only rational question here is not Why? but What? What is the self that I know and will? What is its true nature, and what is implied therein? What is the self that I am to make actual, and how is the principle present, living, and incarnate in its particular modes of realization?

ESSAY III

PLEASURE FOR PLEASURE'S SAKE

IT is an old story, a theme too worn for the turning of sentences, and yet too living a moral not to find every day a new point and to break a fresh heart, that our lives are wasted in the pursuit of the impalpable, the search for the impossible and the unmeaning. Neither to-day nor yesterday, but throughout the whole life of the race, the complaint has gone forth that all is vanity; that the ends for which we live and we die are 'mere ideas', illusions begotten on the brain by the wish of the heart—poor phrases that stir the blood, until experience or reflection for a little, and death for all time, bring with it disenchantment and quiet. Duty for duty's sake, life for an end beyond sense, honour, and beauty, and love for the invisible—all these are first felt and then seen to be dream and shadow and unreal vision. And our cry and our desire is for something that will satisfy us, something that we know and do not only think, something that is real and solid, that we can lay hold of and be sure of, and that will not change in our hands. We have said good-bye to our transcendent longings, we have bidden a sad but an eternal farewell to the hopes of our own and of the world's too credulous youth; we have parted for ever from our early loves, from our fancies and aspirations beyond the human. We seek for the tangible, and we find it in this world; for the knowledge which can never deceive, and that is the certainty of our own well-being; we seek for the palpable, and we feel it; for the end which will satisfy us as men, and we find it, in a word, in happiness.

Happiness! Is that climax, or bathos, or cruel irony? Happiness is the end? Yes, happiness is the end which indeed we all reach after; for what more can we wish than that all should be well with us—that our wants should be filled, and the desire of our hearts be gratified? And happiness can not escape us, we must know it when we find it? Oh yes, it would be strange indeed to come to such a consummation, and never to know it. And happiness is real and palpable, and we can find it by seeking it? Alas! the one question which no one can answer is, What is happiness?—which every one in the end can answer is, what happiness is not. It has been called by every name among men, and has been sought on the heights and in the depths; it has been wooed in all the shapes on earth and in heaven, and what man has won it? Its name is a proverb for the visionary object of a universal and a fruitless search; of all the delusions which make a sport of our lives it is not one, but is one common title which covers and includes them all, which shows behind each in turn, but to vanish and appear behind another. The man who says that happiness is his mark aims at nothing apart from the ends of others. He seeks the illusory goal of all men; and he differs from the rest that are and have been, not at all, or only in his assertion that happiness is to be found by seeking it.

'But happiness', will be the reply, 'is vague, because it has been made so—is impalpable, because projected beyond the solid world into the region of cloud and fiction—is visionary, because diverted from its object, and used as a name for visions. Such ends are not happiness. But there is an end which men can seek and do find, which never deceives, which is real and tangible and felt to be happiness; and that end is pleasure. Pleasure is something we can be sure of, for it dwells not we know not where, but here in ourselves. It is found, and it can be found; it is the end for man and for beast, the one thing worth living for, the one thing they do live for and do really desire, and the only thing they ought to set before them. This is real, because we feel and know it to be real; and solely by partaking, or seeming to partake, in its reality do other ends pass for, and impose on the world as, happiness.'

We said that to answer the question, what happiness is, has been thought impossible; that there are few who, in the end, are unable to say what happiness is not. And if there

be any one thing which well-nigh the whole voice of the
world, from all ages, nations, and sorts of men, has agreed
to declare is *not* happiness, that thing is pleasure, and the
search for it.   Not in the school alone, but round us in life,
we see that to identify in the beginning pleasure and happiness, leads in the end to the confession that there ' is nothing in it ', εὐδαιμονίαν ὅλως ἀδύνατον εἶναι.   The ' pursuit of
pleasure ' is a phrase which calls for a smile or a sigh, since
the world has learnt that, if pleasure is the end, it is an end
which must not be made one, and is found there most where
it is not sought.   If to find pleasure is the end, and science
is the means, then indeed we must say

> Die hohe Kraft
> Der Wissenschaft
> Der ganzen Welt verborgen!
> Und wer nicht denkt,
> Dem wird sie geschenkt,
> Er hat sie ohne Sorgen. [1]

Common opinion repeats its old song, that the search for
pleasure is the coarsest form of vulgar delusion, that if you
want to be happy in the sense of pleased, you must not think
of pleasure, but, taking up some accredited form of living,
must make that your end, and in that case, with moderately
good fortune, you will be happy ; if you are not, then it
must be your own fault ; but that, if you go further, you are
like to fare worse.   You had better *not* try elsewhere, or, at
least, not for pleasure elsewhere.

So far the weight of popular experience bears heavily
against the practicability of Hedonism.   But Hedonism, we
shall be told, does not of necessity mean the search by the
individual for the pleasure of the individual.   It is to such
selfish pleasure-seeking alone that the proverbial condemna-

---

[1] Thus rendered in Mr. C. Kegan Paul's version of *Faust* :
> The highest might
> Of science quite
>   Is from the world concealed!
> But whosoe'er
> Expends no care,
>   To him it is revealed.

tion of Hedonism applies. The end for modern Utilitarianism is not the pleasure of one, but the pleasure of all, the maximum of pleasurable, and minimum of painful, feeling in all sentient organisms, and not in my sentient organism; and against the possibility of realizing such an end common opinion has nothing to say. This we admit to be true, but in this shape the question has never fairly come before the popular mind; and it would be well to remember that if the individual, when he seeks pleasure, fails in his individual aim, such a fact ought at least to inspire us with some doubt whether, when mankind seek the pleasure of the sentient world, that end be so much more real and tangible.

Opinion, then, as the result of popular experience, so far as it has touched on the question, would appear to be against the practicability of Hedonism. Still vulgar opinion must not count against philosophical theory, though it certainly may against the still more vulgar preconception as to the reality and palpable character of pleasure.

But Hedonism, we must remember, does not assert itself simply as a theory which can be worked. It puts itself forward as moral, as the one and only possible account of morality. The fact is the moral world, Hedonism is the supposed explanation; and if we find that non-theoretical persons, who have direct cognizance of the fact, with but few exceptions reject the explanation, that ought to have great weight with us. And the case stands thus undeniably. When moral persons without a theory on the matter are told that the moral end for the individual and the race is the getting a maximum surplusage of pleasurable feeling, and that there is nothing in the whole world which has the smallest moral value except this end and the means to it, there is no gainsaying that they repudiate such a result. They feel that there are things 'we should choose even if no pleasure came from them'; and that if we choose these things, being good, for ourselves, then we must choose them also for the race, if we care for the race as we do for ourselves. We may be told, indeed, that a vulgar objection of this sort is founded on a misunderstanding, and to this

we shall have to recur ; but for the present we prefer to
believe that never, except on a misunderstanding, has the
moral consciousness in any case acquiesced in Hedonism.
And we must say, I think, that, supposing it possible that
Hedonism could be worked, yet common moral opinion is
decided against its being, what it professes to be, a sufficient
account of morals.

For morality and religion believe in some end for the man
and for the race to be worked out ; some idea to be realized
in mankind and in the individual, and to be realized even
though it should not be compatible [1] with the minimum
of pain and maximum of pleasure in human souls and
bodies, to say nothing at all about other sentient organisms.
The end for our morality and our religion is an idea (or call
it what you will), which is thought of both as the moving
principle and final aim of human progress, and that idea
(whatever else it may be, or may not be) most certainly is
not the mere idea of an increase of pleasure and a diminution
of pain.   What we represent to ourselves as the goal of our
being we must take as a law for the guidance alike both
of this and that man, and of the race as a whole ; and if you
do not use the vague phrase ' happiness', but say fairly and
nakedly that you mean ' feeling pleased as much as possible
and as long as possible', then you can not, I think, bring the
Hedonistic end before the moral consciousness without a
sharp collision.

Now I am not saying that what is commonly believed
must be true.   I am perfectly ready to consider the possibility
of the ordinary moral creed being a mistaken one ; but the
point which I wish to emphasize is this: The fact is the
moral world, both on its external side of the family, society,
and the State, and the work of the individual in them, and
again, on its internal side of moral feeling and belief.
The theory which will account for and justify these facts
as a whole is the true moral theory ; and any theory which
can not account for these facts may, in some other way,

[1] [This is very doubtful. 'Without considering its compatibility'
might stand, cf. p. 136. The question is not actually raised, I should say.]

perhaps, be a very good and correct theory, but it is *not* a *moral* theory. Supposing every other ethical theory to be false, it does not follow that therefore Hedonism is a true ethical theory. It does not follow, because it has refuted its 'intuitive moralists' (or what not?), that therefore it accounts for the facts of the moral consciousness. Admitted that it is workable, it has still to be proved moral—moral in the sense of explaining, not explaining away, morality. And it can be proved moral by the refuting of some other theory only on the strength of two assumptions. The first is, that there must be some existing theory which is a sufficient account of morals, and that is an unproved assumption ; the second is, that the disjunction, that the 'either—or' of 'intuitive' and 'utilitarian' is complete and exhaustive, and that is a false assumption.[1]

At the cost of repetition, and perhaps of wearisomeness, I must dwell a little longer on the ordinary consciousness. There are times, indeed, when we feel that increase of progress means increase of pleasure, and that it is hard to consider them apart. I do not mean those moments (if there are such) when the music-hall theory of life seems real to us, but the hours (and there must be such) when advance in goodness and knowledge, and advance in the pleasure of them, have been so intermingled, and brought home as one to our minds (in our own case or in that of others), that we

---

[1] 'Whoever would disprove the theory which makes utility our guide, must produce another principle that were a surer and better guide.'

'Now if we reject *utility* as the index to God's commands, we must assent to the theory or hypothesis which supposes a *moral sense*. One of the adverse theories which regard the nature of that index is certainly true.' Austin's *Jurisprudence*, i. 79; ⟨i. 147, ed. iii⟩.

If we wished to cross an unknown bog, and two men came to us, of whom the one said, 'Some one must know the way over this bog, for there must be a way, and you see there is no one here beside us two, and therefore one of us two must be able to guide you. And the other man does not know the way, as you can soon see; therefore I must'—should we answer, 'Lead on, I follow'? Philosophy would indeed be the easiest of studies, if we might arrive at truth by assuming that one of two accounts must be true, and prove the one by disproving the other; but in philosophy this is just what can not be done.

feel it impossible to choose one and not also choose the other. And there doubtless are hours again, when all that is called progress seems so futile and disappointing, that we bitterly feel ' increase of knowledge ' is indeed ' increase of sorrow', and that he who thinks least is happiest ; when we envy the beasts their lives without a past or a future, their heedless joys and easily forgotten griefs ; and when for our-selves, and if for ourselves then for others, we could wish to cease, or to be as they are 'von allem Wissensqualm entladen'· These are the extremes ; but when in the season neither of our exaltation, nor of our depression, we soberly consider the matter, then we choose most certainly for ourselves (and so also for others) what we think the highest life, i.e. the life with the highest functions ; and in that life we certainly include the feeling of pleasure ; but if the alternative is presented to us of lower functions with less pains and greater pleasures, or higher functions with greater pains and less pleasures, then we must choose the latter.

And the alternative is conceivable. If it is impossible in fact that a stage of progress could come, where, by advancing further in the direction of what seems to it highest, humanity would decrease its surplus of pleasure (and I do not see how it is to be proved impossible) [1]—yet, at all events, the

---

[1] Mr. Mill's assertion that ' most of the great positive evils of the world are in themselves removable ' (*Utilitarianism*, p. 21) calls for no remark ; but the reader may perhaps think that Mr. Spencer's doctrine of the Evanescence of Evil (*Social Statics*, p. 73, fol., ed. 1868) should be noticed. His proof seems (so far as I understand it) to rest on the following assumptions :

(1) The natural environment of mankind is stationary. Can this be proved ?

(2) The spiritual environment of mankind is stationary. Not only can this not be proved, but the opposite is, or ought to be, supposed by the doctrine of evolution. Progress must alter the environment.

(3) Apparently children are to be born in harmony with their sur-roundings, and remain so till death.

(4) Moral evil, in the sense of moral badness, is to disappear. It will be impossible to oppose one's private good to the general good, and act according to the former. Self-will will cease, and with it the pain it brings.

All these assumptions, I think, are wanted. Nos. 3 and 4 represent

alternative can be brought directly before the mind : advance in this direction (the higher) at the cost of pleasure, on the whole, after the pleasure of advance is counted in ; advance in that direction (the lower), with the gain of pleasure, on the whole, even after the regrets of the non-advance have been subtracted. The necessity for choice can be imagined; and there is no doubt, on the one side, what the choice of the moral man would be ; there is no doubt, on the other side, what, if pleasure were the end, it ought to be. In such a case, what we think the most moral man and people would be therefore the most certain to act immorally, if Hedonism is morality.

But these consequences, it will be urged, do not apply to modern Utilitarianism. That creed, we shall be told, whether for the man or the race, is high and self-sacrificing. For not only does it place the end in the pleasure of all, not the pleasure of one, but in addition it distinguishes pleasures according to their quality. The greatest quantity of pleasure is not the end ; there are pleasures we desire in preference to others, even at the cost of discontent and dissatisfaction. These pleasures, then, are to be preferred, and these are the higher pleasures. Such a doctrine, it will be added, is surely moral.

The doctrine, we admit, has done homage to popular opinion, so far as, for the sake of it, to sacrifice its own consistency and desert its principle. This we shall have to prove later on. But yet we can not for a moment think that it has succeeded in satisfying the demands of morality. Virtue is still a mere means to pleasure in ourselves or others, and, as anything beyond, is worthless, if not immoral; is not virtue at all. What is right is determined by that which is most 'grateful to the feelings' of connoisseurs in pleasures, who have tried them all. No compromise is possible on

absolute impossibilities, so far as I understand the matter. No. 2 is impossible on the supposition of continual progress. No other supposition can be proved to be true; and No. 1 can not, I believe, be proved. How far Mr. Spencer's own teaching contradicts these assumptions is of no importance here.

this point.   Ordinary morality is clear that, when it aims
at virtue for itself and others, it has not got its eye on wages
or perquisites; its motive, in the sense of the object of its
conscious desire, is not the anticipated feeling of pleasure.
What it has before its mind is an object, an act or an event,
which is not (for itself at least) a state of the feeling self, in
itself or others.   To say that, in desiring the right, it proposes
to itself a pleasure to be got by the right, is to assert in the
face of facts.   To the moral mind that feeling is an accompaniment or a consequent, and it may be thought of as such.
But to think of it as more, to propose it as the end to which
the act or objective event is the means, and nothing but
the means, is simply to turn the moral point of view upside
down.   You may argue psychologically, if you will, and say
that what *is* desired is pleasure (this is false, as we shall show
in another Essay), and we are ready for argument's sake to
admit it here; for here it makes not the smallest difference.
The moral consciousness does not *think* it acts to get pleasure,
and the point here at issue is not whether what it believes,
and must believe, is or is not a psychological illusion, but
whether Utilitarianism is in harmony therewith.

Hedonism in any form must teach 'Morality is a means
to pleasure'; and whether that pleasure is to be got *in*
morality, or merely *by* morality, yet the getting of the pleasure is the ultimate aim.   Pleasure for pleasure's sake is the
end, and nothing else is an end in any sense, except so far
as it is a means to pleasure.   This, we repeat once more, is
absolutely irreconcilable with ordinary moral beliefs.   And
not only is Hedonism repudiated by those beliefs as immoral,
but, as we saw, so far as the popular mind has pronounced
upon it, it is also declared to be impracticable.   These two
points we wished to make clear, and with this result we
have finished the first or introductory part of our undertaking.

It remains to ask in the second place, Why is it that
pleasure-seeking, as the search for my pleasure, is declared
vain, and pleasure itself impalpable and misleading, a something which gives us no standard to work by, and no end to

aim at, no system to realize in our lives? We must look for an answer to the nature of pleasure.

Pleasure and pain are feelings, and they are nothing but feelings. It would perhaps be right to call them the two simple modes of *self*-feeling; but we are not here concerned with psychological accuracy. The point which we wish to emphasize, and which we think is not doubtful, is that, considered psychically, they are nothing whatever but states of the feeling self. This means that they exist in me only as long as I feel them, and only as I feel them, that beyond this they have no reference to anything else, no validity, and no meaning whatever. They are 'subjective' because they neither have, nor pretend to, reality beyond this or that subject. They are as they are felt to be, but they tell us nothing. In one word, they have no content: they are as states of us, but they have nothing for us.[1]

[1] [This is unsatisfactory. If you abstract from all content but pleasure and pain, you have obviously no content but pleasure and pain. But is that *no* content at all?

And, *if* you view pleasure and pain merely as this or that particular passing feeling, naturally it is no more. But for Hedonism *must* you do this? Why do it because Hedonists who know no better do it? See the foot-note to p. 95. Our mere feeling self is an abstraction, but why must you also make it a series?

The 'subjective' ⟨l. 12, above⟩ is very doubtful. And the 'self-feeling', if true, seems irrelevant.

I seem to have assumed that the Hedonistic End can't be formulated as a general character, because it can't exist except psychically, and so as momentary and particular. But this does not follow.

The Hedonistic End (cf.⟨and contrast⟩ pp. 245–6) is the attainment of a state of things such as to produce, throughout whatever period of time we are able to foresee, the greatest surplus of pleasure within our power to reach, whatever it may be.

The conception of a period of existence may be self-contradictory, but is absolutely necessary for morality, whatever view you take. Otherwise growth to perfection becomes meaningless.

There is no trouble about 'our power to produce', unless you adopt something like fatalism, and deny that our efforts and aims make a difference.

In short, the objection to Hedonism comes to this, that (i) it abstracts and denies all but its abstraction, and (ii) you really do want something like a whole, and clearly all that side of the End falls outside the abstraction of mere pleasure.]

I do not think it is necessary to dwell on this matter. Let us proceed to the application. The practical end, if it is to be a practical goal and standard, must present itself to us as some definite unity, some concrete whole that we can realize in our acts, and carry out in our life. And pleasure (as pain) we find to be nothing but a name which stands for a series of this, that, and the other feelings, which are not except in the moment or moments that they are felt, which have as a series neither limitation of number, beginning nor end, nor in themselves any reference at all, any of them, beyond themselves. To realize, as such, the self which feels pleasure and pain, means to realize this infinite perishing series.[1] And it is clear at once that this is not what is required for a practical end. Let us see the problem a little closer.

On the one side our Hedonist is aware, however dimly, of himself not as this, nor that, nor the other particular feeling or satisfaction, but as something which is not this, that, or the other, and yet is real, and is to be realized. Self-realization, as we saw, was the object of desire; and so, as above, on the one hand is the self, which we are forced to look on as a whole which is in its parts, as a living totality, as a universal present throughout, and constituted by its particulars: and this self is setting out, however unaware, to find itself as such and to satisfy itself as such, or not to find itself and not to satisfy itself at all. On the other side is the mere feeling self, the series of particular satisfactions, which the self has come (how we need not here inquire) to take as its reality, and as the sole possible field for its self-realization.

The point to observe is the heterogeneous nature of the self to be satisfied, and of the proposed satisfaction, and the

[1] It is an abstraction, no doubt, to consider pleasurable feelings as mere pleasures, but it is not our abstraction but the Hedonist's. It is an abstraction, again, to consider feelings as merely particular. They can not be that, if they are *our* feelings, if they are the feelings of a self. But we can make our mere feeling self, as the self which feels mere pleasure and pain, an object only in the series of its feelings, and these (as such a series) have no relations, each either within itself or beyond itself.

consequent impossibility of a solution for the problem. The practical difficulty is soon forced on the seeker after pleasure.

Pleasures, we saw, were a perishing series. This one comes, and the intense self-feeling proclaims satisfaction. It is gone, and *we* are not satisfied. It was not that one, then, but this one now; and this one now is gone. It was not that one, then, but another and another; but another and another do not give us what we want; we are still left eager and confident, till the flush of feeling dies down, and when that is gone there is nothing left. We are where we began, so far as the getting happiness goes; and we have not found ourselves, and we are not satisfied.

This is common experience, and it is the practical refutation of Hedonism, or of the seeking happiness in pleasure. Happiness, for the ordinary man, neither means a pleasure nor a number of pleasures. It means in general the finding of himself, or the satisfaction of himself as a whole, and in particular it means the realization of his concrete ideal of life. '*This* is happiness', he says, not identifying happiness with one pleasure or a number of them, but understanding by it, '*in* this is become fact what I have at heart.' But the Hedonist has said, Happiness is pleasure, and the Hedonist knows that happiness is a whole.[1] How, then, if pleasures make no system, if they are a number of perishing particulars, can the whole that is sought be found

[1] I am quite aware that with *some* Hedonistic writers 'happiness' is not distinguished from 'pleasure'. They are said to be simply the same. This is an outrage on language, which avenges itself in the confusion described below, foot-note, p. 120. But the argument of the text is not affected by it. If happiness = pleasure, then 'get happiness' = 'get pleasure'. What is pleasure? It is a general name, and 'get happiness' will mean 'get a general name'. But a general name is not a reality, and can not be got. The reality is the particular. 'Get happiness' will mean then, 'get some one pleasure'. Is that it? No, we are to get all the happiness we can. And so, after all our quibbling, 'get happiness' *does* mean 'get the largest possible sum or collection of pleasures'. Mr. Green, in his Introduction to Hume's *Treatise* (ii. 7) ⟨Green's *Works*, i, pp. 307 foll.⟩, has made this so clear, that one might have hoped it could not have been misunderstood. On the whole subject of this Essay let me recommend the student to consult him.

in them? It is the old question, how find the universal in mere particulars? And the answer is the old answer, In their sum. The self is to be found, happiness is to be realized, in the sum of the moments of the feeling self. The practical direction is, get *all* pleasures, and you will have got happiness; and we saw above its well-known practical issue in weariness and dissatisfaction.

The theoretical reason is simple. The sum, or the All of pleasures is a self-contradiction, and therefore the search for it is futile. A series which has no beginning, or, if a beginning, yet no end, can not be summed; there *is* no All, and yet the All is postulated, and the series is to be summed. But it can not be summed till we are dead, and then, if we have realized it, we, I suppose, do not know it, and we are not happy; and before death we can not have realized it, because there is always more to come, the series is always incomplete. What is the sum of pleasures, and how many go to the sum? All of how many is it, and when are we at the end? After death or in life? Do you mean a finite number? Then more is beyond. Do you mean an infinite number? Then we never reach it; for a further pleasure is conceivable, and nothing is infinite which has something still left outside of it. We must say, then, that no one ever reaches happiness. Or do you mean as much pleasure as a man can get? Then every one at every point is happy, and happiness is always complete, for, by the Hedonistic theory, we all of us get as much as we can.[1]

---

[1] I am anxious that the reader should not pass by this argument as a verbal puzzle. Beside it there is certainly much more to be said against Hedonism; but the root of Hedonism is not understood, until it is seen, (1) That pleasure, as such, is an abstraction (cf. Essay VII); (2) That the sum of pleasures is a fiction. On this latter head I fear that I must further enlarge.

'Get all you can' is a familiar phrase, and is very good sense. I say to a boy, 'Go into that room, and fetch out all the apples you can carry'; and there is no nonsense in that. There is a given finite sum of apples, which I do not know, but which, under all the conditions, is the maximum. This is got and brought, and the task is accomplished. Why then not say, 'Get all the pleasures you can'? For these reasons. (i) Let it be granted that there is a given finite sum of pleasures for the man to get; yet *he* never *has* got it. Only death puts an end to the

The Hedonist has taken the universal in the sense of all the particulars, and in this sense, here as everywhere, since the particulars are arising and perishing, the universal has no truth nor reality. The true universal, which unconsciously he seeks, is infinite, for it is a concrete whole concluded within itself, and complete; but the false universal is infinite in the sense of a process *ad indefinitum*. It is a demand for, a would-be, completeness, with everlasting present incompleteness. It is always finite, and so never is realized. The sum is never finished; when the last pleasure is reached, we stand no nearer our end than at the first. It would be so, even if the pleasures did not die; but in addition the past pleasures have died; and we stand with heart unsatisfied and hands empty, driven on and beyond for ever in pursuit of a delusion, through a weary round which never advances. There remains, then, to Hedonism either the assertion that happiness is completed in one intense moment, or the con-

work; and after death nothing, or the same unfinished task. (ii) There is really no such sum. A pleasure *is* only in the time during which I feel it. A past pleasure means either an idea, or *another* (secondary) impression. *Itself* is nothing at all: I did get it, I have not got it; and the 'did get' is not the pleasure. In order to have the sum of pleasures, I must have them all *now*, which is impossible. Thus you can not reach the end, and the effort to reach it is not in itself desirable. You may say, if you please; The end is an illusion, and the effort worthless in itself, but this particular effort gives a specific pleasure, which is the end. But if you do this, then you either (*a*) sink considerations of quantity, and the *greatest* happiness principle is given up; or (*b*) the same problem as above breaks out with respect to the sum of specific pleasures.

If you admit that to get the greatest sum in life is unmeaning, then arises the question, Can you approximate, and make approximation the end? I will not raise the question, Can you approximate to a confessed fiction? and to avoid that, let us say, The end is for me, at any given moment of life, to be having then the greatest possible number of units of pleasure. Here we fall into the dilemma given in the text. Either happiness is never reached, or there is no one who does not reach the most perfect happiness imaginable.

(i) *If* happiness means the greatest possible number of units, then I *never* reach it. Whatever I have is finite, and beyond every finite sum another unit is conceivable.

(ii) *If* happiness means having all I can get, no matter how much or

fession that happiness is impossible, or the attempt to place it elsewhere than in the sum of pleasures.

The first is the '*nullo vivere consilio*'. It is the giving up of any practical goal or any rule of life, and we are not called upon to consider it further. The second is inevitable, if happiness is equal to the sum, or the greatest possible amount, of pleasures; for one and the other are the same unreal fiction. The end, in this sense, exists only in the head of the Hedonistic moral man. His morality is the striving to realize an idea, which can never be realized, and which, if realized, would be *ipso facto* annihilated. He would feel it no objection to his theory, nor any comfort in his sorrow, if we said to him that, if happiness could be, then the tale would be made up, the end would be reached, the search would be over, and with it all morality; for his morality is nothing to him as an end, but only as a means; and the bitterness of his lot is filled up by the thought, that the means he does not care for are always with him, and the end he lusts after away from him. His morality says, get what you never can get; never rest, never be satisfied, strive beyond the present to an impossible future.

how little, then, given the truth of the common Hedonistic psychology, every man at every moment has absolute happiness. This is very obvious. 'Why so ?' comes the objection; 'if Mr. A. had done otherwise, he would have had more pleasure.' 'You mean', I answer, '*if* he had been Mr. B.' When, in ordinary language, we say, 'He did not do what he could, or what was possible,' we mean, 'His energy did expend itself in this direction, failed to do so in that,' and we impute inability as a fault, where it is the result of previous misdirection [pp. 45-6]. But the common Hedonist can not say this, because, according to him, there is only one possible direction of expenditure, i. e. the greatest seeming pleasure. You have no choice between pleasure and something else, you can do nothing but gravitate to what seems most pleasant, and you can not alter what seems except by your will, i. e. by gravitation to what seems most pleasant. Every one has done his conceivable utmost to approximate, and therefore is absolutely happy.

I think the better plan for the Hedonist would be to make happiness a fixed finite sum, which can be got, and beyond which nothing counts ; and similarly to fix an unhappiness point on the scale ; but we have pursued the subject far enough.

The question of the approximative character of all morality will be discussed in another place.

The above is the proverbial experience of the voluptuary. His road to happiness is well known to be the worst, since pleasure there can not be, where there is no satisfaction ; and he must end (whatever else may become of him) by giving up his earnest search for the sum of pleasures.

The third alternative is not to give up pleasure as an end, but to place happiness elsewhere than in the greatest possible amount of 'grateful feeling'. This is what the prudent man of the world, with a love for pleasure, generally does do. We take a certain quantity of pleasure, and absence of pain, as a fair amount, which we may call happiness, because we feel we can do with it : and to get this amount we take up some way of living, which we follow, in general without thinking of pleasure. If opportunity offers for delights by the way, we take them, but without inconveniencing ourselves, without leaving the road too far, and without thinking too much about it. It is a good rule to get more, but a rule we must not make too much of, or follow to the point of endangering our happiness, i. e. the fixed and fair amount which comes to us from our course of life.

Pleasure is still ostensibly the end ; but really it has ceased to be so, and, whether we know it or not, our way of living is an end to our minds, and not a mere means. In short, we have got interests, and these are objects of desire not thought of as means to pleasure. We have adopted happiness in the vulgar sense, and really have given up Hedonism, as the consistent hunt after pleasure for pleasure's sake. Yet pleasure is still nominally the end, and hence the above view of life lies open to the following objections :

'You tell me that pleasure is my end ; and yet you tell me not to make it my end, but to make some accredited type of life my end, and take the pleasure as it comes from that. I am to make getting pleasure my aim, though only by the way and at odd times. And in this manner you assure me that, in the long run, I shall secure the greatest amount of pleasurable feeling. It seems strange to have a mark one must not look at, but I should not care for that if I were sure to hit. Yet this is what I can not tell if I shall do.

I see men die, having reaped for themselves a harvest of painful self-denial; and the pleasure they made by it was but gleanings for others, when they were in the grave. Did they attain their end? And I, since our life at any moment may cheat us, shall I put off a present certainty for the sake of a doubtful future?'

The answer must be, That is true enough: there is no certainty in life; but still it is more reasonable to act on probabilities. You may die, but the chances are you will live. You had better suppose that it will be so, and, taking the rules for living, the moral 'Nautical Almanack',[1] direct your course by them; for, if you live as long as most men, you will certainly in this way get the most pleasure.

And perhaps this answer may satisfy. But a new and serious difficulty arises. It being admitted that life is to be regulated on probabilities, the question then occurs, Who is to judge of the probabilities? The moral end is for me to get the most pleasure I can; the moral rule is, 'Act on the probability of your living, and therefore live for life as a whole'; but this moral rule tells me nothing about the moral Almanack. Why is that to be to me a law? What does it rest upon? What others have done and found? Will others be responsible for me, then? Am I to act upon my own opinion, or am I to follow the Almanack even against my opinion? Is the latter course right and justifiable? Will it, so to speak, excuse me in the Hedonistic judgement-day, when charged with having missed my end by misconduct, to plead that I did what others did, and that, when my own belief would have brought me right, I followed the multitude, and therefore did evil?

It appears to me that, if I am to seek my pleasure, it must be left to me to judge concerning my pleasure; and, this being so, the Almanack is not a law to me. It was made to be used by me according to my private views, not to be followed against them. And herewith all moral legislation disappears.[2]

---

[1] Mill's *Util.*, pp. 35-6.

[2] [But surely, on any view, the right and duty of private judgement must remain (cf. p. 106 foll.).]

For obviously, (1) circumstances get into strange tangles, which can not be provided against ; and the course laid down in the Almanack as a law may, in peculiar cases, lead to pain instead of pleasure ; and here I must disregard the Almanack. And obviously, (2) not outward situations only, but men's temperaments differ. What brings pleasure to one brings none to another ; and so with pain. You can speak generally beforehand, but it may not apply to this or that man. And the consequence is, that the Almanack and its moral rules are no authority. It is right to act according to them. It is right to act diametrically against them. In short they are not laws at all; they are only rules, and rules, as we know, admit of and imply exceptions. As Mr. Stephen has said,[1] ' A given road may be the direct way from one place to another, but that fact is no reason for following the road when you are offered a short cut. It may be a good rule not to seek for more than 5 per cent. in investments, but if it so happens that you can invest at 10 per cent. with perfect safety, would not a man who refused to do so be a fool ? '

And with this, if Hedonism be taken as the seeking my private pleasure, we have come to the end of Hedonism as a practical creed. Its aim was the getting for myself a maximum surplus of pleasurable feeling, and it gave me rules which it was my duty to follow. But it is not in earnest with its rules ; they may hold good, or they may not hold good ; I may keep them, or break them, whichever I think most likely to issue in pleasure in my particular case. And it is not in earnest with its end. To aim at pleasure is not to get it, and yet the getting of it is a moral duty. We must aim at it then by the way, without caring or trying too much to get it. We are not to think about the rules, except as servants which may be useful or worthless ; and about the end perhaps the less we think the better. We are to please ourselves about the rules ; we are to please ourselves about the end ; for end and rules are neither end nor rules.

---

[1] *Liberty*, &c., pp. 362-3, ed. ii. Mr. Stephen has put this part of the case so strongly that I have not thought it worth while to enlarge upon it. Kant is very clear and successful on this point.

Our positive aim in life is given up; we may content ourselves, as a substitute, with the resolve to live our life as we
find it, to sink useless theories, and follow the bent of our
practical leanings; or, saddened at our disenchantment,
may embrace the conclusion that, if pleasure can not be
found, yet pain at least can be avoided. Not only in the
school, but in life around us, does the positive beginning
conduct to the negative result, to the making a goal of an
absence, to the placing the end in a mere negation.

We have shown, in the first place, the collision between
popular opinion and Hedonism as the search for pleasure;
we have shown, in the second place, the reason why the
seeking of *my* pleasure gives no practicable end in life. On
both points we have dwelt, perhaps, at unnecessary length;
but we have not yet done justice to the doctrine which
makes virtue a means, not to my pleasure, but to the pleasure
of the ' whole sentient creation'—to modern Utilitarianism,
which may be called, I suppose, our most fashionable moral
philosophy. This we must now notice, but only so far as
our subject compels us. A more detailed examination is
not called for here, and, as we think, would not repay us
anywhere.

The end, as before, is the greatest amount of pleasurable
feeling, yet not now in me, but in the sentient world as a
whole. The first thing to observe is that (as we noticed
above), if happiness means this, happiness is unrealizable—
it can by no possibility be reached. If the greatest happiness,
in the sense of the maximum of pleasure, was, as applied to
the individual, a mere ' idea', or rather a self-contradictory
attempt at an idea, which we saw by its very nature could
not exist as a fact; then *a fortiori*, I should say, the realization of a maximum of pleasure in the ' whole sentient
creation' (which stands, I suppose, for what particular
animal organisms are now and are to be hereafter) is nothing
but a wild and impossible fiction.

Happiness, in the sense of ' as much as you can ', we saw,
is never and nowhere realized; or, if any one prefers it, is
realized everywhere and without any drawback. In both

cases, as a something set to be gained, it has no signification. Happiness, in the meaning of a maximum of pleasure, can never be reached ; and what is the sense of trying to reach the impossible ? Happiness, in the meaning of always a little more and always a little less, is the stone of Sisyphus and the vessel of the Danaides—it is not heaven, but hell. Whether we try for it or not, we always have got a little more and a little less [1] (than we might have), and never at any time, however much we try for it, can we have a little more or a little less than we have got.

But theoretical considerations of this sort are likely neither to be understood nor regarded. Our morality, we shall hear, 'is a practical matter'. And I should have thought it indeed a practical consideration, whether our chief good be realizable or no, whether it be πρακτὸν καὶ κτητὸν ἀνθρώπῳ, or exist only in the heads of certain theorists. But let this pass. We can avoid, I dare say, practical inconvenience, by not meaning what we say or saying what we mean.

Whatever, then, we may think about the possibility of the actual existence of the end, and the satisfactoriness (or otherwise) of aiming at the impossible and unmeaning, at all events our moral law and precept is clear : Increase the pleasure, i.e. multiply in number, and intensify in quality, the pleasurable feelings of sentient beings, and do the opposite by their pains.

We have already noticed, but it may not be amiss to call attention once more to the fact, that a doctrine of this sort is directly opposed to popular morality. If, by being changed into pigs, we secured an absolute certainty of a greater amount of pleasure with a less amount of pain, we (I speak for the ordinary person) should decline the change,

---

[1] To define happiness as 'increase in pleasure', or 'the having more than we had', would not extricate us from our difficulties. For then no stationary state could be happy at all, and no man would be happier than another, save in respect of being in more intense transition. The actual amount of pleasure would go for nothing. But it is not worth while to develop the absurdities consequent on such a possible definition.

either for ourselves or the race, and should think it our
duty to do so.[1]   But, if we believe that the greatest amount
of pleasure is the end, it would be our duty to strive after
and accept such a change.   And some such choice is not
a mere theoretical possibility.   Unless Fourier be much
belied, his scheme of 'phalansteries' was a practical proposal to seek for pleasure as the end, and all else as means.
The ordinary moral man refuses to discuss such a proposal.
He repudiates the end, and the means with it.   But the
'greatest amount of pleasure' doctrine must accept the end,
and calmly discuss the means; and this is not the moral
point of view.   It is surely imaginable (I do not say it is
likely), that we might have to say to a large and immoral
majority, 'If I wanted to make you happy, which I do not,
I should do so by pampering your vices, which I will not '.
(Stephen, *Liberty*, pp. 287–8.)

So much for the morality of the theory.   Let us now
consider its practicability and consistency.   The end, as the
pleasure of all, is, like my pleasure, not something which
I can apprehend and carry out in my life.   It is not
a system, not a concrete whole.   There are no means included in it: there are none which, in themselves, belong to
the end.   Wanting to know what I am to do, ' Increase the
pleasure of all' gives me, by itself, no answer.   ' But there
is no need that it should ', will be the reply ;   ' The experience
of mankind has discovered the means which tend to increase
pleasure ;   these are laid down in the moral Almanack
(Mill, *Util.*, p. 36), and they may fairly be considered as
included in the end.'

Here I think that Hedonism does not see a most serious
difficulty.   It is the old question, What is the nature of the
authority of the Almanack, and are its rules laws?   If they
are laws, on what do they rest?   If they are not, are there
any other moral laws ;   and without laws can you have
morality ?   Let me explain the objection.   You can not,
I object to the Hedonist, make these laws part of the end,

[1] [Yes, but this issue is never *clearly* raised by ordinary morality (cf.
pp. 136–7, l. 4).]

and identify them therewith; for the end was clearly laid down as pleasurable feeling, and there is no essential connexion between that end and the laws as means. If the laws or rules are not feelings (and they are not), they must be mere means to feeling. The relation of the two, of the end and the means, is external. You can not, from the conception of the end as such, conclude in any way to the rules as such. This seems to me quite clear; and, if it is so, then you can in your mind put the end on one side and the rules on the other, and contemplate the possibility of going to the end without these particular means. You may say you do not care for possibilities; experience shows the connexion of means and end, and that is enough. This point I wish especially to emphasize: such an observed connexion is not sufficient; or it is sufficient only if we are prepared to make one of the two following assumptions. The first is that the general opinion of mankind, which we suppose to exist and be embodied in these rules, is infallible; that it takes the only way, or the best way, to the given end; and also that I have no excuse for thinking otherwise. The second is that, whether I think the rules the best means to the end or not, I have in any case to sink my own view as to the right means to the given end, and take the rules as something which is not to be departed from. One of these two supposable assumptions is necessary.

(1) Now with respect to the first, I see no ground upon which the Hedonist, were he so disposed, could maintain and justify such a strong assertion of the ὃ πᾶσι δοκεῖ. Why am I bound to consider these laws infallible, in such a sense that any departure from them, in any case, must contribute less to the given end than a corresponding observance? And how to me is such a truth (if it be a truth) not to be an open question? How is my doubt or my denial of the truth to be *ipso facto* immorality? An example will help us. Let us take the precept, Do not commit adultery. How are we to prove that no possible adultery can increase the overplus of pleasurable feeling? How are we to show that a man's honest and probable view to the contrary is an

immoral view? And, if we can not show these things, what becomes of this first supposable assumption?

(2) Then, if mankind may err, if the right of private judgement is not to be suppressed, if the supposed general experience is not infallible,[1] how can it be moral for me always to follow it even in the teeth of my own judgement? I may be perfectly aware that acting on rules is, speaking generally, the way to reach the end. I may even admit that the departure from rules in most cases has produced, and must produce, an effect detrimental to the end. I might, if I pleased, for argument's sake admit (though it would be contrary to fact, and no one could ask for such an admission) that every previous departure from rules has been a failure, and has decreased the surplus. But now the matter stands thus: I have taken all pains to form an opinion, and I am quite certain that my case is an exception. I have no doubt whatever that in this instance the breaking of a rule will increase the surplus. To say that I am a fool does not touch the question; to say that I must be mistaken does not touch the question; to say that I ought not to think as I do, or ought not to act accordingly, begs the question. The moral end is clear; I, after having thought over all considerations up to my lights, am clear as to the means. What right have you, what right has the world to tell me to hold my hand, to make your uncertain opinion the standard rather than the certain end? How shall I answer for it to my own conscience[2] if I do? What is this rule that is to come between me and my moral duty? Let us repeat our illustration. The rule says, Do not commit adultery. I wish to commit adultery. I am sure I do not want to please myself at all; in fact rather the contrary. I am as positive as I can be of anything, that the case is either not contemplated by the rule, or, if it is, that the rule is wrong, that the proposed act must diminish the

---

[1] [Certainly, but on *any* theory we have a corresponding difficulty (cf. pp. 101-2).]

[2] 'And to my God', I might add, against those who drag the Deity into the question.

sum of the pain and must increase the sum of the pleasure of the sentient world as a whole, and this too after all consequences that I can reckon (and I can reckon no more) have been counted in. Is it immoral then to break the rule; or rather is it not immoral to keep it, to sacrifice a real good to a mere idea? My conscience is clear; and my dreams will not be broken by ' the groans' of an 'abstraction'. (Mill, *Dissert.*, i. 21.)

Now, if it be answered here that, on any theory of morals, collisions must arise—that I fully admit to be true; and again, that on any theory collisions *of this kind* must arise (i. e. not the conflict of moral ends, but the conflict of diverse reflective calculations as to the means to a given moral end)— that (though I absolutely deny it) I will admit for argument's sake, and argument's sake alone. But (1) it belongs to the essence of Hedonism to provoke such collisions, and to justify the raising of casuistical questions on well-nigh every point of conduct, and this not merely theoretically, but with a view to one's own immediate practice.[1] The reason is simple,

[1] [This is perhaps exaggerated. But still
(1) the ordinary moral judgement is not merely intellectual.
  (a) It is the reaction of our moral nature on the concrete case, and this makes the selection the important point here. Even in the last resort in a doubtful case it is not reflective, except to some extent. In the main it is *not* so.
And (b) it is not merely perceptive, even intuitionally.
In the last resort the Hedonistic moral judgement must
  (a) be *merely* perceptive (as the concrete individual case has *no* value in itself *as* concrete, but only as means).
And (b) it must be largely reflective.
    The only answer to this is to say that the moral judgement represents through past habit the best judgement as to the means to pleasure, and so *serves*, though blindly and irrationally and in principle fallaciously. This answer, even if true in general, cannot hold universally, since custom cannot be the final arbiter for Hedonism.
And (2) the Hedonistic judgement must be in the end mainly reflective, and the lowering of the concrete case to mere means is a constant provocation to that.
On the other side *no* moral law is absolute, and hence all are liable to 'exceptions' (where there is a collision of duties), and this point I should not have slurred.]

and we have stated it already. The end for Hedonism has
no means which belong to it and are inseparable from it.
The means are external; and so long as you get the end
the means are immaterial. The relation of the means to
the end is matter of opinion, and it can not be more than
matter of opinion. The opinion of any number of persons
is still only an opinion. The end I am certain of. As to
the means, I have nothing but the opinion of myself and
others. The last appeal is to my private judgement. Now
my private judgement may assure me that in 999 cases out
of 1,000 it contributes more to the end that I should not
exercise my private judgement. It *may* assure me that,
being what I am, it will contribute to the surplus if I never
use my private judgement. But it need not so assure me.
It may assure me that in the thousandth case I had better
use my private judgement. And it may go a great deal
further than this. The question is not, *Do* I and others act
as a rule from habit, and according to general opinion? for
that is a mere question of fact. The question is one of morals:
ought my private judgement ever to come into collision
with general opinion, as in fact it sometimes does and must?
If not, why not? If it may, then ought I in such cases ever
to follow it? and, if not, why not? If I may follow it in my
own case once, why not twice? If here, why not there?
And if anybody is ever to use his private judgement on
any moral point, why may not I be the man, and this
the case where I may? To put the whole matter in two
words; the precepts of Hedonism are only rules, and rules
may always have exceptions: they are not, and, so far as
I see, they can not be made out to be laws. I am not their
servant, but they are mine. And, so far as my lights go,
this is to make possible, to justify, and even to encourage,
an incessant practical casuistry; and that, it need scarcely
be added, is the death of morality. Before I proceed, however, let me entreat the reader to remember that the
question, Are Utilitarians immoral? is one question, and
the question, Is their theory immoral? altogether another,
and the only one which we are concerned with.

And (2), if it were true that no other moral theory was in a happier plight, what are we to say but 'so much the worse for all moral theories', and not 'so much the better for Hedonism'? The moral consciousness is the touchstone of moral theories, and that moral consciousness, I appeal to it in every man, has laws which are a great deal more than rules. To that consciousness 'Do not commit adultery' is a law to be obeyed; it is not the prescription of a more or less questionable policy. It is not a means, which in the opinion of A, B, and C will or may conduce to an end other than itself, and in the opinion of D may or will not do so. Let the Hedonist refute thrice or four times over, if he pleases, his rival theories; but he does not thereby establish his own, and is no nearer doing so than before.

To proceed—the conclusion we have reached is that, supposing it to be certain that the end is the maximum surplus of pleasure in the sentient world, that end gives no standard for morality. The end is in itself most abstract and impalpable. The means are external and in themselves immaterial to the end; and the fixing the relation of means to end must always be matter of opinion; in the last resort it is, and (what is most important) it *ought* to be, matter of my private opinion. As it turned out before, so here also the rules are not laws; I can please myself about them: and a standard which is no standard, a law which is no law, but which I may break or keep, which is at the mercy of changing judgement and fleeting opinion, is no practical basis for me to regulate my life by.[1]

---

[1] To bring the matter home to the reader, I will produce an example or two of cases where Hedonism gives no guidance.* If in certain South Sea Islands the people have not what we call 'morality', but are very happy, is it moral or immoral to attempt to turn them from their ways? If by an immoral act, which probably will not be discovered, I can defeat a stroke of pernicious policy on a large scale, what am I to do? Is prostitution a good or a bad thing? To prove that it is bad we must prove that it diminishes the surplus of pleasant sensations, and is not this a fair subject for argument? Do I or do I not add to

---

* [But does *any* moral view 'give guidance' in such cases?]

The Utilitarian, I am perfectly aware, does not wish me to keep the end continually before me, but rather to have my eye on the accredited means. The question is not, however, what the Utilitarian wishes, but what his theory justifies and demands. One of the most serious objections to Hedonism is that, as we have seen, it is not in earnest with its own conclusions. It is no argument in favour of a theory, it is surely rather an argument against it, that it can not teach the legitimate consequences of its principles.

The greatest amount of pleasure then, if we take it for our end, we have found to be unrealizable, to be non- or immoral, and lastly, in practice to be an unworkable doctrine. All this time we have taken the end for granted. But now we are to ask, What ground is there for taking the pleasure of the sentient creation as the moral end? What possible

the surplus of 'grateful feeling' by a given act or acts of sexual irregularity? This is a serious practical question, and I know that in many cases it is honestly answered in the affirmative; and in some of these cases, so far as such impalpable questions can be judged of, I should say the affirmation was correct. Is suicide ever allowable, and if so, when? and when not? Is murder? and if not, why not? and so on with all the crimes in the decalogue and out of it. If any given act is to be shown immoral, you must, if called on, exhibit the probability of its producing more pain than pleasure in the world, and is not this again and again a hopeless problem? Of course the Hedonist does not *want* the question raised. Of course he *wants* people to go by rules always, and no one to ask any questions, except it be himself. That we quite understand. The point is, if I *choose* to raise such questions, on what ground can he say I may not? On what ground can he refuse to discuss the case? On what ground can he blame me, if I take and act on a view which is other than his view?

'The beliefs which have thus come down are the rules of morality for the multitude, and for the philosopher until he has succeeded in finding better. That philosophers might easily do this, even now, on many subjects . . . I admit, or rather earnestly maintain' (Mill, *Util.*, p. 34). From the author of the *Essay on Liberty* this should mean a good deal. If the philosopher may make new rules, I suppose he may modify old ones. And who is 'the philosopher'? Are we (as proposed for the franchise) to have an examination, passing in which shall entitle a man to try 'experiments in living'? Or shall we leave it to private judgement? Then I should like to know in these days of 'advanced thinking' who would *not* be a 'philosopher', and how many would be left in the 'multitude'.

reason is there why I should look on this as that for which everything else must be given up, even my own pleasure and my own life? And here I think Hedonism is altogether helpless. The consistent, and the only consistent position, is to say that I desire my own pleasure, that the pleasure of others is in many ways conducive to my own, and that desiring the end I must desire the means also. But this is a return to the doctrine we discussed above, viz. that my pleasure is the end ; and to accept this doctrine is to leave the standpoint of modern Utilitarianism, and to say, Its end is not an end ; it is or it may be a mere means.

The Hedonist in his distress may turn himself in various directions.

(1) He may say, 'The end is not provable because too good to be provable. It is self-evident, and nothing else is more certain.' But having noticed already that the moral consciousness repudiates the claim of his end to be the chief good, and it being clear that selfishness often in its practice, and sometimes in its theory, rejects its claim to be anything more than a means, I think we need not trouble ourselves with its pretence to self-evidence ; more especially as, according to the psychology of the ordinary Hedonist, to desire the end as such is a psychological impossibility.

(2) The next resource is the *Deus ex machina*. Not only on a certain stage, but also with certain theorists the maxim seems to hold good, 'When in trouble bring in the Deity'. God, we shall be told, wills the greatest amount of pleasure of the whole sentient creation, and therefore we ought to do so likewise. Now, even if I were capable of it, I am not disposed to enter into the speculative theology of our 'inductive' moralists ; I will say to them merely,

Lasst unsern Herrgott aus dem Spass,

and go on.

(3) But now I have to meet no less an antagonist than Mr. Mill himself ; and he has proved that the Utilitarian end is desirable. Let us hear him ;

'No reason can be given why the general happiness is desirable, except that each person, so far as he believes it to be attainable, desires his own happiness.   This, however, being a fact, we have not only all the proof which the case admits of, but all which it is possible to require, that happiness is a good ; that each person's happiness is a good to that person, and the general happiness, therefore, a good to the aggregate [1] of all persons' (*Util.*, p. 52).

Whether our 'great modern logician' thought that by this he had proved that the happiness of all was desirable for each, I will not undertake to say.   He either meant to prove this, or has proved what he started with, viz. that each desires his own pleasure.   And yet there is a certain plausibility about it.   If many pigs are fed at one trough, each desires his own food, and somehow as a consequence does seem to desire the food of all ; and by parity of reasoning it should follow that each pig, desiring his own pleasure, desires also the pleasure of all.[2]   But as this scarcely seems conformable to experience, I suppose there must be something wrong with the argument, and so likewise with the argument of our philosopher.[3]

[1] ['I merely meant in this particular sentence to argue that, since A's happiness is a good, B's a good, C's a good, &c., the sum of all these goods must be a good.' *Letters*, ii, p. 116. (From Davidson, *Political Thought in England*, p. 185.)

But, surely, in this explanation (even if we accept it) the 'since' implies a difference between the 'sum' and the several goods, and that the 'sum' is a good to the 'aggregate' of persons as distinguished from the several persons.

If we suppose Mill to be thinking only of the 'ascetic' * we may take him to argue thus : 'There must be in an aggregate *at least* what there is in the individuals ; therefore pleasure, as an end, belongs to the aggregate.'   This is correct, but it ignores the question 'belongs *how* ?'   And here Egoistic Hedonism comes in and wrecks the desired consequence.]

[2] [This is from Kant, *not* (as has been suggested by a critic) from Carlyle.]

[3] Either Mill meant to argue, '*Because* everybody desires his own

---

* ⟨*Utilitarianism*, p. 23.   '*All honour to those who can abnegate for themselves the personal enjoyment of life, when by such renunciation they contribute worthily to increase the amount of happiness in the world ; but he who does it, or professes to do it, for any other purpose, is no more deserving of admiration than the ascetic mounted on his pillar.*'—ED.⟩

The End as the pleasure of all is, starting from the theories of our Utilitarian moralists, not only unprovable but impossible. If my self is something which exists by itself and independent of other selves, if all that I desire and can desire is my pleasure, and if that pleasure is an isolated feeling of this particular self, then the sole desirable is a state or states of my own feeling, and in the second place whatever is a means to that. To desire an object which is not the idea of my pleasure is psychologically impossible, and no torturing and twisting of phrases will make a connexion from such an idea to any such object. And such an object is the idea of the pleasure of others considered not as conducing to mine. I may happen to desire the pleasure of others, and I may happen not to do so. To tell me the pleasure of others is desirable for me, is to tell me you think it will conduce to my own; to tell me I ought to desire it either says that again, or it is nonsense. Ought is the feeling of obligation,[1] and 'when the feeling ceases the obligation ceases'. The Utilitarian believes on psychological grounds that pleasure is the sole desirable: he believes on the strength of his natural and moral instincts that he must live for others: he puts the two together, and concludes that the pleasure of others is what he has to live for. This is not a good theoretical deduction,[2] but it is the generation of the Utilitarian

pleasure, *therefore* everybody desires his own pleasure'; or '*Because* everybody desires his own pleasure, *therefore* everybody desires the pleasure of everybody else'. Disciples may take their choice. To us it matters not which interpretation be correct. In the one case Mill has proved his point by a pitiable sophism; in the other he has not proved any point at all.

[1] [I think this is not fair, since 'obligation' means here presumably 'the obliging force', cf. (however) pp. 122-3. I should have said 'or it is nonsense, unless it is desired to insist once more that I can desire only the pleasant idea of my own pleasure'.]

[2] It is monstrous to argue thus: 'Because (1) on psychological grounds it is certain that we can desire nothing but our own private pleasure; because (2) on some other grounds something *else* (whatever it may be), something not my feeling of pleasure, something other than my private self, is desired and desirable; therefore (3) this something else which is desired and desirable is the pleasure of others, since, by (1), only pleasure can be desired.' If we argue in this way, we may as well

monster, and of that we must say that its heart is in the right place, but the brain is wanting.

Its heart, its 'natural sentiment', does tell it that its substance is one with the substance of its fellows; that in itself and by itself it is not itself at all, and has no validity except as a violent and futile attempt at abstraction.   And yet if we deny that a universal can be more than 'an idea', if we are sure that the merely individual and the real are one and the same, and in particular that the self is exclusive of other selves, and is in this sense a mere individual; and if further, for morality at all events, we can not do without something that is universal, something which is wider and stronger than this or that self—then here, as in all other spheres, we are face to face with the problem, How out of mere individuals (particulars), which are fixed as such, can you get a universal?   And the problem put in this way is insoluble.   The self can desire in the end, as we too think, nothing but itself, and if the self it is to realize is an atom, a unit which repels other units, and can have nothing in itself but what is exclusively *its*, its feeling, its pleasure and pain—then it is certain that it can stand to others, with their pleasures and pains, only in an external relation; and since it is the end, the others must be the means, and nothing but the means. On such a basis morality is impossible; and yet morality does exist.   But if the head could follow the heart, not with

go a little further to—' (4) and therefore we can and do desire something not our own private pleasure, and therefore (1) is false, and therefore the whole argument disappears, since it is upon (1) that the whole rests'.

I am ashamed to have to examine such reasoning, but it is necessary to do so, since it is common enough.   Is it not palpable at first sight that (1) and (2) are absolutely incompatible, that each contradicts the other flatly?   You must choose between them, and, whichever you choose, the proof of Utilitarianism goes, because that springs from the unnatural conjunction of both.

The only escape that I can see is to say in (2) that something is desirable though not desired, and write 'not desired but desirable' for 'desired and desirable'.   But not only is this perhaps altogether unmeaning, but also the conclusion now disappears; you can get nothing from the premises.   Because A is desired and B is desirable, it does not follow, I suppose, that a hash of A and B is desired and desirable.

a wretched compromise but altogether; if the self to be realized is not exclusive of other selves, but on the contrary is determined, characterized, made what it is by relation to others; if my self which I aim at is the realization in me of a moral world which is a system of selves, an organism in which I am a member, and in whose life I live—then I can not aim at my own well-being without aiming at that of others.[1] The others are not mere means to me, but are involved in my essence; and this essence of myself, which is not only mine but embraces and stands above both me and this man and the other man, is superior to, and gives a law to us all, in a higher sense than the organism as a whole gives a law to the members. And this concrete and real universal makes the morality, which does exist, possible in theory as well as real in fact. It is this which modern Utilitarianism is blindly groping after, but it will not find it till it gives up the Hedonism of its end, and the basis of its psychology, which stands upon uncriticized, violent, and unreal metaphysical abstractions.

So much in passing, and here we might well end. We have dwelt too long on the efforts of Hedonism to compromise with morality, but we are forced to notice one last attempt. This consists in distinguishing pleasures, according to their quality,[2] into higher and lower. The former are

---

[1] [Except, of course, so far as in selfish action I make my abstracted and isolated self my main aim and end. And this is, in a sense, inconsistent. See Essay VII on *Selfishness and Self-sacrifice*.]

[2] There is a point which might be raised here, and which is of considerable importance. It is this. Are pleasures, *as* pleasures, distinguishable by anything else than quantity? The pleasure, as such, is not the whole pleasant feeling, not the whole of *what* is felt. Then we have to ask, Does this '*what* is felt', which qualifies the pleasure, and makes it of one sort and not of another, make part of the mere pleasure itself, *as* pleasure? Or have we to say, Pleasure is itself always one and the same, and differs only in degree; sorts of pleasures are degrees of the same pleasure in reference to sorts of other feelings, which, as such, are *not* pleasures as such? Or more briefly, Has pleasure any content in itself? If not, then it has no qualitative distinctness in itself, but only by its reference to that which it goes with.

superior, the latter are inferior; and hence, in preferring the higher pleasures, we are true to Hedonism, and yet are at one with the moral consciousness. We must briefly examine this doctrine.

It has two forms. One of these takes quality simply as quality; the other takes quality in relation to quantity, and looks on it as the index or result of quantity. The latter, we shall find, keeps true to the principle of the greatest surplus of pleasure, but it says nothing new. The former leaves the principle unawares, and moves unknowingly to other ground, but can get no standing-place for morality. Let us first discuss the latter; but, before we begin, we must call attention to the phrases 'higher' and 'lower'.

Higher and lower (forgive me, dear reader) are 'relative': they are comparatives, and they hence mean more or less of something. Higher means nearer some top, or it means nothing. Lower means nearer some bottom, or it means nothing. This being established, when we talk of 'higher' and 'lower' pleasure, we ought to know what our top and our bottom are, or else we risk talking nonsense.

Next let me observe (and forgive me, if you can, reader) that top and bottom, as a rule, are 'relative', and depend on the way in which you look at the matter. If the top is the 'end', you may put the end anywhere: benevolence is (morally) higher than selfishness, murder is higher (as a crime) than larceny. You may speak of the height of goodness, badness, pleasure, pain, beauty, and ugliness. And so, when a man talks to us of 'higher' and 'lower', he says nothing to us at all, till we know what end or summit he has in his mind.

Is not pleasure, as such, the abstraction of one element of a whole psychical state from that state; and when so abstracted, are there differences of *kind* in it, or only of degree? Not wishing to give a positive opinion on this point, I have not introduced it into the text as affecting the argument. But the thoughtful reader will at once perceive its bearing. Hedonism, when it ceases to aim at pleasure as such and nothing but pleasure, is false to its principle and becomes incoherent. But if pleasure, as such, is not qualitatively distinguishable, then we must have regard to nothing but quantity.

Again, higher and lower, as comparative terms, refer to degree. What is higher has a greater degree (or it has a greater number of degrees) of something definite ; what is lower has a less degree or number of degrees. Their quality, as higher and lower, is referable to quantity.[1] So that apart from quantity, apart from degree, there is no comparison, no estimation, no higher and lower at all.

The result of these perhaps trivial considerations is that, if we are confined to *mere* quality, the words higher and lower have no meaning. If of two pleasures I can not say one is higher than the other in degree (as intenser), or as the result or producer of degree (as accompaniment of higher function, or as connected with approximation to some end), then the words higher and lower can not be applied to them. The sphere of mere quality is the world of immediate perception ; and here we may say A or we may say B, but we can not make comparisons between A and B without leaving our sphere. I may take this and not that, I may choose that and not the other, but if, because of this and on the mere strength of this, I call one higher and one lower, I am not simply arbitrary and perhaps wrong in my opinion, but I am talking sheer and absolute nonsense.

To proceed then with one of our two views, (1) the theory which takes quality either as = intensive quantity, or as a means to quantity in general. The ' higher pleasure ' is here the pleasure which contains in itself most degrees of pleasure, or which contributes on the whole to the existence of a larger number of degrees of pleasure. Here the principle of the greatest amount of pleasure is adhered to ; that is the top, and what approaches to it or contributes to it is

---

[1] Speaking roughly and inaccurately, we may say they are of this quality, as containing more or fewer degrees of somewhat, or as the result of more or fewer degrees, or (what comes to the same thing) as producing a qualitative result which is referred to more or fewer degrees ; e. g. a certain warmth is higher, because containing more degrees of objective heat ; a piece of work is higher if it is the result of more skill ; and A's skill stands higher than B's, if A produces a result which B can not produce, and if the result must be referred to the amount of skill in the performer.

nearer the top.   But since the moral 'higher' is here, as we
see, the more pleasurable or the means to the more pleasurable, we come in the end to the amount, the quantity of
pleasure without distinction of kind or quality; and having
already seen that such an end is not a moral end, we get
nothing from the phrases 'higher' and 'lower' unless it be
confusion.

(2) The second view is that which distinguishes pleasures
by their *mere* quality.   The 'higher' pleasure here is not
the more intense pleasure; it is not the pleasure connected
with the maximum of pleasure on the whole without distinction of kind.   It is the preferable kind of pleasure (Mill,
Util., p. 12).

The first point to be noticed is that our theory gives up
and abandons the greatest amount of pleasure principle.   If
you are to prefer a higher pleasure to a lower without
reference to quantity—then there is an end altogether of the
principle which puts the measure in the surplus of pleasure
to the whole sentient creation.   It is no use saying all pleasures are ends, only some are more ends.   It is no use talking
of 'estimation' and 'comparison' (Mill, pp. 12, 17).   You
have no standard to estimate by, no measure to make
comparisons with.   Given a certain small quantity of higher
pleasure in collision with a certain large quantity of lower,
how can you decide between them?   To work the sum you
must reduce the data to the same denomination.   You must
go to quantity or nothing; you decline to go to quantity,
and hence you can not get any result.   But if you refuse to
work the sum, you abandon the greatest amount of pleasure
principle.

There is no harm in doing that: but what else have we
to go to? The higher pleasures? And what are the higher
pleasures? We find higher pleasure means nothing but the
pleasure which those who have experienced both it and
others do as a fact choose in preference.   Higher then, as
we saw above, has no meaning at all, unless we go to something *outside* pleasure, for we may not go to quantity of
pleasure.   But, if we go outside pleasure, not only have we

given up the greatest amount theory, but we have thrown over Hedonism altogether.[1]

Let us drop the word higher then, as we must. The end is pleasures in order, as they are preferred by men who know them. The objection which at once arises (p. 14) is, Is there not any difference of opinion? Do not different men, and does not even the same man at different times, prefer different pleasures? What is the answer? It is not very intelligible, and is too long to quote (pp. 14, 15). What it comes to would appear, however, to be either Yes, or No. Let us consider these alternatives one at a time.

(1) If we say 'Yes, not only do different men prefer different pleasures, but so does the same man at different times', then what basis have we left for a moral system? Merely this. Most men at most times do prefer one sort of pleasure to another; and from this we have to show that I ought to prefer one sort of pleasure to others at all times. We need not ask how the transition is to be made from what most men do to what I am to do. I think it can be made on no view of human nature, and I am quite sure it can not be made on Mill's view. Supposing then that in Mill's mouth moral obligation had a meaning, yet there is no reason why it should attach itself to the average pleasures of the average man.

(2) And if we say No, if, having accepted the Platonic doctrine that the judge of pleasures is he who knows them all, we go further and assert with Sokrates that no man is

---

[1] Mill is unaware that he has done so, because of the various senses in which he uses the word happiness. Happiness is (pp. 8, 10) simply identified with pleasure. Then (13, 14) appears the doctrine that happiness may exist without contentment, and (I suppose) contentment without happiness. We hear (13) that the 'sense of dignity' is 'part' of happiness, and (19) we see happiness means a desirable kind of life. It is a 'concrete whole', with 'parts' (55). It has ' ingredients' (53), and appears not to be a mere 'aggregate' or 'collective something'. Instead of pleasure, it has plainly come to mean something like the life we prefer, and hence greatest happiness will stand for the widest and intensest realization of such an ideal. This is to leave Hedonism altogether. [My references throughout are to *Utilitarianism*, ed. i, the only one I have at hand.]

willingly evil, that you can not prefer bad to good, that, if
you take the bad, it is because you never have known or
now do not know the good, we then, I think, are in good
company, but in no better case.   For an opponent will hold
to the fact that he does knowingly prefer what is called bad
to good, and will hence, by our argument, conclude first
that bad is really good, and next that nothing can be either
good or bad, since bad to one man is good to another.
And if we, on the other hand, persist that the fact is impossible (I do not know how we are to prove it so), and that no
one ever did or could choose what we call bad, when he
had in his mind what we call good, then we identify immorality with ignorance, and moral obligation disappears.   For
every man not only does, but must do, the best on every
occasion, so far as he knows it ; his knowledge is an accident
which has nothing to do with his will ; he must act up to
the ought, so far as he has an ought, and he can not do
what he thinks is wrong.

To proceed—the basis of our moral theory is now, There
is a scale of pleasures ; some persons know all, and others
only some ; but you necessarily choose the pleasures you
know according to the scale. I, e. g., know the alphabet of
pleasures, always or sometimes, up to M.   'Immoral man
to choose M, when you should have chosen P or R or even
X.'   But I do not know what they are.   'And therefore
you are immoral, for I and a good many other people do.'
But let us drop the matter here ; on such a theory, the
reader will assent, moral obligation is unmeaning.[1]

[1] At the risk of hypercriticism I will make one or two further remarks
on Mill's view. According to it, pleasures must stand in a kind of
order of merit, represented, let us say, by the letters of the alphabet.
All pleasures, because pleasures, are good in themselves. A pleasure is
immoral only when taken where a higher was possible, now or as a
consequence. Then every pleasure is moral, because it has a supposable pleasure below it ; every pleasure is immoral, because there is
always a supposable pleasure above it. No man is moral, because his
knowledge is limited, and he therefore can not always take the highest
conceivable pleasure ; but if so, then all men are equally moral, for
they all take the highest pleasure they know. Or, passing by this, let
us suppose the pleasures divided into two classes, higher and lower.

On either supposition, then, these preferable pleasures found no 'ought' in the moral sense :[1] you have them or you have them not ; you like them or you do not like them ; you know them or you do not know them ; and there is an end of it. If A, B, and C call D immoral, D may return the epithet, and if he likes to say 'ignorance is morality' or to make any other assertion whatever, he can do it, as it appears to me, on precisely the same ground as A, B, and C have for their assertions, viz. no ground at all but likes and dislikes.

If the lower are to be considered at all, then, as we have said, in the event of a collision the problem is insoluble, because what is not of the same denomination can not be compared. Let us suppose then that the lower are not to be considered, and we are left with the higher. Here the same problem breaks out. For these pleasures are no system ; if you make the idea of a system your end, and regulate the pleasures by that, you have deserted Hedonism. The pleasures are no system, and they are not all of equal value. Hence, as above, they can not be calculated quantitatively. In the event of collisions then (such as must take place) between e. g. the pleasures of philosophy, pleasures of natural science, pleasures of virtue, pleasures of love, pleasures of the table, pleasures of the 'theopathic affections', pleasures of fine art, pleasures of history, &c., you have again a problem which can not be solved except by the caprice of the individual, who will prefer for himself and others what he likes best.

Another point of interest is that the theory which begins with the most intense democracy, wide enough to take in all life that feels pleasure and pain, ends in a no less intense Platonic aristocracy. The higher pleasure is to be preferred to any amount of the lower, and I suppose is to constitute the moral standard. But clearly the beasts are incapable of refined pleasures ; the vulgar are better, but still very low ; the only man who knows the highest pleasure is the philosopher. He is moral, the universe below is immoral in increasing degree. And, since no amount of lower can weigh against higher, and, since the highest pleasures (and only the philosopher can judge what they are, for only he knows all) are realizable only in the few, therefore we must live for the few, and not for the many. And I suppose the same argument might be used by the artist, or well-nigh any one else. But it is not worth while to pursue the matter further.

[1] [This is probably indefensible (cf. note 1 on p. 114) as 'obligation &c.' means 'the obliging or compelling force'. But I must read Mill again to see what is meant (p. 123, l. 24) by ' *only* a feeling in my own mind '. This looks as if Mill denied any 'restraining force' of anything *but* the feeling, i.e. abstracted *that* from what possesses it and acts through it.]

And here I think we might leave the matter; but, having gone so far, we may as well go a little further. Not only has moral obligation nothing in Mr. Mill's theory to which it can attach itself save the likes or dislikes of one or more individuals, but in the end it *is* itself nothing more than a similar feeling.

'The ultimate sanction of all morality' is 'a subjective feeling in our own minds' (p. 41), and the 'moral faculty' is 'susceptible by a sufficient use of the external sanctions, and of the force of early impressions, of being cultivated in almost any direction; so that there is hardly anything so absurd or so mischievous that it may not, by means of these influences, be made to act on the human mind with all the authority of conscience' (p. 44). The feeling of obligation then, we see, does not refer itself essentially to anything in particular. And further, 'this sanction has no binding efficacy on those who do not possess the feelings it appeals to' (p. 42). 'The sanction, so far as it is disinterested, is always in the mind itself, and the notion, therefore, of the transcendental moralists must be that this sanction will not exist *in* the mind, unless it is believed to have its root out of the mind, and that, if a person is able to say to himself, This which is restraining me and which is called my con-science, is only a feeling in my own mind, he may possibly draw the conclusion that when the feeling ceases the obliga-tion ceases, and that, if he find the feeling inconvenient, he may disregard it and endeavour to get rid of it' (pp. 42, 43). This is a serious matter; and I should say that any theory which maintains that a man may get rid of his sense of moral obligation if he can, and that, if he does so, the moral obligation is gone, is as grossly immoral a theory as ever was published. Does Mr. Mill repudiate the doctrine? Not at all; he evidently accepts it, though he prefers not to say so. The passage goes on: 'But is this danger confined to the Utilitarian morality?' &c. Now I am ashamed of repeating it so often, but I must entreat the reader not to have dust thrown in his eyes in this way, and not to be dis-tracted by 'transcendental moralists' or any other bugbears.

The question is, Is theory A true, or are we obliged to say that either theory A is false or the facts are a lie? The question is not, Have theories B and C the same fault as A? When we have done with A, we will then, if we choose, go to B and C; and if they turn out *all* false, that does not prove *one* true. These pleader's devices are in place in a law-court, but philosophy does not recognize them.

If then all that the moral 'ought' means is that I happen to have a feeling which I need not have, and that this feeling attaches itself now to one set of pleasures and now to another set according to accident or my liking, would it not be better altogether to have done with the word, and, as some have done, openly to reject it and give it up, since already we have given up all that it stands for? But if we give up the word, then we have confessed that, as a theory of morals, Hedonism is bankrupt, and we are left with nothing but our 'natural sentiment'.

Hedonism *is* bankrupt; with weariness we have pursued it, so far as was necessary, through its various shapes, from the selfish doctrine of the individual to the self-sacrificing spirit of modern Utilitarianism. We have seen that in every form it gives an end which is illusory and impalpable. We have seen that its efforts to compromise with the moral consciousness are useless; that in no shape will it give us a creed that holds water, and that will justify to the inquiring mind those moral beliefs which it is not prepared for the sake of any theory to relinquish. Whatever we may think of those who embrace the doctrine, whatever may be its practical results, yet theoretically considered we have seen, I trust, that it is immoral and false, and are ready to endorse the saying, Ἡδονὴ τέλος, πόρνης δόγμα.

Modern Utilitarianism has a good object in view. Though we understand it differently, we have the same object in view, and that is why we are at issue with Utilitarianism.

We agree that it is desirable to have a standard of virtue which is palpable and 'objective'; and therefore we refuse to place the end in what is most impalpable, what is absolutely and entirely ' subjective'.

We agree that the end is not the realization of an abstract idea ; and therefore we refuse to take as our end the greatest amount of pleasure ; for that is an abstract idea, and it is altogether unrealizable.

We agree that the end is not a 'thing-in-itself', is not Heaven knows what or where, but is the end for us as men, τἀνθρώπινον ἀγαθόν ; and therefore we refuse to find it in that element of the mind which is *least* distinctively human, and shared with us by the beasts that perish.

We agree that it must be κτητὸν ἀνθρώπῳ ; and therefore we refuse to seek for it in that which has become a proverb for its fallaciousness.

We agree in the refusal to separate actions and consequences ; and therefore we refuse to abstract from action one moment, viz. the accompanying or the consequent feeling, and put our test in the more or less of that.

We agree that happiness is the end ; and therefore we say pleasure is not the end.

We agree that pleasure is *a* good ; we say it is not *the* good.

We agree (strange fellowship !) with the author of the *Essay on Liberty* in affirming the ὃ πᾶσι δοκεῖ τοῦτ᾽ εἶναί φαμεν ; and therefore we dissent from a theory which gives the lie to the moral consciousness, and whose psychological basis destroys and makes unmeaning the maxim.

We agree to make the self-evolution of ourselves and of humanity the end. We refuse to place progress in the greater or less amount of ' grateful feeling'. We repeat the good old doctrine that the test of higher and lower can not lie in a feeling which accompanies the exercise of every function, but is to be found in the quality of the function itself. To measure that, we are to go to our idea of man, and to his place in creation and his evolution in history.

In one single word, the end and the standard is self-realization, and is not the feeling of self-realizedness.

May we suggest, in conclusion, that of all our Utilitarians

there is perhaps not one who has not still a great deal to learn from Aristotle's *Ethics*?[1]

[1] Since the above was written Mr. Sidgwick's book ⟨*Methods of Ethics*, ed. i⟩ has appeared. I am far from wishing to deny to it a certain value, but on the subject of Hedonism I can not honestly say more than that he seems to me to have left the question exactly where he found it. As other people, however, seem to think otherwise, I am forced to define my position against him. But I labour here under two difficulties—the first, want of space; the second, my inability to make sure of Mr. Sidgwick's meaning.

The latter arises in great measure from the character of the work. Ostensibly critical, it goes throughout upon preconceptions, which not only are not discussed, but which often are not even made explicit. With some of these we must begin.

(1) It is tacitly assumed that the individual and the universal are two independent things (p. 473). Hence the *mere* individual is not (as with us) an abstraction in our heads, but a real existence.

(2) The practical result of this dogmatic preconception is seen on p. 374. To find a man's ultimate end we are to suppose 'only a single sentient conscious being in the universe'. This supposition *pre*-supposes either that the universe is real out of relation to all consciousness, or is real in relation to one finite consciousness. An author no doubt has a right to maintain these or any other propositions, but whence he gets a right quietly to take them for granted I should be glad to be informed.

(3) But let us suppose the possibility of a finite subject alone in a material universe, and then let us look at Mr. Sidgwick's views from the ground of common sense.

On this ground I say (*a*) for myself, I can not imagine myself into the position of this solitary sentient, and doubt if the author, or any one else, can do so. (*b*) Passing this by, we come to the assertion that such a supposed being would consider itself to have some rational end, some ultimate good, something right and reasonable as such, for which to live. All I can say here is that, so far as I can imagine myself absolutely alone in a material world, I do not think it would occur to me that I had anything to live for. (*c*) Supposing, however, that, being forced so to continue, I did avoid pain and get pleasure, it would not occur to me to say that therefore I was realizing the 'intrinsically and objectively desirable', the 'end of Reason', the 'absolutely Good or Desirable'.

Surely common sense must see that, to find what end we ought to pursue in the human life we live, by seeing what would be left us to pursue in an unimaginable and inhuman predicament, is not common sense at all, but simply bad metaphysics. No doubt a mere quantity is no more than the sum of its units, and to find the value of each unit no doubt you must isolate it by division. But tacitly to assume that the moral world is a mere sum of units, whose value can be found separately, is really nothing but an enormous piece of dogmatism.

Starting from these preconceptions as to the nature of the individual, we have to get to the conclusion that the pleasure of all is the end for each, which problem we have seen above is insoluble. Mr. Sidgwick has an argument whereby he 'suppresses Egoism', which, so far as I can take it in, is as follows :

(1) We *do*, as a fact, desire objects other than our pleasures. But

(2) Our private pleasure is for us the sole ultimate or rational desirable. But

(3) Our private pleasure as such is not rational. Therefore

(4) It is rational for us to desire something other than it. And, because

(5) Pleasure is the only thing we *can* desire (?), therefore

(6) We desire, and are to desire, pleasure as rational. But that means pleasure in general, i. e. pleasure without reference to any feeling subject in particular.

(This is, of course, not Mr. Sidgwick's statement, but my understanding, or very likely my misunderstanding, of him ; so I shall not examine it in this form.)

He takes from Utilitarianism the pleasure of all as my end, whether I happen to want it or not. He takes from the popular interpretation of the moral consciousness the desire for 'the right and reasonable as such'. These seem to go well together, and we say, 'I am to desire the pleasure of all as right and reasonable as such'. This assertion being emphatically repudiated, it is necessary to prove it. How to do this? As before, isolate a man, and you will see that he perceives intuitively that it is right and reasonable for him to pursue pleasure. This means that he perceives two things, (1) that he desires his private pleasure ; (2) that he desires the reasonable. Put them together, and you get the argument ; (*a*) The reasonable is not my private pleasure. (*b*) Other people's pleasure is not my private pleasure. Therefore (*c*) other people's pleasure is reasonable. Or, if this is not meant, perhaps the assertion is that the isolated man sees two things together, both that his pleasure is the reasonable end, and that not *his* pleasure, but pleasure as such, is so. In that case would it not be better to say at once, 'I intuitively perceive that the Utilitarian conclusion is right'? For then the reply, 'But I do not', would end the argument.

However Mr. Sidgwick may get to his conclusion, he has to make it good against two parties—(1) those who assert the right and reasonable, but deny that it is pleasure ; (2) those who deny the right and reasonable, but assert pleasure as *my* private pleasure. (1) The first party (so far as I can represent them) have spoken already. We deny the intuition, and the reasoning we have sufficiently refuted by stating it ; and if we wished to do more, we should do well to press for some further account of the phrases 'objectively desirable', 'real end of reason', &c. If my pleasure is my sole end, if the objective is (also) my end, then I should say there is a hopeless contradiction in which we stick. (2) But Mr. Sidgwick's attitude towards Egoism is more instructive. Having first (after Butler) rightly denied the basis of Hedonism, viz. the assertion that I desire nothing but pleasure, he throws himself repentant into the arms of the true faith, and says, 'Though as a fact other things are or seem to be desired, yet nothing but my pleasure is *desirable*'. 'My pleasure is the end.' Here we have Egoism. 'But', says Mr. Sidgwick, 'the right and reasonable is objectively desirable.' 'Not so,' replies the Egoist. 'The *objectively* desirable is a fiction. The distinction of desir*ed* and desir*able* is wholly fallacious, unless "desirable" is a clumsy name for the means to what I desire. The end is what I do desire, and that is just what I happen to like; "reasonable" is what I correctly conclude is a means to that; and as for "right" and "ought", if they are not a misleading way of saying this over again, they are as nonsensical as "objective end of reason".' And against this Mr. Sidgwick, having left the only true line, has nothing to say, but that he hopes the Egoist will be good enough to admit that something is objectively desirable as an end. If the Egoist does so, he is 'suppressed' certainly, and deserves to be. But will he do so? I recommend the reader to peruse Stirner's book, *Der Einzige und sein Eigenthum.*

Mr. Sidgwick asserts that only my pleasure is desirable, and that I desire this as objectively desirable. But (1) *if* I desire my pleasure as mine in particular, is it not a flat contradiction to say I desire it as *not* mine in particular? and (2) *can* I desire *my* pleasure as pleasure in general? Is not that a pure fiction invented to support a weak compromise—a fiction which neither of the parties opposed would, if they understood their position, attend to for a moment? Is my feeling pleased anything *but* my feeling pleased? Can you put the 'feeling pleased' on the one side, and the 'my' on the other? I know but one theory on which this is possible, and that is the view which, while it regards the distinctions of 'me' and 'you' as mere illusion or 'Maja', nevertheless maintains that the pleasure and pain are not mere illusion. Against this view I am not called on to argue, and Mr. Sidgwick is, I imagine, no more a friend to it than I am.*

I have criticized Mr. Sidgwick sharply, not from want of respect, but because I must be brief and fear to be obscure. Whether I understand him or not, I do not know; and with respect to what Mr. Bain has said on the same subject this again is my case. As to what he means by 'disinterested action' I have not the least idea.† He speaks of

---

* [There may be errors in this account of Sidgwick, but in the main it holds, I think.] ⟨*On this subject see further the pamphlet by the author,* 'Mr. Sidgwick's Hedonism', *1877; and a short note,* 'H. Sidgwick on Ethical Studies', *in Mind, Old Series, ii. 122.*—ED.⟩

† [Certainly *most* obscure, because apparently he denies it to be volition (below, p. 261).]

entering into the feelings of another being, which, on his view, is to me much as if he said, 'One bag of marbles enters into the marbles of another bag'; and again (*Emotions*, &c., ed. iii, p. 267), he talks of 'pleasures whose nature is to take in other sentient beings', which, again, is as if he said, 'There are some marbles whose nature it is to take in other bags of marbles'. Either these things are illusions or not. If they are not, it seems to me they revolutionize the whole of Mr. Bain's pyschology. If they are, I want to know whether and why we are to rest our Ethics upon them. What seems clear to me is this—Pleasure is the one end, or it is not. If it is not, then Hedonism goes. If it is, then *my* pleasure is my end. The pleasure of others is neither a feeling in me, nor an idea of a feeling in me. If it seems to be so, this is a mere illusion. If what is not my feeling or its idea is my end, then the root of Hedonism is torn up. If so, the argument from the individual to the race disappears, because pleasure is *not* the sole end of the individual.

In this plight, nothing is left to Hedonism but an appeal to the facts of society. If these show that progress so far involves increase of pleasure (and here, on the question of fact, Hedonism has to meet Pessimism), that does not prove it will be always so; still less does it prove that the idea of increase of pleasure *is* the moving cause of progress, and even less that it *ought* to be.

NOTE TO ESSAY III

THERE are two questions suggested by the above— (1) Is pleasure good, and if so, in what sense is it good? (2) Is pain evil, and in what way is it evil? Let us take the latter first.

Considered psychically pain is an evil, because it is the feeling of the negation of the self or life.[1] The good is the affirmation of the self, and hence pain is counter to the good. If we are asked to suppose a pain which is a feeling of negation, but not a felt negation, i. e. which is not really in any way the negation of function or the cause of such negation, and are then asked, Is such hypothetical pain an evil? we can not say it would be, because we can say nothing about it at all. It seems to us to be an unreal abstraction. Real pain is the feeling of the negatedness of the self, and therefore, as such, it is bad. It is bad also, because it further acts in the direction of the general lowering of life. Both as felt diminution of the good, and as the cause of further diminution, it is an evil.

If, where pain comes from negated function, but the function is supposed to be indifferent, we are asked, Is then the pain bad? we reply that it is so, because the whole self is negated; *I* feel pain, and am therein lowered directly or indirectly.

In passing we may ask, Is then pain on the whole an evil? We can not say that. We know that pain often is a good; and we should have a right to say of any pain that it was an absolute evil, only if we knew that it was pain *per se*, i. e. mere negation. But that is what we can not know. Speaking generally, you can not have mere pain, the negative without the positive; painlessness means death;

---

[1] [This is too dogmatic. You can't show in fact that pain is always the feeling of negation, though you can see that its effect is always alterative and so negative. You can't show (p. 131, l. 1) that 'wherever there is an active conscious self' there is pain. And (p. 131, l. 7) 'without some pain' is exaggerated.

The general answer is, however, right. Pain is an evil so far as you, by an abstraction, take it as merely painful, as without an affirmative reaction which it conditions. Whether, taken apart from any effects at all, it is evil, is hard or impossible to say, because that is such an abstraction. You *may* say Yes, but your answer amounts to nothing unless you add that, in reality, pain can be taken by itself as absolutely real.]

pain appears to involve reaction ; and again, wherever there is an active conscious self, it seems there must be pain. To say that pain is an absolute evil, we should have to answer in the affirmative the question, Can you have the positive without the negative, or the negative in this form ? And I do not see how we can give this answer. We know that pain is often a stimulus ; without some pain little is produced—perhaps nothing. We know that the pain of the part is often the good of the whole ; that that good demands sometimes even the destruction of the part. The life of the whole is the end, and for this all must be sacrificed. And so the question is, Is the negation of the part always a condition of the affirmation of the whole, or is it sometimes not ? (And we should remember that the affirmation of the whole may be in the part, or without the part.) Can we ever say, Here is an overplus of the negative ; here is negation of function, which, in itself and its results, is negation of the good, or of life as a whole ? I do not see how we are to say this, because I do not see how we can know enough about the whole of things. For anything I can tell pain *per se* may be always an unreal abstraction, as I know it often is. What is bad for this or that relative totality may be good for a higher ; and above the highest relative totality may be (for anything I know to the contrary) an absolute totality, in which and for which pain is the mere condition of affirmation and in no sense the diminution of life, but whose life (as I suppose all life) involves in itself a subordinated negation. This I do not assert to be the case ; but I wished to point out that no man has a right to say pain is an evil absolutely, unless he knows that there is no such life of the whole, or that pain is a negative which limits its functions, and is not a negative condition of those functions.[1]

To return from our digression. We have seen that pain is bad whenever it is not necessary as a condition of good. Turning now to pleasure, we ask, Is pleasure, generally speaking, good ? Doubtless it is good. It is the felt assertion of the will or self. It is felt self-realizedness. It is good because it accompanies and makes a whole with

---

[1] [It is impossible—I should say—to show positively from the particular facts (*a posteriori*) that pain is *not* in the end an evil. On the other hand, to show *a posteriori* that it is so is obviously impossible. The question, to my mind, turns on whether we have, or have not, a *general* view on which to go. Without that—one way or the other—we are helpless.]

good activity, because it goes with that self-realization which is good; or secondly, because it heightens the general assertion of self, which is the condition of realizing the good in self.

Pleasure is the psychical accompaniment of exercise of function, and a distinction is required in order to think of function apart from some pleasure. Perhaps there is really no such thing. The function brings its own pleasure, however small, though the whole state may be painful.

Pleasure, then, is generally good; but the questions which now arise are, Can pleasure exist without function? If so, is it good? Or, to put it otherwise; Are all pleasures of activity good? Are all pleasures of passivity good? Are any pleasures neither good nor bad? And finally, Is any pleasure good *per se*, or simply as pleasure?

Can pleasure exist without function? We could not enter here on a psychological investigation of the point, even were we able to treat the matter satisfactorily. But taking pleasure to be the feeling of the realizedness of the will or self, we should doubt if apart from some present function or activity pleasure could exist. The questions to be answered would be, how far in what seem the most, or mere, 'passive pleasures' of sense function is concerned; how far in contemplative pleasures activity of contemplation comes in; how far, lastly, the very feeling of self, which is pleasure, in being felt implies an activity. To a tired man, for instance, the pleasure of lying down in bed is great; he wants no more; it is complete affirmation of his will, perfect satisfiedness. But as he grows more and more sleepy, does his pleasure increase? When he is asleep does he feel pleasure? On the other hand, is he less satisfied; and, if so, in what sense? If his pleasure has been diminished or has ceased, is not that because the reaction, the function of the feeling centre, has ceased or been diminished; and is not that reaction what is felt when pleasure is felt?

Let us, however, pass by this question, as without answering it decidedly we hope to show how far pleasure is good. Roughly speaking, we can distinguish pleasures of activity and passivity; pleasure which comes with our doing something, and pleasure which we do nothing to get.[1] Let us ask with each class when pleasure is good, and when it is bad, if it is bad. We will first take pleasures of activity.

---

[1] We need not distinguish further the pleasure of having something done to us. It will, I think, be covered by our answer, and it is a somewhat complicated state of mind.

(1) (*a*) When are they good? When the activity is good the pleasure is good, because the two are a psychical whole. You can not have the function without the pleasure: the absence of the pleasure would weaken and perhaps destroy the function, and also generally lower the self to the detriment of other functions; whereas presence of pleasure tends to the heightening of functions in general, beside its own function.— Then what activities are good? Detail is impossible; but, generally, those which directly realize the good will in a living man, or which indirectly increase life and so the possibility of a higher realization of the good in a living man or men. Or rather the two can not be divided. Life is a whole; and life is not only the condition of the good, but may be taken as another name for it. 'The end of life is life', and (speaking generally) what heightens life heightens the good. Pleasure then is not a means to the good, but is included in it and belongs to it.

(*b*) What pleasures of activity are bad then (for admittedly there are such)? The pleasure is bad when the activity is bad; and the activity is bad when, in its immediate or ulterior results, it lowers the life of the individual, or of a larger totality, and so diminishes realization of good, or prevents a higher and fuller realization. Here pleasure is bad because it strengthens and intensifies a bad activity. The pleasure *per se* is not bad, but then there is no such thing except in our heads.

(2) Next as to pleasures of passivity. Let us for short-ness' sake exclude artistic pleasures, and take pleasures of sensuous satisfaction. Are passive sensuous pleasures good or bad? In themselves, I think, they are neither good nor bad. Or we may say roughly, they are good when they are not bad.

(*a*) When are they bad? This is not hard to answer. They are bad when they prevent or retard the realization of the good life in us by preventing action. This they do when they produce special results which hinder the good, or when they generally contribute towards a habit of self-indulgence, which is bad because it retards or opposes the activity of the good. In short, they are bad when they lower life or prevent its progress. They are not bad *per se*, but then here again they do not exist *per se*.

(*b*) When are they good? They are good when (without the evil results just mentioned) they increase what is ordinarily called happiness, a feeling of general content with one's existence. That is good, because existence is good, and because without happiness existence is impaired, and with it the good ; and because happiness (generally speaking) increases activity. Discontent and unhappiness are great evils, for (even if they do not lead to immorality) they lower life and activity for good. 'Life is the end of life', and so what makes life more liveable is good ; and life further must be realized in living men, the basis of whose nature is and must remain animal. To neglect the basis is to make as great a mistake as to regard it as the crown and summit. Life is a whole ; and hence pleasures inseparable from life, and pleasures that maintain and heighten a feeling of well-being and joy in living (which again heightens life), are good, because life is good—supposing, that is, that they are not bad, in the sense described above.

We come now to the two questions—Are any pleasures neither good nor bad ? Are any pleasures good *per se* ?

(1) Are any pleasures neither good nor bad? The ordinary man would say Yes. A certain amount of pleasure is undeniably good ; and (as a rule), if you want more, the more is good (where it is not bad), and this because the satisfaction of the want is good for you, or the non-satisfaction bad. Then again undeniably there is (speaking generally) a too much of any particular pleasure, and that too much is bad. But between enough and too much, as in the pleasures of eating and drinking, there comes a neutral territory. It is probably good for you to have, say, not less than two glasses of wine after dinner. Six on ordinary occasions is perhaps too many ; but, as to three or four, they are neither one way nor the other. If asked, is the pleasure of these intermediates bad? we say No. If asked, is it good ? I do not think we can say Yes. If asked, is it not a positive addition to the surplus of pleasure?[1] I do not think we can say No. We should put the whole question aside as idle. We should say the pleasure is neither good nor bad, or at least we do not know that it is. So far the ordinary man.

Now whether this margin is scientifically defensible, whether there must not be a point, say, of number of drops or fractions of drops, which is good, and beyond which acme you fall at once into badness, we shall not discuss.

---

[1] [The right answer here (cf. p. 136) is : Yes, it *is* good *if* it is not in any way bad. But in these cases there is a doubt about the '*if*'. So we hesitate.]

It is not an easy question; and fortunately the answer matters nothing to our argument. But for the ordinary man clearly some pleasures are neither good nor bad, and this because (for him) they do neither harm nor good.

(2) To come now to the question, Is any pleasure a good *per se*? we are in a position, I think, to answer it in the negative. Ordinarily it does sound absurd to say mere pleasure is not an end, since at first sight it seems desirable. The foregoing, however, should have removed this difficulty. We have seen that the pleasures pronounced desirable are so because they are inseparable from and heighten life; and hence these pleasures are not pleasures *per se*. And further, if the doctrine of the indifferent margin were indefensible (we believe that it is not so), then *no* pleasure could be a pleasure *per se*, and our present question would disappear.

But supposing that there exist pleasures which are only pleasurable and, so to speak, end in themselves, then these may certainly be desired, but I think they are not considered desirable or good. And, if that is so, then, in denying that pleasure in itself is good, we are not in collision with the ordinary consciousness. To illustrate. Having had three glasses of wine, I may say I think so much was desirable. I certainly may have another if I like, and I suppose it will give me a certain amount of pleasure and no pain, or lessening of pleasure, now or afterwards. Is the surplus good?[1] Is it desirable? Clearly, though a pleasure, and though not bad, it may not be good; and such is the case, I think, with all innocent pleasures, as e.g. those of physical exercise, sports and games, sightseeing, &c. If this be so, however, then common consciousness does *not* hold pleasure *per se* to be desirable or good. And as for philosophical arguments, what and where are they?

We have now seen that pleasure is good so far as inseparable from life, and so far as it results in the heightening of life. But in itself, if and so far as we separate it by an abstraction or find it apart from its good qualities, it is not good, it is in no sense an end in itself.

Here we might cease, but further elucidations will perhaps not be superfluous.

Life is an end in itself. It is true that life implies

---

[1] [If the surplus is *mere* surplus it *is* good. But, as we are not sure that in fact it *is* mere bare surplus, without other aspects, we can not say if it is good or not.]

pleasure. Pessimism notwithstanding, it implies, speaking generally, a surplus of pleasure; and I am not called upon to deny (though I certainly neither assert nor admit it) that higher life means always a greater surplus.[1]

If so, have we come back to Hedonism? Since pleasure and life are inseparable, can we say that to aim at the realization of life is to aim at pleasure? No, in the sense of making it an object, it is not to aim at pleasure; and this distinction is a vital difference, which we must never slur. Function carries pleasure with it as its psychical accompaniment, but what determines, makes, and is good or bad, is in the end function. Function, moreover, is something comparatively definite. It gives something you can aim at, something you can do. Not so the pleasure. Further, so far as function and pleasure are separable objects of choice, we must, if we are moral, choose the former. If they are inseparable, are one whole, why are we to aim at the indefinite side, at the subjective psychical sequent and accompaniment, when we have an objective act which we can see before us and perform, and which is the prius of the feeling? It is the act carries with it the pleasure, not the pleasure the act.

'Yes, but', it will be said, 'we want *more* pleasure, more than we get with present function; and we will alter the function to get the pleasure.' Then you must take one of these three positions. You (a) wholly reject the idea that one function is in itself higher than another; or, while believing in higher and lower functions, you say (b) pleasure is separable, or (c) inseparable from the higher.

On the first supposition (a) you break at once with common morality, which does not believe that lower and higher stand for mere means to less or more pleasure. And (b) on the second you are confessedly immoral; for, while believing in a higher, you propose to sacrifice it to pleasure. 'Let us have pleasure, even at the cost of function' is not a moral point of view.[2]

[1] [Higher life and greater surplus, not denied or admitted (cf. p. 138 first paragraph and p. 135). I should now assert it.]

[2] Nor can you reconcile yourself to common morality by saying, 'But we will *only* increase the pleasure'. For (1) either the increase of pleasure does issue in the heightening of function, and will be good in this sense and not in yours; or else (2), as we have seen, if pleasure neither raises nor lowers function, then common opinion * considers it neither desirable nor undesirable.

* [Cf. pp. 134-5. The truth is that common opinion never makes the abstraction at all.]

Thirdly (*c*) if you maintain more pleasure and higher function to be on the whole inseparable, you may at once be challenged as to the truth of that assertion ; and if you are not allowed to assume it, you can not assume that more pleasure is an end.

But allowing you for the present to assume that higher function and more pleasure go together, so that to have one is to have the other, why (I would ask), if these two are one whole, will you persist in isolating one side of that whole ; since surely it is the less knowable side ? The coincidence of the two is an extremely general truth ; it need not (*presumably*, that is) be true for this man or generation ; and, if so, how is it possible to aim at progress except by aiming at function ? The function must (on the whole and in the end) carry the pleasure with it, and it is surely a more definite mark. Is it not preposterous to think of aiming at more pleasure, in the end and on the whole (not in any future that we can see), in order, by making this the end, to get along with it some higher function which we know nothing about ? Is it not (e. g.) hopelessly vague, if we want to find out what the divine will is, to attempt to define it by some idea of pleasure in the end and on the whole, and not to ourselves or any one else in any time that we can see ? Is it not less vague to study that will by considering the previous evolution of it, and to accept what seems a higher step in that evolution, as an end in itself ? Must we not say that this going together of function and pleasure is a mere general faith, which we can not verify by experience in every case, and so can not use to determine our particular course ?

Of course one sees quite clearly that, generally speaking, it is a good thing to aim at the increasing of pleasure and diminishing of pain ; but it is a good thing because it increases the actuality and possibility of life. To make function the end justifies and demands the increase of pleasure and gives you all you can fairly ask in that way. But to say more pleasure is all the end, and life a mere accompaniment to that, is another matter.

And again, when we are doubtful what is higher in progress, it may be a safe course to increase pleasure and diminish pain, because that heightens the good function we have. But to look on the increase of pleasure as the mark to aim at always and simply, when we aim at progress, is again a very different course.

But, leaving this subject, we must observe that we have no right to assume that higher function and more pleasure do on the whole go together.[1] We have bitter proof that in particular cases and stages of progress this is not the case, and so are forced to separate the two in our minds. We can *imagine* function without pleasure, since we have experienced decrease of pleasure proportionate to heightening of quality of function. But, when the two come thus before the mind separately, we feel we must choose function and not pleasure.

In conclusion, there is one way in which pleasure may be used as a test of function. It shows whether function is impeded in discharge or not. But by it you can not tell higher from lower function ; and, if you go by it, you must prefer a lower state of harmony to a higher state of self-contradiction.

For the sake of clearness I have run the risk of wearisome length and repetition. In the foregoing Essay I have sharply, not I hope too sharply, criticized Hedonism. From a somewhat more positive consideration I have reached the same result. And now in a spirit of conciliation I would ask the Utilitarian, whose heart is in the right place, who does not care about pleasure, but who wants something definite, to consider this—whether to take life as the end, the highest and ever a higher life, be *more* vague than Hedonism ; whether it does not give him all he wants ; and whether, beside being more in harmony with morality, it is not equally antagonistic to Asceticism.

If our end is to realize the life or the self which is realized in all life, and to develop this in more distinctively human forms, and if we consider that this life to be realized *must* be realized in living individuals, we shall be far enough from asceticism. There is here no abstract negation of human nature, no sacrifice of detail and fullness to a barren formula. The universal is realized only in the free self-development of the individual, and the individual can only truly develop his individuality by specifying in himself the common life of all. As we repudiate the liberty of Individualism (better, Particularism), so we repudiate the tyranny of the (abstract) universal. The member is no member but a parasitical excrescence, if it does not live with the life of the whole ;

---

[1] [Here we open a grave question. *Are* we wrong to 'prefer a lower state'? *Is* it a lower state, if it were possible? I have modified my opinion here : cf. p. 105.]

the whole life does not exist except in the life of the members. And here, in the moral sphere, the members are self-conscious. It is then only in the intensity of the self-consciousness of the members that the whole can be intensely realized. Furthermore, these members are spiritualized animals ; everything human stands on the basis of animal life ; and to make self-realization the end not only justifies but demands attention to the well-being and happiness of man as a spiritualized animal, because the feeling of inner harmony is required for, is the psychical condition of, maintenance and progress of function. So far as this we go and must go, but no further ; we ought not to sacrifice what seems to be maintenance or progress of function to prospect of increased pleasure. But I do not think that the Utilitarian *wishes* to teach that doctrine ; and whatever he wants to teach he can teach without making pleasure the end. To repeat it once more, if self-realization is the end, then pleasure is a relative end and good, because a condition without which good is impossible ; and hence to increase pleasure is good, though we need not add ' for pleasure's sake '. And unhappiness is evil, if it is a psychical state which tends to exclude the good, and may be treated as an evil, which it is our bounden duty to fight against, without our being forced to say ' it is the evil itself, and there is no evil beyond it '.

If again it is objected that the end is vague and has no content, the following Essays will to a certain extent, I hope, remove the objection. Here we may reply that to take human progress as the end, and to keep our eye on past progress, is not a useless prescription ; and if any one wants a moral philosophy to tell him what in particular he is to do, he will find that there neither is nor can be such a thing, and at all events will not find it in Hedonism.

One word on the unconscious or latent Hedonism of society in its progress. That is no argument for making pleasure the end, as the reader who has followed me so far will, I trust, at once see. Taking for granted the asserted fact, that society tends to identify what brings pleasure with what is good, we altogether deny the Hedonistic inference. If society tends to realize life more highly and perfectly, it is obvious that it must also realize the conditions of such life. The fact that life can not exist without pleasure does not prove pleasure to be the end of life, unless we are prepared to say (the illustration is not a good one) that *because* as a man rises in society he wears better clothes, *therefore* to be dressed like a gentleman was the conscious or unconscious end of his advancement. Of course it might have been, but do we say that it was? Or, again, a mother *may* have desired her daughter's health not for her health's sake, but for the sake of her looks; but would it not be an unfounded inference to conclude that it *must* have been so? The argument we have noticed holds against asceticism, but we must entreat the reader to bear in mind that the opposite of a false view may be every whit *as* false; and that you could argue from the denial of asceticism to the assertion of Hedonism only if you had previously made good your alternative, your 'either—or' of the two.

Finally (as we have already gone beyond all bounds), let us make a remark on the phrase 'Utilitarianism'. It is a thoroughly bad name, and misleads a great many persons. It does indeed express the fact that, for Hedonism, virtue and action are *not* the end, but are useful as mere means to something outside them. But surely it would be better to call the theory after its end (as we have done),[1] since to not a few persons 'Utilitarianism' conveys the notion that the end is the useful, which, besides being strictly speaking sheer nonsense, is also misleading. The associations of the useful are transferred to Hedonism, and if these are in some ways unfavourable (Mill's *Util.*, p. 9), they seem to me in other and more ways to be favourable. The practical man hears of 'the useful', and thinks he has got something solid, while he really is embracing (as I have shown) the cloud of a wild theoretical fiction, from which he would shrink if he saw it apart from its false lights and colours. And on whichever side the balance of advantage lies, no respectable writer can wish to rest on a basis of misunderstanding. The two words 'useful' and 'happiness' delude not only the public, but perhaps all Utilitarian writers. While they are the terms employed, the question can not possibly be brought to a clear issue; and let me say for myself that I see no good reason why 'Utilitarianism' should stand for Hedonism. If 'happiness' means wellbeing or perfection of life, then I am content to say that, with Plato and Aristotle, I hold happiness to be the end; and, although virtue is not a *mere* means, yet it can be regarded as a means, and so is 'useful'. In this sense we, who reject

---

[1] Since Mr. Sidgwick's book has appeared this has grown more common, and is a step in the right direction.

Hedonism, can call ourselves Utilitarians, and the man who thinks he is pushing some counter view by emphasizing 'happiness' and 'usefulness' does not touch us with his phrases, but rather perhaps confirms us. But pleasure for pleasure's sake, and life and virtue for the sake of pleasure, is another doctrine, which we repudiate.

ESSAY IV

DUTY FOR DUTY'S SAKE

IN our answer to the question, Why should I be moral? we found that, explicitly or by implication, all Ethics presupposed something which is the good, and that this good (whatever else may be its nature) has always the character of an end. The moral good is an end in itself, is to be pursued for its own sake. It must not be made a means to something not itself. We have now seen further that pleasure is not the good, is not the end; that, in pursuing pleasure as such, we do not pursue the good. Hedonism we have dismissed, and may banish it, if we please, from our sight, while we turn to develop a new view of the good, another answer to the question, What is the end? In Hedonism we have criticized a onesided view; we shall have to do here with an opposite extremity of onesidedness. The self to be realized before was the self or selves as a maximum quantity or number of particular feelings: in the theory which awaits us the self to be realized has a defect which is diametrically opposed to the first, and yet is the same defect. Its fault is the opposite, since for mere particular it substitutes mere universal; we have not to do with feelings, as this and that, but with a form which is thought of as not this or that. Its fault is the same fault, the failing to see things as a whole, and the fixing as real one element which yet is unreal when apart from the other. In a word, we find in both a onesided view, and their common vice may be called abstractness.[1] So much by way of anticipation, and now we must betake ourselves to our task.

[2] What is the moral end? We know already in part

[1] ['*Abstractness*' as the common vice. This I have repeated in *Essays on Truth and Reality*.] ⟨*p. 470.*—ED.⟩

[2] What follows, the reader must be warned, is very far from being meant to be a statement of Kant's main ethical view; as such it would be neither complete nor accurate, though it will be found to be an

what it is not. It is not a state or collection of states of
the self, as feeling pleasure, to be produced either in me
or outside me. To know what it *is* we must go to the
moral consciousness. We find there that the end is for me
as active, is a practical end. It is not something merely to
be felt, it is something to be done.

And it is not something to be done, in which, when done,
the doer is not to be involved. The end does not fall
outside the doer. I am to realize myself; and, as we saw,
I can not make an ultimate end of anything except myself,
can not make myself a mere means to something else.
Nor, again, does the end fall outside the activity. If the
production in me of a mere passive state were the end, the
activity would be a mere means to that. But the moral
consciousness assures us that the activity is an end in itself.
The end is a doing which is to be done; the activity is
good in itself, not for the sake of a result beyond. The
end, then, is not to be felt, but is to be done: it is to be
done and not made; it falls not outside the self of the doer,
nor further outside his activity.

In short, the good is the Good Will. The end is will
for the sake of will; and, in its relation to me, it is the
realization of the good will in myself, or of myself as the
good will. In this character I am an end to myself, and
I am an absolute and ultimate end. There is nothing
which is good, unless it be a good will.

This is no metaphysical fiction. It is the truth of life
and of the moral consciousness. A man is not called good
because he is rich, nor because he is handsome or clever.
He is good when he is moral, and he is moral when his
actions are conformed to and embody a good will, or when
his will is good.

But 'good will' tells us little or nothing. It says only

applicable criticism. We could not give a statement of Kant's view
without giving all the sides of it; and, were we prepared to do that,
not only would considerable space be required, but also we should be
obliged to consider topics which lie outside our present undertaking.
We have stated a view for purposes of criticism, but that criticism is
at the same time a criticism that holds against more than our statement.

that will is the end. It does not say *what* will is the end; and we want to know what the good will is.

What is the good will? We may call it indifferently the Free will, or the Universal will, or the Autonomous will, or finally the Formal will.

(1) It is the universal will. The very notion of the moral end is that it should be an end absolutely, not conditionally. It is not an end for me without being one also for you, or for you and me and not for a third person; but it is, without limitation to any this or that, an end for us all. And so the will, as end, is not the particular will of particular men, existing as this, that, and the other series of states of mind. It is the same for you and me, and, in the character of our common standard and aim, it is above you and me. It is thus objective and universal.

(2) It is the free will. It is not conditioned by, it does not owe its existence and attributes to, it is not made what it is by, and hence it can not (properly speaking) be called forth by, anything which is not itself. It exists because of itself and for the sake of itself. It has no end or aim beyond itself; is not constituted or determined by anything else.

Hence we see it is not determined by anything in particular. For, as we saw, it was universal; and universal means not particular; and so no more than a verbal conclusion is wanted to show that, if determined by something particular, it would be determined by something not itself. And this we have already taken to be false.

(3) It is autonomous. For it is universal and an end to itself. The good will is the will which wills the universal as itself and itself as the universal, and hence may be said to be a law to itself and to will its own law. And, because it is universal, hence in willing what is valid for itself it wills what is valid for all. It legislates universally in legislating for itself, since it would not legislate for itself did it not legislate universally.

(4) And lastly, it is formal. For, in willing itself, it wills the universal, and that is not-particular. Any pos-

sible object of desire, any wished-for event, any end in the
shape of a result to be attained in the particular existence
of myself or another, all are this or that something: they
have a content, they are 'material'. Only that will is
good which wills itself as not-particular, as without content
or matter, in a word, which wills itself as form.

The good will, then, is the will which is determined by
the form only, which realizes itself as the bare form of the
will. And this formal will is now seen to be the true
expression for all the foregoing characteristics, of universality, freedom, and autonomy. In formality we see they
are all one. I am autonomous only because I am free,
free only because I am universal, universal only because
not particular, and not particular only when formal.

That the good must be formal we might have seen by
considering its character of a universal standard or test.
Such a standard is a form or it is nothing. It is to be
above every possible this and that, and hence can not be
any this or that. It is by being *not* this or that, that it
succeeds in having nothing which is not common to every
this and that. Otherwise there would be something which
would fall without its sphere; it would be only one thing
among others, and so would no longer be a standard. But
that which can be common to everything is not matter or
content, but form only. As no material test of truth, so
no material test of morality is possible.

The good will, then, is the bare form of the will, and this
is the end. This is what I have to realize, and realize in
myself. But I am not a mere form; I have an 'empirical' nature, a series of particular states of the 'this me',
a mass of desires, aversions, inclinations, passions, pleasures,
and pains, what we may call a sensuous self. It is in this
self that all content, all matter, all possible filling of the
form must be sought; for all matter must come from 'experience', must be given in and through the perception of
the outer world or of the series of my own internal states,
and is in either case sensuous, and the opposite of the
insensible form.

The 'empirical' self. the this me, is, no less than the self which is formal will, an element of the moral subject. These elements are antithetical the one to the other; and hence the realization of the form is possible only through an antagonism, an opposition which has to be overcome. It is this conflict and this victory in which the essence of morality lies. Morality is the activity of the formal self forcing the sensuous self, and here first can we attach a meaning to the words 'ought' and 'duty'.[1]

If our self were nothing beyond the series of its states, if it were nothing above and beyond these coexistent and successive phenomena, then the word 'ought' could have no meaning. And again, if our self were a pure, unalloyed will, realizing itself apart from a sensuous element, the word 'ought' would still be meaningless. It is the antagonism of the two elements in one subject which is the essence of the ought. The ought is a command; it expresses something which neither simply is nor is not, but which both is and is not; something, in short, which is to be. Further, when addressed to myself, it puts before me something which is to be done, and which I am to do. A command is the doing of something by me, which doing is willed by a will, not me, and presented as such by that will to me.[2] In the ought the self is commanded, and that self is the sensuous self in me, which is ordered, and which, if I obey, is forced by the non-sensuous formal will which stands above the empirical element, and, equally with that, is myself. The ought is the command of the formal will,

---

[1] In a lower sense we can use, and do use, 'ought' outside the moral world. Wherever 'law' has a meaning, 'ought' has also a meaning. Where the particular phenomenon does not answer to its conception, we say 'ought'. 'A man (e. g.) "ought" to have two eyes.' 'Ice of that thickness "ought" to have borne.' Something has interfered in the case, so that the fact is not an exhibition of the law. But the moral 'ought' means much more than this. There the particular fact or phenomenon is this or that *will*, which, moreover, is or can be *aware of its position* as such in relation to the law or general conception. This makes an enormous difference.

[2] A command *may* contain a promise or threat. It is not of its essence that it should do so.

and duty is the obedience, or, more properly, the compulsion of the lower self by that will, or the realization of the form in and against the recalcitrant matter of the desires.

Duty must be for duty's sake, or it is not duty. It is not enough that my acts should realize and embody the universal form, and so far be conformable thereto. It is not enough that the act commanded be done by me. The end, as we have seen, is not a result beyond and outside the activity. It is not the realizedness of the form which is the good, but rather the realization of it; because only as active is it negative, only as negative is it real. And further, the good is not merely the realization of the form by a foreign subject, but its own realization of itself by itself. That does not take place unless the act ordered to be done in the field of the lower self is done by me in the character of the formal self. If that is so, I must know that it is so; and if I do not know that it is so, then it is not so. Duty is not duty unless, in every case and in every act, it is consciously done for the sake of duty, and that means for the sake of the realization of the bare form, and of nothing whatever besides the bare form. And hence we see that an act, done from pleasure in or desire for the bare form, can in no case be dutiful; for that would be the lower nature, for some liking of its own, choosing to realize the form; it could not be the form realizing itself; and hence such an act is not in any degree moral, since in no degree does it attain the end. The lower self in morality is not led, nor coaxed, nor consulted, but forced.

Here again we appeal to the moral consciousness to bear testimony to our conclusion. Every moral man knows that to do right is to do one's duty for its own sake, and that, if duty is done for the sake of some ulterior object, that act may be legal but is certainly not moral.

Having found ourselves in accord with practical morality, and resting on the conclusion that no act is moral except that which is consciously done for the sake of the universal form, we have now to state the rule which is to guide our practice in life, and which is too simple to occasion any trouble in the working. We have to realize the good will, the will that is an end in itself, and that is universally valid ; and, as we saw, these characteristics are summed up in formality. The standard, we saw, must be formal; it must exclude all possible content, because content is diversity ; and hence the residue left to us for a standard is plainly identity, the identity which excludes diversity ; and of this we can say only that it is, and that it does not contradict itself. Our practical maxim, then, is, Realize non-contradiction. Realize, i. e. act and keep acting ; do not contradict yourself, i. e. let all your acts embody and realize the principle of non-contradiction ; for so only can you realize the formal will which is the good will. Whatever act embodies a self-contradiction is immoral. Whatever act is self-consistent is legal. Whatever act is self-consistent, and is done for the sake of realizing self-consistency, and for the sake of nothing else, is moral. This is simple, this is practical ; and there surely is cause for thankfulness in the arrangement of things which has placed the standard and test of all that is most important, of everything which really is important, in a form which even the unlettered can understand, and a child can apply.

¹ Stated as we have stated it above, the theory of duty for duty's sake carries with it little or no plausibility. Criticism of it may appear to the reader to be superfluous, but nevertheless it will repay us to see briefly set forth the inner contradictions in which it loses itself, and which destroy its claim to practical value.

The theory contradicts itself ; and, reduced to a simple form, the contradiction is as follows : Self-realization is the end, and the self to be realized is the negative of reality ; we are to realize, and must produce nothing real.

¹ As I said before, this is not a statement of the Kantian view; that view is far wider, and at the same time more confused. As a system it has been annihilated by Hegel's criticism (*Philosophische Abhandlungen, Werke*, i, pp. 343 foll. (1832) and *Phänomenologie, Werke*, ii, pp. 451 foll. (1832)), to which I owe most of the following. Compare also Schopenhauer, iv. *Grundprobleme*, pp. 117–78. But the reader must bear in mind that only I am responsible for what I say.

Let us explain. The good is the will. The will is the carrying of the inner mind out into the world of fact ; it is the identity of thought and existence, the process in which the ideal passes over into reality, and where the content on both sides is the same, subject always to the diversity of the two different elements. Mere thought, *as* thought, is not will—that is the inner side only. Mere existence in time and space, or time, is not will—that is the outside only. For will we want both sides, and both sides in one. And from the above we see at once that, if the two sides are to correspond, there must be some correspondence in the nature of what they contain ; and, starting here from the side of existence, we may say, you can realize nothing, unless that which you are to realize have in it already the character which distinguishes reality.

To realize means to translate an ideal content into existence, whether it be the existence of a series of events in time only,[1] as in mere psychical acts, or existence both in space and time, as is the case in all outward acts.

Neither to give a proper definition of the real, nor to discuss the nature of existence in space and time, and its relation to thought in general, and in particular to human thought, even were I competent to do it, would be possible here. But I do not suppose I shall find much contradiction if I say that the predominant character of existence in space and time is, in one word, its particularness, what is ordinarily called its concreteness, the infinitude of its relations. An existing thing and the mere thought of a thing are not the same, if that be taken to mean that there is no differ-

---

[1] This is true of course only so long as psychical events are considered simply as such. Every psychical state *has* also, I suppose, its existence in space. In this connexion let me add in passing, that whether the will has *direct* control over the thoughts * or not is an open question in psychology. It is indifferent to us here what answer be given.

---

* ['Whether the will has *direct* control over the thoughts, or only fixes attention on the subject, and inhibits *other* developments' is meant, I presume.]

ence between them ; and, especially in morals, the distance between theory and fact is as immeasurable as the distance between what is thought and what is willed, between a definition and the thing defined. As I have said before, we can not go into these fundamental questions, but so much seems clear—that, as against a theory, definition, or abstract principle, the main character of existence in space and time is the endless detail of its particular relations. You can not particularize a definition so as to exhaust any sensible object, since that object stands in relation to every other thing in the world.

Let us say then that to realize (whatever else it is besides) is at least to particularize, and we shall see how the theory of duty for duty's sake contradicts itself. (1) It says you are not to do what it says you are to do ; what you have to effect is the negation of the particular ; and so it says in a breath, realize and do not realize. (2) It gives you no content; and that which has no content can not be willed, since in volition we must have the same content on each side. (3) Psychically considered, an act of will is a particular act, and hence a formal act of will is impossible.

To explain—(1) You are to realize the good will, and that means the formal will, or the universal will. But universal means the opposite of particular. 'Realize the particular' means realize the opposite of the universal ; and so, if you particularize the universal, you have not realized *it*, i. e. not the universal you had to realize ; or, in other words, if you materialize the form, it is no longer formal. On the other hand, 'realize' *means* materialize, it *means* particularize. 'Realize' *asserts* the concrete identity of matter and form which 'formal will' denies ; and we are left with the hopeless contradiction of an order, which tells us in one breath that only the formal (i. e. the *not*-real) will is good, and that for the sake of the good we are to realize (i. e. unformalize) the formal will.

Or less abstractly—we have two elements in one subject, the sensuous nature and the pure will. The pure will is to be kept pure ; it is for its sake that we act, and action consists in the forcing of the sensuous nature. The order is here, 'Realize the pure will in the sensuous nature', and the contradiction is as above. The pure will means the non-sensuous will, and 'realize it' means translate it into an element which destroys its essence. The formal will, when realized, is no longer formal, is materialized, is sensualized, is no longer pure. If you do not want to sensualize the will, why do you say make it real? What is the use and meaning of realizing? Or if you say the will is and means realization, then do you not see that the will means the identity of the pure and sensuous nature, that it implies the two sides, and that 'formal will' says 'have both sides, but be sure you have only one'; or, more briefly, that pure or formal will is nonsense?

In its simplest form the contradiction is this. 'Realize non-contradiction' is the order. But 'non-contradiction' = bare form; 'realize' = give content to: content contradicts form without content, and so 'realize non-contradiction' means 'realize a contradiction'.[1]

(2) In our remarks on the self-contradiction of the principle, its abstract negation of reality on the one side, and its demand for realization on the other, we have perhaps rendered further detail needless; but it may be instructive to repeat more specially the general refutation.

We saw that an act of will has two sides, an inner and an outer, what (in one meaning of these much-misused terms) we may call a 'subjective' and an 'objective' side. There is a certain content, which on one side is to be done, on the other side is done. The killing of a man, for instance,

---

[1] The hopeless inconsistencies of the dualistic moral theory, the standing contradictions of its moral theology and practical postulates generally, are beyond our subject. The whole point of view has been criticized in the second of the passages from Hegel referred to above.

We may remark in passing a contradiction involved in the doctrine of the imperative. A command is addressed by one will to another, and must be obeyed, if at all, by the second will. But here the will that is commanded is not the will that executes; hence the imperative is never obeyed; and, as it is not to produce action in that to which it is addressed, it is a mere sham-imperative.

is not, properly speaking, an act of my will, unless I meant to kill him and did kill him. Neither the mere movement of my body, nor the mere thought of my mind, constitutes an act.[1]

There are two sides, and on each side the content is the same. The doing *what* one wills is acting, and nothing else is acting. The act is the process of translation from the inside world to the outside world (or from the thought to the fact of an event in the inside world), and the translation would not be a translation, unless it implied the identity of the translated.

The immediate corollary from this is that no act can be the mere carrying out of an abstract principle. The content on each side must be the same, and it is at once obvious that no abstraction is a content which is capable of real existence. To take its place in the outward world, the principle must be specialized into a concrete individual, which can then be carried over into existence in time and space. Hence, on the inside (the 'subjective' side), the abstraction must have become concrete, and in itself have two sides, be in short individualized; or else there is no possibility of action, because nothing that can be carried over.[2]

Everybody knows that the only way to do your duty is to do your duties; that general doing good may mean doing no good in particular, and so none at all, but rather perhaps the contrary of good. Everybody knows that the setting out, whether in religion, morals, or politics, with the intent to realize an abstraction, is a futile endeavour; and that what it comes to is that either you do nothing at all, or that the particular content which is necessary for action is added to the abstraction by the chance of circumstances or caprice. Everybody suspects, if they do not

---

[1] This statement is subject to the qualifications mentioned in Essay I, p. 7.

[2] Our statement must not be taken to deny the possibility of the will having a content which is *merely* this or that. We say nothing about that, because we are not concerned with it.

feel sure, that the acting consciously on and from abstract principles means self-deceit or hypocrisy or both.

(3) A more psychological consideration leads us still to the futility of duty for duty's sake. A will which does not act is no will, and every act is a particular event : an act is this or that act, and an act in general is nonsense. But how can a formal act be this or that act? Even where the abstraction has been specialized into definite 'material' ends and aims to be accomplished, yet even there for the particular volition the special circumstances of time, place, &c., are wanted. They may not be essential to the act; they may make no practical difference to the content. If I have resolved to kill a man in a certain way, the place, time, &c., are psychically necessary for the particular act of killing, but they may not enter into the essence of the act. (So it is with one's ordinary duties.) The more specialized and materialized the previous intent, the less is added to it by the particular circumstances; and the less specialized the content, the more is added. If I run out into the street to kill a man, chance [1] decides who it is I kill. So with duty. If I intend to do duty generally, chance decides what duty I do; for what falls outside the preconceived intent is chance, and here everything falls outside saving the bare form.

To act you must will something, and something definite. To will in general is impossible, and to will in particular is never to will nothing but a form. It must at best be to will a chance case of the form, and then (speaking psychologically) what moves is chance (desire). The bare form can not move. Will, when one wills nothing in particular, is a pure fiction ; and (to put the same thing differently) so is will without desire, conscious or unconscious, special or habitual. It is simply a psychological monster. It is admitted that, if real, it is inexplicable; it is admitted to be in no single case verifiable ; and surely Schopenhauer (op. cit. p. 168) is not wrong when he says that, if what is

---

[1] Chance, that is to say, relatively to my intent; because my intent does not essentially involve the particular person killed.

neither conceivable nor to be found in experience is not incredible, then nothing is incredible. If any theory requires such a supposition, then that proves the theory to be false.

We have shown that a formal will is self-contradictory, since the essence of will is that it should not be formal. Duty for duty's sake is false and impossible. It may not be superfluous to show in addition that, even if such a principle of action were possible, yet it would be worthless and of no avail for practice.

The maxim of non-contradiction is useless. We have seen that it contradicts itself, since it posits a content which is the contradiction of its bare form; but, apart from that, it gives us no information. What am I to do? 'Produce a tautology' is the answer. 'Everything which contradicts itself is wrong. Everything which is tautological is right. Nothing which is tautological is wrong.' Then what does contradict itself? Everything in one sense; nothing in another.

The principle of non-contradiction does not mean, Do not contradict your*self*; produce a harmony, a system in your acts and yourself; realize yourself as an organic whole. That would be vague enough without further directions; but what our principle here says is not that. It says the *act* must not contradict itself. What does this mean? It means that the matter realized, the determination posited by the act, must be self-consistent. Property, e. g., is self-consistent. Theft of property is a contradiction.

In the first place, however, is any determination free from contradiction? Take what you will, you must take something definite, and the definite is what it is by the negation of something else. It belongs to the essence of any possible A that it should not be B, C, D, &c., and without this negation it would not be A. A mere positive affirmative is a fictitious abstraction. 'Affirm A' means 'negate B, C, D, &c.' Property, e. g., implies in its appropriation a negation, an exclusion. In this sense not only is the definite content in contradiction with the form, but it also in itself involves contradiction.

This, however, is not the meaning of the rule of non-contradiction. The meaning of that is that you must not posit a determination and with it its own negation. You must not have an act which embodies the rule to negate anything, for that is a self-contradiction. A rule 'negate A' contradicts itself, for if A is negated you can not negate it. 'Steal property' is a contradiction, for it destroys property, and with it possibility of theft.

We have no need here to push further a metaphysical argument against this view, for it supplies us at once with a crushing instance against itself. The essence of morality was a similar contradiction.[1] 'Negate the sensuous self.' But if the sensuous self *is* negated, possibility of morality disappears. Morality is thus as inconsistent as theft. 'Succour the poor' both negates *and* presupposes (hence posits) poverty: as Blake comically says,

> Pity would be no more,
> If we did not make somebody poor.

If you are to love your enemies, you must never be without them; and yet you try to get rid of them. Is that consistent? In short, every duty which presupposes something to be negated is no duty; it is an immoral rule, because self-contradictory.

No rule must be stated negatively then, but all positively; and then comes the very serious question, whether there is any rule which can *not* be stated positively. The canon is an empty form, 'Let A be A'. It is a tautology; and it requires no great skill to put anything and everything into the form of a tautology, and so to moralize it. 'Let property be', 'let no-property be'; 'let law be', 'let no-law be'; 'let love be', 'let hate be'; 'be brave', 'be cowardly'; 'be kind', 'be cruel', 'be indifferent'; 'let succour be', 'let no-succour be'; or riches, or poverty, or pleasure,

---

[1] Hegel (loc. cit.) pushes this ruthlessly even against the postulate of immortality. In what immediately follows we are drawing from him very largely.

or pain. Where is the canon? It is nowhere. Poverty
is poverty, and is an affirmative tautology. Hate is hate,
as much as love is love. They become contradictory only
when you say, 'hate your friends', or 'love your enemies';
or when, instead of affirming, you analyse them, and see
that each is the affirmation of a negation, or the negation
of an affirmation. Hate we can all see is so, and deeper
thinkers tell us the same of love.

What duty for duty's sake really does is first to posit
a determination, such as property, love, courage, &c., and
then to say that whatever contradicts these is wrong.
And, since the principle is a formal empty universal, there
is no connexion between it and the content which is brought
under it. That connexion is made from the outside, and
rests on arbitrary choice, or considerations of general well-
being and perhaps pleasure. The morality of pure duty
turns out then to be either something like a Hedonistic
rule,[1] or no rule at all, save the hypocritical maxim that,
before you do what you like, you should call it duty; and
this outdoes Probabilism.

Thus to get from the form of duty to particular duties is
impossible. The particular duties must be taken for granted,
as in ordinary morality they are taken for granted. But
supposing this done, is duty for duty's sake a valid formula,
in the sense that we are to act always on a law and nothing
but a law, and that a law can have no exceptions, in the
sense of particular cases where it is overruled? No, this
takes for granted that life is so simple that we never have
to consider more than one duty at a time; whereas we
really have to do with conflicting duties, which as a rule
escape conflict simply because it is understood which have
to give way. It is a mistake to suppose that collision of
duties is uncommon; it has been remarked truly that *every*
act can be taken to involve such collision.[2]

To put the question plainly—It is clear that in a given
case I may have several duties, and that I may be able to

---

[1] Schopenhauer has some characteristic and piquant criticism on
this head.   [2] [Collision of Duties: cf. p. 226, l. 13.]

do only one. I must then break some 'categorical' law, and the question the ordinary man puts to himself is, Which duty am I to do? He would say, ' All duties have their limits and are subordinated one to another. You can not put them all in the form of your " categorical imperative " (in the shape of a law absolute and dependent on nothing besides itself) without such exceptions and modifications that, in many cases, you might as well have left it alone altogether. We certainly have laws, but we may not be able to follow them all at once; and to know which we are to follow is a matter of good sense which can not be decided in any other way. One should give to the poor—in what cases and how much? Should sacrifice oneself—in what way and within what limits? Should not indulge one's appetites—except when it is right. Should not idle away one's time—except when one takes one's pleasure. Nor neglect one's work—but for some good reason. All these points we admit are in one way matter of law; but if you think to decide in particular cases by applying some "categorical imperative", you must be a pedant, if not a fool.'

Ordinary morality does not hold to each of its laws as inviolable, each as an absolute end in itself. It is not even aware of a collision in most cases where duties clash; and, where it perceives it, and is confronted with collisions of moral laws, each of which it has been accustomed to look on as an absolute monarch, so to speak, or a commander-in-chief, rather than as a possible subordinate officer, there it does subordinate one to the other, and feels uneasiness only in proportion to the rarity of the necessity, and the consequent jar to the feelings. There are few laws a breach of which (in obedience to a higher law) morality does not allow, and I believe there is none which is not to be broken in conceivable (imaginable) circumstances,[1] though the necessity of deciding the question does not practically occur. According to ordinary morality (the fact is too palpable to be gainsaid), it is quite right to speak falsely with intent to

[1] [Except of course the universal law to do the best we can in the circumstances.]

deceive under certain circumstances, though ordinary morality might add, ' I don't call that a lie '. It *is* a lie ; and when Kant and others maintained that it must always be wrong to lie, they forgot the rather important fact that in some cases to abstain from acting *is* acting, is wilful neglect of a duty, and that there are duties above truth-speaking, and many offences against morality which are worse, though they may be less painful, than a lie. So to kill oneself, in a manner which must be called suicide, *may* not only be right but heroic ;[1] homicide may be excusable, rebellion in the subject and disobedience in the soldier all morally justifiable, and every one of them clear breaches of categorical imperatives, in obedience to a higher law.

All that it comes to is this (and it is, we must remember, a very important truth), that you must never break a law of duty to please yourself, never for the sake of an end not duty, but only for the sake of a superior and overruling duty. Any breach of duty, as duty, and not as *lower* duty, is always and absolutely wrong; but it would be rash to say that any one act must be in all cases absolutely and unconditionally immoral. Circumstances decide, because circumstances determine the manner in which the over-ruling duty must be realized. This is a simple fact which by the candid observer can not be denied, and which is merely the exposition of the moral consciousness, though I am fully aware that it is an exposition which that consciousness would not accept, simply because it must necessarily misunderstand it in its abstract form. And if moral

---

[1] The story of the imprisoned Italian who, knowing that he was being drugged to disorder his intellect and cause him to betray his comrades, opened a vein, is a good instance. It is a duty for various persons continually to give themselves to certain or well-nigh certain death, and no one has ever called it anything but heroically right and dutiful. Excusable killing is illustrated by the well-known story told in the Indian Mutiny of the husband who killed his wife. Rebellions and mutinies need no illustration. It is noticeable that Berkeley urged passive obedience on the ground that a moral law was absolute.*

* [Cf. Berkeley, *Passive Obedience* (Fraser's edition of Berkeley's Works, vol. iii).]

theory were meant to influence moral practice and to be dabbled in by 'the vulgar' (and there are not so many persons who in this respect are *not* the vulgar), then I grant this is a fact it would be well to keep in the background. None the less it is a fact.[1]

So we see 'duty for duty's sake' says only, 'do the right for the sake of the right'; it does not tell us what right is; or 'realize a good will, do what a good will would do, for the sake of being yourself a good will'. And that is something; but beyond that it is silent or beside the mark. It tells us to act for the sake of a form, which we saw was a self-contradictory command; and we even saw that in sober sadness the form did exist for form's sake, and in literal truth remained only a form. We saw that duty's universal laws are not universal, if that means they can never be overruled, and that its form and its absolute imperative are impracticable. What after all remains is the acting for the sake of a good will, to realize oneself by realizing the will which is above us and higher than ours, and the assurance that this, and not the self to be pleased, is the end for which we have to live. But as to that which the good will is, it tells us nothing, and leaves us with an idle abstraction.

[1] We shall come upon this again in Essays V and VI.

ESSAY V

MY STATION AND ITS DUTIES

WE have traversed by this time, however cursorily, a considerable field, and so far it might appear without any issue, or at best with a merely negative result. Certainly, in our anticipatory remarks (Essay II), we thought we found some answer to the question, What is the end? But that answer was too abstract to stand by itself. And, if we may be said to know thus much, that the end is self-realization, yet at present we do not seem to have learnt anything about the self to be realized. And the detail of Essays II and III appears at most to have given us some knowledge of that which self-realization is not.

We have learnt that the self to be realized is not the self as this or that feeling, or as any series of the particular feelings of our own or others' streams or trains of consciousness. It is, in short, not the self to be pleased.[1] The greatest sum of units of pleasure we found to be the idea of a mere collection, whereas, if we wanted morality, it was something like a universal that we wanted. Happiness, as the effort to construct that universal by the addition of particulars, gave us a futile and bastard product, which carried its self-destruction within it, in the continual assertion of its own universality, together with its unceasing actual particularity and finitude; so that happiness was, if we chose, nowhere not realized; or again, if we chose, not anywhere realizable. And, passing then to the opposite pole, to the universal as the negative of the particulars, to the supposed pure will or duty for duty's sake, we found that too was an unreal conception. It was a mere form which, to be will, must give itself a content, and which could give itself a content only at the cost of a self-contradiction: we saw, further, that any such content was in addition arbitrarily

---

[1] [For this refer back. We might better have said, 'not the mere feeling self of this or that moment, or of a number of such moments'.]

postulated, and that, even then, the form was either never realized, because real in no particular content, or always and everywhere realized, because equally reconcilable with any content. And so, as before with happiness, we perceived that morality could here have no existence, if it meant anything more than the continual asseveration of an empty formula. And, if we had chosen, we might have gone on to exhibit the falsity of asceticism, to see that the self can not be realized as its own mere negation, since morality is practice, is will to do something, is self-affirmation; and that a will to deny one's will is not self-realization, but rather is, strictly speaking, a psychical impossibility, a self-contradictory illusion. And the possibility, again, of taking as the self to be realized the self which I happen to have, my natural being, and of making life the end of life in the sense that each should live his life as he happens to find it now, and from time to time, in his own nature, has been precluded beforehand by the result derived from the consideration of the moral consciousness, viz. that morality implies a superior, a higher self, or at all events a universal something which is above this or that self, and so above mine. And, to complete the account of our negations, we saw further, with respect to duty for duty's sake, that even were it possible (as it is not) to create a content from the formula, and to elaborate in this manner a system of duties, yet even then the practice required by the theory would be impossible, and so too morality, since in practice particular duties must collide; and the collision of duties, if we hold to duty for duty's sake, is the destruction of all duty, save the unrealized form of duty in general.

But let us view this result, which seems so unsatisfactory, from the positive side; let us see after all with what we are left. We have self-realization left as the end, the self so far being defined as neither a collection of particular feelings nor an abstract universal. The self is to be realized as something not simply one or the other; it is to be realized further as will, will not being merely the natural will, or the will as it happens to exist and finds itself here or there, but the will as the *good* will, i. e. the will that realizes an end which is above this or that man,[1] superior to them, and capable of confronting them in the shape of a law or an ought. This superior something, further, which is a possible law or ought to the individual man, does not depend for its existence on his choice or opinion. Either there is no morality, so says the moral consciousness, or moral duties exist independently of their position by this or that person: my duty may be mine and no other man's, but I do not make it mine. If it is duty, it would be the duty of any person in my case and condition, whether he thought so or not: in a word, duty is 'objective', in the sense of not being contingent on the mere opinion or choice of this or that subject.

What we have left then (to resume it) is this—the end is the realization of the good will which is superior to ourselves; and again the end is self-realization. Bringing these together, we see the end is the realization of ourselves as the will which is above ourselves. And this will (if morality exists) we saw must be 'objective', because not dependent on 'subjective' liking; and 'universal', because not identifiable with any particular, but standing above all actual and possible particulars. Further, though universal, it is not abstract, since it belongs to its essence that it should be realized, and it has no real existence except in and through its particulars. The good will (for morality) is meaningless, if, whatever else it be, it be not the will of living finite beings. It is a concrete universal, because it not only is above but is within and throughout its details, and is so far only as they are. It is the life which can live only in and by them, as they are dead unless within it; it is the whole soul which lives so far as the body lives, which makes the body a living body, and which without the body is as unreal an abstraction as the body without it. It is an organism and a moral organism; and it is conscious self-realization, because only by the will of its self-conscious members can the moral organism give itself reality. It is the self-realization of the whole body,

[1] [i. e. merely as this or that man.]

because it is one and the same will which lives and acts in the life and action of each. It is the self-realization of each member, because each member can not find the function, which makes him himself, apart from the whole to which he belongs ; to be himself he must go beyond himself, to live his life he must live a life which is not *merely* his own, but which, none the less, but on the contrary all the more, is intensely and emphatically his own individuality. Here, and here first, are the contradictions which have beset us solved—here is a universal which can confront our wandering desires with a fixed and stern imperative, but which yet is no unreal form of the mind, but a living soul that penetrates and stands fast in the detail of actual existence. It is real, and real for me. It is in its affirmation that I affirm myself, for I am but as a 'heart-beat in its system'. And I am real in it ; for, when I give myself to it, it gives me the fruition of my own personal activity, the accomplished ideal of my life which is happiness. In the realized idea which, superior to me, and yet here and now in and by me, affirms itself in a continuous process, we have found the end, we have found self-realization, duty, and happiness in one— yes, we have found ourselves, when we have found our station and its duties, our function as an organ in the social organism.[1]

'Mere rhetoric', we shall be told, 'a bad metaphysical dream, a stale old story once more warmed up, which can not hold its own against the logic of facts. That the state was prior to the individual, that the whole was sometimes more than the sum of the parts, was an illusion which preyed on the thinkers of Greece. But that illusion has been traced to its source and dispelled, and is in plain words exploded. The family, society, the state, and generally every community of men, consists of individuals, and there is nothing in them real except the individuals. Individuals have made them, and make them, by placing themselves and by stand-

---

[1] ['A' for 'the' would perhaps be better, as 'the' perhaps limits 'social organism' to the state.] ⟨*Cf. Note on p. 173, l. 33.*—ED.⟩

ing in certain relations. The individuals are real by themselves, and it is because of them that the relations are real. They make them, they are real *in* them, not because of them, and they would be just as real *out* of them. The whole is the mere sum of the parts, and the parts are as real away from the whole as they are within the whole. Do you really suppose that the individual would perish if every form of community were destroyed? Do you think that anything real answers to the phrases of universal and organism? Everything is in the organism what it is out, and the universal is a name, the existing fact answering to which is particular persons in such and such relations. To put the matter shortly, the community is the sum of its parts, is made by the addition of parts; and the parts are as real before the addition as after; the relations they stand in do not make them what they are, but are accidental, not essential, to their being; and, as to the whole, if it is not a name for the individuals that compose it, it is a name of nothing actual. These are not metaphysical dreams. They are facts and verifiable facts.'

Are they facts? Facts should explain facts; and the view called 'individualism' (because the one reality that it believes in is the 'individual', in the sense of this, that, and the other particular) should hence be the right explanation. What are the facts here to be explained? They are human communities, the family, society, and the state. Individualism has explained them long ago. They are 'collections' held together by force, illusion, or contract. It has told the story of their origin, and to its own satisfaction cleared the matter up. Is the explanation satisfactory and verifiable? That would be a bold assertion, when historical science has rejected and entirely discredited the individualistic origin of society, and when, if we turn to practice, we find everywhere the state asserting itself as a power which has, and, if need be asserts, the right to make use of and expend the property and person of the individual without regard to his wishes, and which, moreover, may destroy his life in punishment, and put forth other powers such as no theory of contract will explain except by the most palpable fictions, while at the same time no ordinary person calls their morality in question. Both history and practical politics refuse to verify the 'facts' of the individualist; and we should find perhaps still less to confirm his theory if we examined the family.

If, then, apart from metaphysic, one looks at the history and present practice of society, these would not appear to establish the 'fact' that the individual is the one reality, and communities mere collections. 'For all that', we shall be told, 'it is the truth.' True that is, I suppose, not as fact but as metaphysic; and this is what one finds too often with those who deride metaphysic and talk most of facts. Their minds, so far as such a thing may be, are not seldom mere 'collective unities' of metaphysical dogmas. They decry any real metaphysic, because they dimly feel that their own will not stand criticism ; and they appeal to facts because, while their metaphysic stands, they feel they need not be afraid of them. When their view is pushed as to plain realities, such as the nature of gregarious animals, the probable origin of mankind from them, the institutions of early society, actual existing communities with the common type impressed on all their members, their organic structure and the assertion of the whole body as of paramount importance in comparison with any of the members, then they must fall back on their metaphysic. And the point we wish here to emphasize is this, that their metaphysic is mere dogmatism. It is assumed, not proved. It has a right to no refutation, for assertion can demand no more than counter-assertion ; and what is affirmed on the one side, we on the other side can simply deny, and we intend to do so here.

A discussion that would go to the bottom of the question, What is an individual ? is certainly wanted. It would certainly be desirable, showing first what an individual is, to show then that 'individualism' has not apprehended that, but taken an abstraction for reality. But, if I could do that (which I could not do), this would not be the place ;

nor perhaps should I have to say very much that has not been said before, and has been not attended to.

But we are not going to enter on a metaphysical question to which we are not equal; we meet the metaphysical assertion of the 'individualist' with a mere denial; and, turning to facts, we will try to show that they lead us in another direction. To the assertion, then, that selves are 'individual' in the sense of exclusive of other selves, we oppose the (equally justified) assertion, that this is a mere fancy. We say that, out of theory, no such individual men exist; and we will try to show from fact that, in fact, what we call an individual man is what he is because of and by virtue of community, and that communities are thus not mere names but something real, and can be regarded (if we mean to keep to facts) only as the one in the many.

And to confine the subject, and to keep to what is familiar, we will not call to our aid the life of animals, nor early societies, nor the course of history, but we will take men as they are now; we will take ourselves, and endeavour to keep wholly to the teaching of experience.

Let us take a man, an Englishman as he is now, and try to point out that, apart from what he has in common with others, apart from his sameness with others, he is not an Englishman—nor a man at all; that if you take him as something by himself, he is not what he is. Of course we do not mean to say that he can not go out of England without disappearing, nor, even if all the rest of the nation perished, that he would not survive. What we mean to say is, that he is what he is because he is a born and educated social being, and a member of an individual social organism; that if you make abstraction of all this, which is the same in him and in others, what you have left is not an Englishman, nor a man, but some I know not what residuum, which never has existed by itself, and does not so exist. If we suppose the world of relations, in which he was born and bred, never to have been, then we suppose the very essence of him not to be; if we take that away, we have taken him away; and hence he now is not an individual, in the sense of owing nothing to the sphere of relations in which he finds himself, but does contain those relations within himself as belonging to his very being; he is what he is, in brief, so far as he is what others also are.

But we shall be cut short here with an objection. 'It is impossible', we shall be told, 'that two men should have the *same* thing in common. You are confusing sameness and likeness.' [1] I say in answer that I am not, and that the too probable objector I am imagining too probably knows the meaning of neither one word nor the other. But this is a matter we do not intend to stay over, because it is a metaphysical question we can not discuss, and which, more-over, we can not be called on to discuss. We can not be called on to discuss it, because we have to do again here with sheer assertion, which either is ignorant of or ignores the critical investigation of the subject, and which, therefore, has no right to demand an answer. We allude to it merely because it has become a sort of catchword with 'advanced thinkers'. All that it comes to is this; first identity and diversity are assumed to exclude one another, and therefore, since diversity is a fact, it follows that there is no identity. Hence a difficulty; because it has been seen long ago, and forces itself upon every one, that denial of all identity brings you into sharp collision with ordinary fact, and leads to total scepticism; [2] so, to avoid this, while we yet maintain the previous dogma, 'resemblance' is brought in—a conception which (I suppose I need not add) is not analysed or properly defined, and so does all the better. Against these assertions I shall put some others: viz. that identity and diversity, sameness and difference, imply one another, and depend for their meaning on one another; that mere diversity is non-sense, just as mere identity is also nonsense; that resemblance or likeness, strictly speaking, falls not in the objects, but in

---

[1] [Cf. *Appearance and Reality*, p. 348.]

[2] Even from Mr. Mill (in controversy) we can quote, 'If every general conception, instead of being "the One in the Many", were considered to be as many different conceptions as there are things to which it is applicable, there would be no such thing as general language.'—*Logic*, i. 201, ed. vi ⟨i. 199, ed. vii⟩.

the person contemplating (likening, ver-gleichend) ; that 'is A really like B?' does not mean 'does it seem like?' It may mean 'would it seem like to everybody?' but it generally means 'is there an "objective identity"'? Is there a point or points the same in both, whether any one sees it or not?' We do not talk of cases of 'mistaken likeness'; we do not hang one man because he is 'exactly like' another, or at least we do not wish to do so. We are the same as we were, not merely more or less like. We have the same faith, hope, and purpose, and the same feelings as another man has now, as ourselves had at another time—not understanding thereby the numerical indistinguishedness of particular states and moments, but calling the feelings one and the same feeling, because *what* is felt is the same, and not merely like. In short, so far is it from being true that 'sameness' is really 'likeness', that it is utterly false that two things are really and objectively 'like', unless that means 'more or less the same'. So much by way of counter-assertion ; and now let us turn to our facts.

The 'individual' man, the man into whose essence his community with others does not enter, who does not include relation to others in his very being, is, we say, a fiction, and in the light of facts we have to examine him. Let us take him in the shape of an English child as soon as he is born ; for I suppose we ought not to go further back. Let us take him as soon as he is separated from his mother, and occupies a space clear and exclusive of all other human beings. At this time, education and custom will, I imagine, be allowed to have not as yet operated on him or lessened his 'individuality'. But is he now a mere 'individual', in the sense of not implying in his being identity with others? We can not say that, if we hold to the teaching of modern physiology. Physiology would tell us, in one language or another, that even now the child's mind is no passive 'tabula rasa'; he has an inner, a yet undeveloped nature, which must largely determine his future individuality. What is this inner nature? Is it particular to himself? Certainly not all of it, will have to be the answer. The child is not fallen from heaven. He is born of certain parents who come of certain families, and he has in him the qualities of his parents, and, as breeders would say, of the strains from both sides. Much of it we can see, and more we believe to be latent, and, given certain (possible or impossible) conditions, ready to come to light. On the descent of mental qualities, modern investigation and popular experience, as expressed in uneducated vulgar opinion, altogether, I believe, support one another, and we need not linger here. But if the intellectual and active qualities do descend from ancestors, is it not, I would ask, quite clear that a man may have in him the same that his father and mother had, the same that his brothers and sisters have? And if any one objects to the word 'same', I would put this to him. If, concerning two dogs allied in blood, I were to ask a man, 'Is that of the same strain or stock as this?' and were answered, 'No, not the same, but similar', should I not think one of these things, that the man either meant to deceive me, or was a 'thinker', or a fool?

But the child is not merely the member of a family; he is born into other spheres, and (passing over the subordinate wholes, which nevertheless do in many cases qualify him) he is born a member of the English nation. It is, I believe, a matter of fact that at birth the child of one race is not the same as the child of another; that in the children of the one race there is a certain identity, a developed or undeveloped national type, which may be hard to recognize, or which at present may even be unrecognizable, but which nevertheless in some form will appear.[1] If that be the fact, then again we must say that one English child is in some points, though perhaps it does not as yet show itself, the same as another. His being is so far common to him with others; he is not a mere 'individual'.

We see the child has been born at a certain time of parents of a certain race, and that means also of a certain degree of

---

[1] [Perhaps, but 'race' and 'nationality' are not conterminous. This paragraph can hardly stand without large qualification. How far is identity of race an effective bond of union?]

culture. It is the opinion of those best qualified to speak
on the subject, that civilization is to some not inconsiderable
extent hereditary ;[1] that aptitudes are developed, and are
latent in the child at birth ; and that it is a very different
thing, even apart from education, to be born of civilized and
of uncivilized ancestors. These 'civilized tendencies', if we
may use the phrase, are part of the essence of the child : he
would only partly (if at all) be himself without them ; he
owes them to his ancestors, and his ancestors owe them to
society. The ancestors were made what they were by the
society they lived in. If in answer it be replied, 'Yes, but
individual ancestors were prior to their society', then that,
to say the least of it, is a hazardous and unproved assertion,
since man, so far as history can trace him back, is social ;
and if Mr. Darwin's conjecture as to the development of man
from a social animal be received, we must say that man has
never been anything but social, and society never was made
by individual men. Nor, if the (baseless) assertion of the
priority of individual men were allowed, would that destroy
our case ; for certainly our more immediate ancestors were
social ; and, whether society was manufactured previously
by individuals or not, yet in their case it certainly was not
so. They at all events have been so qualified by the common
possessions of social mankind that, as members in the organism, they have become relative to the whole. If we suppose
then that the results of the social life of the race are present
in a latent and potential form in the child, can we deny that

---

[1] [Are civilized tendencies hereditary? How far is very doubtful.
What you can say is, 'There are hereditary tendencies which come from
the fact of social existence, not the existence of this or that society,
specially and particularly, but still the fact of past existence in *some*
society'. So, further, l. 26, above. 'The social life of the race' is
a doubtful expression for either 'the human race', or '*this* human race',
or '*this* human *race*', or 'this human *community*'. See also p. 204.

So again, on p. 171, the same doubt remains. It all holds good
against individualism, but does *not* all hold in favour of this or that
particular community as distinct from others of more or less the same
general character.

So again, p. 173, l. 22, 'The social state'. The transition is made
in the next paragraph.]

they are common property? Can we assert that they are
not an element of sameness in all? Can we say that the
individual is this individual, because he is exclusive, when,
if we deduct from him what he includes, he loses characteristics which make him himself, and when again he does
include what the others include, and therefore does (how
can we escape the consequence?) include in some sense the
others also, just as they include him? By himself, then,
what are we to call him? I confess I do not know, unless
we name him a theoretical attempt to isolate what can not
be isolated; and that, I suppose, has, out of our heads, no
existence. But what he is really, and not in mere theory,
can be described only as the specification or particularization of that which is common, which is the same amid
diversity, and without which the 'individual' would be so
other than he is that we could not call him the same.

Thus the child is at birth; and he is born not into a
desert, but into a living world, a whole which has a true
individuality of its own, and into a system and order which
it is difficult to look at as anything else than an organism,
and which, even in England, we are now beginning to call
by that name. And I fear that the 'individuality' (the
particularness) which the child brought into the light with
him, now stands but a poor chance, and that there is no help
for him until he is old enough to become a 'philosopher'.
We have seen that already he has in him inherited habits,
or what will of themselves appear as such; but, in addition
to this, he is not for one moment left alone, but continually
tampered with; and the habituation which is applied from
the outside is the more insidious that it answers to this inborn
disposition. Who can resist it? Nay, who but a 'thinker'
could wish to have resisted it? And yet the tender care that
receives and guides him is impressing on him habits, habits,
alas, not particular to himself, and the 'icy chains' of universal
custom are hardening themselves round his cradled life. As
the poet tells us, he has not yet thought of himself; his earliest
notions come mixed to him of things and persons, not distinct
from one another, nor divided from the feeling of his own

existence.   The need that he can not understand moves him
to foolish, but not futile, cries for what only another can give
him ; and the breast of his mother, and the soft warmth and
touches and tones of his nurse, are made one with the feeling of
his own pleasure and pain ; nor is he yet a moralist to beware
of such illusion, and to see in them mere means to an end
without them in his separate self.   For he does not even
think of his separate self; he grows with his world, his
mind fills and orders itself; and when he can separate himself from that world, and know himself apart from it, then
by that time his self, the object of his self-consciousness, is
penetrated, infected, characterized by the existence of others.
Its content implies in every fibre relations of community.
He learns, or already perhaps has learnt, to speak, and here
he appropriates the common heritage of his race, the tongue
that he makes his own is his country's language, it is (or it
should be) the same that others speak, and it carries into
his mind the ideas and sentiments of the race (over this
I need not stay), and stamps them in indelibly.   He grows
up in an atmosphere of example and general custom, his
life widens out from one little world to other and higher
worlds, and he apprehends through successive stations the
whole in which he lives, and in which he has lived.   Is he
now to try and develop his ' individuality ', his self which is
not the same as other selves?   Where is it ?   What is it ?
Where can he find it ?   The soul within him is saturated, is
filled, is qualified by, it has assimilated, has got its substance,
has built itself up from, it *is* one and the same life with the
universal life, and if he turns against this he turns against
himself ; if he thrusts it from him, he tears his own vitals ;
if he attacks it, he sets his weapon against his own heart.
He has found his life in the life of the whole, he lives that
in himself, ' he is a pulse-beat of the whole system, and
himself the whole system '.

' The child, in his character of the form of the possibility
of a moral individual, is something subjective or negative ;
his growing to manhood is the ceasing to be of this form,
and his education is the discipline or the compulsion thereof.

The positive side and the essence is that he is suckled at the breast of the universal Ethos, lives in its absolute intuition, as in that of a foreign being first, then comprehends it more and more, and so passes over into the universal mind.' The writer proceeds to draw the weighty conclusion that virtue 'is not a troubling oneself about a peculiar and isolated morality of one's own, that the striving for a positive morality of one's own is futile, and in its very nature impossible of attainment; that in respect of morality the saying of the wisest men of antiquity is the only one which is true, that to be moral is to live in accordance with the moral tradition of one's country; and in respect of education, the one true answer is that which a Pythagorean gave to him who asked what was the best education for his son, If you make him the citizen of a people with good institutions'.[1]

But this is to anticipate. So far, I think, without aid from metaphysics, we have seen that the 'individual' apart from the community is an abstraction. It is not anything real, and hence not anything that we can realize, however much we may wish to do so. We have seen that I am myself by sharing with others, by including in my essence relations to them, the relations of the social state. If I wish to realize my true being, I must therefore realize something beyond my being as a mere this or that; for my true being has in it a life which is not the life of any mere particular, and so must be called a universal life.

What is it then that I am to realize? We have said it in 'my station and its duties'. To know what a man is (as we have seen) you must not take him in isolation. He is one of a people, he was born in a family, he lives in a certain society, in a certain state. What he has to do depends on what his place is, what his function is, and that all comes from his station in the organism.[2] Are there then such organisms

[1] Hegel, *Philosophische Abhandlungen, Werke*, i, pp. 399–400 (1832).

[2] [We pass here from negation of individualism, and assertion of social life as essential to the 'organism' and the individual's place in it (cf. also pp. 204, 198); (i) The family, (ii) social position, and particular profession, (iii) the state, (iv) and a still wider society are all mentioned. The transition seems then made mainly to the state, and the individual's

in which he lives, and if so, what is their nature? Here we come
to questions which must be answered in full by any complete
system of Ethics, but which we can not enter on. We must
content ourselves by pointing out that there are such facts
as the family, then in a middle position a man's own profession and society, and, over all, the larger community of
the state. Leaving out of sight the question of a society
wider than the state, we must say that a man's life with its
moral duties is in the main filled up by his station in that
system of wholes which the state is, and that this, partly by
its laws and institutions, and still more by its spirit, gives
him the life which he does live and ought to live. That objective institutions exist is of course an obvious fact; and it is
a fact which every day is becoming plainer that these
institutions are organic, and further, that they are moral.
The assertion that communities have been manufactured by
the addition of exclusive units is, as we have seen, a mere
fable; and if, within the state, we take that which seems
wholly to depend on individual caprice, e. g. marriage,[1] yet
even here we find that a man does give up his self so far as
it excludes others; he does bring himself under a unity
which is superior to the particular person and the impulses
that belong to his single existence, and which makes him
fully as much as he makes it. In short, man is a social
being; he is real only because he is social, and can realize
himself only because it is as social that he realizes himself.
The mere individual is a delusion of theory; and the attempt
to realize it in practice is the starvation and mutilation of
human nature, with total sterility or the production of
monstrosities.

Let us now in detail compare the advantages of our
present view with the defects of 'duty for duty's sake'. The
objections we found fatal to that view may be stated as

function in that as social organism. But this should have been
explained and enlarged on.]

[1] Marriage is a contract, a contract to pass out of the sphere of
contract; and this is possible only because the contracting parties are
already beyond and above the sphere of mere contract.

follows: (1) The universal was abstract. There was no content which belonged to it and was one with it; and the consequence was, that either nothing could be willed, or what was willed was willed not because of the universal, but capriciously. (2) The universal was 'subjective'. It certainly gave itself out as 'objective', in the sense of being independent of this or that person, but still it was not real in the world. It did not come to us as what *was* in fact, it came as what in itself merely was to be, an inner notion in moral persons, which, at least perhaps, had not power to carry itself out and transform the world. And self-realization, if it means will, does mean that we, in fact, do put ourselves forth and see ourselves actual in outer existence. Hence, by identifying ourselves with that which has not necessarily this existence, which is not master of the outer world, we can not secure our self-realization; since, when we have identified ourselves with the end, the end may still remain a mere inner end which does not accomplish itself, and so does not satisfy us. (3) The universal left a part of ourselves outside it. However much we tried to be good, however determined we were to make our will one with the good will, yet we never succeeded. There was always something left in us which was in contradiction with the good. And this we saw was even necessary, because morality meant and implied this contradiction, unless we accepted that form of conscientiousness which consists in the simple identification of one's conscience with one's own self (unless, i. e., the consciousness of the relation of my private self to myself as the good self be degraded into my self-consciousness of my mere private self as the good self); and this can not be, if we are in earnest with morality. There thus remains a perpetual contradiction in myself, no less than in the world, between the 'is to be' and the 'is', a contradiction that can not be got rid of without getting rid of morality; for, as we saw, it is inherent in morality. The man can not realize himself in himself as moral, because the conforming of his sensuous nature to the universal would be the radical suppression of it, and hence not only of himself, but also of the morality which is constituted by the relation of himself to the universal law. The man then can not find self-realization in the morality of pure duty; because (1) he can not look on his subjective self as the realized moral law; (2) he can not look on the objective world as the realization of the moral law; (3) he can not realize the moral law at all, because it is defined as that which has no particular content, and therefore no reality; or, if he gives it a content, then it is not the law he realizes, since the content is got not from the law, but from elsewhere. In short, duty for duty's sake is an unsolved contradiction, the standing 'is to be', which, therefore, because it is to be, is *not*; and in which, therefore, since it is *not*, he can not find himself realized nor satisfy himself.

These are serious defects: let us see how they are mended by 'my station and its duties'. In that (1) the universal is concrete; (2) it is objective; (3) it leaves nothing of us outside it.

(1) It is concrete, and yet not given by caprice. Let us take the latter first. It is not given by caprice; for, although within certain limits I may choose my station according to my own liking, yet I and every one else must have some station with duties pertaining to it, and those duties do not depend on our opinion or liking. Certain circumstances, a certain position, call for a certain course. How I in particular know what my right course is, is a question we shall recur to hereafter—but at present we may take it as an obvious fact that in my station my particular duties are prescribed to me, and I have them whether I wish to or not. And secondly, it is concrete. The universal to be realized is no abstraction, but an organic whole; a system where many spheres are subordinated to one sphere, and particular actions to spheres. This system is real in the detail of its functions, not out of them, and lives in its vital processes, not away from them. The organs are always at work for the whole, the whole is at work in the organs. And I am one of the organs. The universal then which I am to realize is the system which penetrates and subordinates to itself the particulars of all

lives, and here and now in my life has this and that function
in this and that case, in exercising which through my will
it realizes itself as a whole, and me in it.

(2) It is 'objective'; and this means that it does not stand
over against the outer world as mere 'subject' confronted
by mere 'object'. In that sense of the words it is neither
merely 'objective' nor merely 'subjective'; but it is that
real identity of subject and object, which, as we have seen,
is the only thing that satisfies our desires. The inner side
does exist, but it is no more than the inside; it is one factor
in the whole, and must not be separated from the other
factor; and the mistake which is made by the morality
which confines itself to the individual man, is just this
attempt at the separation of what can not be separated.
The inner side certainly is a fact, and it can be distinguished
from the rest of the whole; but it really is one element of
the whole, depends on the whole for its being, and can not
be divided from it. Let us explain. The moral world, as
we said, is a whole, and has two sides. There is an outer
side, systems and institutions, from the family to the nation;
this we may call the body of the moral world. And there
must also be a soul, or else the body goes to pieces; every
one knows that institutions without the spirit of them are
dead. In the moral organism this spirit is in the will of the
organs, as the will of the whole which, in and by the organs,
carries out the organism and makes it alive, and which also
(and this is the point to which attention is requested) is, and
must be felt or known, in each organ as his own inward
and personal will. It is quite clear that a nation is not
strong without public spirit, and is not public-spirited unless
the members of it are public-spirited, i. e. feel the good of
the public as a personal matter, or have it at their hearts.
The point here is that you can not have the moral world
unless it is willed; that to be willed it must be willed by
persons; and that these persons not only have the moral
world as the content of their wills, but also must in
some way be aware of themselves as willing this content.
This being inwardly aware of oneself as willing the good

will falls in the inside of the moral whole; we may call it the soul; and it is the sphere of personal morality, or morality in the narrower sense of the consciousness of the relation of my private self to the inwardly presented universal will, my being aware of and willing myself as one with that or contrary to that, as dutiful or bad. We must never let this out of our sight, that, where the moral world exists, you have and you must have these two sides; neither will stand apart from the other; moral institutions are carcasses without personal morality, and personal morality apart from moral institutions is an unreality, a soul without a body.

Now this inward, this 'subjective', this personal side, this knowing in himself by the subject of the relation in which the will of him as this or that man stands to the will of the whole within him, or (as was rightly seen by 'duty for duty's sake') this consciousness in the one subject of himself as two selves, is, as we said, necessary for all morality. But the form in which it is present may vary very much, and, beginning with the stage of mere feeling, goes on to that of explicit reflection. The reader who considers the matter will perceive that (whether in the life of mankind or of this or that man) we do not begin with a consciousness of good and evil, right and wrong, as such, or in the strict sense.[1] The child is taught to will a content which is universal and good, and he learns to identify his will with it, so that he feels pleasure when he feels himself in accord with it, uneasiness or pain when his will is contrary thereto, and he feels that it is contrary. This is the beginning of personal morality, and from this we may pass to consider the end. That, so far as form went, was sufficiently exhibited in Essay IV. It consists in the explicit consciousness in myself of two elements which, even though they exist in disunion, are felt to be really one; these are myself as the will of this or that self, and again the universal will as the will for good; and this latter I feel to be my true self, and desire my other self to be subordinated to and so identified with it; in which case I feel the

[1] On this point see more in Essay VII.

satisfaction of an inward realization. That, so far as form goes, is correct. But the important point on which 'duty for duty's sake' utterly failed us was as to the content of the universal will. We have seen that for action this must have a content, and now we see where the content comes from. The universal side in personal morality [1] is, in short, the reflection of the objective moral world into ourselves (or into itself). The outer universal which I have been taught to will as my will, and which I have grown to find myself in, is now presented by me inwardly to myself as the universal which is my true being, and which by my will I must realize, if need be, against my will as this or that man. So this inner universal has the same content as the outer universal, for it *is* the outer universal in another sphere; it is the inside *of* the outside. *There* was the whole system as an objective will, including my station, and realizing itself here and now in my function. *Here* is the same system presented as a will in me, standing above my will, which wills a certain act to be done by me as a will which is one with the universal will. This universal will is not a blank, but it is filled by the consideration of my station in the whole with reference to habitual and special acts. The ideal self appealed to by the moral man is an ideally presented will, in his position and circumstances, which rightly particularizes the general laws which answer to the general functions and system of spheres of the moral organism. That is the content, and therefore, as we saw, it is concrete and filled. And therefore also (which is equally important) it is not merely 'subjective'.

If, on the inner side of the moral whole, the universal factor were (as in would-be morality it is) filled with a content which is not the detail of the objective will particularizing itself in such and such functions, then there would be no true identity of subject and object, no need why that which is moral should be that which is real, and we

---

[1] ['Personal morality.' This is here provisionally identified with oneness with the will of the 'objective moral world'. This is *only* provisionally. The reader should have been warned of this.]

should never escape from a practical postulate, which, as we saw, is a practical standing contradiction. But if, as we have seen, the universal on the inside is the universal on the outside reflected in us, or (since we can not separate it and ourselves) into itself in us; if the objective will of the moral organism is real only in the will of its organs, and if, in willing morally, we will ourselves as that will, and that will wills itself in us—then we must hold that this universal on the inner side is the will of the whole, which is self-conscious in us, and wills itself in us against the actual or possible opposition of the false private self. This being so, when we will morally, the will of the objective world wills itself in us, and carries both us and itself out into the world of the moral will, which is its own realm. We see thus that, when morals are looked at as a whole, the will of the inside, so far as it is moral, *is* the will of the outside, and the two are one and can not be torn apart without *ipso facto* destroying the unity in which morality consists. To be moral, I must will my station and its duties; that is, I will to particularize the moral system truly in a given case; and the other side to this act is, that the moral system wills to particularize itself in a given station and functions, i. e. in my actions and by my will. In other words, my moral self is not simply mine; it is not an inner which belongs simply to me ; and further, it is not a mere inner at all, but it is the soul which animates the body and lives in it, and would not be the soul if it had not a body and *its* body. The objective organism, the systematized moral world, is the reality of the moral will; my duties on the inside answer to due functions on the outside. There is no need here for a pre-established or a postulated harmony, for the moral whole is the identity of both sides; my private choice, so far as I am moral, is the mere form of bestowing myself on, and identifying myself with, the will of the moral organism, which realizes in its process both itself and myself. Hence we see that what I have to do I have not to force on a recalcitrant world; I have to fill my place—the place that waits for me to fill it; to make my private self the means, my life the sphere and the function of the soul of the whole, which thus, personal in me, externalizes both itself and me into a solid reality, which is both mine and its.

(3) What we come to now is the third superiority of 'my station and its duties'. The universal which is the end, and which we have seen is concrete and does realize itself, does also more. It gets rid of the contradiction between duty and the 'empirical' self; it does not in its realization leave me for ever outside and unrealized.

In 'duty for duty's sake' we were always unsatisfied, no nearer our goal at the end than at the beginning. There we had the fixed antithesis of the sensuous self on one side and a non-sensuous moral ideal on the other—a standing contradiction which brought with it a perpetual self-deceit, or the depressing perpetual confession that I am not what I ought to be in my inner heart, and that I never can be so. Duty, we thus saw, was an infinite process, an unending 'not-yet'; a continual 'not' with an everlasting 'to be', or an abiding 'to be' with a ceaseless 'not'.

From this last peevish enemy we are again delivered by 'my station and its duties'. There I realize myself morally, so that not only what ought to be in the world is, but I am what I ought to be, and find so my contentment and satisfaction. If this were not the case, when we consider that the ordinary moral man is self-contented and happy, we should be forced to accuse him of immorality, and we do not do this; we say he most likely might be better, but we do not say that he is bad, or need consider himself so. Why is this? It is because 'my station and its duties' teaches us to identify others and ourselves with the station we fill; to consider that as good, and by virtue of that to consider others and ourselves good too. It teaches us that a man who does his work in the world is good, notwithstanding his faults, if his faults do not prevent him from fulfilling his station. It tells us that the heart is an idle abstraction; we are not to think of it, nor must we look at our insides, but at our work and our life, and say to ourselves, Am I fulfilling my appointed function or not? Fulfil it we can, if we will: what we have to do is not so much better than the world that we can not do it; the world is there waiting for it; my duties are my rights. On the one hand, I am not likely to be much better than the world asks me to be; on the other hand, if I can take my place in the world I ought not to be discontented. Here we must not be misunderstood; we do not say that the false self, the habits and desires opposed to the good will, are extinguished. Though negated, they never are all of them entirely suppressed, and can not be. Hence we must not say that any man really does fill his station to the full height of his capacity; nor must we say of any man that he can not perform his function better than he does, for we all can do so, and should try to do so. We do not wish to deny what are plain moral facts, nor in any way to slur them over.

How then does the contradiction disappear? It disappears by my identifying myself with the good will that I realize in the world, by my refusing to identify myself with the bad will of my private self. So far as I am one with the good will, living as a member in the moral organism, I am to consider myself real, and I am not to consider the false self real. That can not be attributed to me in my character of member in the organism. Even in me the false existence of it has been partly suppressed by that organism; and, so far as the organism is concerned, it is wholly suppressed, because contradicted in its results, and allowed no reality. Hence, not existing for the organism, it does not exist for me as a member thereof; and only as a member thereof do I hold myself to be real. And yet this is not justification by faith,[1] for we not only trust, but see, that despite our faults the moral world stands fast, and we in and by it. It is like faith, however, in this, that not merely by thinking ourselves, but by willing ourselves as such, can we look on ourselves as organs in a good whole, and so ourselves good. And further, the knowledge that as members of the system we are real, and not otherwise, en-

---

[1] ['Justification by faith.' This, however, must come in again in ideal morality, cf. p. 189, l. 4.]

courages us more and more to identify ourselves with that
system; to make ourselves better, and so more real, since
we see that the good is real, and that nothing else is.

Or, to repeat it, in education my self by habituation has
been growing into one with the good self around me, and by
my free acceptance of my lot hereafter I consciously make
myself one with the good, so that, though bad habits cling
to and even arise in me, yet I can not but be aware of myself
as the reality of the good will. That is my essential side;
my imperfections are not, and practically they do not matter.
The good will in the world realizes itself by and in imperfect instruments, and in spite of them. The work is done,
and so long as I will my part of the work and do it (as I do),
I feel that, if I perform the function, I *am* the organ, and
that my faults, if they do not matter to my station, do not
matter to me. My heart I am not to think of, except to tell
by my work whether it is in my work, and one with the
moral whole; and if that is so, I have the consciousness of
absolute reality in the good because of and by myself, and
in myself because of and through the good; and with that
I am satisfied, and have no right to be dissatisfied.

The individual's consciousness of himself is inseparable
from the knowing himself as an organ of the whole; and the
residuum falls more and more into the background, so that
he thinks of it, if at all, not as himself, but as an idle appen-
dage. For his nature now is not distinct from his 'artificial
self'. He is related to the living moral system not as to a
foreign body; his relation to it is 'too inward even for faith',
since faith implies a certain separation. It is no other-world
that he can not see but must trust to: he feels himself in it,
and it in him; in a word, the self-consciousness of himself
is the self-consciousness of the whole in him, and his will is
the will which sees in him its accomplishment by him; it is
the free will which knows itself as the free will, and, as this,
beholds its realization and is more than content.

The non-theoretical person, if he be not immoral, is at
peace with reality; and the man who in any degree has

made this point of view his own, becomes more and more reconciled to the world and to life, and the theories of 'advanced thinkers' come to him more and more as the thinnest and most miserable abstractions. He sees evils which can not discourage him, since they point to the strength of the life which can endure such parasites and flourish in spite of them. If the popularizing of superficial views inclines him to bitterness, he comforts himself when he sees that they live in the head, and but little, if at all, in the heart and life; that still at the push the doctrinaire and the quacksalver go to the wall, and that even that too is as it ought to be. He sees the true account of the state (which holds it to be neither mere force nor convention, but the moral organism, the real identity of might and right) unknown or 'refuted', laughed at and despised, but he sees the state every day in its practice refute every other doctrine, and do with the moral approval of all what the explicit theory of scarcely one will morally justify. He sees instincts are better and stronger than so-called 'principles'. He sees in the hour of need what are called 'rights' laughed at, 'freedom', the liberty to do what one pleases, trampled on, the claims of the individual trodden under foot, and theories burst like cobwebs. And he sees, as of old, the heart of a nation rise high and beat in the breast of each one of her citizens, till her safety and her honour are dearer to each than life, till to those who live her shame and sorrow, if such is allotted, outweigh their loss, and death seems a little thing to those who go for her to their common and nameless grave. And he knows that what is stronger than death is hate or love, hate here for love's sake, and that love does not fear death, because already it is the death into life of what our philosophers tell us is the only life and reality.

Yes, the state is not put together, but it lives; it is not a heap nor a machine; it is no mere extravagance when a poet talks of a nation's soul. It is the objective mind which is subjective and self-conscious in its citizens: it feels and knows itself in the heart of each. It speaks the word of command and gives the field of accomplishment, and in the

activity of obedience it has and bestows individual life and
satisfaction and happiness.

First in the community is the individual realized.   He is
here the embodiment of beauty, goodness, and truth : of
truth, because he corresponds to his universal conception ;
of beauty, because he realizes it in a single form to the senses
or imagination ; of goodness, because his will expresses and
is the will of the universal.

' The realm of morality is nothing but the absolute
spiritual unity of the essence of individuals, which exists in
the independent reality of them. . . . The moral substance,
looked at abstractedly from the mere side of its universality,
is the law, and, as this, is only thought ; but none the less is
it, from another point of view, immediate real self-consciousness or custom : and conversely the individual exists as this
single unit, in as much as it is conscious in its individuality
of the universal consciousness as its own being, in as much
as its action and existence are the universal Ethos. . . . They
(the individuals) are aware in themselves that they possess
this individual independent being because of the sacrifice of
their individuality, because the universal substance is their
soul and essence : and, on the other side, this universal is their
individual action, the work that they as individuals have
produced.

' The merely individual action and business of the separate
person is concerned with the needs he is subject to as a
natural being, as an individuality which exists.   That even
these his commonest functions do not come to nothing, but
possess reality, is effected solely by the universal maintain-
ing medium, by the power of the whole people.   But it is
not simply the form of persistence which the universal substance confers on his action ; it gives also the content—
what he does *is* the universal skill and custom of all.   This
content, just so far as it completely individualizes itself,
is in its reality interlaced with the action of all.   The work
of the individual for his needs is a satisfaction of the needs
of others as much as of his own ; and he attains the satisfaction of his own only through the work of the others.

The individual in his individual work thus accomplishes a universal work—he does so here *unconsciously* ; but he also further accomplishes it as his *conscious* object : the whole as the whole is his work for which he sacrifices himself, and from which by that very sacrifice he gets again his self restored. Here there is nothing taken which is not given, nothing wherein the independent individual, by and in the resolution of his atomic existence, by and in the negation of his self, fails to give himself the positive significance of a being which exists by and for itself.   This unity—on the one side of the being for another, or the making oneself into an outward thing, and on the other side of the being for oneself—this universal substance speaks its universal language in the usages and laws of his people : and yet this unchanging essence is itself nought else than the expression of the single individuality, which seems at first sight its mere opposite ; the laws pronounce nothing but what every one *is* and does. The individual recognizes the substance not only as his universal outward existence, but he recognizes also himself in it, particularized in his own individuality and in that of each of his fellow citizens.   And so in the universal mind each one has nothing but self-certainty, the assurance of finding in existing reality nothing but himself.   In all I contemplate independent beings, that are such, and are for themselves, only in the very same way that I am for myself ; in them I see existing free unity of self with others, and existing by virtue of me and by virtue of the others alike. Them as myself, myself as them.[1]

[1] Let me illustrate from our great poet :

> So they loved, as love in twain
> Had the essence but in one ;
> Two distincts, division none :
> Number there in love was slain.
>
> Hearts remote yet not asunder ;
> Distance, and no space was seen—
> So between them love did shine. . . .
> Either was the other's mine.
>
> Property was thus appalled,
> That the self was not the same ;

' In a free people, therefore, reason is realized in truth ; it is present living mind, and in this not only does the individual find his destination, i. e. his universal and singular essence, promulgated and ready to his hand as an outward existence, but he himself is this essence, and has also reached and fulfilled his destination. Hence the wisest men of antiquity have given judgement that wisdom and virtue consist in living agreeably to the Ethos of one's people.'— (Hegel, *Phänom. d. G., Werke*, ii. 256–8 (1841).)

Once let us take the point of view which regards the community as the real moral organism, which in its members knows and wills itself, and sees the individual to be real just so far as the universal self is in his self, as he in it, and we get the solution of most, if not all, of our previous difficulties. There is here no need to ask and by some scientific process find out what is moral, for morality exists all round us, and faces us, if need be, with a categorical imperative, while it surrounds us on the other side with an atmosphere of love.

The belief in this real moral organism is the one solution of ethical problems. It breaks down the antithesis of despotism and individualism ; it denies them, while it preserves the truth of both. The truth of individualism is saved, because, unless we have intense life and self-consciousness in the members of the state, the whole state is ossified. The truth of despotism is saved, because, unless the member

> Single nature's double name
> Neither two nor one was called.
>
> Reason, in itself confounded,
> Saw division grow together :
> To themselves yet either neither
> Simple were so well compounded,
>
> That it cried, How true a twain
> Seemeth this concordant one !
> Love hath reason, reason none,
> If what parts can so remain.
> —(*The Phœnix and the Turtle.*)

Surely philosophy does not reach its end till the ´ reason of reason ' is adequate to the ' reason of love '.

realizes the whole by and in himself, he fails to reach his own individuality. Considered in the main, the best communities are those which have the best men for their members, and the best men are the members of the best communities. Circle as this is, it is not a vicious circle. The two problems of the best man and best state are two sides, two distinguishable aspects of the one problem, how to realize in human nature the perfect unity of homogeneity and specification ; and when we see that each of these without the other is unreal, then we see that (speaking in general) the welfare of the state and the welfare of its individuals are questions which it is mistaken and ruinous to separate. Personal morality and political and social institutions can not exist apart, and (in general) the better the one the better the other. The community is moral, because it realizes personal morality ; personal morality is moral, because and in so far as it realizes the moral whole.

It is here we find a *partial* answer to the complaint of our day on the dwindling of human nature. The higher the organism (we are told), the more are its functions specified, and hence narrowed. The man becomes a machine, or the piece of a machine ; and, though the world grows, 'the individual withers'. On this we may first remark that, if what is meant is that, the more centralized the system, the more narrow and monotonous is the life of the member, that is a very questionable assertion. If it be meant that the individual's life can be narrowed to 'file-packing', or the like, without detriment to the intensity of the life of the whole, that is even more questionable. If again it be meant that in many cases we have a one-sided specification, which, despite the immediate stimulus of particular function, implies ultimate loss of life to the body,[1] that, I think, probably is so, but it is doubtful if we are compelled to think it always must be so. But the root of the whole complaint is a false view of things, which we have briefly noticed above (pp. 79–80). The moral organism is not a mere animal organism. In the

---

[1] [Is the body the social organism or the individual man ? I think the first is meant, but it really is *both*.]

latter (it is no novel remark) the member is not aware of itself as such, while in the former it knows itself, and therefore knows the whole in itself. The narrow external function of the man is not the whole man. He has a life which we can not see with our eyes; and there is no duty so mean that it is not the realization of this, and knowable as such. What counts is not the visible outer work so much as the spirit in which it is done.[1] The breadth of my life is not measured by the multitude of my pursuits, nor the space I take up amongst other men; but by the fullness of the whole life which I know as mine. It is true that less now depends on each of us, as this or that man; it is not true that our individuality is therefore lessened, that therefore we have less in us.

Let us now consider our point of view in relation to certain antagonistic ideas; and first against the common error that there is something 'right in itself' for me to do, in the sense that either there must be some absolute rule of morality the same for all persons without distinction of times and places, or else that all morality is 'relative', and hence no morality. Let us begin by remarking that there is no such fixed code or rule of right. It is abundantly clear that the morality of one time is not that of another time, that the men considered good in one age might in another age not be thought good, and what would be right for us here might be mean and base in another country, and what would be wrong for us here might there be our bounden duty. This is clear fact, which is denied only in the interest of a foregone conclusion. The motive to deny it is the belief that it is fatal to morality. If what is right here is wrong there, then all morality (such is the notion) becomes chance and convention, and so ceases. But 'my station and its duties' holds that *unless* morals varied, there could be no morality; that a morality which was *not* relative would be futile, and I should have to ask for something 'more relative than this'.

[1] [But here, if so, we *seem* driven to justification by faith; cf. p. 182, l. 29.]

Let us explain. We hold that man is φύσει πολιτικός, that apart from the community he is θεὸς ἢ θηρίον, no man at all. We hold again that the true nature of man, the oneness of homogeneity and specification, is being wrought out in history; in short, we believe in evolution. The process of evolution is the humanizing of the bestial foundation of man's nature by carrying out in it the true idea of man; in other words, by realizing man as an infinite whole (p. 74). This realization is possible only by the individual's living as member in a higher life, and this higher life is slowly developed in a series of stages. Starting from and on the basis of animal nature, humanity has worked itself out by gradual advances of specification and systematization; and any other progress would, in the world we know, have been impossible. The notion that full-fledged moral ideas fell down from heaven is contrary to all the facts with which we are acquainted. If they had done so, it would have been for their own sake; for by us they certainly could not have been perceived, much less applied. At any given period to know more than he did, man must have been more than he was; for a human being is nothing if he is not the son of his time; and he must realize himself as that, or he will not do it at all.

Morality is ' relative', but is none the less real. At every stage there is the solid fact of a world so far moralized. There is an objective morality in the accomplished will of the past and present, a higher self worked out by the infinite pain, the sweat and blood of generations, and now given to me by free grace and in love and faith as a sacred trust. It comes to me as the truth of my own nature, and the power and the law, which is stronger and higher than any caprice or opinion of my own.

' Evolution', in this sense of the word, gives us over neither to chance nor alien necessity, for it is that self-realization which is the progressive conquest of both. But, on another understanding of the term, we can not help asking, Is this still the case, and is 'my station' a tenable point of view?

Wholly tenable, in the form in which we have stated it,

it is not. For if, in saying Morality has developed, all we mean is that something has happened different from earlier events, that human society has changed, and that the alterations, so far as we know them, are more or less of a certain sort; if 'progress' signifies that an advance has been set going and is kept up by chance in an unknown direction; that the higher is, in short, what *is* and what before was not, and that what will be, of whatever sort it is, will still be a step in progress; if, in short, the movement of history towards a goal is mere illusion, and the stages of that movement are nothing but the successes of what from time to time somehow happens to be best suited to the chance of circumstances—then it is clear in the first place that, teleology being banished, such words as evolution [1] and progress

[1] With respect to 'evolution' I may remark in passing that, though this word may of course be used to stand for anything whatever, yet for all that it has a meaning of its own, which those who care to use words, not merely with *a* meaning, but also with *their* meaning, would do well to consider. To try to exhibit all that is contained in it would be a serious matter, but we may call attention to a part. And first, 'evolution', 'development', 'progress', all imply something identical throughout, a subject of the evolution, which is one and the same. If what is there at the beginning is not there at the end, and the same as what was there at the beginning, then evolution is a word with no meaning. Something must evolve itself, and that something, which is the end, must also be the beginning. It must be what moves itself to the end, and must be the end which is the 'because' of the motion. Evolution must evolve itself to itself, progress itself go forward to a goal which is itself, development bring out nothing but what was in, and bring it out, not from external compulsion, but *because* it is in.

And further, unless what is at the end is different from that which was at the beginning, there is no evolution. That which develops, or evolves itself, both is and is not. It *is*, or it could not be *it* which develops, and which at the end has developed. It *is not*, or else it could not become. It becomes what it is; and, if this is nonsense, then evolution is nonsense.

Evolution is a contradiction; and, when the contradiction ceases, the evolution ceases. The process is a contradiction, and only *because* it is a contradiction can it be a process. So long as progress lasts, contradiction lasts; so long as anything becomes, it is not. To be realized is to cease to progress. To be at the end (in one sense) is to lose the end (in another), and that because (in both senses) all then comes to the end. For the process is a contradiction, and the solution of the contradiction is in every sense the *end* of the process.

have lost their own meaning, and that to speak of humanity realizing itself in history, and of myself finding in that movement the truth of myself worked out, would be simply to delude oneself with hollow phrases.

Thus far, we must say that on such a view of 'development' the doctrine of 'my station' is grievously curtailed. But is it destroyed? Not wholly; though sorely mutilated, it still keeps its ground. We have rejected teleology, but have not yet embraced individualism. We still believe that the universal self is more than a collection or an idea, that it is reality, and that apart from it the 'individuals' are the fictions of a theory. We have still the fact of the one self particularized in its many members; and the right and duty of gaining self-realization through the real universal is still as certain as is the impossibility of gaining it otherwise. And so 'my station' is after all a position, not indeed satisfactory, but not yet untenable.

But if the larger doctrine be the truth, if evolution is more than a tortured phrase, and progress to a goal no mere idea but an actual fact, then history is the working out of the true human nature through various incomplete stages towards completion, and 'my station' is the one satisfactory view of morals. Here (as we have seen) all morality is and must be 'relative', because the essence of realization is evolution through stages, and hence existence in some one stage which is not final; here, on the other hand, all morality is 'absolute', because in every stage the essence of man *is* realized, however imperfectly: and yet again the distinction of right in itself against relative morality is not banished, because, from the point of view of a higher stage, we can see that lower stages failed to realize the truth completely enough, and also, mixed and one with their realization, did present features contrary to the true nature of man as we now see it. Yet herein the morality of every stage is justified for that stage; and the demand for a code of right in itself, apart from any stage, is seen to be the asking for an impossibility.

The next point we come to is the question, How do I get to know in particular what is right and wrong? And here again we find a strangely erroneous preconception. It is thought that moral philosophy has to accomplish this task for us; and the conclusion lies near at hand, that any system which will not do this is worthless. Well, we first remark, and with some confidence, that there cannot be a moral philosophy which will tell us what in particular we are to do, and also that it is not the business of philosophy to do so. All philosophy has to do is 'to understand what is', and moral philosophy has to understand morals which exist, not to make them or give directions for making them. Such a notion is simply ludicrous. Philosophy in general has not to anticipate the discoveries of the particular sciences nor the evolution of history; the philosophy of religion has not to make a new religion or teach an old one, but simply to understand the religious consciousness; and aesthetic has not to produce works of fine art, but to theorize the beautiful which it finds; political philosophy has not to play tricks with the state, but to understand it; and ethics has not to make the world moral, but to reduce to theory the morality current in the world. If we want it to do anything more, so much the worse for us; for it can not possibly construct new morality, and, even if it could to any extent codify what exists (a point on which I do not enter), yet it surely is clear that in cases of collision of duties it would not help you to know what to do. Who would go to a learned theologian, as such, in a practical religious difficulty; to a system of aesthetic for suggestions on the handling of an artistic theme; to a physiologist, as such, for a diagnosis and prescription; to a political philosopher in practical politics; or to a psychologist in an intrigue of any kind? All these persons no doubt *might* be the best to go to, but that would not be because they were the best theorists, but because they were more. In short, the view which thinks moral philosophy is to supply us with particular moral prescriptions confuses science with art, and confuses, besides, reflective with intuitive judgement. That which tells us what in particular is right and wrong is not reflection but intuition.[1]

We know what is right in a particular case by what we may call an immediate judgement, or an intuitive subsumption. These phrases are perhaps not very luminous, and the matter of the 'intuitive understanding' in general is doubtless difficult, and the special character of moral judgements not easy to define; and I do not say that I am in a position to explain these subjects at all, nor, I think, could any one do so, except at considerable length. But the point that I do wish to establish here is, I think, not at all obscure. The reader has first to recognize that moral judgements are not discursive; next, that nevertheless they do start from and rest on a certain basis; and then if he puts the two together, he will see that they involve what he may call the 'intuitive understanding', or by any other name, so long as he keeps in sight the two elements and holds them together.

On the head that moral judgements are not discursive, no one, I think, will wish me to stay long. If the reader attends to the facts he will not want anything else; and if he does not, I confess I can not prove my point. In practical morality no doubt we *may* reflect on our principles, but I think it is not too much to say that we *never* do so, except where we have come upon a difficulty of particular application. If any one thinks that a man's *ordinary* judgement, 'this is right or wrong,' comes from the having a rule *before* the mind and bringing the particular case under it, he may be right; and I can not try to show that he is wrong. I can only leave it to the reader to judge for himself. We say we 'see' and we 'feel' in these cases, not we 'conclude'. We prize the advice of persons who can give us no reasons for what they say. There is a general belief that the having a

---

[1] I must ask the reader here not to think of 'Intuitionalism', or of 'Organs of the Absolute', or of anything else of the sort. 'Intuitive' is used here as the opposite of 'reflective' or 'discursive', 'intuition' as the opposite of 'reasoning' or 'explicit inferring'. If the reader dislike the word, he may substitute 'perception' or 'sense', if he will; but then he must remember that neither are to exclude the intellectual, the understanding and its implicit judgements and inferences.

reason for all your actions is pedantic and absurd.   There is a general belief that to try to have reasons for all that you do is sometimes very dangerous.   Not only the woman but the man who ' deliberates' may be ' lost '.   First thoughts are often the best,[1] and if once you begin to argue with the devil you are in a perilous state.   And I think I may add (though I do it in fear) that women in general are remarkable for the fineness of their moral perceptions [2] and the quickness of their judgements, and yet are or (let me save myself by saying) ' may be' not remarkable for corresponding discursive ability.

Taking for granted then that our ordinary way of judging in morals is not by reflection and explicit reasoning, we have now to point to the other side of the fact, viz. that these judgements are not mere isolated impressions, but stand in an intimate and vital relation to a certain system, which is their basis.   Here again we must ask the reader to pause, if in doubt, and consider the facts for himself.   Different men, who have lived in different times and countries, judge or would judge a fresh case in morals differently.   Why is this?   There is probably no ' why ' before the mind of either when he judges ; but *we* perhaps can say, ' I know why A said so and B so ', because we find some general rule or principle different in each, and in each the basis of the judgement.   Different people in the same society may judge points differently, and we sometimes know why.   It is because A is struck by one aspect of the case, B by another ; and one principle is (not *before*, but) *in* A's mind when he judges, and another in B's.   Each has subsumed, but under a different head ; the one perhaps justice, the other gratitude.   Every man has the morality he has made his own in his mind, and he ' sees ' or ' feels ' or ' judges '

---

[1] It is right to remark that second thoughts are often the offspring of wrong desire, but not always so.   They may arise from collisions, and in these cases we see how little is to be done by theoretical deduction.

[2] Not, perhaps, on *all* matters.   Nor, again, will it do to say that *everywhere* women are pre-eminently intuitive, and men discursive.   But in *practical* matters there seems not much doubt that it is so.

accordingly, though he does not reason explicitly from data to a conclusion.

I think this will be clear to the reader; and so we must say that on their perceptive or intellectual side (and that, the reader must not forget, is the one side that we are considering) our moral judgements are intuitive subsumptions.

To the question, How am I to know what is right? the answer must be, By the αἴσθησις of the φρόνιμος; and the φρόνιμος is the man who has identified his will with the moral spirit of the community, and judges accordingly. If an immoral course be suggested to him, he 'feels' or 'sees' at once that the act is not in harmony with a good will, and he does not do this by saying, 'this is a breach of rule A, *therefore*, &c.'; but the first thing he is aware of is that he 'does not like it'; and what he has done, without being aware of it, is (at least in most cases) to seize the quality of the act, that quality being a general quality. Actions of a particular kind he does not like, and he has instinctively referred the particular act to that kind. What is right is perceived in the same way; courses suggest themselves, and one is approved of, because intuitively judged to be of a certain kind, which kind represents a principle of the good will.

If a man is to know what is right, he should have imbibed by precept, and still more by example, the spirit of his community, its general and special beliefs as to right and wrong, and, with this whole embodied in his mind, should particularize it in any new case, not by a reflective deduction, but by an intuitive subsumption, which does not know that it is a subsumption;[1] by a carrying out of the self into a

[1] Every act has, of course, many sides, many relations, many 'points of view from which it may be regarded', and so many qualities. There are always several principles under which you can bring it, and hence there is not the smallest difficulty in exhibiting it as the realization of either right or wrong. No act in the world is without *some* side capable of being subsumed under a good rule; e. g. theft is economy, care for one's relations, protest against bad institutions, really doing oneself but justice, &c.; and, if all else fails, it probably saves us from something worse, and therefore is good. Cowardice is prudence and a duty,

new case, wherein what is before the mind is the case and not the self to be carried out, and where it is indeed the whole that feels and sees, but all that is seen is seen in the form of *this* case, *this* point, *this* instance. Precept is good, but example is better; for by a series of particulars (as such forgotten) we get the general spirit, we identify ourselves

courage rashness and a vice, and so on. The casuist must have little ingenuity, if there is anything he fails to justify or condemn according to his order. And the vice of casuistry is that, attempting to decide the particulars of morality by the deductions of the reflective under-standing, it at once degenerates into finding a good reason for what you mean to do. You have principles of all sorts, and the case has all sorts of sides; *which* side is the essential side, and which principle is *the* principle *here*, rests in the end on your mere private choice; and that is determined by heaven knows what. No *reasoning* will tell you which the moral point of view *here* is. Hence the necessary immorality and the ruinous effects of practical casuistry. (Casuistry used not as a guide to conduct, but as a means to the theoretical investigation of moral principles, the casuistry used to discover the principle *from* the fact, and not to deduce the fact from the principle—is, of course, quite another thing.) Our moralists do not like casuistry; but if the current notion that moral philosophy has to tell you what to do is well founded, then casuistry, so far as I can see, at once follows, or should follow.

But the ordinary moral judgement is not discursive. It does not look to the right and left, and, considering the case from all its sides, consciously subsume under one principle. When the case is presented, it fixes on one quality in the act, referring that unconsciously to one principle, in which it feels the whole of itself, and sees that whole in a single side of the act. So far as right and wrong are concerned, it can perceive nothing but *this* quality of *this* case, and anything else it refuses to try to perceive. Practical morality means singlemindedness, the having one idea; it means what in other spheres* would be the greatest narrowness. Point out to a man of simple morals that the case has other sides than the one he instinctively fixes on, and he suspects you wish to corrupt him. And so you probably would if you went on. Apart from bad example, the readiest way to debauch the morality of any one is, on the side of principle, to confuse them by forcing them to see in all moral and immoral acts other sides and points of view, which alter the character of each; and, on the side of parti-culars, to warp their instinctive apprehension through personal affection for yourself or some other individual.

---

[1] * [Not wholly so, for in the intellectual world also the relevant, and here essential, is often seized intuitively and not reflectively]

on the sides both of will and judgement with the basis, which basis (be it remembered) has not got to be explicit.[1]

There are a number of questions which invite consideration[2] here, but we can not stop. We wished to point out briefly the character of our common moral judgements. This (on the intellectual side) is the way in which they are ordinarily made; and, in the main, there is not much practical difficulty. What is moral *in any particular given case* is seldom doubtful.[3] Society pronounces beforehand;[4] or, after some one course has been taken, it can say whether it was right or not; though society can not generalize much, and, if asked to reflect, is helpless and becomes incoherent. But I do not say there are no cases where the morally-minded man has to doubt; most certainly such do arise, though not so many as some people think, far fewer than some would be glad to think. A very large number arise from reflection, which wants to act from an explicit principle, and so begins to abstract and divide, and, thus becoming one-sided, makes the relative absolute. Apart from this, however, collisions must take place; and here there is no guide whatever but the intuitive judgement of oneself or others.[5]

This intuition must not be confounded with what is sometimes mis-called 'conscience'. It is not mere individual opinion or caprice. It presupposes the morality of the

[1] It is worth while in this connexion to refer to the custom some persons have (and find useful) of calling before the mind, when in doubt, a known person of high character and quick judgement, and thinking what they would have done. This no doubt both delivers the mind from private considerations and also is to act in the spirit of the other person (so far as we know it), i. e. from the general basis of his acts (certainly *not* the mere memory of his particular acts, or such memory plus inference).

[2] One of these would be as to how progress in morality is made.

[3] [This is too optimistic.]

[4] ['Society', see pp. 173–4, 222–3.]

[5] I may remark on this (after Erdmann, and I suppose Plato) that collisions of duties are avoided mostly by each man keeping to his own immediate duties, and not trying to see from the point of view of other stations than his own.

community as its basis, and is subject to the approval thereof.   Here, if anywhere, the idea of universal and impersonal
morality is realized.   For the final arbiters are the φρόνιμοι,
persons with a will to do right, and not full of reflections and
theories.   If they fail you, you must judge for yourself, but
practically they seldom do fail you.   Their private peculiarities
neutralize each other, and the result is an intuition which does
not belong merely to this or that man or collection of men.
'Conscience' is the antipodes of this.   It wants you to have
no law but yourself, and to be better than the world.   But
this intuition tells you that, if you could be as good as your
world, you would be better than most likely you are, and
that to wish to be better than the world is to be already on
the threshold of immorality.

This perhaps 'is a hard saying', but it is least hard to
those who know life best ; it is intolerable to those mainly
who, from inexperience or preconceived theories, can not
see the world as it is.   Explained it may be by saying that
enthusiasm for good dies away—the ideal fades—

> Dem Herrlichsten, was auch der Geist empfangen,
> Drängt immer fremd und fremder Stoff sich an ;

but better perhaps if we say that those who have seen most
of the world (not one side of it)—old people of no one-sided
profession nor of immoral life—know most also how much
good there is in it.   They are tolerant of new theories and
youthful opinions that everything would be better upside
down, because they know that this also is as it should be,
and that the world gets good even from these.   They are
intolerant only of those who are old enough, and should be
wise enough, to know better than that they know better
than the world ; for in such people they can not help seeing
the self-conceit which is pardonable only in youth.

Let us be clear.   What is that wish to be better, and to
make the world better, which is on the threshold of immorality ?   What is the 'world' in this sense ?   It is the morality
already existing ready to hand in laws, institutions, social

usages, moral opinions and feelings. This is the element in
which the young are brought up. It has given moral content to themselves, and it is the only source of such content.[1]
It is not wrong, it is a duty, to take the best that there is,
and to live up to the best. It is not wrong, it is a duty,
standing on the basis of the existing, and in harmony with
its general spirit, to try and make not only oneself but also
the world better, or rather, and in preference, one's own
world better. But it is another thing, starting from oneself,
from ideals in one's head, to set oneself and them against
the moral world. The moral world with its social institutions, &c., is a fact; it is real; our 'ideals' are not real.
'But we will make them real.' We should consider what
we are, and what the world is. We should learn to see the
great moral fact in the world, and to reflect on the likelihood
of our private 'ideal' being anything more than an abstraction,
which, because an abstraction, is all the better fitted for our
heads, and all the worse fitted for actual existence.

We should consider whether the encouraging oneself in
having opinions of one's own, in the sense of thinking differently from the world on moral subjects, be not, in any person
other than a heaven-born prophet, sheer self-conceit. And
though the disease may spend itself in the harmless and
even entertaining sillinesses by which we are advised to
assert our social 'individuality', yet still the having theories
of one's own in the face of the world is not far from having
practice in the same direction; and if the latter is (as it often
must be) immorality, the former has certainly but stopped at
the threshold.

But the moral organism is strong against both. The
person anxious to throw off the yoke of custom and develop
his 'individuality' in startling directions, passes as a rule into
the common Philistine, and learns that Philistinism is after
all a good thing. And the licentious young man, anxious
for pleasure at any price, who, without troubling himself
about 'principles', does put into practice the principles of
the former person, finds after all that the self within him

[1] [This forgets literature for one thing.]

can be satisfied only with that from whence it came.   And some fine morning the dream is gone, the enchanted bower is a hideous phantasm, and the despised and common reality has become the ideal.

We have thus seen the community to be the real moral idea, to be stronger than the theories and the practice of its members against it, and to give us self-realization.   And this is indeed limitation; it bids us say farewell to visions of superhuman morality, to ideal societies, and to practical 'ideals' generally.   But perhaps the unlimited is not the perfect, nor the true ideal.   And, leaving 'ideals' out of sight, it is quite clear that if anybody wants to realize himself as a perfect man without trying to be a perfect member of his country and all his smaller communities, he makes what all sane persons would admit to be a great mistake. There is no more fatal enemy than theories which are not also facts; and when people inveigh against the vulgar anti-thesis of the two, they themselves should accept their own doctrine, and give up the harbouring of theories of what should be and is not.   Until they do that, the vulgar are in the right; for a theory of that which (only) is to be, is a theory of that which in fact is not, and that I suppose is only a theory.

There is nothing better than my station and its duties, nor anything higher or more truly beautiful.   It holds and will hold its own against the worship of the 'individual', whatever form that may take.   It is strong against frantic theories and vehement passions, and in the end it triumphs over the fact, and can smile at the literature, even of senti-mentalism, however fulsome in its impulsive setting out, or sour in its disappointed end.   It laughs at its frenzied apotheosis of the yet unsatisfied passion it calls love; and at that embitterment too which has lost its illusions, and yet can not let them go—with its kindness for the genius too clever in general to do anything in particular, and its adoration of star-gazing virgins with souls above their spheres, whose wish to be something in the world takes the form of wanting to do something with it, and who in the end do badly what they might have done in the beginning well ; and, worse than all, its cynical contempt for what deserves only pity, sacrifice of a life for work to the best of one's lights, a sacrifice despised not simply because it has failed, but because it is stupid, and uninteresting, and altogether unsentimental.

And all these books (ah! how many) it puts into the one scale, and with them the writers of them ; and into the other scale it puts three such lines as these :

> One place performs like any other place
> The proper service every place on earth
> Was framed to furnish man with ——

κόκκυ, μεθεῖτε· καὶ πολύ γε κατωτέρω
χωρεῖ τὸ τοῦδε.

> Have we still to ask,
> καὶ τί ποτ᾽ ἐστὶ ταἴτιον ;[1]

———————

The theory which we have just exhibited (more or less in our own way), and over which perhaps we have heated our-selves a little, seems to us a great advance on anything we have had before, and indeed in the main to be satisfactory. It satisfies us, because in it our wills attain their realization ; the content of the will is a whole, is systematic ; and it is the same whole on both sides. On the outside and inside alike we have the same universal will in union with the particular personality ; and in the identity of inside and outside in one single process we have reached the point where the ' is to be ', with all its contradictions, disappears, or remains but as a moment in a higher ' is '.

None the less, however, must we consider this satisfaction neither ultimate, nor all-inclusive, nor anything but pre-carious. If put forth as that beyond which we do not need to go, as the end in itself, it is open to very serious objections, some of which we must now develop.

———————

[1] Arist. *Frogs*, 1384. *Dionysos.*—Cuckoo ! Let go the scales ; Aeschylos' side goes down, oh, much much the lowest. *Euripides.*— Why, what ever is the reason ?

The point upon which 'my station and its duties' prided itself most was that it had got rid of the opposition of 'ought' and 'is' in both its forms; viz. the opposition of the outer world to the 'ought' in me, and the opposition of my particular self to the 'ought' in general. We shall have to see that it has not succeeded in doing either, or at least not completely.

1. Within the sphere of my station and its duties the opposition is not vanquished; for,

(a) It is impossible to maintain the doctrine of what may be called 'justification by sight'. The self can not be so seen to be identified with the moral whole that the bad self disappears. (i) In the moral man the consciousness of that unity can not be present always, but only when he is fully engaged in satisfactory work. Then, I think, it is present: but when he is not so engaged, and the bad self shows itself, he can scarcely be self-contented, or, if he is so, scarcely because he *sees* that the bad self is unreal. He can only forget his faults when he is too busy to think of them; and he can hardly be so always. And he can not always *see* that his faults do not matter to the moral order of things: when it comes to that he can only trust. Further, (ii) the more or less immoral man who, because of past offences, is now *unable* to perform his due function, or to perform it duly, can not always in his work gain once more the self-content he has lost; because that very work tells him of what should have been, and now is not and will not be: and the habits he has formed perhaps drag him still into the faults that made them. We can not, without taking a low point of view, ask that this man's life, morally considered, should be more than a struggle; and it would be the most untrue Pharisaism or indifferentism to call him immoral because he struggles, and so far as he struggles. Here justification by sight is out of the question.

(b) Again, the moral man need not find himself realized in the world. (i) It is necessary to remark that the community in which he is a member may be in a confused or rotten condition, so that in it right and might do not always go together. And (ii) the very best community can only ensure that correspondence in the gross ; it can not do so in every single detail. (iii) There are afflictions for which no moral organism has balm or physician, though it has alleviation ; and these can mar the life of any man. (iv) The member may have to sacrifice himself for the community. In none of these cases can he *see* his realization ; and here again the contradiction breaks out, and we must wrap ourselves in a virtue which is our own and not the world's, or seek a higher doctrine by which, through faith and through faith alone, self-suppression issues in a higher self-realization.

2. Within the sphere of my station and its duties we see the contradiction is but partially solved : and the second objection is also very serious. You can not confine a man to his station and its duties. Whether in another sense that formula would be all-embracing is a further question : but in the sense in which we took it, function in a 'visible' community, it certainly is not so. And we must remark here in passing that, if we accept (as I think we must) the fact that the essence of a man involves identity with others, the question what the final reality of that identity is, is still left unanswered : we should still have to ask what is the higher whole in which the individual is a function, and in which the relative wholes subsist, and to inquire whether that community is, or can be, a visible community at all.

Passing by this, however, let us develop our objection. A man can not take his morality simply from the moral world he is in, for many reasons. (a) That moral world, being in a state of historical development, is not and can not be self-consistent ; and the man must thus stand before and above inconsistencies, and reflect on them. This must lead to the knowledge that the world is not altogether as it should be, and to a process of trying to make it better. With this co-operates (b) what may be called cosmopolitan morality. Men nowadays know to some extent what is thought right and wrong in other communities now, and what has been thought at other times ; and this leads to a notion of goodness not of any particular time and country. For numbers of persons no doubt this is unnecessary; but it is necessary for others, and they have the moral ideal (with the psychological origin of which we are not concerned) of a good man who is not good as member of this or that community, but who realizes himself in whatever community he finds himself. This, however, must mean also that he is not perfectly realized in any particular station.

3. We have seen that the moral man can to a certain extent distinguish his moral essence from his particular function; and now a third objection at once follows, that the content of the ideal self does not fall wholly within any community, is in short *not* merely the ideal of a perfect social being. The making myself better does not always directly involve relation to others. The production of truth and beauty (together with what is called 'culture') may be recognized as a duty; and it will be very hard to reduce it in all cases to a duty of any station that I can see. If we like to say that these duties to myself are duties to humanity,[1] that perhaps is true; but we must remember that humanity is not a visible community. If you mean by it only past, present, and future human beings, then you can not show that in all cases my culture is of use (directly or indirectly) to any one but myself. Unless you are prepared to restrict science and fine art to what is useful, i. e. to common arts and 'accomplishments', you can not hope to 'verify' such an assertion. You are in the region of belief, not knowledge; and this equally whether your belief is true or false. We must say then that, in aiming at truth and beauty, we are trying to realize ourself not as a member of any visible community.

And, finally, against this ideal self the particular person remains and must remain imperfect. The ideal self is not fully realized in us, in any way that we can see. We are aware of a ceaseless process, it is well if we can add progress, in which the false private self is constantly subdued but never disappears. And it never can disappear: we are

---

[1] ['Humanity', pp. 231–2. Is all morality social? Cf. pp. 214, 231–2.]

never realized. The contradiction remains; and not to feel it demands something lower or something higher than a moral point of view.

Starting from these objections, our next Essay must try to make more clear what is involved in them, and to raise in a sharper form the difficulties as to the nature of morality. And our Concluding Remarks will again take up the same thread, after we have in some measure investigated in Essay VII the difficult problems of the bad self and selfishness.

NOTE TO ESSAY V

RIGHTS AND DUTIES

To handle this subject properly, more space would be wanted than I have at command. But I will make some remarks shortly and in outline.

A great to-do has been made about the ambiguity of the word 'right'; as I think, needlessly. Right is the rule, and what is conformable to the rule, whether that rule be physical or mental; e. g. a right line, a 'right English bull-dog' (Swift), a right conclusion, a right action.

Right is, generally, the expression of the universal. It is the emphasis of the universal side in the relation of particular and universal. It implies particulars, and therefore possibility of discrepancy between them and the universal. Hence right means law; which law may be carried out or merely stated. 'Is it right to do this?' means 'is the universal realized in this?' 'Have I a right?' means 'am I in this the expression of law?'

In the moral sphere, with which alone we are concerned, right means always the relation of the universal to the particular will. The emphasis is on the universal. Possibility of discrepancy with a conscious subject makes law here *command*.

Command is the simple proposal of an action (or abstinence) to me by another will, as the content of that will. Or, from the side of the commander, it is the willing by me of some state of another will, such willing being presented by me as a fact to that will. Threat is not the essence of command: command need not imply the holding forth or the anticipation of consequences.

To *have* rights is not merely to be the object with respect to which commands (positive or prohibitory) are addressed to others. If that were so, inanimate matter would have rights; e. g. the very dirt in the road would 'have a right' to be taken up or let lie—and this is barbarous. To have rights is to be (or to be presumed to be) capable of realizing the universal command consciously as such.[1] This answers

[1] 'I have rights against others', or 'I have a right to this or that from others', means, (1) it is right, it is the expression of the universal, that they should do this or that in reference to me: I am the object of

the question, Has a beast rights? He is the object of duties, not the subject of rights. Right is the universal in its relation to a will capable of recognizing it as such, whether it remain mere command or is also carried out in act.

Wherever in the moral world you have law you have also right and rights. These may be real or ideal. The first are the will of the state or society, the second the will of the ideal-social or non-social ideal. (*Vide* Essay VI.)

It is in order to secure the existence of rights in the acts of particular wills that compulsion is used. But compulsion is not necessary to the general and abstract definition of right, and it can not be immediately deduced from it.

What is duty? It is simply the other side of right. It is the same relation, viewed from the other pole or moment. It is the relation of the particular to the universal, with the emphasis on the particular. It is *my* will in its affirmative relation to the objective will. Right is the universal, existing for thought alone or also carried out. Duty is my will, either merely thought of as realizing this universal, or actually also doing so. 'This is my duty' means 'in this I identify, or am thought of as identifying, myself with right'.

Duty, like right, implies possible discordance of particular and universal. Like right, too, it implies more than this. It implies the consciousness (or presumed capacity for consciousness) of the relation of my will to the universal as the right. Hence a beast has no duties in the proper sense. If he has, then he has also rights.

Right is the universal will implying particular will. It is the objective side implying a subjective side, i. e. duty. Duty is the particular will implying a universal will. It is the subjective side implying an objective side, i. e. right. But the two sides are inseparable. No right without duty; no duty without right and rights. (To this we shall return.)

Right and duty are sides of a single whole. This whole is the good. Rights and duties imply the identity, and non-identity, of the particular and universal wills. Right may remain a mere command, duty a mere 'ought to be', the non-agreement of the particular and universal. They are both

their duty. But this by itself does not give me 'rights'. To 'have a right' to anything from another, I must (2) be a subject which knows the universal as such, both (*a*) in its *immediate* relation to my will, in its expression through my acts; and (*b*) also here in its expression through the acts of others, which acts may concern me. When my will as the universal, and the universal as my will, calls for these acts, then I 'have a right' to them in the proper sense; but not otherwise.

abstractions. They are both, if fixed and isolated one from the other, self-contradictions. Each by itself is a mere ' is to be ', each a willed idea, which, so long as apart from the other, remains a *mere*, i.e. a *not*-willed, idea. Each is a single side of one and the same relation, fixed apart from the other side. In the good the sides come together, and in the whole first cease to be abstractions and gain real existence. The right is carried out in duty. The duty realizes itself in the right.

But in the good rights and duties as such disappear. There is no more mere right or mere duty, no more particular and universal as such, no external relation of the two. They are now sides and elements in one whole; and, if they appear, it is only as, within the movement and life of the whole, here one element and there another has its relative emphasis. But outside the whole their reality fades into ' mere idea', into legend and fable.

Rights and duties do not exist outside the moral world; and that world does not exist where there is not a sphere of inner morality, however immediate, the consciousness, however vague, of the relation of the private will to the universal, whether that universal be presented as outer (in the shape of tribal custom or of some individual) or again as inner. Where there is no morality there is no right: where there is no right there are no rights. Just so, where there are no rights there is no right, and where no right there no morality. Inner morality without an objective right and wrong is a self-delusion. Right and rights outside morality are a mere fiction.

It is here that every partial theory of morals and politics is wrecked and seen to be worthless. False theories of right either (1) fail to get to any objective universal except by some fond invention (of contract), which, besides being an invention, presupposes what it is to create. (A contract outside the sphere of right and morality is nonsense.) Or (2) they take an objective universal (as positive law, will of the monarch, or what seems most convenient to the majority); and here they fail because their right is mere force, and is not moral, not right at all; and hence they can not show that I am *in* the right to obey it, or in the wrong to disobey it, but merely that, if I do not obey it, it may (or may not) be inconvenient for me. So again in morals they either (1) posit a universal, such as the will of the Deity or of other human beings; and this fails because in it I do not affirm *my* self; or else (2) there is nothing anywhere objective and universal at all; and here I affirm nothing *but* myself. In either case there is no duty and no morality.

'But rights and duties', we shall be told, 'collide.' They collide only as rights do with rights or duties with duties. Rights and duties of one sphere collide with those of another sphere, and again within each sphere they collide in different persons, and again in one and the same person. But that right as such can collide with duty as such is impossible. There is no right which is not a duty, no duty which is not a right. In either case right would cease to be right, and duty duty.

This will be denied. It will be said, (1) There are duties without rights; (2) rights without duties. As to the first (1) we say, If we have not a right to do anything, it is not right for us. If it is not right for us, then it is not our duty. It is quite true that *moral* duty may not be *legal* right, nor *legal* duty *moral* right, but this is not to the point.

As to the second (2), it seems harder to see that where I have no duties I have no rights. In the spheres of the state, of society, of ideal morality, I have a right to do this and not that, that and not the other. But can it be said that all these things that I have a right to do are my duties? Is not that nonsense?

No doubt there is much truth in this. It is almost as bad to have nothing *but* duties as it is to have no duties at all. For free individual self-development we must have both elements. Where the universal is all there is ossification; where the particular is all there is dissolution; in neither case life.

Is it true then that there are rights where there are no duties? No. In a sense, rights are wider than duties: but what does this mean? Does it mean there are rights outside the moral sphere? Certainly not. We shall see (Essay VI) that there is no limit to the moral sphere; and if there were a limit, then outside that rights would cease to be rights. 'More rights than duties' then must be true, if at all, *within* the moral sphere. Does it hold there that there are more rights than duties? It is not a very hard puzzle. To make it easier let us double it, and say 'there are more duties than rights'. A man, for instance, has a certain indivisible sum to spend in charity. He has a duty to A, B, and C, but not a right to more than one, because it is wrong if he gives more than his indivisible limited sum. Hence there are more duties than rights. All that it comes to is that, when you look on duties as possible, they are wider than what, when actually done, is right and actual duty.   Just so possible rights are wider than what is actually duty and actually right.

The reason why this is noticed on the side of rights, and not on the side of duty, is very simple.   We saw above that in right the emphasis is on the universal side.   Now every act is a determined this or that act, and what makes it a this or that act is the particularization.   What I have a right to do thus depends on what my duty is; for duty, we saw, emphasized the particular side.   Now, where there are no indifferents and no choice between them, rights are never wider than duties.   It is where indifferents come in (cf. Essay VI) that possibility is wider than actuality.   And because right emphasizes the side common to all the indifferents, i. e. the undetermined side, it is therefore wider than duty, which emphasizes the particular side, and hence is narrower.[1]

Thus, where the choice of my particular will comes in, that has rights and must be respected.   But it has rights only because the sphere of its exercise, and therefore what it does therein, is duty.   And it must be respected by others only so far as it thus expresses the universal will.   If it has not right on its side, it has no rights whatever.

There is indeed a sphere where rights seem in collision with right.   Wherever you have law you have this, since it comes from the nature of law.   Thus, within limits, I am *just*ified in returning evil for evil; I have a right to do it, even where it is not right but wrong to do it.   The same thing is found in the spheres of state-law, social law, and mere moral law alike.   This does not show that in these cases there is *no* moral universal; it shows that we are keeping to nothing *but* the universal.   We have here the distinction of justice and equity.   A merely just [2] act may (we all

---

[1] [Where a man has competing duties he *may* say, 'I feel that I have (or " as if I had ") no right to neglect any of them'.   This, however, is moral illusion due to confusion, but so far the claims are wider than the rights.   Really, the man has here a right to 'please himself'.   He also has a duty to do so, in the interest of his mental and moral development, rather than leave it to chance.   The emphasis falls on the 'right' because this 'duty' probably does not occur to him *as* duty. But there *is* a duty here and elsewhere 'to please oneself'.   Cf. pp. 212-17.]

[2] What is justice?   I have no space to develop or illustrate, but will set down what seems to be the fact.   The just does not = right; injustice does not = wrong.   Justice does not = giving to each his deserts : 'nothing but justice' may be less or more than my deserts.

know) be most unjust. The universal as law must be the same for all : it can not be specified to meet every particular case. Hence, in keeping to this unspecified universal, I have ' right ' on my side ; but again, failing to specify it in my case, I do what is not right for me to do. I fail in duty, do not do, and am not, right.

The sphere of mere private right in the state can not exist out of the moral whole. It is, for the sake of the develop-ment of the whole, created and kept up in the whole, but merely at the pleasure of the whole. Just so in morals there is a sphere of private liking, the sphere of indifferents, but this exists only because it ought to exist, only because duty is realized in its existence, though not by its particulars as particulars, i. e. as this one against that one. The sphere of private right has rights only so long as it is right and is duty. It exists merely on sufferance ; and the moment the right of the whole demands its suppression it has no rights. Public right everywhere overrides it in practice, if not in theory. This is the justification of such things as forcible expropriation, conscription, &c. The only proper way of regarding them is to say, In developing my property, &c., as this or that man, I am doing my duty to the state, for the state lives in its individuals : and I do my duty again in another way by giving up to the use of the state my property and person, for the individual lives in the state. What other view will justify the facts of political life ?

To repeat then : Right is the assertion of the universal will in relation to the particular will. Duty is the assertion of the particular will in the affirmation of the universal. Good is the identity, not the mere relation, of both. Right may be real,[1] may actually exist ; or be only ideal, merely thought of. So may duty. Rights and duties are elements in the good ; they must go together. The universal cannot

---

Justice is not *mere* conforming to law: injustice is not *mere* acting against law ; e. g. murder is not called ' unjust '. Justice and injustice mean this, but they imply something more.

Injustice is, while you explicitly or implicitly profess to go on a rule, the not going merely on the rule, but the making exceptions in favour of persons. Justice is the really going by nothing but one's ostensible rule in assigning advantage and disadvantage to persons.*

What the rule is, is another matter. The rule may be the morally right. This is ideal justice. All lower sorts of law furnish each its own lower justice and injustice.

[1] [See p. 211.]

---

* [' Ostensible ' should be ' recognized and approved '. And ' ad-vantage and disadvantage ' should include ' approval and disapproval '.]

be affirmed except in the particular, the particular only affirms itself in the universal; but they should be suppressed in the good as anything more than elements, which reciprocally supplement each other, and should be regarded as two sides to one whole.   It is not moral to stand on one's rights with the right; i.e. right should not be *mere* right : nor moral to make a duty of all one's duties; i.e. duty should not be *mere* duty.

We maintain the following theses. (1) It is false that you can have rights without duties. (2) It is false that you can have duties without rights. (3) It is false that right is merely negative.[1] (4) It is false that duty depends on possible compulsion, and a mere mistake that command always implies a threat; and (5) It is absolutely false that rights or duties can exist outside the moral world.

[1] Schopenhauer has developed this view with great clearness. He goes so far as to make wrong the original positive conception, right the mere negation of it.

ESSAY VI

IDEAL MORALITY

IN our criticism of the view developed in Essay V we saw that, however true the main doctrine of that Essay may be, it is no sufficient answer to the question, What is morality? and, guided by its partial failure, we must try to find a less one-sided solution.

We saw (in Essay II) that the end was the realizing of the self; and the problem which in passing suggested itself was, Are morality and self-realization the same thing,[1] or, if not altogether the same, in what respect are they different?

That in some way they do differ is clear from the popular views on the subject. Every one would agree that by his artistic or scientific production an artist or a man of science does realize himself, but no one, not blinded by a theory, would say that he was moral just so far as, and because, what he produced was good of its sort and desirable in itself. A man may be good at this or that thing, and may have done good work in the world; and yet when asked, 'But was he a good man?' we may find ourselves, although we wish to say Yes, unable to do more than hesitate. A man need not be a good man just so far as he is a good artist; and the doctrine which unreservedly identifies moral goodness with any desirable realization of the self can not be maintained.

Can we then accept the other view, which, as it were, separates morality into a sphere of its own; which calls a man moral according as he abstains from direct breaches of social rules, and immoral if he commits them; while it forgets that the one man may be lazy, selfish, and without a wish to improve himself, while the other, with all his faults, at least loves what is beautiful and good, and has striven towards it? We can not do that unless, while we

[1] [Cf. p. 228, and note, pp. *244*, 218–19.]

recognize the truth of the doctrine, we shut our eyes to its accompanying falsity.

And, finding in neither the expression of our moral consciousness, we thankfully accept the correction which sees in 'conduct' nine-tenths of life, though we can not expect the main question to be answered by a coarse and popular method, which divides into parts instead of distinguishing aspects; and though, in the saving one-tenth and the sweeping nine-tenths alike, we can see little more than the faltering assertion of one mistake, or the confident aggravation of another.

A man's life, we take it, can not thus be cut in pieces. You can not say, 'In this part the man is a moral being, and in that part he is not'. We have not yet found that fraction of his existence in which the moral goodness of the good man is no more realized, and where 'the lusts of the flesh' cease to wage their warfare. We have heard in the sphere of religion, 'Do *all* to the glory of God', and here too we recognize no smaller claim. To be a good man in all things and everywhere, to try to do always the best, and to do one's best in it, whether in lonely work or in social relaxation to suppress the worse self and realize the good self, this and nothing short of this is the dictate of morality. This, it seems to us, is a deliverance of the moral consciousness too clear for misunderstanding, were it not for two fixed habits of thought. One of these lies in the confining of a man's morality to the sphere of his social relations; the other is the notion that morality is a life harassed and persecuted everywhere by 'imperatives' and disagreeable duties, and that without these you have not got morality. We have seen, and have yet to see, that the first has grasped only part of the truth; and on the second it is sufficient to remark that it stands and falls with the identification of morality with unwilling obedience to law, and that, according to the common view, a man does not cease to be good so far as goodness becomes natural and pleasant to him.

But we shall be met at this point with an absurdity

supposed to follow. Work of any sort, it will be said, is, we grant you, a field for morality, and so is most of life in relation to others; but there must be a sphere where morality ceases, or else it will follow that a man is moral in all the trifling details of his own life which concern him alone, and no less again in his amusements. If morality does not stop somewhere, you must take it to be a moral question not only whether a man amuses himself, but also how he amuses himself. There will be no region of things indifferent, and this leads to consequences equally absurd and immoral.[1] We answer without hesitation that in human life there is, in one sense, no sphere of things indifferent, and yet that no absurd consequences follow. If it is my moral duty to go from one town to another, and there are two roads which are equally good, it is indifferent to the proposed moral duty *which* road I take; it is not indifferent *that* I do take one or the other; and whichever road I do take, I am doing my duty on it, and hence it is far from indifferent : my walking on road A is a matter of duty in reference to the end, though not a matter of duty if you consider it against walking on road B; and so with B—but I can escape the sphere of duty neither on A nor on B. In order to realize the good will in a finite corporeal being it is necessary that certain spheres should exist, and should have a general character; this is a moral question, and not indifferent. The detail of those spheres within certain limits does not matter; not that it is immaterial that there *is* a detail of trifles, and hence not that this and that trifle has no moral importance, but that this trifle has no importance *against that trifle.* Qualify a trifle by subordinating it to a good will, and it has moral significance;

---

[1] Expressed in other language the objection is, 'There is a sphere of rights which falls outside the sphere of duty, or else it will follow that all my rights are my duties, which is absurd.'—For the answer, see p. 210. Here we may say, it is right and a duty that the sphere of indifferent detail should exist. It is a duty that I should develop my nature by private choice therein. Therefore, *because* that is a duty, it is a duty *not* to make a duty of every detail; and thus in every detail I have done my duty.

qualify it by contrast with another trifle, and morally it
signifies nothing. This is plain enough, and, so far as it
goes, will I hope be sufficient. The reader no doubt will see
that, if a class of acts is morally desirable, then whatever falls
within that class is also morally desirable, so far as falling
therein ; though in its other relations it may be indifferent.

But the difficulty which remains will be something of
this sort. The reader will feel that, to a certain extent, the
regulation of the times and fields of amusements, &c., and,
to a still larger extent, the choice of trifling details therein,
involves no reflection, no deliberate choice, is not made
a matter of conscience, is in a word done naturally ; and he
may find a difficulty in seeing how, if this is so, it can be
said to fall within the moral sphere. Morality, he may
feel, does tell me it is good to amuse myself, and more
decidedly that I may *not* amuse myself beyond certain
limits ; but within those limits it leaves me to my natural
self. In this, it seems to us, there is a twofold misapprehension, a mistake as to the limits, and a mistake as to the
character of the moralized self. It is, first, an error to
suppose that in what is called human life there remains
any region which has not been moralized. Whatever has
been brought under the control of the will, it is not too
much to say, has been brought into the sphere of morality ;
in our eating, our drinking, our sleeping, we from childhood
have not been left to ourselves ; and the habits, formed in
us by the morality outside of us, now hold of the moral
will which in a manner has been their issue. And so in
our lightest moments the element of control and regulation
is not wanting ; it is part of the business of education to
see that it is there, and its absence, wherever it is seen to
be absent, pains us. The character shows itself in every
trifling detail of life ; we can not go in to amuse ourselves
while we leave it outside the door with our dog ; it is ourself, and our moral self, being not mere temper or inborn
disposition, but the outcome of a series of acts of will.
Natural it is indeed well to be ; but that is because by this
time morality should be our nature, and good behaviour its

unreflecting issue; and to be natural in any sense which excludes moral habituation is never, so far as I know the world, thought desirable. In a good and amiable man the good and amiable self is present throughout, and that self is for us a moral self. This brings us to the second mistake, which also rests on the same misapprehension of the cardinal truth that what is natural can not be moral, nor what is moral natural. 'What is natural does not reflect, and without reflection there is no morality. Hence, where we are natural *because* we do not reflect, there we can not be moral.' So runs the perversion. But here it is forgotten that we *have* reflected; that acts which issue from moral reflection have qualified our will; that our character thus, not only in its content, but also in the form of its acquisition, is within the moral sphere; and that a character, whether good or bad, is a second nature. The man to whom it 'comes natural' to be good is commonly thought a good man, and the good self of the good man is present in and determines the detail of his life not less effectually because unconsciously. So far facts speak loudly, and the only path which remains open to the objector is to deny that the good self is necessarily a moral self, on the ground not that its content is non-moral, but that its genesis is so; in other words, because, though moral in itself, it is not so for the agent. We may be told, the genesis of the good self generally is not a moral genesis, or in this and that sphere or relation it is not so, and hence, though good, it need not, so far as good, be moral. To the consideration of this question we shall have to come later, and at present can only observe that we refuse to separate goodness conscious or unconscious from the will to be good, or the will to be good from morality; and we assert that, because the good self shows itself everywhere, therefore there is no part of life at which morality stops and goes no further. Thus much against the notion that in our amusements, &c., we cease to be moral beings, that there is a tenth part of life where conduct is not required. But as to the remaining nine-tenths we need surely say no more : wherever

there is anything to be done not in play but in earnest,
there the moral consciousness tells us it is right to do our
best, and, if this is so, there can be no question but that
here is a field for morality.[1]

It is a moral duty to realize everywhere the best self,
which for us in this sphere is an ideal self; and, asking
what morality is, we so far must answer, it is coextensive
with self-realization in the sense of the realization of the
ideal self in and by us. And thus we are led to the
inquiry, what is the *content* of this ideal self.[2]

From our criticism on the foregoing Essay we can at
once gather that the good self is the self which realizes
(1) a social, (2) a non-social ideal; the self, first, which
does, and, second, which does not directly and immediately
involve relation to others. Or from another point of view,
what is aimed at is the realization in me (1) of the ideal
which is realized in society, of my station and its duties, or
(2) of the ideal which is not there fully realized; and this
is (*a*) the perfection of a social and (*b*) of a non-social self.
Or again (it is all the same thing) we may divide into (1)
duties to oneself which are not regarded as social duties, (2)
duties to oneself [3] which are so regarded, these latter being

[1] It may even be my moral duty to be religious in the sense of
acting with a view to the support and maintenance of the religious
consciousness, the faith which is to reissue in religious-moral practice.
Hence though morality, as we shall see, does not include everything,
yet nothing in another sense falls outside of it.

[2] On the genesis of the ideal self and of the good self, or the self
whose will is identified with its ideal, we shall say what seems necessary
in other connexions.

[3] I may remark that a duty which is *not* a duty to myself can not
possibly be a moral duty. When we hear of self-regarding duties we
should ask what is meant.* A '*self*-regarding duty' in one sense of
the word says no more than 'a duty'; in another sense it says 'a duty
which is the direct opposite of what a duty is', i.e. a *selfish* duty: or
again, it means a non-social duty. Confusion on this head leads to
serious mistakes.

* [This *might* mean a duty towards myself as this or that member
of society.]

(*a*) the duties of the station which I happen to be in, (*b*) duties beyond that station. Let us further explain.

The content of the good self, we see, has a threefold origin; and (1) the first and most important contribution comes from what we have called my station and its duties, and of this we have spoken already at some length. We saw that the notion of an individual man existing in his own right independent of society was an idle fancy, that a human being is human because he has drawn his being from human society, because he is the individual embodiment of a larger life; and we saw that this larger life, of the family, society, or the nation, was a moral will, a universal the realization of which in his personal will made a man's morality. We have nothing to add here except in passing to call attention to what we lately advanced, viz. that the good man is good throughout all his life and not merely in parts; and further to request the reader to turn to himself and ask himself in what his better self consists. He will find, if we do not mistake, that the greater part of it consists in his loyally, and according to the spirit, performing his duties and filling his place as the member of a family, society, and the state. He will find that, when he has satisfied the demands of these spheres upon him, he will in the main have covered the claims of what he calls his good self. The basis and foundation of the ideal self is the self which is true to my station and its duties.

But (2) we saw also that, if we investigate our good self, we find something besides, claims beyond what the world expects of us, a will for good beyond what we see to be realized anywhere. The good in my station and its duties was visibly realized in the world, and it was mostly possible to act up to that real ideal; but this good beyond is only an ideal; for it is not wholly realized in the world we see, and, do what we may, we can not find it realized in ourselves. It is what we strive for and in a manner do gain, but never attain to and never possess. And this ideal self (so far as we are concerned with it here) is a social self. The perfect types of zeal and purity, honour and love, which, figured and presented in our own situation and circumstances, and thereby unconsciously specialized, become the guides of our conduct and law of our being, are social ideals. They directly involve relation to other men, and, if you remove others, you immediately make the practice of these virtues impossible.[1]

This then is the ideal self which in its essence is social; and concerning this many difficulties arise which we can not discuss. Among these would be the two inquiries, What is the origin, and what the content of this ideal self? In passing we may remark that the first contains two questions which are often confused, viz. (a) How is it possible for the mind to frame an ideal; or, given as a fact a mind which idealizes, what must be concluded as to its nature? Can anything idealize unless itself in some way *be* an ideal? This, we need not say, suggests serious problems which we can not even touch upon here. Then (b) it contains also the questions, What was the historical genesis of the ideal; by what steps did it come into the world? And again, What is its genesis in us? And these can scarcely be separated from one another, or from the further inquiry, What is its content?

The historical genesis we shall not enter on; and as to the genesis in the individual, we will merely remark that we seem first to see in some person or persons the type of what is excellent; then by the teaching, tradition, and imagination of our own and other countries and times, we receive a content which we *find* existing realized in present or past individuals, and finally detach from all as that which is realized wholly in none, but is an ideal type of human perfection. At this point we encounter a question of fact, namely, how far the ideal which serves as a guide to conduct is presented in an individual form. No doubt two extremes exist. A large number of men have, I think, no

---

[1] Virtues such as chastity, which might be practised in solitude, are either negative of the bad self, or conditions of the good will. If you wrongly consider them by themselves, they are not positively desirable. We may call them, if we will, the ' ascetic virtues '.

moral ideal beyond the station they live in, and of these some are even satisfied with the presentation of this or that known person as a type; while again in the highest form of morality the ideal is not figured in the shape of an individual.[1] But between the extremes must be endless gradations.

We have previously said something as to the way in which the ideal is made use of in moral judgements, and what remains is to call attention to the content of this social ideal. It is obvious at once that it is a will which practises no other kind of virtues than those which we find in the world; and we can see no reason for supposing this presented ideal self to be anything beyond the idealization of what exists in human nature, the material idealized being more or less cosmopolitan, and the abstraction employed being more or less one-sided.

And with these cursory and insufficient remarks we must dismiss the ideal of a perfect social being.

But (3) there remains in the good self a further region we have not yet entered on; an ideal, the realization of which is recognized as a moral duty, but which yet in its essence does not involve direct relation to other men.[2] The realization for myself of truth and beauty, the living for the self which in the apprehension, the knowledge, the sight, and the love of them finds its true being, is (all those who know the meaning of the words will bear me out) a moral obligation, which is not felt as such only so far as it is too pleasant.

It is a moral duty for the artist or the inquirer to lead

---

[1] The difficulty everywhere is, Is the embodiment used to fire the imagination, while the type is not that of this or that individual; or is it otherwise? The solution is to be found in the answer to the question, Is the impersonation modified; and if modified, how, and by what, and to suit what is it modified?

[2] Morality, on its own ground at least, knows nothing of a universal and invisible self, in which all members are real, which they realize in their own gifts and graces, and in realizing which they realize the other members. Humanity as an organic whole, if a possible point of view, is not strictly speaking a moral point of view. See more below.

the life of one, and a moral offence when he fails to do so. But on the other hand it is impossible, without violent straining of the facts, to turn these virtues into social virtues or duties to my neighbour. No doubt such virtues do as a rule lead indirectly to the welfare of others, but this is not enough to make them social; their social bearing is indirect, and does not lie in their very essence. The end they aim at is a single end of their own, the content of which does not necessarily involve the good of other men. This we can see from supposing the opposite. If that were true, then it would not be the duty of the inquirer, as such, simply to inquire, or of the artist, as such, simply to produce the best work of art; but each would have to consider ends falling outside his science or art, and would have no right to treat these latter as ends in themselves. 'Nor has he', may be the confident answer. I reply that to me this is a question of fact, and to me it is a fact that the moral consciousness recognizes the perfecting of my intellectual or artistic nature by the production of the proper results, as an end in itself and not merely as a means. The pursuit of these ends, apart from what they lead to, is approved as morally desirable, not perhaps by the theory, but, I think, by the instinctive judgement of all persons worth consider- ing; and if, and while, this fact stands, for me at least it is not affected by doctrines which require that it should be otherwise. To say, without society science and art could not have arisen, is true. To say, apart from society the life of an artist or man of science can not be carried on, is also true; but neither truth goes to show that society is the ultimate end, unless by an argument which takes the basis of a result as its final cause, and which would prove the physical and physiological conditions of society to be the end for which it existed. Man is not man at all unless social, but man is not much above the beasts unless more than social.

If it be said that, morally considered, the realization of the social self is an end, and that of the non-social nothing but an outward means, and that hence science and art are not to be pursued independently, no doubt it would be possible to meet such an assertion by argument from and upon its own ground. We might urge that science is most useful, when treated as more than useful. But we decline by doing this to degrade and obscure the question. We repeat that the assertion is both unproven and false, and the decision is left to the moral consciousness of the reader.

And if again it be said that the social self is the one end, but yet none the less science and art are ends in themselves, and to be pursued independently; they are included in the social self, and therefore, as elements in the end, are themselves ends and not mere means—then, in answer, I will not reply that this is false (for indeed I hope it may be true), but only that it is utterly unproven. It is on the assertor that the burden of proof must lie. To us it seems plain that the content of the theoretical self does not in its essence involve relation to others: nothing is easier than to suppose a life of art or speculation which, as far as we can see, though true to itself, has, so far as others are concerned, been sheer waste or even loss, and which knew that it was so. This is a fairly supposable case, and no one, I think, can refuse to enter on it. Was the life immoral? I say, No, it was not *therefore* immoral, but may have been *therefore* moral past ordinary morality. And if I am told Yes, it was moral, but it was social: it did in its essence involve relation to others, because there is a *necessary* connexion (nothing short of this proves the conclusion) between theoretic realization in this and that man, and the realization of him therein and thereby in relation to others, and perhaps also of society as a whole—then I answer, You are asserting in the teeth of appearances; you must prove this necessary connexion, and, I think I may add, you can not do it. What you say may be true, but science, or at all events your science, can not guarantee it; and it is not a truth for the moral consciousness, but leads us further into another region.

Our result at present is as follows. Morality is co-extensive with self-realization, as the affirmation of the self which is one with the ideal; and the content of this self is furnished

(1) by the objective world of my station and its duties, (2) by the ideal of social, and (3) of non-social perfection. And now we have to do with the question, How do these spheres stand to one another? And this is in some ways an awkward question, because it brings up practical every-day difficulties. They are something of this sort. May a man, for the sake of science or art, venture on acts of commission or omission which in any one else would be im-moral; or, to put it coarsely, may he be what is generally called a bad man, may he trample on ordinary morality, in order that he may be a good artist? Or again, if the perhaps less familiar question of the relation of (1) to (2) comes up, the doubt is, Must I do the work that lies next me in the world, and so serve society, even, as it seems, to the detriment of my own moral being? May I adopt a profession considered moral by the world, but which, judged by my ideal, can not be called moral?

The first point to which we must call attention is that all these are cases of colliding duties. In none of them is there a contest between the claims of morality and of something else not morality. In the moral sphere such a contest is impossible and meaningless. We have in all of them a conflict between moral duties which are taken to exclude one another, e. g. my moral duty as artist on the one hand and as father of a family on the other, and so on: we have nothing to do with examples where morality is neglected or opposed in the name of anything else than an other and higher morality.

And the second point, which has engaged us before (pp. 156-9, 193 foll.), and on which we desire to insist with emphasis, is, that cases of collision of duties are not scientific but practical questions. Moral science has nothing what-ever to do with the settlement of them; that would belong, did such a thing exist, to the moral art. The difficulties of collisions are not scientific problems; they arise from the complexity of individual cases, and this can be dealt with solely by practical insight, not by abstract conceptions and discursive reasoning. It is no use knowing that one class of duties is in the abstract higher than another: moral practice is not *in abstracto*, and the highest moral duty for *me* is *my* duty; *my* duty being the one which lies next me, and perhaps not the one which would be the highest, supposing it were mine. The man who can give moral advice is the man of experience, who, from his own knowledge and by sympathy, can transport himself into another's case; who knows the heart and sees through moral illusion; and the man of mere theory is in the practical sphere a useless and dangerous pedant.

And now in particular the relation of the two ideal spheres to the real sphere is precisely what subsists inside the real sphere between its own elements. We saw (pp. 156–7) that, as in no one action can all duties be fulfilled, in every action some duties must be neglected. The question is what duty is to be done and left undone *here*; and so in the world of my station neglect of duties is allowed. And, apart from the difficulty (often the impossibility) of distinguishing omission and commission from a moral point of view, we saw (ibid.) that positive breaches of moral law were occasionally moral. And hence if an artist or man of science considers himself called upon, by his duty to art or science, to neglect, or to commit a breach of, ordinary morality, we must say that, in the abstract and by itself, that is not to be condemned. It is a case of colliding duties, such as happens every day in other fields, and its character is not different because extraordinary.

And further, if a claim be set up, on the ground of devotion to no common end, to be judged in one's life by no common standard, we must admit that already within the sphere of my station that claim is usually allowed. We excuse in a soldier or sailor what we do not excuse in others, from whom the same duties are not expected. The morality of the pushing man of business, and still more of the lawyer and the diplomatist in the exercise of their calling, is not measured by the standard of common life; and so, when the service of the ideal is appealed to in justification of neglect and breaches of law, we say that the claim is valid in itself, the abstract right is undeniable, the case is a case of collision, and the question of moral justification is a question of particular fact.

Collision of duties carries all this with it on the one side, but we must not forget what it carries on the other. In raising that excuse we are saying, 'I neglect duty because of duty'; and this means we recognize two duties, one higher than the other. And first it implies that we are acting, not to please ourselves, but because we are bound by what we consider moral duty. It implies again that we consider what we break through or pass by, not as a trifle, but as a serious moral claim, which we disregard solely because, if we do not do so, it prevents us from performing our superior service.

Common social morality is the basis of human life. It is specialized in particular functions of society, and upon its foundation are erected the ideals of a higher social perfection and of the theoretic life; but common morality remains both the cradle and protecting nurse of its aspiring offspring, and, if we ever forget that, we lie open to the charge of ingratitude and baseness. Some neglect is unavoidable; but open and direct outrage on the standing moral institutions which make society and human life what it is, can be justified (I do not say condoned) only on the plea of overpowering moral necessity. And the individual should remember that the will for good, if weakened in one place, runs the greatest risk of being weakened in all.

Our result then is that ideal morality stands on the basis of social, that its relation thereto is the same relation that subsists within the social sphere, and that everywhere, since duty has to give way to duty, neglect and breaches of ordinary in the name of higher morality are justifiable in the abstract (and that is all we are concerned with); but if the claim be set up, on account of devotion to the ideal, for liberty to act thus not in the name of moral necessity, or to forget that what we break through or disregard is in itself to be respected, such a claim is without the smallest moral justification.[1]

[1] I have not entered on the questions whether as a fact breaches of

The highest type we can imagine is the man who, on the basis of everyday morality, aims at the ideal perfection of it, and on this double basis strives to realize a non-social ideal. But where collisions arise, there, we must repeat, it is impossible for mere theory to offer a solution, not only because the perception which decides is not a mere intellectual perception, but because no general solution of individual difficulties is possible.

To return to our main discussion—the field of morality we find is the whole field of life; its claim is as wide as self-realization, and the question raised before (p. 64) now presents itself, Are morality and self-realization the same and not different? This appears at first sight to be the case. The moral end is to realize the self, and all forms of the realizing of the self are seen to fall within the sphere of morality; and so it seems natural to say that morality is the process of self-realization, and the most moral man is the man who most fully and energetically realizes human nature. Virtue is excellence, and the most excellent is the most virtuous.

If we say this, however, we come into direct collision with the moral consciousness, which clearly distinguishes moral from other excellence, and asserts that the latter is not in itself moral at all; and, referring back (p. 143), we find the deliverance of that consciousness in the emphatic maxim that nothing is morally good save a good will. This maxim we shall forthwith take to be true, and so proceed.

Morality then will be the realization of the self as the good will.[1] It is not self-realization from all points of

common morality are demanded by the service of the ideal, and, if so, when they are to be committed. The first is a matter of fact it would not profit us to discuss in connexion with the abstract question; and the second in our opinion can not be theoretically determined. Which duty or duties weigh heaviest in this or that case is an affair for perception, not reasoning. We may remark, however, that the doctrine of the text will not be found to err on the side of laxity.

[1] [Morality and Self-realization, how different? See pp. 309-10, 214, 232-7, 244.

'Morality' is Self-realization, or the production (and existence) of

view, though all self-realization can be looked at from this one point of view; for all of it involves will, and, so far as the will is good, so far is the realization moral. Strictly speaking and in the proper sense, morality is self-realization within the sphere of the personal will. We see this plainly in art and science, for there we have moral excellence, and that excellence does not lie in mere skill or mere success, but in single-mindedness and devotion to what seems best as against what we merely happen to like. Θεωρία is at the same time πρᾶξις, and so far as it is πρᾶξις, so far is it moral or immoral.[1] And even in the sphere of my station and its duties, when in the stricter sense you consider it morally, you find that the same thing holds. From the highest point of view you judge a man moral not so far as he has succeeded outwardly, but so far as he has identified his will with the universal, whether that will has properly externalized itself or not. Morality has not to do immediately with the outer results of the will: the results it looks at are the habits and general temper produced by acts, and, strictly speaking, it does not fall beyond the subjective side, the personal will and the heart. Clearly a will which does not utter itself is no will,[2] but you can not measure a will morally by external results: they are an index, but an index that must be used with caution.

excellences, so far as they can be taken as the expression (if not the result) of the will for good.

There is a difficulty as to how far the merely 'natural' still comes in here really. Clearly not all the 'admirable' is moral. There is a difficulty, again, as to what is 'the will for good'. Is it *any* willing so far as good? Or is it only what can be taken as the willing *against* the bad? And in what sense *bad*? Cf. p. 237, second paragraph.]

[1] Cf. Aristotle, *Pol.* vii. 1325, b. 14–23.

[2]   Thyself and thy belongings
Are not thine own so proper, as to waste
Thyself upon thy virtues, them on thee.
Heaven doth with us, as we with torches do,
Not light them for themselves: for if our virtues
Did not go forth of us, 'twere all alike
As if we had them not. Spirits are not finely touch'd
But to fine issues.

We shall return to the question, What is the measure of a man's morality?

The general end is self-realization, the making real of the ideal self; and for morality, in particular, the ideal self is the good will, the identification of my will with the ideal as a universal will. The end for morals is a will, and my will, and a universal will, and one will. Let us briefly refer on these heads to the moral consciousness.

Nothing, we have seen, is good but a good will. The end for morals is not the mere existence of any sort of ideal indifferently, but it is the realization of an ideal will in my will. The end is the ideal willed by me, the willing of the ideal in and by my will, and hence an ideal will. And my will as realizing the ideal is the good will. A will which obeys no law is not moral, a law which is not willed is nothing for morality. Acts, so far as they spring from the good will, are good, and a temper and habits and character are good so far as they are a present good will, result from it and embody it; and what issues from a good character must thus likewise be morally good.

That the good will for morality is my will is obvious enough, and it is no less plain (pp. 144, 162) that it is presented as universal. That does not mean that everybody does or has to do what I do, but it means that, if they were I, they must do as I have to do, or else be immoral; it means that my moral will is *not* the mere will of myself as this or that man, but something above it and beyond it And further, again, the good will is presented as one will; in collisions, going to our moral consciousness, we are told that, if we knew it, there is a right, that the collision is for us, and is not for the good will. We can not bring before us two diverse good wills, or one good will at cross purposes and not in harmony with itself; and we feel sure that, if our will were but one with the universal, then we too should be one with ourselves, with no conflict of desires, but a harmony and system.

Such is the will presented to itself by the moral consciousness, but for the moral consciousness that is ideal and not real. Within the sphere of morality the universal remains but partially realized : it is something that for ever wants to be, and yet is not.

We saw that the will of the social organism might be called a universal will, and a will which was visibly real, as well as ideal ; but we saw too that the sphere of my station and its duties did not cover the whole good self ; and further, even within that sphere, and apart from diffi- culties of progress, for morality in the strict sense ideal and real remain apart. The bad self is not extinguished, and in myself I see an element of will wherein the universal is unrealized, and against which it therefore remains (so far as my morality is concerned) a mere idea ; for, even if we assume that society gets no hurt, yet I do not come up to my special type.

For morals then the universal is not realized within my station, and furthermore the moral consciousness does not say that it is realized anywhere at all. The claim of the ideal is to cover the whole field of reality, but our con- science tells us that we will it here, and that there again we do not will it, here it is realized, and there it is not realized, and we can not point to it in ourselves or others and say, Here is the universal incarnate, and fully actual by and as the will of this or that man ; and indeed we see that for the ideal self to be in the world as the expressed will of this or that spiritualized animal is quite out of the question.

Of course if religion, and more particularly if Christianity be brought in, the answer must be different. The ideal here is a universal, because it is God's will, and because it therefore is the will of an organic unity, present though unseen, which is the one life of its many members, which is real in them, and in which they are real ; and in which, through faith for them, and for God we do not know how, the bad self is unreal. But all this lies beyond morality : my mere moral consciousness knows nothing whatever about it. And we must give the same answer, if we are told on other grounds that humanity is an actually existing organic community, in which we are members, and whose will is present in us.[1] For supposing that the identity (not mere likeness) of the best self in all men is proved, and further the right established to use the word 'humanity', not as an abstract term for an abstract idea, nor as a name for an imaginary collection of all past, present, and future individuals, but for a real corporate unity, yet still we must say, My conscience tells me that my bad self is real; and whether on speculative grounds you try to show that it is unreal, or bring in faith, yet in either case you have gone beyond morality; for morality the good is still only realized in part, and there is something against which it still remains a mere idea.

The ideal self then for morals is not visibly universal nor fully actual. It is not visibly and in the world seen to be an harmonious system, but in the world and in us realizes, it would seem, itself against itself. And in us it is not a system; our self is not a harmony, our desires are not fully identified with the ideal, and the ideal does not always bring peace in its train. In our heart it clashes with itself, and desires we can not exterminate clash with our good will, and, however much we improve (if we do improve), we never are perfect, we never are a harmony, a system, as our true idea is, and as it calls upon us to be.

Thus morality, because its end is not completely realized, is after all ideal; and what we have next to see is that it is not simply positive; it is also negative. The self, which, as the good will, is identified with our type, has to work against the crude material of the natural wants, affections, and impulses, which, though not evil in themselves, stand in the way of good, and must be disciplined, repressed, and encouraged. It is negative again of what is positively evil, the false self, the desires and habits which embody a will directly contrary to the good will. And further it belongs to its essence that it should be so negative of both, because a being not limited, and limited by evil in himself, is not

[1] [Humanity as invisible organism : see p. 205.]

what we call moral. (Cf. pp. 145–6.) A moral will must be finite, and hence have a natural basis; and it must to a certain extent (how far is another matter) be evil, because a being which does not know good and evil is not moral, and because (as we shall see more fully hereafter) the specific characters of good and evil can be known only one against the other, and furthermore can not be apprehended by the mere intellect, but only by inner experience. Morality, in short, implies a knowledge of what the 'ought' means, and the 'ought' implies contradiction and moral contradiction.

So we see morality is negative; the non-moral and the immoral must exist as a condition of it, since the moral is what it is only in asserting itself against its opposite. But morality is not merely negative; it is a great mistake to suppose that the immoral is there already,[1] and that morality consists simply in making it not to be. The good will is not that which merely destroys the natural or the immoral; it does indeed destroy them as such, but this by itself is not morality. It is when it destroys them by its own assertion, and destroys them by transmuting the energy contained in them, that the will is moral.[2]

The good self is not real as the mere abolition of reality. On its affirmative side (and it is moral only when it is affirmative) it is the position of the universal will, as the true infinite, in the personal will of this or that man; and here it has reality, not complete, not adequate, but still certain. You can not separate negation and affirmation

---

[1] By its very essence immorality can not exist except as against morality: a purely immoral being is a downright impossibility. The man who has become entirely immoral has ceased to know good and evil, has ceased to belong to the moral sphere, is morally speaking dead.

[2] [This in general is wholly true. There are, however, cases of repression of bad impulses where it is true perhaps only *generally*. The positive assertion, that is, is always there, but can it always be said to use up the *particular* impulse, and transmute *that*? It asserts the good will in *that* general sphere—yes! but *more*, perhaps not.]

without destroying the moral world. The abstract non-existence of the non-moral is nothing; and the existence of nothing (if that were possible) is not a moral end. The assertion of the moral, the positive realization of the good will to the negation of the natural and bad will, is morality, and no one element of this whole is so; for in the destruction of the bad it is only the affirmation of the good which is desirable (cf. p. 27).

The realization of the good in personal morality is the habituated will, the moral character of individuals. It is actual in the virtues of the heart, and those virtues are the habits which, embodying good acts of will, have become part of the man's self, and which answer to the various sides of his station, or more generally to his various relations to the ideal.

Morality then is a process of realization, and it has two sides or elements which can not be separated; (1) the position of an ideal self, and the making of that actual in the will; (2) the negation, which is inherent in this, the making unreal (not by annihilation but transformation) of the for ever unsystematized natural material, and the bad self. And this account removes many of the difficulties we encountered in Essay IV.

It does not remove them all. Morality does involve a contradiction; it does tell you to realize that which never can be realized, and which, if realized, does efface itself as such. No one ever was or could be perfectly moral; and, if he were, he would be moral no longer. Where there is no imperfection there is no ought, where there is no ought there is no morality, where there is no self-contradiction there is no ought. The ought is a self-contradiction. Are we to say then that that disposes of it? Surely not, unless it also disposes of ourselves; and that can not be. At least from this point of view, we are a self-contradiction: we never are what we feel we really are; we really are what we know we are not; and if we became what we are, we should scarcely be ourselves. Morality aims at the cessation of that which makes it possible; it is the effort after non-

morality, and it presses forward beyond itself to a super-
moral sphere where it ceases as such to exist.[1,2]

It is at this point we find problems too great for us, and,
if we follow any further, it will be only in our Concluding
Remarks, and merely with a view to clear up what has gone
before. But at our present point of view we must remain,
till we have answered some objections and attempted to
remove some difficulties. The rest of this Essay will have
to do with ἀπορίαι which arise in respect of morality, and
the next one will try to make more clear what we mean by
the bad self which opposes the good.

The first one-sided view of morality which must engage
us may be put as follows: 'Morality is not the realization
of a content, but the identification of the will with the
universal. The moral end is consequently the production
of a system, a harmony in the desires, the heart and will;
and therefore we may and must suppress aspiration in
order to get moral harmony.' We answer—It is true
morality is not the mere realization of a content, since in
itself that content is not, strictly speaking, moral. The
performance is not moral apart from the will. That is one
side. But on the other side the will which is not the will
to perform is not moral at all. To try to be good not in
science, art, or any other ideal pursuit, nor to be good
socially, but to be virtuous simply in oneself, or to realize
the good will with no content to it, is not to be moral in
any way. A mere formal harmony is not a moral end:

---

[1] It does not concern me to go out of my way to say more on endless
moral progress. I have already (p. 155) referred to Hegel's annihilating
criticism. Progress to an end which is completeness and the end of
progress and morality, is one thing. Endless progress is progress
without an end, is endless incompleteness, endless immorality, and is
quite another thing.

[2] [To some extent this is even realized in and through morality.
We can and do admire, in some cases, the goodness which is, or has
(in part) become, 'natural instinct', and admire it *more* than the
'moral' (strictly). Of course this, however, is only partial, and is
based on, and ready to return to, what *is* moral (strictly).]

the end is not system, but the systematic realization of the self whose will is in harmony with the ideal. For example, if the question arises, Am I to advance as a good man or a good artist? morality says, 'Of course as a good man'; but then the whole matter turns on this, What line of action, the doing of what, does make me the best man? In collision of morality with morality it does not hold that the higher the morality the more harmonious the self. You may have harmony of a sort (*not perfect* harmony) without any morality, and you may have morality with but little harmony.

There are other one-sided views, from which consequences follow opposed to the moral consciousness. We may state them so; 'The most systematic man is not the most moral, since he need not have done what he could and therefore should have done; is then the most energetic realization of the good self the most moral man? Suppose we say Yes. Then (1) the difference of capacity and circumstances is left out of the account, and the stronger and more successful nature will be the more moral; and again (2) the different amount of drawbacks is not considered: no credit is given to a man for moral struggles however severe; and in both cases we are in collision with the moral consciousness.

'Or if we say, No, you must look not to the positive realization but to the negative, to the victory over the bad self;—that, again, is against morality, because it unjustly favours the weaker nature; the more energetic may, because he is more energetic, have therefore more bad self to conquer.

'Again if we say, Neither negative nor positive realization is to be looked to, for morality is a struggle, and it is the struggle which is of importance—then it will follow that, to increase the struggle and with it morality, the bad self must not be allowed to decrease beyond a certain point; and, further, it will follow that either all men are morally equal, since all struggle, and no one can do more than struggle; or else, if the most moral man is the man who struggles most, the quantity (intensive and extensive) of the struggle, and not the degree in the scale of qualitative advance, will count for morality.   And of these, as of the other conclusions, every one is immoral.'

It would not repay us to investigate these difficulties in detail; they arise from doctrines which are not false in themselves, but each of which is false if taken as the expression of the whole truth, and their solution will come readily from the answer to the question, Who for the moral consciousness is the most moral man? [1]

Who is the most moral man?   'Moral' with an emphasis. We do not ask who is the most perfect man.   We do not say, Whose will is most identified with *the* ideal human type? but, Whose will is most identified with *his* ideal?

For the moral consciousness tells us that a man is not good morally according as he stands in the scale of human progress; that a man's morality may in one sense be higher than another man's, yet he himself may be, strictly speaking, morally lower.   It tells us that, if we judge by a purely moral standard, the low savage may be, not a higher, but a better man than the civilized European; and, we see, (1) the most moral man is the man who tries most to act up to what his light tells him is best.   But in that we must remember is included the getting the best light which, up to his light, he can.

(2) Suppose now that the lights of two men are equal, can we then look to the greater or lesser realization of their ideal, and judge them accordingly?   Morality says, No. It says the formal energy in all men is not the same; and, unless selves are equal to start with, they can not be morally compared simply with an eye to their respective realization.

(3) And again men vary, not only in light and in formal energy, but also in disposition.   Disposition no doubt is not moral character; that does not begin until a man is self-conscious, and by volition the good and bad selves get their

---

[1] [Degrees of morality.   Here we see again that the Good is wider than the *moral* Good.   It is not true that nothing is good but a good will.   (Cf. p. 228.)]

specific character one against the other;[1] but none the less is natural disposition the material from which the moral self is built up. And dispositions or natures vary indefinitely: some are more harmonious than others, and some again are more chaotic and lead inevitably to jars and painful contradictions. The material of some men offers more resistance to the systematizing good will, and gives more openings for the increase and strengthening of the bad self, than does that of others. And, unless in this too individuals are equal, you can not simply compare them by the result.

(4) And further we have to consider external circumstances in relation to disposition, as bearing on the facility of appropriating the good, and again on the difficulty of controlling the bad self; and our conclusion at present is this. Men equal in light, formal energy, natural disposition, and circumstances, and equal also in present extent and intent of their good and bad selves, are morally equal.

Even here we are not at the end:[2] but this is enough to show that for us to make an accurate comparison is scarcely possible, and fully to justify the saying that 'only God sees the heart', if we mean by that not that morality is a matter of the heart in the sense of staying there, but that the data for solving the psychological problem are not accessible to us. This is not to be regretted: in morality we have nothing to do with others and what they do or neglect; we have nothing to do with what we ourselves may in past time have succeeded with or failed in, except so far as it is present in our will; what is before us is the relation of our private will to the good will, what we are and do and have still to do.

To resume, after making these four qualifications we may say men are equal morally, whose good and bad selves are equal in extent and intent; but here we have two sides to consider and not one, and it does not appear how these stand to one another, and how the problem is to be worked.

---

[1] See more in following Essay.
[2] [See what follows in the next paragraph.]

You can not measure by comparative lessness of bad self, because morality is not merely negative; nor again by moreness of good self, because it is not merely affirmative. You can not go by severity of struggle between bad and good, because, other things being equal, the more of good against less of bad, and hence lessness of struggle, is the better. Greater or less struggle is a test only when it points to greater or less affirmation, when, being a negative condition,[1] the moreness of it points to the moreness of the positive, the condition of which it is. It is a serious mistake to argue, 'because more *sine qua non*, therefore more'. Nor again can you go by relative absence of struggle, because that may mean relative absence of the good will, and moral deadness.

To measure morality you must take the two sides, good and bad together, and then comes up the question of their relation. May we (1) say the bad self is in itself indifferent, and so measure simply by the good; or must we (2) treat it as a minus quantity and subtract it from the good?

(1) In 'in itself indifferent' the *in itself* is the important point. So far as the bad self thwarts the good by direct opposition, no one would call it indifferent. And then, beside its open hostility, it creates consequences which thwart the good, and in addition appropriates to itself a share of the general energy which should have gone to the good, and so weakens it. And all this no one would call indifferent.

But 'in itself indifferent' does not mean this.[2] It means, the bad self matters so far as it lessens the good, but by itself it is only a negation; and, after you have allowed for

---

[1] A condition is negative when, not its existence as such, but the negation of its existence is necessary to that of which it is the condition.

[2] The reader no doubt is aware that there is a view which reduces the distinction of good and bad to a mere *quantitative* difference; virtue and vice differ only in being a little more or a little less of the same thing. This view makes great play with its 'all is relative', 'it all depends on which way you look at it', and the rest of the phrases behind which shallowness tries to look like wisdom. But we shall not stop to discuss it.

its negative properties, you need not consider it at all. The more or less of position of the good self in relation to light, energy, disposition, and circumstances, constitutes the more or less of morality. The bad self only takes from that position ; so that you need only find out what position after all you have, and then there is no occasion to consider the bad self. If in two men with equal light, energy, &c., the good selves are equal, it does not matter whether one has more bad self than the other, and we can strike that out of the account. This is the first proposal. Is it satisfactory?

I think we must say it is not. Practically it might never mislead us, because the consequences of the affirmation of the bad self in immoral acts result in a weakening of the good will far more extensive than might seem at first sight. The doctrine might not take us wrong, but we are asking, Is it theoretically accurate as an exposition of the moral consciousness? And this we must deny, since for that consciousness the bad self is not in itself indifferent.

(2) Considered otherwise, and not in relation to morality, the bad self may be *only* the negative condition of the affirmation of the good ; the presence of which is necessary for morality, but of which anything more than the mere presence is the decrease of the affirmation. It may be something to work against, a resistance which is good for the reaction of energy, but the greater resistance of which does not carry more reaction with it. But this, if a possible point of view, is not a (mere) moral point of view, and as such is here untenable. The bad self for morality is not simply a negation, but the positive assertion of self. The self-conscious self which is positive, which is the very affirmation we know, is in the bad self, feels and knows itself therein as really as it does in the good self. Evil deeds are not mere comings-short, but, apart from their consequences, they are (I do not say sins, for they are that only in and for religion, but) offences, over-steppings, crimes. The bad self is the positive assertion of evil by and in the self; and the will, so far as bad, is not a defect of will, nor a non-moral natural will, but it is an immoral

will, and for the moral consciousness it is as real[1] as the good will.

Hence I am moral not only according to the relative extensive and intensive affirmation of the good will in me, but from that result must be further deducted the relative assertion of the bad will in me, as something which not only takes up space, uses energy, and so starves the good will, besides thwarting it and creating consequences (psychical and physical) which thwart it, but which also, as a positive minus, must be deducted from the plus of the good self, in order to arrive at the final result.

That result can not be worked out with accuracy. On the side of the good you can not reduce intent to extent, so as to count the plus quantity; and on the side of the bad for the same reason you can not count the minus quantity; and even if you could, yet you could not reduce the minus units and the plus units to a common denomination, so as to get by subtraction a quantitative result. But, though practically useless, our answer so far will I hope be found to be the solution of the foregoing ἀπορίαι.

It is perhaps necessary to say something on another point, viz. as to whether a man is moral because of his present or also because of his past state. When we put it in this way the question seems to admit of but one answer; for clearly I am moral because I *am*, and not because I have been, good. But in a different form it may occasion difficulty. Suppose we have three men equal at the start, and one of them has been good and now has fallen away, another has before fallen away and now is trying to be good, and a third has never been far either one way or the other; how do we judge these morally? Is it fair not to count the past?

The answer is that a man's morality, on the one hand, is not the summing up of a past result; and we can consider only the present state, can look only at the will as it is now. This is one side. But on the other hand the will is what it has done; and the present is thus also the past. Evil deeds

---

[1] [Yes, I think so, *for the moral consciousness*. On the bad self see Essay VII.]

must survive in a present evil will which is a positive evil, just as good deeds are not lost, but live in a present good will. No one becomes bad or good all at once, however much men may sometimes seem to do so. And we believe that at the last the existing positive bad and positive good available energy of will (after making all the proper qualifications and allowances, which include, of course, bodily changes) is the true representative of the good and evil the man has done.[1] If in the sphere of morality we are to measure men's lives morally as wholes, this perhaps is how we are to do it, if we do it at all; though from another point of view, and not by us, it may perhaps be done differently.

In conclusion, we must warn the reader against supposing that morality is to be estimated by the intensity of the moral consciousness. It is true that a man who has never known himself to be good or bad is as yet not strictly either, is not yet within the moral sphere. Knowledge of good and evil is necessary for morality, and that (see Essay VII) depends on a self-conscious volition with which responsibility begins, and after which we are answerable for acts of will not self-conscious, because now we know their character, and ought to have them under our control. Self-consciousness is necessary for a moral being, but it is a dangerous mistake to think that all morality must therefore be self-conscious. To be moral, a man need not know that he is acting rightly; still less need he know that he is acting rightly for the sake of morality, and for no other sake. It does not follow, because self-consciousness is the condition of imputation, that therefore everything which is imputed must be done with self-consciousness. The will both for good and evil need not be deliberate volition, still less the deliberate volition of the good simply because it is good, or the evil because it is evil. To will the evil because it is evil is, we think, impossible; to will the moral because it is moral, and for the sake of morality, demands a certain pitch of culture, and then is not common. To will the right as the right, though not for the sake of rightness, is common

[1] [This perhaps cannot be shown.]

enough; but, in most of our moral actions, we do not do
so much as this, because we act from habit and without
reflection. Habits are all-important, and habits need not
be self-conscious; and yet habits are imputable, because
what makes the habit is within the region of conscious
volition, and can not be disowned by it. The habits we
encourage or suffer, we are aware of or might be aware of;
we know their moral quality, and hence are responsible for
them. Our character formed by habit is the present state
of our will, and, though we may not be fully aware of its
nature, yet morally it makes us what we are.[1] Our will is
not this, that, or the other conscious volition, nor does it
exist just so far as we reflect upon it. It is a formed habit
of willing, such a potential will as, apart from counteracting
causes, and given the external conditions which we have
a right to expect, must issue in acts of a certain sort. It is
such a will as this which makes a man moral, and it need not
everywhere and in all its acts be aware of what it is doing.

To sum up, in estimating morality you take the amount
of the present extent and intent (conscious or unconscious)
of the will for good, less the present extent and intent of
will (conscious or unconscious) for bad, and all in relation
to what may be called chance, i. e. the amount of obtainable
light, formal energy, natural disposition, and external circumstances of every kind, under which head must come
that increase or decrease of general energy for which we are
not accountable. Morality, in the sense of personal morality,
may either be self-conscious or not so. It wills the end
explicitly and directly as a moral end, as one not outside
the heart and inner will, and, so far, it is self-conscious. Or
again, it wills the end for its own sake, simply and directly,
and, so far, not as an end within the heart and will; and
further, it need not always even be aware that it is acting

---

[1] We have consciously, and with knowledge of their moral character,
committed ourselves to volitions with which our habits are essentially
connected, or have failed to do so when we might have done so; and
hence those habits are ours, and constitute our standing will.

rightly: in these cases it is not self-conscious. But *morally* considered one morality is not higher than the other.

Personal morality, then, is the process of the assertion of the ideal self, considered not directly as the position of its content, but with respect to the intensity of the process as will. And it must be taken in relation to natural energy, disposition, and all circumstances; and again with respect to the intensity of the negation of the false self, since this negation is an inseparable element. It further includes the willing of psychical changes in the self, in the way of systematization, since these are means to the assertion of the ideal, and the negation of the bad self. And the ground and result of morality is habit or state, which answers to process as its psychical embodiment and basis, and which, as standing will in a man for good, is virtue, just as the habitual will for bad is vice.

Or otherwise, morality is the systematization of the self by the realization therein of the ideal self as will; such ideal taking its content from (1) the objective realized will, (2) the not yet realized objective will, (3) an ideal, the content of which can not (without going beyond morality) be realized as objective will.

It is the process of self-realization from one point of view, i. e. as the negation of the will which has a content other than the true content of the self, and the affirmation of the will whose content is that ideal in which alone the self can look for true realization.

And being a process, involving a contradiction as the *sine qua non* of its existence, it tries to realize the for ever unreal, and it does desire its own extinction, as mere morality, in desiring the suppression of its finitude.[1]

---

[1] [The doctrine that nothing is good but the Good Will is clearly untenable. There are excellences for which we admire this or that man which yet cannot fairly be brought under the Good Will—health, strength, luck, and, still more, beauty. These are in various senses admirable, and, if so, desirable; and, if so, they surely must be good, though certainly not so morally. Again, when, and so far as, moral goodness becomes instinctive and natural, we do not admire it less,

Morality is approximative; and, before we proceed, we
must learn more accurately how this is to be understood.
The reader, recalling our criticism of the Hedonistic chief
good (pp. 97–8), may now object that the contradiction we
discovered there is inherent in all morality: that in all
we aim at a mark we do not hit, and endeavour to get nearer
to an impossibility. We must try to clear up this matter.

(1) That in morality we fail *altogether* to realize the end
is not true. If it were so we should not be moral. In our
hearts and lives the ideal self is actually carried out, our
will is made one with it and does realize it, although the
bad self never disappears and the good self is incoherent
and partial. 'Well but', comes the objection, 'Hedonism
can say this too. There too the end is partially realized.'
Not so, we reply. Asking for this partial reality, we
are told to look at that fraction of the sum of pleasures
which has been reached; and we say at once, that is not

---

but often more. It tends to become good as the beautiful is good—
τὸ καλόν.

We cannot, as to goodness, identify the man with his morality if we
take that in the strict sense. And this obviously raises the question
how the morality stands to the man, how far they do not coincide, and
how the man comes to have the Good Will which he has, or which (we
are tempted to say) falls to his lot.

The moral judgement is here in a difficulty, and is not consistent.
It mainly identifies the man with his moral goodness or badness, so
far as this is willed or comes from will in the past. It tends so to
judge the man, but it also tends to make *some* allowances.

In the main it does not raise the question how the man comes to
will or not to will, or how in one man the will is able to be victorious,
in another man not. The man *is* or *is not* so, as to his moral will,
however we take that, i. e. whether as struggle only or as success.

But how such or such a moral will is allotted to such or such a man,
and on what principle (if any), morality does not ask. And yet to
make the allotment come from the Will would clearly be ridiculous, as
the fact that the Will, or so much Will, is there must 'come first', and
cannot follow from the Will *before* that is there.

Hence moral imputation in the end breaks down in principle (if you
take it as ultimate and final), and we see this in the 'allowances'
made morally, as we see it again in the religious point of view; i. e. the
Grace of God makes all the difference between one man and another.
'There, but for the Grace of God, goes—&c.']

actual at all; in that you have got nothing whatever. The
past is past, and to have had a feeling is not to have it; so
that in ordinary Hedonism I do but try to heap up what
dies in the moment of its birth, and can not thus get nearer
to the possession of anything.[1] In morality on the other
hand the past is present now in the will, and the will is
the reality of the good. Common Hedonism can not say
this.

(2) But the question remains, Does not morality pursue
a fallacious object? Is it not a mere quantitative approach
to zero? We answer, No, it is a great deal more. On the
side of the bad self the moral end is certainly to produce
the nothingness of *that*, and mere negative morality is destroyed by our objector's question. But, as we have explained above (p. 234), true morality is the positive assertion
of the good will. It aims then, we may say, at the zero of
morality *as such* (i. e. as struggle against the bad), but not
at the zero of the positive will for good.

(3) But, let this be as it may, is not morality the approximation to an endless quantity; does it not labour in
vain for the false infinite? Again we say, No. The moral
end is not a sum of units: it is qualitative perfection. What
I want is not mere increase of quantity; but, given a certain
quantum of energy in my will, I desire the complete expenditure of that in behalf of the ideal. The object is for
me to become an infinite whole by making my will one
with an infinite whole. The size of the whole, as such,
is not considered at all. It is true that, though mere quantity is not the end, yet the end implies quantity. Perfect
good means zero of badness, and zero of neutral or undeveloped energy. Hence degrees of advance to moral
perfection can be measured by the lessening extent of the
non-moral and the immoral. But the suppression of these
negatives as such is not the end; and though the good will
can legitimately be considered from one point of view as
a number of units of a certain sort of energy, yet mere size
is not the essence of the matter, and to say that moral

[1] [See note, p. 94.]

perfection must rise and fall with the addition or subtraction of such units would be absolutely false.

These questions at every point have done their best to draw us beyond our depth into the abstract metaphysic which in the end they turn upon. And now we come to one which threatens to involve us more deeply, and our answer to which must remain superficial. What sense have the words 'higher' and 'lower' when applied to morality?

(1) In the strict meaning of 'moral' we have discussed this above (pp. 237–8). Strictly speaking, a higher stage in historical progress is not more *moral* than a lower stage. For in personal morality we consider not the relative complete-ness of the ideal aimed at, but the more or less identifica-tion of a given sum of energy with the particular ideal. And on this head we have dwelt as long as seemed necessary.

(2) But in the wider sense of 'moral' there is a question which we have not properly discussed. If human history is an evolution (p. 189 foll.), how is one stage of it morally higher than another? For in one sense the European certainly is morally a higher being than the savage. He is higher, because the life he has inherited and more or less realized is nearer the truth of human nature. It combines greater specification with more complete homogeneity. And he is higher *morally*, not only because the good will is better according as the type it aims at is truer, but also because that stage of the progressive realization of human nature from which the European gets his being is the historical product of a will which in the main was for good, and now at any rate is the present living embodiment of the good will. Thus if we hold that in evolution one stage is higher than another, we can say also that one stage is more moral than another. But (as before) in the strict sense general human progress is not moral, because it abstracts from the collision of good and bad in the personal self.

And here we might perhaps stop, did not a fresh question irresistibly intrude. Is there such a thing as progress? Does not progress mean the perpetual 'more', the would-be approximation to an endless sum? And, if so, is not

progress the illusion of a journey in the direction of a figment? An infinite quantity we have seen to be a self-
contradiction, and the advance towards it fallacious; so that
'more' does not come any nearer to 'most'. In comparison
of infinity, all finite sums are equal. When you ask for the
difference between each and the infinite, in order to compare these differences one with the other, you get in every
case the same answer, Between the infinite and each finite
alike there is a quantity, about which in no case can we say
more than that it is not any finite sum. Thus against the
infinite there is no difference between the finites, and we
feel the full force of the objection. Progress in the sense
of an advance towards the perfect seems to be a sheer
illusion.

True, we can fall back on our thesis that the end is the
true infinite, the complete identity of homogeneity and
specification (p. 74). This we can insist is not a quantity,
and may repeat that into the definition of perfection mere
size does not enter at all. But still the difficulty remains.
Within the process of evolution the higher is defined as that
which is *more* intensely homogeneous in a *greater* specification, and it does seem as if higher and lower were in the
end reducible to quantity, extensive or intensive, since
the higher man is the man who has *more* of the truth of
human nature. For take an example; suppose a man to
be perfectly self-contained and homogeneous, and then
to get what are called higher qualities, and so become less
self-contained. Is not this an advance, and an advance
because a getting *more*? Is not a wider and deeper truth
a higher truth? And is it not higher because you have
something *beside* what you had before, or *more* of something of which before you had less? And is not, once
again, the conclusion from all this that progress is an illusory
quantitative advance towards a fiction?

How can we escape? Will it do to say that the higher
is such because it contains the lower as an element in
a larger whole; and that the lower is such because, from
the point of view of the higher, it is limited and narrow,

and a position in which the higher would be in contradiction with itself? But is not the question here once more, If quantity is not to be considered, *why* is the more inclusive position higher?

I know of no answer but this, that the perfect is that in which we can rest without contradiction, that the lower is such because it contradicts itself, and so is forced to advance beyond itself to another stage, which is the solution of the contradiction that existed in the lower, and so a relative perfection.[1] If there is a whole which is not finite, and if this whole exists in the finite, the reader will see at once that the finite *must* be discrepant, not only with what is outside itself, but also with itself. The movement towards the solution of this contradiction consists in the extension of the lower so as to take in and resolve its conflicting elements in a higher unity. And this is the reason why the advance consists in greater specification and more intense homogeneity, and therefore, to a certain extent, can be measured by quantity. On this view the higher is above the lower, not because it contains a larger number of units, but because it is the harmony of those elements which in the lower were a standing contradiction. And this conclusion I will ask the reader to take, not as positive doctrine, but as matter for his reflection.

But if any one says he must go further, and objects, ' Well, but in every stage the whole is realized, and in no stage is it realized free from all contradiction. It is actual and complete in the one as in the other—

> As full, as perfect, in a hair as heart,
> As full, as perfect, in vile man that mourns,
> As the rapt seraph that adores and burns ;
> To him no high, no low, no great, no small ;
> He fills, he bounds, connects, and equals all,'

here I confess I can not follow, nor, if I could, would my theme allow of it. For the moral point of view holds good only *within* the process of evolution.

The question, Is evolution or progress the truth from he

---

[1] [On this point see *Essays on Truth and Reality*, Chapter VIII.]

highest point of view? raises problems which nothing but a system of metaphysic can solve. We are forced to believe in the many, we can not help believing in the one; and, whether we desire it or not, these thoughts come together in our minds, and we say, The process of change is the truth. Is then process, still more is evolution, what we can think without contradicting ourselves? To whom in England can we go for an answer? And yet one might have thought that a part of the energy now spent in preaching the creed of evolution would well have been spent on the inquiry, What in the end *is* process in general, and, in particular, what *is* evolution? Is it, or is it not, a self-contradiction? And, if it is, what conclusions follow? But dogma is more pleasant than criticism, and as yet we have no English philosophy whose basis is not dogmatic.

But, whatever evolution may be, Ethics is confined within it. To ask what it is, is to rise above it, and to pass beyond the world of mere morality.

ESSAY VII

SELFISHNESS AND SELF-SACRIFICE

TO say that selfishness and self-sacrifice are equally selfish does seem to the unthinking person a mere foolish remark; which, if suspected to be true, would fill him with astonishment and horror. But the view of such emotions should the rather tend to recommend the doctrine to the thinker. For wonder, as he knows, is the beginning of philosophy; and a shudder comes over the not yet initiated, when the deeper mysteries are unveiled.

But seriously, is it not strange that men can believe in a world of universal self-seeking, and men whose theories (the phrase is not mine) have not come from 'raking into that filthiest of all jakes, a bad mind', but whose lives in many cases were self-denying, and who were better and wiser than ourselves? This on one side is a fact, just as, on the other side, the common belief in self-sacrifice is a fact; and such facts as these should engage our attention. For what we most want, more especially those of us who talk most about facts, is to stand by *all* the facts. It is our duty to take them without picking and choosing them to suit our views, to explain them, if we can, but not to explain them away; and to reason on them, and find the reason of them, but never to think ourselves rational when, by the shortest cut to reason, we have reasoned ourselves out of them.

But our present undertaking has narrow limits. We intend, so far as possible without reference to others, to ask, and in our own way to develop, the question, What is selfishness, and what self-sacrifice? and to include in that the inquiry, What ground is there for the denial of unselfishness? And with this last let us begin, not with

reference to particular theories, but striving to satisfy ourselves.

If selfishness is self-seeking, and to seek self is never to
act apart from desire [1] and *our* desire, never to do anything
but what we want, then surely all deliberate actions must
be considered selfish. For deliberately to act without an
object in view is impossible; duty is done for duty's sake
only when duty is an object of desire; thought as such does
not move; and only the thought of what you like or dislike
brings with it a practical result. Whether we consider
blind appetite, or conscious desire, or circumspect volition,
the result is the same. No act is ever without a reason for
its existence, and the reason is always a feeling of pain
or of pleasure, or both. We seek what we like, and
avoid what we dislike; we do what we want, and this is
selfish.

That others approve or disapprove goes for nothing, for
it does not touch the main fact. You may want to do
what others want you to do, or you may not : but you do
what you want. And so, considered morally and not from
the outside, your action is the same, for the root of it is
in all cases one, your own desire or aversion; and to follow
these is always selfish. What *else* is selfishness? Others
may say to me 'you are agreeable or disagreeable', 'you
are taking the best means to your end', or again 'you are
mistaken', but to me this makes no difference: morality
looks at the heart, and it sees that I please myself in each
one of my acts, and can do nothing else. If I were pleased
to do otherwise, it would only be because I was otherwise
pleased.

Can I sacrifice myself? Oh yes, I can like what others
do not like, and the result may prove painful to myself and

[1] [No act without desire. This is doubtful at least, if not false
psychologically, if taken as universal : see my articles in *Mind*. ⟨*The
definition of Will*; *Mind*, xi, xii, and xiii.⟩ Bain (see *E. S.* pp. 128–9,
note 261) has laid hold of this as to 'disinterested action' and (so far as
I can understand him) has perverted it into the ridiculous doctrine
that 'the disinterested' can not be willed at all. It exists as intellectual
only, just as 'fixed ideas' exist; cf. Notes on pp. 257–8 and 260.]

pleasant to others ; but so it may be with the result of any
other act : or the result may be pleasant to me, though it
would not be so to others.   And so self-sacrifice is a peculiar sort of self-seeking, arising from mistaken notions or
eccentric tastes.   No doubt it may be agreeable to others,
and so be approved by them ; but to conclude that the act
is disagreeable to me when I do it, is to suppose an absurdity.
If it were so I should not do it.   Or if my appetite is perverted to take pain for pleasure (as it really can not be),
this surely does not prove that I have no appetite at all, or
that I do not seek to gratify it.

Illustrations are useful as appeals to the feelings ; but
they do not remove vital facts, though they may remove
our attention from them ; and the vital fact here, to
repeat it again, is this—Without want no action : want
is my want : I do what I want ; and therefore, whatever
my outward act may be, my motive and my heart is selfish ; and for morals the act is qualified by the heart and
motive.

Such is the ground we may assign for the theory of selfishness, and we shall see that, in a certain sense, that ground is
firm.   What would be the answer of the practical man ?

The practical man, I suppose, would say something of
this sort : ' True it is that a man does what he has a mind
to, or, if you will, what he wants to do ; but I call a man
selfish or not according to what it is that he wants and likes.
Some men care to do the right, others to do *only* what they
want, to please no one but themselves ; and the moral
character of each depends on the nature of what pleases
him.'   If we pressed him further and said, ' Yes, but the
difference is superficial ; what pleases a man is what he
desires, and hence in all cases alike he must do what he
likes, and because he likes it : *why* he does it is the point,
and the ' why ' is his personal desire or aversion ; hence he
is always at bottom selfish ',—then I think our supposed
practical man would imagine you wished to impose upon
him.   These questions about the ' why ' he would take to
be misleading nonsense.   He accepts it as a fact that some

men want good and others mere pleasure, and he feels sure
that for that fact there is no further reason, in the sense we
have suggested.　He believes that we are trying to persuade
him that he and others seek the good and avoid the bad, in
all cases, with an ulterior object—as a means, that is to say,
to something else which is the end: and this idea he
indignantly repudiates.　He considers our question of the
motive either an idle triviality, because asking what everybody knows ; or an attempt to mislead, because presupposing
what is palpably false.

And he is right.　That I do what I want to do, is an
idle proposition.　That it should lead to a new result would
be strange, unless truth were to be found in the barest
tautologies.　Like the doctrine of the 'relativity of knowledge', what significance it has, it has only as the negative
of unmeaning fictions, and, as a positive result, it has no
significance at all.　'I know what I know', 'I experience
what I experience', 'I want what I want', indeed 'here be
truths'; much the same as 'I am what I am'; but it is
a poor neighbourhood where such truths can be considered
as making the fortune of a philosopher.　They are not
worthless, because they call attention to a form which may
have been left or thrust out of sight; but, as anything more
than a form, they are more than worthless; they are
positively misleading.　'No object without subject' as
a form is not worthless ; the forgetting of it, or the endeavour
to suppress it, leads and must lead to innumerable errors;
but 'no object without subject' is a mischievous snare when
used as a cover for the statement of some dogmatic preconception of our own on the *nature* of the subject and object,
on the *nature* of experience, on the *nature* of the motive
and the will.　What 'I' means, what my object is, what
'experience' is to stand for, what it is that I do want, and
what we are to say about the self that wants it—these are
questions to which answers can be conjured by no barren formula ; they are questions which, if left unanswered, make our
theories on these subjects futile, and which are not answered
when a formula is used but to distract the attention of the

spectator [1] from the surreptitious introduction of the ready-to-hand result.

And, in particular, to the man who believes that action involves desire, 'I do what I want' says no more than 'I want what I want', or 'I do what I do'. It is a fatal objection against negative morality, against the dream of action without desire or pleasure which asceticism cherishes. For while life lasts and action continues, desire is not destroyed; the ascetic may change the object, but he suppresses his wants so far only as he suppresses life in general; while he *is* (an ascetic) he desires, and he does what he wants; if he desires to destroy desire, yet still that is his desire; if he wills annihilation of his will, yet he wills until with himself his will is annihilated; and the whole question here, as everywhere else, is as to the object of his desire, whether his end is the right end, and whether his means are its means. But it is not our business to discuss this here. To return to the general question, when we are told that we do nothing but that which we want, we answer 'yes, for to us that is tautology'.

But this was not all. 'We do what we want, and we do it *because* we want to do it.' What are we to say to this? We say that it is either senseless or false. If 'because I want' means that it is want or desire which moves me to act, then it is senseless; because, while professing to tell us something, it merely repeats 'I do what I want'. But if 'because I want' means that I do everything as a means to an end, which I represent to myself as the feeling of my private satisfaction, then it is false, and it is grossly false.

Let us dwell on this point, for to do so will repay us. (1) Everybody knows that there are actions which we say we do without a motive; there are acts, in the first place, not preceded even by the (conscious) idea of the act to be done; and in the second place (and these latter are more important),[2] there are acts which are done thinkingly and

---

[1] [As the conjuror with his patter.]

[2] [They are, I presume, the only acts *relevant* here.]

on purpose, and which yet are done without any ulterior intent beyond the act itself. In both of these cases we have no motive before our minds, no thought of any end to be reached, out of and beyond the act itself; and here for our minds there *is* no 'because'—we do what we want, and it is simply a mistake to suppose that in and for our minds there is another or further end represented, which suggests the act, or to which the act is a means. (2) And where we act, as we say, *with* a motive, where we have in our minds a reason, an aim, an object beyond the act, which the act subserves, there these motives, these thoughts of ends or objects to be realized, are of very different kinds. The motive to the act may be the thought of another particular act, or of the whole of a complex scheme; it may be the idea of an end which my action is to bring about, the pleasure or the happiness, the pain or the ruin of another; in a word, the idea of any event the thought of whose realization by certain means excites desire or want, and so is a motive. In none of all these is the thought of my future feeling of satisfaction what I have before me: but this again *may* be my motive, and sometimes is. The pleasant feeling which is to result from an act may be presented in imagination, and thought of as the end to be reached; or the thought of myself to be pleased as much as possible generally, and specially here by such means and in such a way, may be the end which I take as the principle and motive of my action.

Let us illustrate the above: I may eat because I am hungry, instinctively and unthinkingly, or simply purposing to eat this or that dish; and in these cases there is no motive proper. Or I may have a motive. I may wish to please the person who offers it, or to prevent some one else having it; I may eat in illness because, though with present pain and disgust, I have to support my life. Now in every one of these cases it is or it may be incorrect to say that the idea of my pleasure is what moves me to act. I have or I may have no such idea before my mind. I do not say to myself, 'Now it will please me to do this, and *therefore*

I will do it.' This I do only when I think about my food beforehand, when I realize in imagination the taste of what I am about to eat, recognize this as pleasant, and make the pleasantness a motive for eating it ; or when, without calling up any particular image, I know that the eating of this or that will produce pleasure, and, with a view to the pleasure as an end, provide the eatables simply as a means. Here in these two cases my motive is the idea of a pleasure,[1] while in the cases before it was not.

We see, then, that we may act on instinctive impulse or on conscious desire for this or that, either with or without the idea of an ulterior end, or that which we commonly call ' motive ' : and to say that the idea of my feeling of satisfaction is the ' because ' of every action in the sense of its motive, either as the thought of this pleasure which I desire, or of pleasure in general to which this or that is subordinated—is simply to ignore plain facts, as every one may judge for themselves. When I quarrel with a man and stab him, I may act with purpose and intent, and yet altogether without any motive in its ordinary sense of an ulterior end, being moved simply by the negative desire of hate and the positive longing for revenge ; in short, *because* I want to : but most certainly the idea of my want is not present to my mind as my reason or cause for killing ; i. e. I do not say, ' I will kill him in order that I may not feel this want, or may feel it satisfied ', although no doubt it is *possible* that I might.

So much let us now take for granted ; but we have not yet satisfactorily removed the ground for the assertion of universal selfishness. Pleading the cause of that doctrine, we may further say, ' But all this is not to the point. All that is desired is (or, if you will, seems) pleasant, and only what is pleasant is desired.[2] It is the pleasure which moves, and pleasure is *my* pleasure, and therefore it must follow that

---

[1] For further explanation of this phrase see below, pp. 262-3.

[2] To save space I have omitted all consideration of aversion from pain. But to avoid pain is, in respect of selfishness, admittedly the same as to seek pleasure ; so we need not treat it separately.

in this sense my pleasure is my motive, and hence that I always am selfish.' Let us examine this.

'All that is desired is (or seems) pleasant': this is questionable, as we have seen, if extended to instinctive appetites. We may ask, for instance, is it pleasure which first sets the child sucking?—but this by the way. When the assertion is limited to the desire, where objects are before the consciousness, then we think it is always true that in desire the desired is so far pleasant, and nothing but the pleasant can be desired.

'It is the pleasure that moves': then, understanding by this that what immediately determines the will is a feeling of pleasure, let us for argument's sake admit it to be true.[1] *
'And pleasure is my pleasure': yes, undoubtedly—I feel what I feel, and nothing but what I feel; but such a formal assertion, as we saw, tells us nothing about the self which feels; it tells us that the mere feeling self is there, it does not tell us that any other self is not there.

'And hence my pleasure is my motive; for it is my pleasure (or, if you will, my pain) which moves me to act; and therefore I am selfish.' Or, putting it separately, 'My pleasure or pain moves me'; to this we say Yes. 'And my pleasure is my motive'; to this we say No, *non sequitur*.

The reasoning we have developed rests, in a word, on the confusion between a pleasant thought and the thought of a pleasure; between an idea of an objective act or event, contemplation of which is pleasant, and of which I desire the realization, and the idea of myself as the subject of a feeling of satisfaction which is to be. Both ideas move us; both we desire to realize: but the ideas are radically different. One, we repeat, is the mental representation of

---

[1] I believe, on the other hand, that, when put in this way, it is false. What directly moves is a felt contradiction, and this is not pleasant, though it implies an element of pleasure, and though the whole state *may* be pleasant (cf. pp. 67–8, and below, pp. 289 foll., with notes p. 290). This, however, does not matter here.

* [See foot-note. Certainly admit it 'for argument's sake', but not further. There is the tendency of the idea (in will) to realize itself; cf. p. 252 (with Notes and References). For 'motive' cf. p. 267.]

an act of will or thought, or an outward event, the other the mental representation of a state, either general or particular, of our feeling self. And hence we may agree that pleasure attends the idea which moves to action, that it is a necessary concomitant of desire for an object ; we may agree, I say (with the necessary qualifications), to hold this doctrine as substantially true, and yet we need not admit that the motive is always the idea of a pleasure as such.

Surely it is plain that a thought may excite pleasure in us, and yet that such pleasure is not and can not be the thought itself, nor included in the thought. Surely it is plain that when we think of pleasure to be had, and are pleased, the pleasure that we have is not the pleasure we think of. We think of the pleasure we are to have in doing this or that ; the pleasure we think of is our motive ; it is to get it that we act. The getting of it is our idea, and the having that idea pleases us. It is a pleasant thought, and so excites desire (*how* does not here concern us) exactly as another thought, which is not the idea of pleasure as such, also pleases us and so excites desire. But the pleasure we feel is not the motive ; it is not what we want and have *not* got. When the idea of the feeling of satisfaction is the motive, it is the thought of an absent pleasure which produces present pleasure and consequent desire ; but once again that present pleasure is not the motive. Action, if it were, would be inexplicable ; for we should act to get what we have. If my motive were the present pleasure, by action I must lose the motive and hence the pleasure, or at best get instead a pleasure which was not my motive. Motive is that which we want, and which so far we are without.[1] Suppose a motive to be a feeling we have, then so far as we have it, so far as it is a motive, we do not want it, and can not wish for it. I fear I have been, and still may be, wearisome, but I fear still more to leave this point in uncertainty.

---

[1] I may desire the continuance of the present ; but desire for continuance is desire for what is not, what I have not now, what I may have hereafter, what I think, what I do not feel.

The motive, in the ordinary sense of the word 'motive', is always the object of desire, is never the feeling of desire. And the motive, as the object of desire, is never the immediate psychical stimulus to action. What moves to action, whether that action be merely voluntary or also volitional, whether it does or does not involve a formal act of choice or resolve, is in all and every case the desire[1] or the desires: and the real stimulus in desire, the direct and actual mover (whether it be pleasant or painful), is and must be always felt, and can never be thought.[2,3] It is impossible to bring it before the mind in such a way as to make it our object, without, as a consequence, destroying its very nature:[4] the thinking it makes a motive of it, which now, as an idea, is not a desire, but is the object of a new desire.

If it were necessary that the psychical antecedent which directly produces the act should be a motive, then no instinctive act would be possible. And in this respect what holds good of one act holds good of all; the stimulus is a feeling. My pleasure (if it be pleasure), which moves me to act, is, *because* it moves, therefore *not* my motive; and my motive, because it *is* my motive, therefore can *not* be the pleasure which moves. Admit that of several desires the strongest prevails, admit that of alternative pleasant objects we must choose the most pleasant, yet this is not to

---

[1] [Cf. pp. 252, 257–8.]

[2] Of course, while being pleased by the contemplation of an object, you can transfer the pleasure, in idea, to that object, so that they form an integral whole. But then a new feeling must be excited by that whole in order to move you.

[3] [Yes, even when it is the motion of the idea, for that motion (at least actual motion) is not, so far, an idea.] ⟨*It has been thought better to retain this Note, despite its apparent obscurity.*—ED.⟩

[4] I do not mean that it can not be theoretically apprehended, and so transformed by the observing intellect, while at the same time and none the less as feeling it moves us practically. What I mean is that, so far as transformed, it is destroyed. The ideal representation of the feeling, so long as only theoretical, may coexist side by side with the practical feeling; but that representation as practical, i. e. as an idea which generates new practical feeling, is *ipso facto* the destruction of the old feeling as such.

admit that we choose between the ideas of pleasures; it is
not to admit that, if my choice is determined, I therefore
choose that which immediately determines it.   Out of the
present ideas of pleasures, as such, to be had, to choose
always what seems to be the greatest is selfish, but to
choose what pleases me most is not selfish nor unselfish.
It merely means *that* I choose, and says nothing whatever
about *what* I choose.

Let us close this discussion.—Pleasure is the feeling of
self-realizedness; it is affirmative self-feeling, or the feeling
in the self of the harmony of felt self and not-self.   It is
a state of the feeling self; and to make it a motive is to
have present to consciousness the idea of my self as feeling
pleased by this or that means or generally, and is to set
before us such an idea as our practical end, to which all
else conduces; and this once more is not our motive in
every act, or in most acts, nor even (as we shall further see)
in all our selfish acts.

You may say then that I desire only the pleasant, and
that pleasure is my pleasure, and (for argument's sake if
you will) that my pleasure determines me to do in voluntary
acts, and also to choose in volitional acts—yet, with all this,
you have not made one step towards proving me selfish, by
showing that it is the idea of my pleasure, as such, that
I have before me.   The difference is between my finding
my pleasure *in* an end, and my finding means for the end
of my pleasure; and the difference is enormous.

I hope that to the reader by this time it is no less obvious,
and, if this is so, we shall consider the psychological argument for universal selfishness disposed of.   The assertion
that we are all selfish, not perhaps consciously but yet unconsciously, we shall better be able to consider when we
know what selfishness is.   For on this head we are no nearer
a conclusion than when we set out.   All that we have done
has been to show the confusion which surrounds the word
'motive',[1] and to point out that a pleasant thought, or

---

[1] 'The Motives, or Ends of action, are our Pleasures and Pains.'—
Bain, *Mental and Moral Science*, p. 346. And *Emotions*, p. 266, ed. iii,

again the thought of something pleasant is not the same thing with the thought of pleasure, the thinking of something merely as a means to more or less of pleasant feeling as such.

And now what is selfishness? We have just been hearing of the pursuit of pleasure simply as my pleasure, and it naturally occurs to us to identify the two, and say selfishness is this pursuit. Can we do this? Or shall we find that, though the pursuit certainly is selfishness, yet selfishness is more than it, is a wider term than mere pleasure-seeking? That we shall see better, when we know more accurately what pleasure-seeking is, a question which as yet we have not asked.

Confusion here is inevitable unless we are cautious. We talk of pleasure and pleasures as if they were something by themselves, and apart from the pleasant ; as if a pleasant activity were simply a pleasure, and as if a pleasant feeling had no other content than its pleasantness. This is clearly unjustifiable. Pleasure we have called the feeling of self-assertion, but we must remember that there is no such thing as the mere abstract assertion of the self. The self is affirmed in this or that, and the this or that of the particular affirmation must be felt : the self-feeling is not one thing by itself, which is divisible from what is felt in the self: the feeling, and the feeling myself affirmed or denied, are not parts but elements or aspects of one whole, to be distinguished and not divided. It may indeed possibly be maintained that the general feeling of pleasure, which goes with the pleasant,

'The intellect can determine the fitness of means to secure an *end* ; but the end itself must, in the last resort, be some feeling, something desirable or undesirable, some pleasure to be sought, some pain to be avoided, some impulse to be followed out '. To carry confusion further than this would not be easy. The identification of the final with the efficient cause is an object which more than one philosophy has striven to attain. But neither that nor any other problem is cleared up by the simple failure to distinguish between the two.*

* [See pp. 128–9.]

can be distinguished in such a way as to be brought before the imagination by itself, and apart from this or that particular pleasant feeling, and it does not concern us here to contest such a proposition; but what is quite clear, and what we insist upon, is that the representation of this feeling of pleasure as such would not be what is ordinarily called the idea of a pleasure.[1] If the abstraction can be made and brought before the mind, yet people do not commonly do this. A pleasure for them means something pleasant: in a pleasant feeling they do not separate the pleasure from what in particular is felt; they follow ἡδέα and not ἡδονή. This or that pleasant is not aimed at simply as a pleasure; and the pursuit of pleasure in general for pleasure's sake would mean the abstraction from the pleasant of its pleasantness, and the setting that as an object before the mind. Such an end, the notion of the self simply to be pleased, is an intellectual abstraction, and the consistent pursuit of it exists only in theory. The ideal voluptuary desires only pleasure, and the pleasant merely as a means thereto; but this ideal is not to be found, and his supposed consistent hunt is a practical impossibility.

There never was any one who did not desire many things for their own sake; there never was a typical voluptuary: and yet the pursuit of pleasure does to a certain extent exist, and a man approaches the ideal voluptuary so far as he makes abstract pleasantness his object. How it is possible to do this, is a question the answer to which will be found of service to us.

The voluptuary was not always what he is. Children are supposed to pursue the pleasant, but no one ever called a young child a voluptuary, and everybody has been a child. Our voluptuary at first, that is, when his consciousness had arrived at the stage where objects existed for him, and he began to desire them, pursued chance pleasant things without reflection. And to the stage of desire for this or that pleasant thing we may give the name of 'appetite'. What then is an object of appetite, this or that pleasant thing

---

[1] [Pleasure, in and by itself, is an abstraction.]

which is desired? May we say, an object with the sensation or idea of which an idea or ideas of pleasure are associated? This would be most incorrect. Let us take an instance of simple appetite, and see what happens there.

I see on the table a glass of water. In what sense, if any, are ideas of pleasure associated with that? Clearly, as I look at it now, I feel no pleasure at all in myself, and not a pleasant idea do I find which attaches itself to it. I imagine myself drinking it, and call up, so far as I can, all the feelings which that would excite. It makes no difference; there is nothing about it I desire, nothing pleasant at all. But I had forgotten. I remember now how thirsty I was only yesterday, and how glad I was to get a glass of water. Then I was pleased, and now the water has reminded me of it, and I call up before my mind the greedy thirst and the keen pleasure I had. The memory even pleases me. I look again at the water; but do I desire it? No, I want it no more than my dog wants the dry bread which he ate so eagerly an hour ago, and the very existence of which beside him he now does not recognize. Thus we see that first there were no ideas of pleasure associated with the water, and then, even when there were, I yet did not desire it. But now I have gone out in the sun for some hours, and am come in again. My dog, who has drunk by the wayside, now runs up to the bread and eats it; and I am thirsty, see the water and drink. In this case I want the water; before I did not. What makes the difference? Can we say, 'Yes, now I drink because the perceived water suggests ideas of pleasure, and the ideas suggest (directly or through their feelings) the activities with which their archetypes were connected'; or otherwise, 'The pain of thirst suggests through the water the relief from pain, which is the idea of pleasure, and that suggests the action, and so I drink'? All this again (apart from other objections[1]) would be an inaccurate description of the facts.

[1] We are not here concerned with the lowest stages of the will, but we may remark that the 'association' theory is not only helpless before the fact that uneasiness and pain are stimuli to action, and is driven

It is not true as a matter of fact that in the second case, where I drink, the water must have ideas associated with it which it had not associated with it in the first case, where I did not drink. And the whole phraseology is both clumsy and misleading. In more ordinary language this is what really happens. Water has a certain meaning to me; and, when I see water and recognize it, I can have before my mind either all its meaning or only a part. One part of that meaning is that water quenches thirst; i.e. it contains the ideas of certain activities, results, and feelings. These ideas, in the first case, we purposely called up; they were there, and yet that did not move us to drink. In the second case we are moved to drink, but the question is, when we want the water, have we any more ideas than when we did not? 'Yes,' we shall be told, 'you have now the idea of pleasure to be had by drinking, and therefore you drink: that is the new idea, and before you did not drink because you did not have it, or did not have it strong enough.' Taking the last part first, if it were true that we had the idea of future pleasure, then weak and now strong, and it was this which made the difference, then we say this question of the *strength* of an idea points to the fact that what moves is not the mere idea but rather feeling. But passing by that, and going to the first part of the statement, viz. that I have, when I want the water, a new idea, the idea of future pleasure, we say this is not really the case. No

by it to open inconsistencies or palpable fictions (let the reader peruse Bain, *Emotions*, ed. ii, pp. 312–13; ed. iii, pp. 316–18); but that also the real thesis with which it stands and falls, viz. the general priority of activity to all feeling,* it fails even to recognize as the vital question, and obscures it by showing, what is nothing to the point, the priority of general activity to the special sensations of the senses (*Emotions*, 303). But *if* the discharge of energy from the physical centre (lower or higher) be preceded by any specific feeling, and accompanied by any specific feeling, then, *if* this is so, surely here is the place to look for the psychical genesis of the will, and not in the unverified postulate of a discharge, not felt in its origin or itself, and yet followed by pleasure.

---

* [Is this essential to the 'association' theory, or is it only so to Bain? Cf. p. 268, note. It is more or less irrelevant here, cf. pp. 267–8.]

doubt I might have the idea of future pleasure, and so drink; but, if I drink merely because I am thirsty, simply because I want the water, then (as we have seen before) it is false that I have before me any such idea; and hence the difference, supposed to constitute desire, does not exist, although desire does exist. Take the case of simple appetite for water; there what I do really have before my mind is a particular object, recognized as drinkable, i.e. containing the idea of the process of drinking, and the idea of certain accompanying feelings. These feelings may in fact be pleasant, but, in simple appetite, they are not brought before the mind in that character; or again, if that be done by reflection, yet (as we saw) that bringing of pleasant feeling before the mind in idea does not constitute desire. I have this object before me, that is one thing: I want it, and that is another thing, which consists in this. The recognition of the object as water which is drinkable, means the presence of certain ideas before the mind—so far there is no want: there is want when, against the uneasy (or painful) feelings of thirst, I feel in these ideas (through the mediation of the feelings of swallowing liquid, which they more or less faintly excite) a pleasure, which is strong according as the uneasiness is, and *vice versa*. It is the *feeling* of self-assertion in the ideal drinking (known to be ideal partly by its feebleness, but mainly by the non-possession of the object, and the continuance of thirst) against that of negation in the actual uneasiness, which produces such a felt contradiction and tension as leads to a reactionary discharge of energy in the direction of the ideal satisfaction, with its already felt self-affirmation. That discharge carries itself out in the actions connected with the particular idea, in which this mixed and partial satisfaction is felt, those actions being here the drinking the water. Desire is not the idea of a pleasure before the self, it is a felt tension *in* the self. It is an actual pain or uneasiness felt against a felt pleasure in an idea, which moves to make that idea real. This thing to be drunk by me is the idea before the mind; that is the object of desire, and it would be the motive, if it

were the *indirect* object : for motive means an *ulterior* end.[1]
The felt stimulus of pleasure in the idea against pain in the
reality is what moves. i. e. is the immediate psychical *prius*
of the putting forth of energy: and this, as we have seen,
can never be the motive or the object, because a feeling
which is an object is *so far* not a feeling.[2]

Or take the instance of a lump of sugar. That means to
me mainly, or here at least, the sweet-tasting thing ; and
I do not want it. In comes a child ; to him it means also,
as it did to me, the sweet-tasting thing, but he cries for it.
'Yes,' we shall be told, 'in one case there is the idea of a
pleasure, in the other not.' Supposing we have in the child
simple appetite, I deny the statement. In both cases there
is the idea of a sweet taste, and, if that idea is felt to be
pleasant, it moves because it creates want, i. e. a state of
contradiction, where the absence of sweet taste becomes
uneasiness or pain ; such a state as I can produce in myself
perhaps by eating something sour. But it is a mistake to
say that I want the sweet thing because, so to speak, I dis-
count for myself the promised pleasure to be got from eating
it. Whether the pleasure create the uneasiness, or the
uneasiness suggest the pleasure, in any case the essence of
desire is feeling. The child does not cry for the sugar on
Tuesday because he remembers he had a pleasure on
Monday, and thinks he should like another to-day ; but
because the feeling of sweet taste, now transferred as an
idea to the sugar and made objective in it, is recalled in
idea by its perception, and, being recalled, excites a feeling
which, against the felt absence of sweet taste, is felt as
want, and accordingly moves.

An object of simple appetite (using appetite as desire for
recognized objects, not as a name for the lowest form of
want) is this or that thing or process, with the perception
or image of which are connected (directly or through the

---

[1] [Motive : see p. 258 and foll.]

[2] [Yes, but the 'so far' must be emphasized. What is not a feeling
qua object, may be so otherwise in fact. See pp. 252, 261, 264-5.]

idea of activities) certain feelings,[1] which, against the feeling of privation, are pleasant. Whether in any case now want precedes the pleasure, or the pleasure excites the want, makes no difference. Whether the original satisfaction first came unneeded, or was preceded by and followed on the feeling of privation, at the present stage again makes no difference. The feeling of satisfaction which has ensued now at any rate has qualified the object. The object contains in its very notion, not the memory of this or that past satisfaction, but the ideas of the activities or states in which the satisfaction consists, and through them can call up the feeling (as distinct from the idea of the feeling) of a similar satisfaction. These ideas and this feeling are pleasant when want exists, but not otherwise. If I feel hungry, the sight of food pleases me; or the sight of food may, given the unfelt need for it, make me feel hungry; but, if I am satisfied, I do not desire satisfaction, at least while I remain in the stage of mere appetite. No man of simple tastes cares to see food when he is not hungry; e. g. it is not pleasant to live in the public room of an inn where eating goes on all day.[2]

[1] [Whether due or not to certain actual inchoate activities.] ⟨*These words were followed in the MS. by 'Add. ??'*—ED.⟩

[2] As an instance of the collision with fact which follows on false doctrine, I may mention that Mr. Bain, to save his theory, has to assert that, when a child or animal is fed, it goes on eating until compelled to stop by pain (*Senses*, ed. ii, pp. 308–9, ed. iii, 303; *Emotions*, ed. iii, p. 316). No doubt that may and does happen, but that it always does and must happen, will, I think, be recognized by any one who has fed dogs on proper food, and seen eagerness by slow degrees pass into tranquil indifference, as a palpable fiction. Mr. Bain's treatment of the will is thorough and instructive, but, I think, by no means satisfactory. His theory stands on two foundations, (1) the fact of a discharge of energy, preceded by no feeling, and yet followed by pleasure: this 'fact' seems to me nothing whatever but an assertion,[*] which the instances adduced do not verify; (2) the 'law' of 'self-conservation', i.e. the fact that pleasure always promotes and pain always hinders action. Whether it is well to call any and every unrationalized general statement a 'law' I will not ask. Here the

[*] [This is perhaps too strong, but you certainly can't show that no feeling preceded. This is once more irrelevant; cf. p. 264, note.]

But appetite does not remain appetite. Certainly in man (I wish to say nothing further about the lower animals) it tends to pass into what may be called, for convenience' sake, lust.[1] Here it is no longer the ideal satisfaction of appetite,

---

statement of fact is incorrect. Mr. Bain evidently sees that it is so, and yet the theory stands and falls with it. Not being initiated into the 'inductive method', I hardly like to offer an opinion, but I should have said that there were 'three courses' open to Mr. Bain. The first is to revolutionize the theory until it systematically expresses the facts. The second is to say, 'A law is never the worse for a few exceptions'. The third is to torture the facts until they square with the theory. Mr. Bain seems to compromise between the second and third course. But *if* exceptions do not matter, why trouble oneself to get rid of them? If they do matter, why admit a 'supplementary law of Stimulation' (*Emotions*, ed. iii, pp. 311–12) which is the direct denial of the main law? It is *always* wet on half-holidays because of the law of Raininess, but *sometimes* is *not* wet because of the Supplementary Law of Sunshine.

[1] [Lust, cf. p. 283. This is unfortunate because 'Lust' is derogatory. It is meant (I think) to apply only to the satisfaction of appetite when made a permanent end, the desire for other ends being left unnamed. 'Appetite' is used for that which implies the destruction (more or less) of its object, and so is negative in essence, at least in part.

The desire for positive affirmation in a positive object is left unnamed. This has been treated elsewhere in this volume. ⟨*The reference seems to be to the foot-note on pp. 282–3.*—ED.⟩

The point here is that the self feels itself positively affirmed in objects themselves, and not in their mere use destructively. The presence of one's fellows gives heightened self-feeling, as does production of anything in which one feels one's being affirmed and increased, or realization of any ideal in an object, or any kind of self-assertion made real and permanent. Scents might be added as non-destructive enjoyment, and, of course, everything so far as aesthetic. The *gourmet*'s ideal, for example, is not mere satisfied greediness, but largely aesthetic (why *not* an aesthetic of tastes?).

The same applies to any pursuit as assertion of an ideal of positive qualities of oneself. Even the pursuit of women *may*, so far, not be mere lust, but like the huntsman's ideal, or the conquering soldier's. But in all these pursuits, so far as negation predominates, so far they are lower and more worthless, if not wholly false and bad.

N.B. A shared pleasure is, so far, a positive assertion of self, and (no matter what it is otherwise) has become, so far, a positive realization.

These pages, 269–74, are hence one-sided. It would be ridiculous to call the desire for companionship 'Lust'.

felt as pleasant in this or that objective thing or process, which excites desire. The object does not remain sensuous; but by its relation to the permanent self it has been made into an idea, which itself, as against this or that moment of sense, is relatively permanent, and in the absence of perception can yet come before the mind. Hence, by the return of the feeling of satisfaction or the feeling of want, or in other ways, it is suggested to the mind when nothing is before the eyes.[1] But this is not all. Not only is the idea of the object a thought now independent of sense, but the pleasant feeling of satisfaction is reflected on and, as pleasant, is transferred to the object. The feeling of self-affirmation in the possession of the object has now, itself as an idea, become part of the idea of the object; and so not only is the object thought of when absent, but it is thought of as what is wanted, and what pleases when possessed. With the ideal possession of the object is integrated the ideal pleasant satisfaction; it is not the mere idea of the activities and feelings which give satisfaction, but the idea of these as pleasant, which is part of the content of the object. I think of the object habitually as that which gives pleasure when possessed, and hence, from time to time, when I do not possess it, the idea of the pleasant feeling as pleasant excites the feeling of assertion, and this, against the present absence of real assertion, tends to awaken the feeling of privation, and hence desire.[2] The content of the object

However, as to the 'voluptuary', that is all right, in the sense that, whatever the satisfaction, he treats it (or tries to treat it) as a *means* to his own pleasure.

But the limitation of the 'voluptuary' to the satisfaction of sensual appetites (pp. 273, ll. 7–8) is quite wrong; for (as I have just said) the essence of him is not limited to anything in particular, but is *general*.]

[1] We may notice in illustration that what is never absent, what I can always have, seldom becomes an object of lust.

[2] Lust must be based on appetite natural or artificial. The reason further why the water, when by reflection it was thought of as pleasant, did not awake desire was that, though ideas of pleasant feeling were in one way 'associated' with it, yet they did not make part of its meaning; they were not inseparable from it. Desire for water always remains simple appetite, partly because we can get it when we want it,

is now not the idea of certain feelings, pleasant or not as they are wanted or not, but the idea of certain feelings, thought of as pleasant and so creating want.[1]

The object of lust is thus (1) permanent; it is not this or that object.   It is true that what seems to be desired is this or that thing, but the particular is only a case or instance of what is relatively a universal.   This food and this drink disappear with the using; the idea of eating and drinking, and of objects to be eaten and drunk, remains and does not disappear.   And (2) the object is thought of as what pleases; the notion of myself as satisfying myself with it and finding pleasure in that satisfaction, enters, as a distinct element, into the idea of the object.   The consequence of this is that lust is not satisfied with this or that satisfaction of appetite, because the object of lust is not attainable in any one moment of sense.   The ideal possession with the thought of its fore-tasted delight, felt in sharp contrast to the pain of actual emptiness, was there, when the object of sense was absent: it became part of ourselves, that we carried where we went, and that rose perpetually before the mind, which had given to it its own enduring nature.   Then the object of sense was present; and it seemed that it was all that we wanted, and that all that we wanted was this.   Nor did the enjoyment (as we thought) deceive us: yes, this was what our heart was set on, this that we had; we have drained

partly because the ordinary pleasure of drinking is not very great. Hence by reflection and abstraction we may bring the pleasure of drinking before the mind, yet, because the feelings of the process excited by the idea are not pleasant, as against our present state of satisfaction, appetite is not awakened.   The idea of pleasure excited feeling of pleasure, but, because that did not make us feel our present state as privation, therefore it did not move.

[1] Perhaps the readiest way of seeing the transition is, first, to suppose ourselves in a state of appetite for an object of sense. The state we are in is (or may be) pleasant.   Let us delay satisfaction, reflect on the pleasure we feel, and refer it to the object.   The content of the object is now not simply what it was before.   The idea of my feeling pleased is added to it.   And if this were fixed in and became part of the meaning of the object, were integrated with its idea, then the object would now be lusted after.

the cup to the bottom, and there is nothing left us to desire. But we grossly deceived ourselves. The sensuous satisfaction goes and leaves nothing real behind it, but the ideal satisfaction does not go. It remains, made more definite and intense by reflection on the memory of past enjoyment; and, as a thought, it rises again before us when the enjoyment is over, and calls for its reality. Its reality is not there, and the appetite is aroused towards a fresh moment of sense, in which we are to find it. We find again but the old delusion, for our ideal has no reality, and it can have none. The reality it calls for is its own, and it calls for it in that which is alien to its nature. It is permanent, and moments of sense are fleeting; it is objective, and they are not; it stays with us, and they must go. We have tried to find ourselves as this or that, and we are not this or that, and soon discover that not one nor any number of transitory sensations is our realization. We have made an end of the satisfaction of an appetite; the satisfaction of an appetite does not last, but an end does last, because in it we have set ourselves before ourselves to be realized; and, if an end is to satisfy us, it must be a permanent objective something, which when possessed we still have, and find ourselves really there.

We need not repeat how the idea of the act which, as an ideal satisfaction, remains present and survives the particular act, goes on to institute a process with no end (pp. 95-6). We may notice how the thought of an end makes possible the artificial creation of appetite as a means to sensuous satisfaction, and further that here again is the origin of loathing. The perpetual unsatisfied want and disappointment, with their pain, are themselves transferred to and objectified in the idea of that which is lusted after, and now is both longed for and hated.

So far we have seen the nature of lust as compared with appetite; but the ideal voluptuary is not merely the man who lusts and is not satisfied. He reaches a level which, intellectually considered, is still higher. The failure of the objects of lust to give satisfaction, and the disappointment which ensues, provoke reflection which may take this turn. 'My ends are objects in which I am to find pleasure, but I do not find it; and so there must be something wrong somewhere. I have made a mistake as to the end; the deceit was "an illusion of close association"; I wanted pleasure in the ends, and so I thought I wanted the ends; and the ends have fooled me. The attempt to realize the objective ends as ends in themselves was a delusion; [1] I have proved by experience that none of these objects is the end I really want. I want them all, and yet I want none for itself; and that shows there is something in all which I want. What is this? It is my pleasure. The idea of my pleasure, apart from any particular sort of pleasant feeling, and apart from the realization of any object, is the end: all else is means thereto, and to be treated as such.' Here we have at last the typical voluptuary.

We have little to add to what has been said before: the points to which attention must be called are the following. The end is now consciously and explicitly subjective; nothing objective is desired for itself. And, further, the idea of the end is got by a process of reflection and far-reaching abstraction. The end is not the realization of this or that object, either for itself or as that which creates such and such pleasant feelings; nor is it even such and such pleasant feelings for themselves. The end is not the pleasant known as pleasant, but the pleasant apart from its content, and simply in respect of its pleasantness; it is pleasure as pleasure. Such an end, if consciously brought before the mind, is myself as a permanent end to be realized, not in this or that object, nor even in this or that feeling or set of feelings, but, in abstraction from all content, as the self which feels itself affirmed. The feeling of self-realization is the end, which calls for reality, without respect for anything in which the self is to be realized, except as means. It is not necessary to repeat that the abstract feeling of satisfaction, as an end, contradicts the very notion of an end and must fail to satisfy; nor is it necessary to add that

[1] [This is an error; see note, p. 269, and pp. 274-5.]

the voluptuary, as the man who consistently pursues that end, is an impossible character.

To return to our main subject. After this long but, I hope, not useless account of the voluptuary, the question arises, have we found what selfishness is? And the answer is, Certainly not. The voluptuary is selfish, whether he be the ideal one who consciously pursues the abstraction of pleasure, or the real one who to be consistent should do so, the man who makes an end of the pleasant satisfaction of sensual appetites. But the selfish man need not be a voluptuary, for he need not realize for himself beforehand his expectation of pleasures; and we have still to ask what selfishness is.

What first is it not? It is not mere conscious pleasure-seeking, since acts other than this are selfish. It is not doing what you like, because, as we saw, in one sense no one ever does anything else, and yet all are not called selfish. Lastly, it is not a general name for the bad self, because all sorts of wrong-doing are not indiscriminately called selfish. Weak yielding, self-conceit, pride, revenge, and other vices are not so called. It would be absurd, for instance, to say 'how selfish!' when we hear of a murder; and we see at once that, though selfishness belongs to the bad self, it is not co-extensive with it. If we ask what selfishness is, the readiest answer will be perhaps 'thinking only of yourself'; and this appears to be right, though it needs explanation. Thinking only of oneself implies first that we think, that we are self-conscious reflecting beings; and hence it seems a misnomer to call a beast or a young child selfish. Secondly, we think of nothing but ourselves; and this means that the ends we set before us have not an objective content which is desired for itself, and without regard to its relation to our private selves. The selfish man, so far as he is selfish, has objects of desire which are not subordinated to any principle higher than his private satisfaction. If you ask what is the general end which includes his ends, you can point to none; but you find that he treats all objects as means, that he cares for none in itself, but will sacrifice any with readiness; and when you inquire what is common to them all, you find that they minister to his personal comfort; this comfort being a certain quantum of the pleasant and of absence of pain, which satisfies him, and which he either consciously aims at or unconsciously uses as a measure of all objects of desire. The ideal voluptuary consciously pursues pleasure in abstraction; the real voluptuary [1] consciously pursues the pleasant feelings which come from the satisfying of certain desires; the selfish man pursues the generally pleasant, and avoids the painful in general, neither separating the feeling of pleasure as an explicit end, nor troubling himself with hunting for the pleasant for the sake of the pleasant, but making objects his end, either consciously or unconsciously, only so long as they are pleasant.   If he separated pleasure from the pleasant and hunted for the maximum of that, he would be the ideal voluptuary: if he hunted for a certain sort of pleasant feeling as such, he would be the real voluptuary.[1]   He is neither; he is characterized not so much by his end as his absence of end, by his readiness to use anything as a mere means, to be let go when it ceases to serve the end to which the means conduce, i. e. certain objects or feelings which have nothing in common but their pleasantness, and which, if they began to be painful, would at once be neglected.

Selfishness excludes passion: so far as we are selfish we do not lose ourselves in anything, but remain cold-blooded; hence selfishness prevents crimes of a certain sort. It excludes all working for any end which is looked on as what matters, irrespective of our private comfort; hence a man who starved his children that he might pursue his hobby, need not, however immoral in that respect, be selfish—

[1] ['The *real* voluptuary.' This limitation is arbitrary, though supported more or less by common use, cf. '*epicure*'. But the pursuer of pleasant feelings of whatever kind, if, and so far as, these are distinguished from their other content, and pursued consciously or otherwise for themselves, is a voluptuary; e. g. religious emotion, social pleasures, &c., &c.]

at least in the proper sense.[1]   Further, it seems to exclude participation with others ; the pleasures of sexual intercourse or of the table need not be selfish in themselves, but only in their consequences, and so far as all self-indulgence inclines to selfishness.

This, it seems to me, is the description of what is ordinarily called selfishness : it is not co-extensive with the bad, but is a form of it.   But we have not yet properly understood it as immoral and opposed to the good : we must do this, and, to do it, we must know what the bad self and the good self in general are, a task which has now for some time awaited us.

The existence of two selves in a man, a better self which takes pleasure in the good, and a worse self which makes for the bad, is a fact which is too plain to be denied.   In the field of religion we hear of an inward man delighting in God's law, which would have me do what I do not do, and of another self which takes pleasure in what I abhor ; but in morals we have nothing to do with these.   We can not consider either the good or bad self in its relation to the divine will, because that would be to pass at once beyond mere morality.   But, apart from religion, the good and bad selves no doubt exist, and every one knows what they mean. I feel at times identified with the good, as though all my

[1] [This is disputable, however, since selfishness is ambiguous. Negatively it is not so, I think, since it always means undue indifference to the welfare of others. (Of course two or more persons may be selfish together.)   But, as to the positive side of egoism, that need not be mere pleasure or comfort, but may consist in the 'selfish' pursuit of an 'unselfish' end, calling for sacrifice of 'comfort', &c. ; there is, in short, higher and lower selfishness.   Self-realization may be immoral because selfish, if, and so far as, it means undue subordination of others' welfare to one's own, in however high a sense the latter is taken.   If the devotion of oneself to a pursuit involves the sacrifice of others' welfare beyond what is justifiable in the case, that is selfish, though it is not so in the lower sense, nor (perhaps) in the more ordinary sense.   It does mean realizing oneself in a certain way without due regard to others' welfare.   Even if a man gives his life as a martyr, that may be in the above sense a selfish act, just as if he renounced the world by going into a monastery, unjustifiably.]

self were in it; there are certain good habits and pursuits and companies which are natural to me, and in which I feel at home. And then again there are certain bad habits and pursuits and companies in which perhaps I feel no less at home, in which also I feel myself to be myself; and I feel that, when I am good and when I am bad, I am not the same man but quite different, and the world to the one self seems quite another thing to what it does to the other. Nor is it only at different times that I feel so different, but also at one and the same time: I feel in myself impulses to good in collision with impulses to bad, and I feel myself in each of them; and, whichever way I go, I satisfy myself and yet fail to do so. If I yield to the bad self, the good self is dissatisfied; and if I yield to the good self, the bad self is discontented; and I am driven to believe that two souls, two opposing principles, are at war in me, and make me at war with myself; each of which loves what the other hates, and hates what the other loves. In this strife I know that the good is the true self, it is certainly more myself than the other; and yet I can not say that the other is not myself, and when I enter the lists against it, it is at my own breast that I lay my lance in rest.

No doubt this account, as a description of every one, would be much overcharged. There are persons, no doubt, who know the bad self, in the main, not as an active enemy of the good, but merely as particular impulses, or an opposing drag. It is, however, better to see the whole extent of the facts we have to explain.[1]

The two selves do not present themselves as a mere collection of desires and habits, some of which we call good and some bad. We are not only conscious of ourself in them, but in each we are conscious of self in a certain character, as good against bad, bad against good. We are conscious of ourselves as willing them each in that specific character, and we recognize and refer our desires and acts, not to what seem to be certain headings, but rather each to

[1] [Yes, even if this extent is not found usually, or perhaps even normally.]

an apparent active centre, embodied in our will, which has asserted itself and does assert itself in us, and in which we have asserted and do assert ourselves, not as a collection or series, but as a real being, as what we call our good and bad self.

A being which is not self-conscious, and morally self-conscious, can not know a division in himself of good and bad will; and this by itself is a fatal objection against the theory which explains the two selves as hereditary groups of habits, 'egoistic' and 'altruistic', which oppose each other. I am far from denying that this view has a considerable value and sheds light on the subject, but, as a sufficient explanation of the collision in the self, it fails in two ways. In the first place, as we have just seen, the theory fails because the fact to be explained is a double self, and it ignores the self altogether, or recognizes it only as a self-conscious collection; and I do not think that the doctrine of two collections, each of which is aware of itself as antagonistic to the other collection, and both of which are collected in a larger collection, which is aware of itself as one, and yet as what falls into two self-conscious collections which struggle within it—can possibly be made intelligible to any person out of an asylum. The theory stands and falls with the view on the nature of the self which we came upon in Essay I. This is the first objection.

And the second is that the hereditary qualities will not even serve as the natural basis on which the good and bad selves are developed. If in a variety of men you take these selves, and examine their content, you will not find the same in each. The bad self is not entirely composed of habits and desires all of which are 'egoistic'; the content of the good self is not all 'altruistic'. It is mere reckless theorizing to see in the bad self the assertion of propensities in themselves 'egoistic', and nothing in the good self but what is naturally 'altruistic'. I do not know any one inborn propensity which may not be moralized into good or turned into bad. Take the virtues or vices of any man, and we can see that the natural basis of every virtue might under certain conditions have been developed into a vice, and the basis of every vice into a virtue; for vices and virtues have common roots. Illustration in detail would be wearisome, but I will adduce one single instance. Is the hereditary sexual propensity 'egoistic' or 'altruistic'? If egoistic, then all the virtues based on it, to which it supplies the natural material, everything of which it is the root or the nourishment (and how much does not that mean?) is egoistic and bad; and this is in flat contradiction with facts. If altruistic, then the vices it gives origin to (some of the worst we have) are altruistic and good; and that again is against the facts. In any case the theory breaks against the facts and against itself.[1] And I have already contested the assertion that all the good self must be 'altruistic', in the sense of being social.

What, then, is the origin of the two selves? And how are they developed from the crude material of the natural disposition? This is the question we have to answer; but let us first be sure we know what their content is.

The good self is the self which is identified with, and takes pleasure in, the morally good; which is interested in and bound up with pursuits, activities, in a word, with ends that realize the good will. The good will is the will to realize the ideal self; and the ideal self we saw had a three-fold content, the social reality, the social ideal, and the non-social ideal. We need say no more, then, but that the good self is the self whose end and pleasure is the realization of the ideal self.

What is the content of the bad self? Here we find no general head, no objective unity, to which, as an end, its content is subordinated. All we can say is that the content

---

[1] The reader must not misunderstand. I am not saying that good or bad qualities are in no sense transmitted to descendants. I say that these natural good and bad qualities can not be divided into two classes, altruistic and egoistic; and I say further that, if you examine the actual good and bad self in a man, you will not necessarily find all that he has inherited, which was good in his parents, on the good side, and all of the bad in them, which he has inherited, on his bad side. A man's character is not the grouping of two descended heaps.

of the bad self in a man is the habits and pursuits which are antagonistic to the good ; the bad will is the will which is identified with the bad, and the bad is whatever is willed against the good. Its content is not mere pleasure-seeking as such, for that implies abnormal reflection and abstraction : nor, again, is it selfishness, because many bad deeds are done without conscious or unconscious regard to personal comfort. The content of the bad self has no principle, and forms no system, and is relative to no end. Pride, hate, revenge, passionateness, sulkiness, malice, meanness, cowardice, and recklessness have no one thing common to the content of all :[1] I please myself and my worse self in all ; and, if you abstract what is common, you must say, since the worse self as such can not be an end, that hence the end, under which all are subsumed, is private pleasure ;[2] but all that is true in that assertion is that there is no other end. The bad self has indeed, as we have seen and have yet to see, some sort of unity, because we are self-conscious in it ; but that unity does not lie in its content ; the content can be generally described only by reference to the good self, as what contradicts and opposes it, and can not be defined except against it.

Turning now from the question of content to that of origin, we must consider first the genesis of the good self, not in the world in general, but in the will of the individual : and the question here is, how is it possible for the self to identify itself with what seems to be altogether outside it ? How is it that I can feel pleasure in the successes of persons and causes which do not affect my private personality ? How can I desire their furtherance, not as means but as an end ? How can the content of my will be not myself, as this or that exclusive individual ? How, in

---

[1] [It is doubtful if 'no one thing common, &c.' is strictly true. And why leave out sloth ? 'No one *positive* thing' would be better.]

[2] [Even this is not true unless you add 'of the moment'. Vice may be a want of selfishness in the sense of rational egoism (pp. 275-6). It is even *possible* to have such an exaggerated regard for others' welfare as carries 'unselfishness' into a fault.]

a word, can I have interests? We must briefly, and in the merest outline, sketch their origin.[1]

What we start with in the child is the feeling of himself affirmed or negated in this or that sensation; and the next step (a most important one, but one which we must take for granted here) is that the content of these feelings is objectified in things. The ideas of sensations, which were pleasant or painful, are transferred to objects, and, as ideas, form part of the content of those notions of objects by which we recognize them, when presented in perception. These objects are of two kinds. They are partly those which satisfy appetite; and these (if appetite does not pass into lust) remain mere transitory ὀρεκτά, which are desired when wanted, but which are not perpetually thought of as desirable; and whose perceived presence does not necessarily (nor at all, unless want exist) produce in the self a feeling either of affirmation or negation. Their perception or their ideas do not enter into the standing content which is felt in the self, and in which it feels itself permanently affirmed or denied. The objects themselves are not permanent; they disappear in the enjoyment of them; and the making of them permanent, as that in which we are affirmed, necessarily produces lust. But not all the pleasures of the child come from satisfied appetite;[2] and these transitory ὀρεκτά, which are related to recurring natural wants, and disappear in the satisfaction, are not all the objects in which he has made the ideas of his pleasant or painful activities and feelings the content of things. There are other objects round him, which please him apart from appetite, and of these not a few are permanent; they are continually with him, and do not disappear when enjoyed. On the contrary, they remain when possessed; and, so long

---

[1] [Here should come in a discussion of instincts, at least for a complete account of the matter. But, however important for psychology, this point need not, I think, be treated here.]

[2] A complete account of the matter would at this point have to investigate the nature of the satisfaction we get from our different senses, particularly those of sight and hearing. But fortunately our argument is not dependent on this inquiry.

as the child has them, he does not want them or desire them, but feels affirmed and satisfied in them. The feelings they excite, which are pleasant, are transferred to them as ideas, and are made part of their content, so that their mere presence gives pleasure; the will is asserted in them, and their perceived ideas by habituation enter into the content of the child's standing self-feeling (not as yet self-conscious), so that, in their absence, he is uneasy, he feels himself as something which is not fully there; or without them (in the homely phrase) he does not 'feel his self' at all.

Now, here we have not mere appetite, or tension between an actual empty and ideal full self, such as is felt in the presence of this or that sensuous object. The satisfaction is not preceded by a feeling of contradiction, and it is permanent. And further, we have no selfishness, because we have no reflection and abstraction; the presence of the environing pleasant objects excites the general habitual pleasant self-feeling. It is most incorrect and misleading to talk of ideas of pleasure being 'associated' with them. The fact is that the idea of the object (imagined or perceived) gives a feeling of pleasure; and it does so, because for the child its very meaning is objectified pleasant actions and feelings. And the point is that for the child it is a permanent pleasant; it is not a permanent cause of pleasure. It is not a means to an end outside itself. Whether its content is felt to be pleasant, or in addition is known to be so, in neither case is the pleasantness separated in idea from the objective content, and it can not be made an end apart from that. The child likes it for itself, and he will not give it up for another means to the same end, because he has not thought of an end apart from the things he likes.[1]

---

[1] At this point for clearness' sake it may be well to put certain results together. And, passing over the stage of mere want or felt need, not referred to an object, we have

(1) Simple Appetite. Here a sensuous image is presented, with which are integrated the ideas of certain feelings and activities, derived

For the sake of clearness I have put things first; but persons perhaps (if at this stage we have a right to make any such distinction) should have had the precedence. It is a fact which deserves more attention than it receives,

from the pleasant mastering of the object. This image excites a feeling of pleasure, against which the actual state of the subject may be felt as privation. In that case the pleasure felt in the ideal feelings and activities, presented in the object, against the uneasiness of privation, constitutes the tension of desire.

(2) The self is identified with relatively permanent objects, not objects of appetite, so that in the affirmation of these it feels its self-assertion, and in the loss of them privation. This is the beginning of objective interest.

(3) Reflective Desire. Here the object is a relatively permanent thought, the content of which when presented may excite want, and so move.

(a) We have Interests or objective ends, when the content of the object consists of permanent results and activities directed to aims other than the satisfaction of momentary appetites. And here there are two possible cases. (i) The ideas of my pleasant feelings and activities, which make one whole with the content of the object, may have been reflected on and be perceived to be the ideas of what is pleasant to me. Or (ii) there may be no such reflection, and the object, without containing ideas which I recognize as of that which is pleasant to me, may simply excite a feeling of pleasure in me. This distinction is unimportant, so long as there is no *separation in thought* between the ideas of the objective result and of my pleasant feelings. But if this latter takes place, then interest proper ceases, and the object is no longer an end in itself.

(b) In Lust (cf. p. 270) the permanent end is the mastering of the sensuous objects which excite appetite. And my pleasant feelings in that satisfaction are recognized as such, and, as ideas, are made an element (in most cases a distinct element) in the permanent end.

(c) In selfishness there is, properly speaking, no end in itself.* Here the element of what is pleasant to me in general is separated in idea from the objects, and though the former is scarcely made an end, yet the latter are treated as subservient and without intrinsic value.

(d) We have the Voluptuary, when first pleasant feelings, and secondly the pleasantness of pleasant feelings, are made the end to which all else is means, and the abstraction of pleasure for pleasure's sake is pursued.

---

* [Selfishness. See p. 308, l. 27. This is not correct, and seems even admitted to be so. See pp. 270, 276-8, 280, with their respective notes.]

that what satisfies a child's first appetite is endeared in
other ways besides, and is a permanent object. Mother and
nurse satisfy a child's recurring wants ; but they are pleasant to him in other respects, and are always with him, so
that he feels them as part of himself, and, when left alone,
is uneasy and wants them.[1] We see the same thing, mixed
with other feelings, in the relation of the dog, or at least
most dogs, to the master ; and here again the rule is that
the dog a man has brought up is most attached to him.
Even later in life, with regard to some people, we feel
something of the same sort, though here again the feeling
is probably mixed. We like to be with them, their presence
is pleasant. And in all these cases the ideas of pleasure
and their external connexion are fictitious, and the 'illusion of close association' is only there for the deluded
theorist.

Nor is it merely in the absence or presence of what is
dear that the child feels its will negated or affirmed ; it does
so, too, in the negation or affirmation of the object. Natural
sympathy (into the ultimate nature of which we do not
enter) no doubt plays a great part here ; but, apart from
sympathy, there are obvious reasons why the manifested
well-being and pleasure, or again the discomfort, of the
mother or nurse should be identified by the child with what
is enjoyable or painful to itself ; and further again, apart
both from sympathy and this comparatively 'artificial'
connexion, it must happen that the perceived affirmation
or negation of any part of the endeared environment is felt
as the assertion or suppression of the self. When we are
pained by the loss or spoiling of parts of places where we
have been happy, this, I think, does not rest on sympathy ;
and when some childish possession is destroyed or damaged,
and then replaced or repaired, sympathy no doubt may
come in, but the diminution or increase of that which is
perceived (of course, unreflectingly) as the area of self-
assertion, or (if we like the phrase) as 'the objectification

---

[1] Whether the dread of being left alone is natural to a child, or not,
matters nothing to the argument.

of the will ', is essentially and immediately connected with
our own discomfort or pleasure. The self lives in its contents, rises and falls with its world ; things and other persons enter into those contents, and no great advance in
perception is needed to know, for instance, that a mother or
nurse is pleased or annoyed.

At this point we have reached the stage where moral
education begins ; not that the child will be a moral being
as yet, but it is here we can see the unconscious beginnings
of a better and a worse self.

So far the child has felt pleasure or pain in the existence
and well-being, or the absence and hurt of what is not self ;
he has not yet learnt the existence of a will beyond his
own. This he now does ; he finds himself limited and controlled, and controlled by that which is endeared to him.
The pleasure or pain of the mother and nurse has been his
pleasure or pain, and now he learns by experience that this
pleasure and pain are related to certain things which he
does or leaves undone. He sees what displeasure means,
and what it is when others are pleased with him. He learns
that the external, with which he is identified, is a will which
can be asserted against himself with painful consequences,
and that its pleasant or painful assertions in relation to
himself are connected with certain classes of his own
activities. He finds, or should find, that the willing against
the will of the superior is useless and, besides, gives pain to
himself, both by the displeasure of the superior, and also
by more direct unpleasant results. In short, he discovers
that there is a will outside of him, which is not only dear,
but also irresistible ; he learns, in particular, that there are
certain sorts of his activities which are willed by the
superior, and others which are against that will ; and he
learns, in general, that the accordance of his will with the
higher is pleasant, and discord painful. Not that he reflects
much, if at all ; he feels pleasure when in accord with the
superior, pain when antagonistic, and the particular steps
of the process, whereby he has come to do so, are not before
his mind at all. He knows, to a certain extent, what

'good' and what 'naughty' stand for ; and with the one he
is pleased, and pained by the other. He does not distinctly
realize that the superior will is external to him; he does
not bring it before him as the mere will of this or that
person not himself, but as yet his mind is comparatively
simple and run together. He feels the higher will bound
up with his own by affection, and one with himself; and
when he goes against that, then in himself he is unhappy.
The superior is presented as external, but its content is not
so, and it is felt as part of himself.

Obedience to command, pleasing the superior is pleasant
and desired as an end ; disobedience and the superior's displeasure is in itself painful, and is avoided. The child likes
to be good, and hence (no other reason is wanted) the pursuits and activities which are good are liked, and thought of
as desirable for their own sakes, while, by a counter process,
what is disobedient and bad becomes undesirable, and is
thought of as such. For this cause alone the good would
please ; but, in addition, the nature of what the child is
taught to think good is, in the main, what is on the whole
pleasant, while indulgence in the bad brings on the whole
contradiction and pain. The good accords with itself, the
bad does not, and the child soon finds this out. Other
furthering incentives we need not consider ; the fact remains,
that the child finds pleasure in the approval of the superior
and in that which the superior approves of, and pain in the
contrary; and further, that he does so directly and unreflectingly. To will what the superior wills is an end in
itself.

In all this what is there selfish? Of course, if the child
were habitually to say to itself, ' Will doing this be a means
to my pleasure or pain ?' and were to act accordingly, that
question might be awkward. And I do not say that children, more especially when they get older, never do argue
in this way ; nor can I deny that I have heard 'morality'
being taught them so—a lesson, it seems to me, which, if
not perilous, can fail to be so only because understood in
a sense other than its simple meaning. But, roughly

speaking, the process of learning to be good is as I have described it, and such calculating reflections are abnormal, and in infancy impossible ; and the development being in the main what has been sketched above, I repeat the question, Is there anything selfish ?

'Oh yes,' we shall hear, 'what moves is the idea of pleasure'—but of that fiction I think we must really have had enough. A child, when it tries to please its mother, is as unselfish as the hen who faces death for her chickens, as unselfish as the dog who gives his life for his master. The point is once more, what is before the mind in the act ? Are there any ideas of my pleasure, as my pleasure, there or not ? If any one maintains that my dog follows me about, and frets when I leave him, because of ideas of his own private pleasure *as such* which are 'associated' with me, I can not argue with such a man: we split upon a question of fact, and have no common ground. If any one tells me (and I have heard people say it) that a dog loves his master for what he has got from him or expects to get from him, I say this is an ignorant calumny. He may love him *because* he has fed him, in one sense of the word 'because', while in the other sense there is no because about it. The external conditions and psychical origin, in a word, the genesis of a matter, is one thing; its existing essence is another ; and you can not, without throwing philosophy and facts both overboard, argue 'this is how the thing came into the world, and therefore it *is* so'. The fact is that in unselfish love the object that is dear is felt as one with ourselves ; it is loved when the associations which first endeared it can not by any effort be brought before the mind. The man who talks about 'illusion', and says the ideas of private pleasure are there, only we are unable to lay our hand on them, can not, unless he gives reasons, expect to be attended to. I maintain that, in the cases I have mentioned, the original psychical link has been absorbed, the communication is direct ; the object is pleasant in itself, and those ideas are not a part of its content, or, if they are, they are not before the mind. Will any one have the assurance to say that, when you have gained a dog's affection, he must remember the attentions which in one sense *were* the 'because', and still connect them with you, and that they now *are* in this sense still the 'because'? Everybody knows that an animal may be taught to do things by rewarding him with food, but afterwards will do the things partly because he now likes them, and mainly to please you, because he likes you; and he either does not think of the food at all, or conceals his thought with a strange, purposeless, and altogether impossible effort. The association now may have no existence; and, even if the idea does exist, it need not be separated from, but is identified with, the performance.

In these simple attachments there is no more 'because' or 'why' in the sense of 'motive', than there is a because for the love of ourself. We love ourselves, and we love what we feel one with us. The ideas of the pleasant feelings, which did once enter, as such, into the content of the object and were objectified in it, fade away and disappear altogether, as such, or at least (and that is the important point) are no longer ideas before the conscious self. They may cease to be included in the content of the object, but the object, with the rest of its content, gives pleasure directly, and can be thought of as pleasant in itself; we feel ourselves one with it, and in its affirmation our will is affirmed.

We saw above that when the satisfaction of appetite was reflected on, when the self was identified with the pleasant negation of particular sensuous objects, and that as an idea was made an end, then we had lust, with its infinite process and general unsatisfiedness. We have now to see how different it all is, when the self is made one with ideas of a different sort.

The child, as we saw, finds pleasure in accordance with the superior, in the pursuits which are approved by him; and the thought of these activities, which are called good,[1]

---

[1] We shall come upon what may be called bad interests later on in our account of the bad self.

is pleasant and ideally affirms his will. They are ends in
themselves; they are not reached by the excitement of
appetite towards this or that perishing thing of sense ; they
are not merely something to be enjoyed, they are something
to be done.[1] They have a content other than the feeling
of the subject, an objective content ; and that objective
content is by act carried out into the external world. It can
be seen and possessed there ; or, if invisible, yet exists for
thought in its results, or at least in the recognition of others.
The child has done something ; and what he has done he
still in some shape or other has, if it be only in credit; he
possesses an objective issue of his will, and in that not only
did realize himself, but does perpetually have himself
realized. The self, felt permanent and identical within him,
finds its counterpart in the world which is not merely
itself; it has a permanent and identical expression, and, if
it think of itself, it has something to think of, a solid existing
and real content, not the mere memory of the perished and
unreal. Hence there is perpetual satisfaction, not because
desire ceases, but because here desire is pleasant both in
itself and its results. It is necessary, of course, that the
yet to be done, the something more or the something
new, should be presented as ideal assertion against relative
non-assertion. But, in the first place, the privation is
merely relative ; the desire is not, as in lust, the contradiction between fullness and absolute emptiness (in lust we
say, 'if I do not get this now, what matters all that I have
got before? For now it is nothing')—but we start from the
habitual complacency in our known realization, and, if in
one point we fail, yet we still have plenty ; and, secondly,
we have been so accustomed to succeed, that we either do
not think of failing, or, in any case, we know that it is not
this or that moment of sense which matters, since the content

---

[1] [The side of *doing* is here exaggerated. The child's feeling of
harmony and dis-harmony with its 'world', in which it finds satisfaction, obviously does not depend merely on what it does. This, however, does not matter much here : cf. p. 291. The point is that from
the first the child's world does not depend merely on what it *does*:
cf. pp. 285 and 294, l. 25 and foll.]

is objective, and therefore it, or at all events something of the same nature, may be realized another time. So we can feel pleasure already in the ideal success, while the pain of privation disappears or is overpowered.[1] What is always

[1] To the question, 'Is desire pleasant or painful?' no answer can be given. Desire is mixed and, I think, never without both elements.* It is pleasant or painful, as one outweighs the other.

Desire is a contradictory state. I feel in it what I am *not* really, against what I am really, and ideally am not. The actual negation is painful, the ideal affirmation is pleasant, because it excites actual affirmative self-feeling. And I need not remark that in desire pain and pleasure intensify each other.

We need not go far into the matter, for the main features are easy to trace. Is a beast desiring food on the whole pleased or pained? It all depends, and it depends on the preponderance of either element. If they have not a vivid prospect of satisfaction, all beasts that I have noticed seem uneasy and rather pained than pleased when hungry. Show them the food, or in other ways give them the prospect of it, and then there is no doubt that their whole state is pleasant. So with human beings. Notice the face of the hungry man, who is not sure of his dinner or of the time of it; and then notice again that of the hungry man who knows it is coming soon.—Reflection intensifies the pain of want, by keeping the contrast between the actual and ideal before the mind. For the same reason it intensifies the pleasure. Where the attention is directed to the want, that is made intense, and pain predominates: where it is directed to the ideal satisfaction, the pleasure is intensified and outweighs the pain. The cruellest want is where, against the idea of the satisfaction, the reality of the privation is forced on us. The keenest pleasure is where, against the surviving pain of want, the satisfaction is felt or forefelt as actual. It is because the pain so soon disappears that the pleasure of sensuous satisfaction fades so fast. It is not indeed true that the moment the pleasure touches our lips, the pain is gone wholly, but it has even then begun to go, and with it the extreme of pleasure. That is why so often 'the dream is better than the drink'. It must be so where the negation of the sensuous object is the end, i.e. where it is not the permanent assertion of ourselves in a permanent object which is aimed at. Only in the latter case do we keep and have ourselves in what we have. When we do this the pain of want is outweighed. It was partly his failure to consider this, partly his mistake as to the negative

* [I doubt if this is tenable where the fulfilment seems certain, though *possibly* 'desire' proper has ceased here.

And I doubt if the thought of a pleasure, where desire is painful, can be called a felt pleasure.]

with us is the feeling of pleasure in the self which is affirmed permanently and really; what we have done and are, exists apart from our feeling it, and so is objective; and in that habitual reality we have perpetual satisfaction. The ' to be done' means only more of what is done; and the fore-felt pleasure therein dominates the relative privation, which serves only as a freshening and pleasant stimulus, since not only the result but also the activity is an end in itself. Hence, though satisfied, we can desire; and, though we desire, we are not dissatisfied. In lust we have a permanent want occasionally gratified; in interest we have a permanent gratification, where what we want does but add to what we have. In lust the permanent content of the want is not realized, because the objective can not be found in this or that perishing moment of sense; in interest the content is realized, because the moment of sense is not desired as such, but is used as the means and material for the objective result, which, as a result, does not depend on it; the perished past was the condition of translation of the ideal into reality, and a reality which is present. The one object struggles to life, but dies as fast as it is born, and for ever remains a conscious and reluctant death; the other is perpetually born anew, and is for ever the same life, which remains and keeps its past and present.

And we must notice too, what further on will engage us, that the good which the child thus lives itself into and lives in, is in the main harmony with itself. And hence the self, which feels itself to be one and a whole, feels in the good the answering harmony of its own true nature, and divines

character of pleasure (i.e. his seeing in it only the negation of a positive, viz. pain), which was the foundation of Schopenhauer's pessimism. For him life is an oscillation between the pains of want and ennui. Want of permanence again in the realization is the reason why aversion, so often liked, encouraged, and on the whole pleasant mostly cheats itself in the end. When our enemies are destroyed, we have destroyed our pleasure. The whole subject of aversion is difficult and interesting.*

* [Aversion, see Article in *Mind*.] (' *On Pleasure, Pain, Desire, and Volition* ', *vol. xiii, no. 49, p. 21.*—ED.)

that what realizes it as a system realizes itself, and that the jarring and discrepant is false and untrue.

So far we have seen that the self is identified with pursuits and activities as ends to be gained by it, but further it is interested in persons and causes which stand in no direct relation to its personal activity. Apart from anything which it does or has to do, it feels its will affirmed or denied in the success or failure of that which its own action has not to bring about. This result is a mere continuation of the process which drops everything subjective, everything which concerns only me in particular, out of the content of the end, and subordinates my aims to general heads, until on the one hand the mere objective content of the ends, apart from the idea of my activity, is felt as the affirmation of my will, and on the other hand those ends are brought into a harmony, over which presides what, for shortness' sake, we may call the ideal. At this point the understood success or failure of causes and pursuits, which have nothing sensible about them, immediately and in itself asserts or negates my will; and instead of, as at first, taking pleasure in the cause for persons' sakes, I at last am interested in persons for the sake of the cause. The man's self is now wrapped up in the general progress of good, his will is so far by habitua-tion become one with the ideal; and in the realization of that, whether by himself or others, he finds a permanent and everlasting source of pleasure; a cause which brings indeed its own pains with it and, in the absence of faith, can do much to sadden, but in which alone he finds his true self affirmed, and affirmed apart from his private success or failure. After all that has gone before, I will not put the question whether this too is selfish.

The above is a sketch, fragmentary and imperfect, of the growth of the will for good; but, as we said before, good is not moral in the stricter sense, until it knows itself;[1] and it knows itself only in its opposition to evil. It is true in our account we long since passed the stage where the self is conscious of its will as good and as bad, but that was to

[1] [Cf. p. 293, l. 28 and foll.]

avoid confused repetition. We must suppose the child at present to have its will made one with the good, but not to know the good as such, never knowingly to have willed the good as its good will against evil, or evil as its bad will against the good. But, before we pass from unconscious to conscious good, and, with that, to morality, we must trace the growth of the bad self (not known as such), in order to see how the knowledge of good and bad arises from their collision in the self-conscious subject.

What is the origin of the bad self? It is a question that might well make us pause, for it leads directly to the problem of the origin of evil and sin; and that problem leads to innumerable difficulties, of which he who is ready with some crude solution knows but little, though no less perhaps than he (and there are many such) who commits himself offhand to the insolubility of a problem, about the true nature of which he knows as good as nothing. Those ultimate difficulties we intend to pass by. We have nothing to do with what is called natural evil, nothing to do with spiritual evil in its relation to the divine; the false self as sin does not fall within moral philosophy. We have to do with evil solely in the form of the moral bad self, and must attempt in outline to show how it arises, first unconsciously, and then in its specific character; and finally to say something on its nature as against the good.[1] I shall not attempt to mention, much less to criticize, every antagonistic view.

The self, to begin with, is born. morally speaking, neither bad nor good. No doubt it may not be what it should be; it should for instance be a moral being, but I suppose that does not make it one already in any proper sense of the word; and, not being a moral being, it can not be bad. I am far from denying a certain truth to other views on

[1] My knowledge of the literature of the subject is so exceedingly slight that I feel some diffidence in mentioning any work; but I think the reader will find that Vatke's book (*Die Menschliche Freiheit*, Berlin, 1841), if not satisfactory, at all events goes deep into the whole subject.

this point, but, as expressions of the whole, they are one-sided and false. The hereditary theory, in particular, we saw above failed wholly as an account of the good and bad self. We deny that good and evil come to us by nature, but we readily admit that certain qualities are trans-mitted which are the real possibilities of particular forms of both. We allow again the distinction between the purely natural and the potentially moral, and by no means assert that a new-born child is a beast;[1] but we must insist that the child is actually natural, and that the natural is neither immoral nor moral.[2] The child is born with a basis of physical and mental tendencies, more readily developed in some directions, good and bad, than in others, but still at present not developed, and moreover not to be developed by their own necessity. This common ground and material of good and evil we may call natural capacity; and, while by no means passing it over as free from difficulty,[3] we do not propose to enter on it further.

The development of evil from this neutral ground is not, on the whole, very much of a mystery; and we have been over a good deal of the subject already in our account of the growth of lust from appetite. And, presupposing an acquaintance with that process, as well as with the evolution of the unreflecting good will, we can content ourselves with saying very little.—The self, as we saw, objectifies its reac-tions in external things,[4] and rises from satisfaction, as fore-felt in this or that sensuous object, to the thought of ends, the ideas of permanent objects and pursuits, felt or known to be pleasant, and exciting desire by the ideal affirmation which they bring. These, when in harmony with and sub-ordinated to the superior will, we have seen are good. They are evil when they are discrepant with and can not be sub-

---

[1] [I object to the assumption here. It is nonsense to say beasts are not moral in any sense.]

[2] [' A *moral* being.' See p. 293 foll.]

[3] [Certainly as to responsibility (cf. p. 299).]

[4] [This is objectionable, if its ' reactions' are taken as merely ' subjective'.]

ordinated to the superior will,[1] though at this stage neither good nor evil is known as such. The natural material of the bad self is consequently supplied partly by sensuous appetite, partly by other tendencies which oppose the good system (such as violent irascibility, jealousy, laziness, &c.), and, further, by natural inclination to activities and pursuits which lead to collision with the superior. Passionateness or laziness encouraged grows into habit; sensuous appetite reflected on grows into lust, the idea of sensuous satisfaction, and the habit of pursuing that idea; activities and pursuits opposed to the superior may be made objective and relatively permanent sources of pleasure, and become bad interests. The self falls into bad habits in the same way in which it falls into good ones; it becomes identified with bad ends by the same psychical process through which it makes itself one with good ends. It affirms and has affirmed itself in evil, and such bad affirmation is both inevitable and permanent.

It is inevitable for this reason. Let the natural disposition of the child be never so favourable, yet, as against the system which is to be the good self, it is at first a mere chaos[2] of appetites and propensities, which, as they are and exist, can not be systematized. They must be made into a system by repression here and encouragement there; and even then, with all the conditions at the best, some element of the material is sure to give trouble. The will can be made one with the good by nothing but a process of habituation, and this takes time. All the while the child is living from moment to moment what must, under any conditions, be the chance life of a finite being. It is simply impossible that this or that bad satisfaction should not take place; impossible that desire for what is bad should not be awakened, and equally impossible that such temptation

---

[1] Throughout I suppose the superior will to be moral.* Of course all that is opposed to the superior need not form a part of the future moral bad self, but for shortness' sake we must simplify.

[2] [Perhaps exaggerated. So pp. 296-7, 308.]

---

* [But clearly it is *not* so wholly, and can be imitated when bad.]

should not at times be yielded to. And here we have the inevitable affirmation of the self in what is bad; and this is also permanent.

It is permanent because, in one word, the self is permanent, because the self is not a perishing flux or collection. Bad satisfactions are not gone when the moment is by, but in their results they remain in us. Apart from reflection, indulgence strengthens propensity, and, if repeated, forms habit;[1] and, given the presence of positive conditions, and absence of checks, habit will pass into the class of act which produced it. It is a state of the standing will. And reflection makes an idea, independent of this or that sensuous thing, which remains ready to rise before us, and so provokes temptation, and reacts upon habit to the further intensification of both. The self is made one with the bad by abiding habit and lasting idea, and thus gets a content, not past but present, which is discrepant with the content of the good will.

And here we must remark that this content has no unity in itself; it is not subordinated to a single controlling principle. It is a chance collection, united partly by interlacing of habits, partly by relative subordination to this or that bad end; but its various habits and ends are self-contradictory, e.g. lust and laziness, pride and greediness, hatred and cowardice. There is no one end, and there is no identity, no bond of unity in the main, except the

---

[1] It is surprising that a writer of talent could allow himself twice to publish the exquisitely silly remark, 'Failure is to form habits'. The saying is senseless in relation to fact; for every one knows that we can not choose between habits and no habits, but at most between good and bad habits. In connexion with the remaining views of the writer it is, if possible, still more senseless; for habit with him is a word that can mean nothing; and, to be consistent, he must say, 'It matters not what habits you think you have; for they are a delusion, and so are you'.*

---

* [What was meant was, I presume: Form the habit of keeping yourself open to fresh ideas and impressions, subject to the condition that these are not seen to be *bad* ones, and *there* form the habit of closing yourself rigorously.]

affirmative self feeling which, under differences, is the same throughout.[1] The bad is contrary to itself, as well as to the good, and, for these two reasons, is already painful, and, apart from this or that external check, fails to satisfy.

But at this stage in what sense is it contrary to the good? Is the bad known as bad against the good, and in that character willed? Not so, for the moral self-consciousness is not yet awakened. The bad is not brought under the general head of bad against good. Bad actions are attempted or willed, and, when willed, are found in collision with good; there is a sense of jarring and contradiction, accompanied at most by a perception of incompatibility, and followed by pain and dissatisfaction. The good and bad selves do not confront each other as unities: so far as they come explicitly before the mind (especially the bad self), they are only collections. Bad acts are known, as this or that, to be against the will of the superior, but they are not yet done as contrary. Through correction the act may have painful associations, but may be done in despite of these, yet still not consciously against the general good will. As yet the child does not have before it the will of the superior, together with this or that desire, recognized as against the will of the superior, and deliberately realize itself in the known contrary. Hence there is no common predicate for evil things; they are sought because desired as this or that; and the discrepancy with the good is at most felt. And further, we must remember that in the beginning all, and afterwards many, bad actions are done quite innocently, and without the smallest feeling that they are out of harmony with anything else.

So far we have seen the growth of the good and bad wills in what we may call their unconscious and non-moral stage; we have now to pass into the moral sphere. But let us first see clearly what that implies. Three elements are involved in it, knowledge of good, knowledge of bad, and self-conscious volition. You can not, in the full and strict sense,

[1] [Cf pp. 294-5, 299.]

have the first without the second, nor the second without the first, nor either without the third. Evil implies knowledge of good, else it can not be known as opposite to good ; and, where it is not known, there is no morality proper : and the same with good. If a subject does not know what evil is, the words moral goodness are devoid of meaning to it. You can not define moral goodness without bringing in evil : if you leave that out, you have a natural or a superhuman subject ; in either case morality as such goes, because the ' ought' means nothing.[1] And the next point, on which we must insist, is that to know moral good and evil without willing them is simply impossible. These ideas are not ideas of anything external, nor of anything that can by any process of analogy be gathered from the external : their originals are in the subject, and, if he does not know them there first, he will never know them at all. Knowledge of morality is knowledge of specific forms of the will, and, just as will can be known only because we know our will, so these forms of will demand personal and immediate knowledge. Hatred of evil means feeling of evil, and you can not be brought to feel what is not inside you, or has nothing analogous within you. Moral perception must rest on moral experience.

And, lastly, for morality is required self-conscious volition. It will not do for the subject merely to be identified with good on the one side, bad on the other, to perceive their incompatibility and feel their discrepancy. He can not know them, unless he knows them against each other ; and for that he must have them both before him at once. He must have before his mind himself as desiring two things in opposition to each other at one moment, each being seen to belong to a certain class ; he stands above them, and in his conscious identification of his whole self in act with one or the other arises the knowledge of himself, as asserting him-

[1] The question of the exact extent to which evil must go in order to awake conscience has of course (though here again evil takes the form of sin) a considerable interest for theology, but it does not concern us here. It is discussed by Vatke, pp. 275-6.

self as the good or bad will. This is the condition of imputation and responsibility, and here begins the proper moral life of the self.[1]

These are the three elements without which the moral consciousness in the strict sense has no existence; but we can not proceed without guarding against an error in respect of the third. Choice is necessary for morality; but we must not think that good and evil are there, and the subject, standing between, decides and takes whichever he just happens to take, and for no reason at all. Freedom, as the *libertas arbitrii*, not only is not true freedom, but in addition is a fiction. There is no such thing as a mere formal liberty of choice. Did it exist, I may remark in passing, it would be very far from helping to the solution of any problem; but it does not exist. The 'I' in volition is the negation of a content which also determines it: it is no atom nor empty abstraction, but the abstraction from the whole content of the self; from the self which, as identified with good and bad, is before the self; and in addition from the self which is not before the self, the standing will, nay even the passing inclination, of which we are not conscious;[2] in short from the whole content of the self. Formal freedom independent of content is nothing in the real world; the self is filled before volition is possible.

For morality is wanted the self-conscious assertion of the good as good and the bad as bad; and the child, as we left him, had indeed a content to his will which was good and bad, but that content had not been knowingly asserted with the consciousness of its nature. When this is done, both good and bad self assume their specific character.

Let us begin with the bad self. The result of self-conscious volition of this against the good is twofold: it gets a unity; and the particular bad is brought under that

[1] The question of the priority of will or knowledge is discussed by Vatke (p. 259 foll.), to whom I am much indebted here. [Imputation and responsibility: cf. pp. 294-5, 302-3.]

[2] [This seems questionable. I do not see how, if we are not conscious of these *at all*, we can consciously negate them in act.]

unity; it is now done as bad. The collection of evil habits and desires, which before had no identity [1] beside the feeling of self-assertion, is now thought of as one, and gets a general character. It does this of course by its antagonism to the good. The common point in all bad self-assertions, their opposition to good, is recognized, and in all these realizations the self knows it is bad. It knows itself in them as self, because, in volition, it now asserts itself consciously; having willed them, it is aware that they are its will: and it knows itself in them as bad self, because, in the doing of them, the self was asserted in that very character. The particular evil act can now be done as an instance and case of evil; the general is realized as such in the particulars; and, when the particulars are reflected on, they possess within themselves, as their identity, the self-conscious assertion of the self, as the will which is bad and which knows itself bad. This or that evil action or desire is now referred to the general badness; the general badness is carried out in this or that bad act; and, answering to the thought unity, there exists a common specific feeling, which binds all together; so that one evil self is felt in all, and all are felt as one self, which opposes the good, and which acquires its fixity by habit and by the consciousness which reacts on habit.

The unity of the bad self is opposition to the one good self, and it has no other unity. But the good is one, not merely against the bad, but also in itself. We saw that in the good will there was, in the main, subordination and system;[2] and all that is wanted for its self-conscious unity is that, by volition, the self should be asserted in it as one will against particular evil desires, which are recognized in their general character of opposition to it. Good acts are now done as good, and realize a principle which in them is aware of itself. The unity of self-consciousness is bestowed on the good will; but the point to keep in sight is that this will was one before. The good self is now morally good; and there is no need for us to trace its upward development. It knows itself at first as the will

---

[1] [See on pp. 295, 296-7, 308.]   [2] [Cf. p. 303, l. 32.]

which, against the temptation of the bad, wills in its acts, and wills its acts as, the will of a superior outside itself, whether that be a person or tribe. The higher will is here felt, but not yet known, to be also the will of the obeying self; and the process of development, whether in morals or religion, has for its result the end where this higher will is known as the true will of the self, where law ceases to be external and becomes autonomy, and where goodness, or the identity of the particular will with the universal, is only another name for conscious self-realization.

Why in the good self we realize ourselves, and in the bad self we do not do so, is a question we shall discuss lower down. But first (the only one of many difficulties we can notice) there forces itself on us the problem, 'How is the non-moral to pass into the moral?' Apart from the question how the self-feeling, with its merely objective consciousness,[1] passes into consciousness of self as an object, how is the genesis of the moral consciousness explicable? Have we not fallen into a vicious circle? do we not require knowledge of good as a *prius* for the knowledge of evil, and knowledge of evil as a *prius* for the knowledge of good? How is any beginning of morality possible?

We answer, in the first place, that there can be no priority in time, on the one hand or the other. The one side is implicated in the very meaning of the other; and it is one and the same act which gives the knowledge of both alike. Secondly, in answer to the difficulty of the origin of this double knowledge, we say that we do not pretend to trace the exact steps of the process, but that it consists in the gradually increasing specification of the two sides, one against the other, resulting in the increasing performance of actions improperly and relatively good and bad, until at last the two sides come at once to light as two contradictory wills in the self. Let us try to make this clearer.

No one, I believe, can remember the beginning of his moral perceptions, though no doubt a man may think he

---

[1] ['Consciousness' is used here as opposed to feeling, and '*merely objective*' means 'where the self is not yet an object but is only *felt*'.]

does so; but the beginning is probably something of this sort. After the good and bad selves are developed unconsciously by habit, the child does some evil act, and, after the performance, the felt pain of collision, however aroused, causes reflection. It is now seen that the act is opposed to good, and in that perceived contradiction the two wills come to light as contradictories, and, on occasion of the next temptation, the idea of the two opposing sides is present and qualifies the present opposing desires; and so the ensuing volition is done with consciousness of goodness or badness. We may represent the beginning so, but we can not bring before us the slow growth which has led up to it; any more than we can follow in its details the general evolution of human self-consciousness from the beginnings of mere animal feeling. We are forced to say 'here you have this, and before only that', and may be able to see the nature of the transition: but mentally to reproduce and realize the changes is scarcely possible. And here, where a felt discrepancy gradually sharpens itself into a perceived contradiction, we can retrace the general course, but can not recover the detailed experiences, each one of which told, and added to the whole.

From the first the incompatibility of pleasure in the good and in the bad must be in some way felt; and as the two sides by habit harden themselves and grow more connected, this feeling must become more definite. There must come more or less of a perception of the good as a whole, a more or less clear insight that this or that bad act was incompatible, and the disapproval of the superior must to a certain extent be reflected on as attaching to a class of acts. There are dawnings of the moral consciousness which never turn to day, and acts not quite moral, while hardly non-moral; but all that we can hope to do here is to see clearly that the two sides are not perceived as such until perceived in their specific character, one against the other; and that morality proper does not begin until, being so apprehended, they are consciously made the principles of the particular acts.

Growth up to the appearance of the specific moral consciousness is thus not strictly moral, and up to this time, I think, we are not accountable. But, after this time, we must be considered so, although moral growth is still to some extent unconscious. To take the last first, it is quite certain that the awakening of the conscience does not mean its sudden application to the whole of life. It is only by slow degrees that our acts take spontaneously the colour of good and bad, and the process, owing to new material and fresh combinations of the old, remains incomplete to the end of our days. For all that, we are responsible; and if theory must fix some point at which imputation begins,[1] it can not be elsewhere than here. From this time we are a will which knows itself as good and bad, and knows that the good has exclusive claim. We have with full consciousness identified ourselves with good and evil; and from that twofold identification of the will, which begins a new life, and is no transitory accident but a standing self, we are bound to conclude that our particular acts now proceed. The burden of proving the contrary lies in all cases upon ourselves; and, to escape imputation of evil or good, we must show, by establishing compulsion or ignorance, the absence of real connexion between the act and a will morally intelligent, or the standing embodiment of moral intelligence. (Cf. Essay I.)

We have traced, I fear most imperfectly, and I fear too dogmatically, the origin of the good and bad self in a man; and all that remains is to see, from the very nature of each, that the good self is our realization; and that the bad self not only does not realize our true being, but is never, for its own sake and as such, desired at all.

The good self satisfies us because it answers to our real being. It is in the main a harmony,[2] it is subordinated into a system; and thus, in taking its content into our wills and realizing that, we feel that we realize ourselves as the true infinite, as one permanent harmonious whole. Hence its content is at one with itself, and at one with our own

¹ [Perhaps, if it *must* do so: cf. pp. 242, 299.]
² [Cf. p. 300, para. 2.]

felt nature; and again further it is at one with its form. We saw (Essay II) that in volition the ' I ' was a universal, and that it was only when form and content went together that we found self-realization. And now in the will that asserts the good self this is present: the form of self-consciousness, the ' I ' that is drawn back from and reappropriates the content, and the content itself, are both universal; or, in other words, the good self is such that, when confronted with the self-conscious ' I ', it is felt to be identical in nature, and is reasserted as the very self without the smallest discrepancy. ' I ' in the highest sense am present in it, feel and know myself present in it, perpetually reproduce my inmost principle, and see it, however partially, yet truly realized in a positive objectification.

In the bad self on the other hand all is different. Not only is that in contradiction with the good, but it is in contradiction with itself: its content belies the form of the self which is asserted in it, and further its content is in itself discrepant.

As regards the latter point, the content of the bad self, though connected into partial centres, yet has no one centre to which it is subordinated. I need not enlarge on that which has become a familiar theme, that the bad self is anarchical, and that evil lusts and appetites are all each for himself, and wage a war of every one against every one else who stands in the way; and that, from the nature of the case, they must be perpetually in the way of one another. Thus the bad is no unity, no system, no concrete universal. And, secondly, being thus what it is, when formally willed it is contrary to the self that wills it. That self both is, and feels and knows itself to be one, a permanent universal, and a whole; and in the assertion of itself in the bad it puts itself into what does not answer to its nature, and in that objectification must feel that, though the self is gone out, yet the self is not there.

For what in the end is this bad self? It is nothing but a collective self formally asserted as a unity.[1] We have

---

[1] [The bad self is a mere 'collective unity': cf. p. 308.]

come at last, really and in fact, to the collection which is affirmed as not a collection ; but this, we must never forget, is possible only because it belongs to that which is more than a collection. The actual unity of the bad self is a group of centres of bad habits and desires, in which the self-conscious self has affirmed itself, and in which the self feels itself in a specific manner against the good. But the one self is affirmed there formally and not really ; evil deeds are acts of the whole self, but if you ask, 'where then in them is the whole self realized?' you can find it nowhere ; and the specific feeling of being bad, which is common to all the evil, attaches to it by virtue of its opposition to the one good, not in virtue of any one common quality that it has in itself. A specific feeling of contrariness to the good, this or that more or less solid group of associated bad habits, the formal and unreal assertion of the whole self therein, and the reflection on all evil, as what by its general opposition to the good is known as one, this is all the unity of the bad self. It is a universal in the sense of a collection of all, not in the sense of being a whole and an organic system. It is a group of bad tendencies, adhering by the association of habit into relative centres, with nothing common to all save the specific feeling of opposition to the same unity, and by formal self-consciousness and reflection made for our apprehension into a whole, while in reality nothing but a heap of particulars.

The bad self can not as such be self-conscious ; if it were so, it would realize the ideal of a self-conscious collection. It is the whole self which therein is aware of itself as what it is not, as a collection ; and hence the contradiction, hence the indignant refusal to accept one's badness as anything more than a fact which has no business to be a fact, as anything other than a standing self-contradiction and lie. A purely evil being is a sheer impossibility.[1]

The bad self can not be desired for its own sake. Facts, in spite of certain appearances, proclaim that it never is so, that the ἀκόλαστος is a creature of theory, that no one

[1] [Cf. pp. 310–11.]

chooses evil simply on the ground that it is evil, and for its own sake as evil. And we see now the theoretical explanation. But let us guard against error. It is false to say that evil is not done as evil. This or that evil act, when done, is desired for itself, and its content is known to be evil, and under the general head of evil it is committed. But the justification of the mistake is this, that only particular evils are desired; there is no identity in them which is made an end, because there is none to make an end out of. When we are consciously bad, it is because we pursue evils known and done under the head of evil. On the other hand the head of evil, though it seems to be more, is merely a head; it is an abstraction, it is not a system in which the particulars subsist, and there is nothing positive about it which can be taken as an end. Simply to desire evil as such would be simply to hate good as such; but hate and aversion must rest on and start from a positive centre. You can not have a being which is nothing but mere negation; hate must start from a positive internal content, and that would be the positive core of the self, desired for itself as positive, and therefore as good; not desired as mere evil, i. e. as negative of something else.[1]

<hr />

[1] This is a matter which perhaps calls for a remark. We must be careful to remember that the question is, Can I desire evil and hate good in their character as such, and because they are such? Then further, there being nothing whatever in evil as such to desire, desire for evil as such reduces itself to hatred of good. The whole question is then, Can I hate good as such? Certainly in one way I may hate good. I may loathe it, because, though I desire it, it brings me perpetual pain and weariness. I may wish to be rid of it; but this is because I want to sink myself peaceably in such or such lusts. Desiring these I may wish the good away, or, tired of everything, may want simply to be at rest. But in neither case do I hate good simply; what I hate are its accompaniments; remove the annoyances of the good, and I always wish to have it. At the bottom even of the wish for the peace of death lies the positive desire for self-assertion and nothing but self-assertion. And this positive desire can be directed against the good only *per accidens*. The abstract negation of the good we can not really aim at; but, having this or that desire, we negate what opposes it, because and so far as it opposes it, in order to assert ourselves positively. To hate one's life is possible only so

And what is even of more importance is this, that a being which desires evil, not as this, that, and the other evil, but as mere negation of good, is not a being which knows what good is. We have seen that, unless the will is identified with good, good can not be known. If good is not willed, it is not known, and therefore can not as such be hated : and if good is not willed, evil is not known as evil. In short, with the total absence of will for good goes the absence of knowledge both of that and of evil, and, with that, desire for evil as such. The simplest way to put it is to say that to hate good is to hate oneself, and no one can altogether hate himself.

To hate good is to hate oneself, because our being is affirmative all through ; indeed, we are position and affirmation itself, and good is the one and only true form of positive realization. I do not mean that in this and that evil we do not affirm ourselves positively, but I say that we do not do so truly. We know ourselves to be one and a whole, and hence we can know that we have not truly and really produced and got ourselves in any mere this or that as such, or in anything but that which reflects and realizes our nature, as a being which can not believe that its reality is of the

far as one abstracts from it ; and here it is self-affirmation, however abstract, which is our positive end.

There is only one class of facts where evil seems done for its own sake, i.e. to negate the good ; and in these we find a psychological illusion. The illusion is that the good is a foreign will, which represses us from the outside. Breaches of discipline seem done for their own sake ; but they really are done not because evil, but because the self asserts itself in them against what it mistakes for another finite will. Removal of discipline soon destroys the zest of illicit pleasure ; then the subject finds out it does not care for the evil as such, a knowledge bought dear. If the subject goes on to say, 'I wish I could think it wrong, because, since I ceased to do so, the pleasure has gone,' we have the nearest approach to ἀκολασία. But this rests on the illusion as to a foreign will. Other phenomena of the sort can be reduced to the head of the wish 'to spite oneself', a curious state of mind which involves the taking of oneself, in this or that character or quality, to be a self foreign and external to one's present self.*

---

* [Compare here the state of Moral Irony.]

moment, or to be found in the things of the moment. We truly and really are one as a whole; we truly and really are positive; I have shown that the good, and nothing but the good, does realize us as a whole; and we can not resist the conclusion that the good self is the only positive self which is true, that it, and nothing but it, is indeed our very self.

It is a theme which invites reflection; one which, had we space or strength to pursue it, would lead us far. On the one hand, we find ourselves evil; the evil is as much a fact as the good, and without our bad self we should hardly know ourselves. On the other hand, we refuse to accept the bad self as our reality; and the thought, the old thought, which in different forms is common alike to art, philosophy, and religion, is here suggested once more, that all existence is not truth, that all facts are not in the same sense real, or that what is real to one mode or stage of consciousness is not therefore real for an other and higher stage, still less so for that which, present in all, is yet above all modes and stages.

But we must not wander from our depth, nor away from the subject. We have seen, I hope, in some imperfect fashion, what the bad self in general is, and with a fuller meaning we can repeat that selfishness is one form of the bad self. Conscious pleasure-seeking is the pursuit of the idea of the maximum of pleasure as the end, and of all else knowingly as a means. Selfishness is the desiring and pursuing objects, not as ends in themselves, but with a more or less explicit readiness to treat all as means to an end which is private satisfaction, gaining the pleasant or avoiding the painful as such;[1] but it does not imply the striving for the maximum. It is, apart from this, the using all things as a means to happiness in the sense of self-assertion, without regard to objective content for its own sake. The rest of the bad self consists in the will to follow objects and

---

[1] [Selfishness. This won't do. See p. 279 and foll. It is want of due regard for others' welfare.] ⟨See also Notes pp. 276, 280, 283, and references.—ED.⟩

satisfy inclinations which are antagonistic to the good ; but it does not imply the implicit or explicit readiness to treat these as means to an external end. If you insist on subsuming evil under a common end, you must say that end is private satisfaction ; but, at the same time, you must remember that this is only true in the sense that there is no other end to which you can refer it.

What, then, is self-sacrifice ? We have seen that all morality, all identification of the will with the ideal, demands the suppression of the self in some form ; and so, though self-realization, it yet at the same time is self-sacrifice.[1] Can we say, then, that self-sacrifice consists in following the higher and crushing the lower, and that, conversely, all such action is self-sacrifice ?

No, the latter would be false ; for it is not what in the ordinary sense self-sacrifice means. In morality, as a rule, what you give is returned to you with interest ; and the bestowal of the self on the good is rewarded by the general heightening of individual life. If happiness is the realization of one's ideal in one's own existence, the attaining one's end as a whole in the private self, and by and for the private self, then, so far as men can be happy, in the main it is true that virtue is happiness ; and virtue does not necessarily imply self-sacrifice.

Self-sacrifice is more than this. It implies the identification of the will with an object, which entails in the effort to realize it the probable or certain negation of our private existence. And by private existence (other phrases, if this be objected to, will serve) I mean the existence which is ours, I do not say apart from but, distinct from others, what is centred in us as this or that person. The extensive and intensive affirmation of our will, as this ' I ' or that ' You ', whether in bodily well-being, psychical harmony, influence on others, or appropriation of physical or spiritual good things—all these assert our particular personal existence,

---

[1] [Self-sacrifice, what ? Self-realization, what ? Cf. p. 228.] ⟨*An additional note on Self-sacrifice and Self-realization was obviously intended here, but was not written.*—ED.⟩

and all that opposes the actuality or possibility of these lowers it. Self-sacrifice is knowingly to give up, in part or altogether, this existence to that which is higher. In it we bestow our will on what, we believe, either will or may lessen the extensive and intensive assertion of our private self. It is not giving up our will, for that is mere nonsense; nor our will as this or that man, that also is nonsense: if any one likes so to look at it, it is something less, but it is also and therefore a great deal more. It is the will of us, as this or that, to realize an object which means the lessening or total suppression of us as this or that. It is the good self; it is the identification of our will with the ideal; it is self-realization, and as such has a pleasure of its own; it does assert the private will, but it asserts it to its own negation; and the content of the self it realizes, it does not get for itself and have as a personal good of its own, but by sight or faith beholds its accomplishment, if at all, outside of and beyond its individual existence.

Answers to two more questions, and then we have done. The first is, Can there be self-sacrifice for the bad; for the bad, that is, when known as bad? It is perhaps a matter for doubt, but I incline to the negative view. We have seen that the bad is not desired in its quality of bad for the sake of that quality; but the difficulty which remains is that, for the sake of something known to be bad, persons do seem to give up their existence, while aware that they will or may do so. A closer consideration may, however, dispose of these cases. They may be divided into two classes, passionate and deliberate. In the former an element of self-sacrifice is wanting, i. e. the having the consequences in view. Fierce hate and hot lust for a mortal pleasure lead men to death; as the poet says,

> Our natures do pursue,
> Like rats that ravin down their proper bane,
> A thirsty evil; and when we drink we die.

But the point here is this, Is the end only before the mind, with blindness to the possible result; or is that result considered? If it is not considered, there is no self-sacrifice

proper.   The second class is the deliberate pursuit of bad
objects, with a readiness to consider and face all consequences, even one's own death ; sacrifice of oneself, in
short, for a bad cause.   Here the important point is this, Is
the cause really known as bad : or is the conscience confused, so as to take bad for good, or at least to see good in
the bad besides its badness ?   And on our answer to that
question will depend our finding.   Self-sacrifice is admitted,
but the doubt is, was it not after all for the sake of what
seemed good ? [1]   And, unless we remove that doubt, we can
not maintain the possibility of self-sacrifice for evil.

The last inquiry is, whether all self-sacrifice must be
religious ; and here we are decided in the negative.   It
might be urged that the will to suppress the temporal self
implies a will made one with what is above all finite things,
a will identified with a non-temporal will ; and that here
(whether it call itself so or not) we have religion.   But this,
I think, will not hold.   Of course, if self-sacrifice for the
bad be admitted, we can not see in that the assertion of
the divine will.   And further, if the question be narrowed
to self-sacrifice for good, still we must say that it need involve
nothing properly to be called religion.[2]   The cause, with
which the will is identified to the negation of the temporal
self, need not therefore be apprehended as non-temporal, or
that which is above the finite ; but only as a finite realization,
which is above and superior to this or that finite.   And
thus, too, my will may be identified with some bad interest,
which, though finite, is still superior to my finite existence.
The doubt which remains is whether, in cases where the
personal existence is felt as utterly worthless in comparison
of the good to be attained, the good is not so qualified by
the comparison that we have passed into the religious
consciousness, or at least into that which springs from and
depends on it.   Here, however, on the other side we must
take account of the 'abstract self-consciousness', which

[1] [Cf. the 'abstract self-consciousness' and obstinacy, see below, l. 35,
and note 2, and pp. 305-7.]
[2] [Is self-sacrifice religious ?   The answer 'No' is right.]

stakes its existence on a trifle, not because it cares for this or that content, but because, in its abstract assertion, it cares for no particular content as such, not even that of its own finite existence. But this, as well as the consideration of the former difficulty, besides others no doubt which I have omitted or failed to throw light on, I will leave to the reader (if such there be) who, in spite of its treatment by the writer, remains yet unwearied by the subject.

CONCLUDING REMARKS

THE position we are now in can be put very shortly. Morality is an endless process, and therefore a self-contradiction; and, being such, it does not remain standing in itself, but feels the impulse to transcend its existing reality.

It is a self-contradiction in this way: it is a demand for what can not be. Not only is nothing good but the good will, but also nothing is to be real (*so far as willed*) but the good; and yet the reality is not wholly good.[1] Neither in me, nor in the world, is what ought to be what is, and what is what ought to be; and the claim remains in the end a mere claim.

The reason of the contradiction is the fact that man is a contradiction. But man is more; he feels or knows himself as such, and this makes a vital difference; for to feel a contradiction is *ipso facto* to be above it. Otherwise, how would it be possible to feel it? A felt contradiction which does not imply, besides its two poles, a unity which includes and is above them, will, the more it is reflected on, the more be seen to be altogether unmeaning. Unless man was and divined himself to be a whole, he could not feel the contradiction, still less feel pain in it, and reject it as foreign to his real nature.

So we see that the moral point of view, which leaves man in a sphere with which he is not satisfied, can not be final. This or that human being, this or that passing stage of culture, may remain in this region of weariness, of false self-approval and no less false self-contempt; but for the race, as a whole, this is impossible. It has not done it; and, while man is man, it certainly never will do it.

And here we should close these Essays, since here we go beyond morality. But, that we may make the foregoing

---

[1] [Cf. p. 322. 'Real' and 'reality mean here 'existing'.]

plainer, we are tempted to say something more, however fragmentary, however much in the form of an appendix.[1]

Reflection on morality leads us beyond it. It leads us, in short, to see the necessity of a religious point of view. It certainly does not tell us that morality comes first in the world and then religion: what it tells us is that morality is imperfect, and imperfect in such a way as implies a higher, which is religion.

Morality issues in religion: and at this word 'religion' the ordinary reader is upon us with cries and questions, and with all the problems of the day—God, and personal God, immortality of the soul, the conflict of revelation and science, and who knows what besides? He must not expect any answer to these questions here: we are writing a mere appendix; and in that our object is to show that religion, as a matter of fact, does give us what morality does not give; and our method is simply, so far as our purpose requires, to point to the facts of the religious consciousness, without drawing conclusions to the right or left, without trying to go much below the surface, or doing anything beyond what is wanted in this connexion with morality.

We purpose to say nothing about the ultimate truth of religion: nothing again about its origin in the world, or in the individual. We are to take the religious consciousness as an existing fact, and to take it as we find it now in the modern Christian mind,[2] whether that mind recognizes it or whether it does not. And lastly, space compels us to do no more than dogmatically assert what seems to us to be true in respect of it.

That there is some connexion between true religion and morality every one we need consider sees. A man who is 'religious' and does not act morally, is an impostor, or his religion is a false one. This does not hold good elsewhere. A philosopher may be a good philosopher, and yet, taking

[1] Throughout the sequel I have to acknowledge my indebtedness to Vatke's book, *Die Menschliche Freiheit*, 1841.

[2] [The emphasis is on 'modern'.]

him as a whole, may be immoral, and the same thing is true
of an artist, or even of a theologian. They may all be good,
and yet not good men ; but no one who knew what true
religion was would call a man who on the whole was
immoral a religious man.   For religion is not the mere
knowing or contemplating of any object, however high.   It
is not mere philosophy nor art, because it is not mere seeing,
no mere theoretic activity, considered as such or merely
from its theoretical side.   The religious consciousness tells
us that a man is not religious, or more religious, because the
matter of his theoretic activity is religious ; just as the moral
consciousness told us that a man was not moral, or more
moral, simply because he was a moral philosopher.   Religion
is essentially a doing, and a doing which is moral.   It implies
a realizing, and a realizing of the good self.

Are we to say then that morality is religion?   Most
certainly not.   In mere morality the ideal is not : it for ever
remains a 'to be'.   The reality in us or the world is partial
and inadequate ; and no one could say that it answers to
the ideal, that, morally considered, both we and the world
are all we ought to be, and ought to be just what we are.
We have at furthest the belief in an ideal which in its pure
completeness is never real ; which, as an ideal, is a mere
'should be'.   And the question is, Will that do for religion?
No knower of religion, who was not led away by a theory,
would answer Yes.   Nor does it help us to say that religion
is 'morality touched by emotion';[1] for loose phrases of
this sort may suggest to the reader what he knows already
without their help, but, properly speaking, they *say* nothing.
All morality is, in one sense or another, 'touched by
emotion'.   Most emotions, high or low, can go with and
'touch' morality ; and the moment we leave our phrase-
making, and begin to reflect, we see all that is meant is that
morality 'touched' by *religious* emotion is religious ; and
so, as answer to the question What is religion? all that we
have said is, 'It is religion when with morality you have—

[1] ⟨Matthew Arnold ; cf. *Literature and Dogma*, p. 16, Popular
Edition.⟩

religion.' I do not think we learn a very great deal from this.[1]

Religion is more than morality. In the religious consciousness we find the belief, however vague and indistinct, in an object, a not-myself; an object, further, which is real. An ideal which is not real, which is only in our heads, can not be the object of religion: and in particular the ideal self, as the 'is to be' which is real only so far as we put it forth by our wills, and which, as an ideal, we can not put forth, is not a real object, and so not the object for religion. Hence, because it is unreal, the ideal of personal morality is not enough for religion. And we have seen before that the ideal is not realized in the objective world of the state; so that, apart from other objections, here again we can not find the religious object. For the religious consciousness that object is real; and it is not to be found in the mere moral sphere.

But here once more ' culture ' has come to our aid, and has shown us how here, as everywhere, the study of polite literature, which makes for meekness, makes needless also all further education; and we felt already as if the clouds that metaphysic had wrapped about the matter were dissolving in the light of a fresh and sweet intelligence. And, as we turned towards the dawn, we sighed over poor Hegel, who had read neither Goethe nor Homer, nor the Old and New Testaments, nor any of the literature which has gone to form ' culture ', but, knowing no facts, and reading no books, nor ever asking himself[2] 'such a tyro's question as what

---

[1] Compare (Mill, *Dissertations*, i. 70-1) the definition of poetry as ' man's thoughts tinged by his feelings '; where the whole matter again is, *what* feelings? Anything in the way of shallow reflection on the psychological form, anything rather than the effort to grasp the content. All that Mill saw wanting in this ' definition ' was that it missed ' the poet's utter unconsciousness of a listener '. However, to make sure of hitting the mark, he, so to speak, set it down as hit beforehand, and in his own ' definition ' of poetry introduced ' the poet's mind '. This is much as if we were to say, ' Religion is the sort of thing you have in a religious man '.

[2] *Cont. Review*, xxiv. 988 (or ' *God and the Bible* ', *Chap. II, p. 36. Pop Ed. 1888.*—Ed.)

being really was', sat spinning out of his head those foolish logomachies which impose on no person of refinement.[1]

Well, culture has told us what God *was* for the Jews; and we learn that 'I am that I am' means much the same as 'I blow and grow, that I do,' or , 'I shall breathe, that I shall'; and this, if surprising, was at all events definite, not to say tangible. However, to those of us who do not think that Christianity is called upon to wrap itself any longer in 'Hebrew old clothes', all this is entirely a matter for the historian. But when 'culture' went on to tell us what God *is* for science, we heard words we did not understand about 'streams', and 'tendencies', and 'the Eternal' : and, had it been any one else that we were reading, we should have said that, in some literary excursion, they had picked up a metaphysical theory,[2] now out of date, and putting it in phrases, the meaning of which they had never asked themselves, had then served it up to the public as the last result of speculation, or of that 'flexible common sense' which is so much better. And as this in the case of 'culture' and 'criticism' was of course not possible, we concluded that for us once again the light had shone in darkness. But the 'stream' and the 'tendency' having served their turn, like last week's placards, now fall into the background, and we learn at last (*C. R.*, p. 995) that 'the Eternal' is not eternal at all, unless we give that name to whatever a generation sees happen, and believes both has happened and will happen—just as the habit of washing ourselves might be termed 'the Eternal not ourselves that makes for cleanliness', or 'Early to bed and early to rise' the 'Eternal not ourselves that makes for longevity', and so on—that 'the Eternal', in short, is nothing in the world but a piece of literary clap-trap. The consequence is that all we are left

[1] ⟨The two Articles in the *Cont. Review*, xxiv. 794 and 981, to which reference is made in the following pages, are entitled, 'Review of objections to *Literature and Dogma*'. The reader who wishes to follow the matter further will find them reprinted, but with modifications and considerable omissions, in the first two chapters of *God and the Bible*.⟩

[2] [The reference is to Fichte.]

with is the assertion that 'righteousness' is 'salvation' or 'welfare', and that there is a 'law' and a 'Power' which has something to do with this fact ; and here again we must not be ashamed to say that we fail to understand what any one of these phrases means, and suspect ourselves once more to be on the scent of clap-trap.

If what is meant be this, that what is ordinarily called virtue does always lead to and go with what is ordinarily called happiness, then so far is this from being 'verifiable '[1] in everyday experience, that its opposite is so ; it is not a fact, either that to be virtuous is always to be happy, or that happiness must always come from virtue. Everybody knows this, Mr. Arnold 'must know this, and yet he gives it, because it suits his purpose, or because the public, or a large body of the public, desire it ; and this is clap-trap ' (*C. R.*, p. 804).

It is not a fact that to be virtuous is always, and for that reason, to be happy ; and, even were it so, yet such a fact can not be the object of the religious consciousness. The reality which answers to the phrases of culture is, we suppose, the real existence of the phrases as such in books or in our heads ; or again a number of events in time, past, present, and future (i. e. conjunctions of virtue and happiness).

We have an abstract term to stand for the abstraction of this or that quality ; or again we have a series or collection of particular occurrences. When the literary varnish is removed, is there anything more ?[2] But the object of the re-

---

[1] We hear the word 'verifiable ' from Mr. Arnold pretty often. What is to verify ? Has Mr. Arnold put 'such a tyro's question' to himself? If to verify means to find in outward experience, then the object of true religion can not be found as this or that outward thing or quality, and so can not be verified. It is of its essence that in this sense it should be unverifiable.

[2] 'Is there a God?' asks the reader. 'Oh yes,' replies Mr. Arnold, 'and I can verify him in experience.' 'And what is he then?' cries the reader. 'Be virtuous, and as a rule you will be happy', is the answer. 'Well, and God?' 'That is God'; says Mr. Arnold ; 'there is no deception, and what more do you want?' I suppose we do want a good deal more. Most of us, certainly the public which Mr. Arnold addresses, want something they can worship ; and they will not find that

ligious consciousness must be a great deal more. It must be what is real, not only in the heads of this person or set of persons, nor again as this or that finite something or set of somethings. It is in short very different from either those thin abstractions or coarse ' verifiable ' facts, between which and over which there is for our ' culture ' no higher third sphere, save that of the literary groping which is helpless as soon as it ceases to be blind.

But let us turn from this trifling, on which we are sorry to have been forced to say even one word ; let us go back to the religious consciousness.

Religion, we have seen, must have an object; and that object is neither an abstract idea in the head, nor one particular thing or quality, nor any collection of such things or qualities, nor any phrase which stands for one of them or a collection of them. In short it is nothing finite. It can not be a thing or person in the world ; it can not exist in the world, as a part of it, or as this or that course of events in time ; it can not be the ' All ', the sum of things or persons, —since, if one is not divine, no putting of ones together will beget divinity. All this it is not. Its positive character is that it is real; and further, on examining what we find in the religious consciousness,[1] we discover that it is the ideal self considered as realized and real.[2] The ideal self, which in morality is to be, is here the real ideal which truly is.

For morals the ideal self was an ' ought ', an ' is to be ' that is not ; the object of religion is that same ideal self, but here it no longer only ought to be, but also is. This is the nature

in an hypostasized copy-book heading, which is not much more adorable than ' Honesty is the best policy ', or ' Handsome is that handsome does ', or various other edifying maxims, which have not yet come to an apotheosis.*

[1] The reader must carefully distinguish what is *for* (or before) the religious consciousness, and what is only *in* it, and *for us* as we investigate it.

[2] [It is that *at least*. It is, however, also *more* than realized morality. ' Ideal self ' is used, I think, to include realized ideals of every kind.]

* [These other maxims may, however, be taken as falling under the first.]

of the religious object, though the manner of apprehending it may differ widely, may be anything from the vaguest instinct to the most thoughtful reflection.

With religion we may here compare science and art. The artist and poet, however obscurely, do feel and believe that beauty, where it is not seen, yet somehow and somewhere is and is real; though not as a mere idea in people's heads, nor yet as anything in the visible world. And science, however dimly, starts from and rests upon the preconception that, even against appearances, reason not only ought to be, but really is.

Is then religion a mere mode of theoretic creation and contemplation, like art and science? Is it a lower form or stage of philosophy, or another sort of art, or some kind of compound mixture? It is none of these, and between it and them there is a vital difference.

In the very essence of the religious consciousness we find the relation of our *will* to the real ideal self. We find ourselves, as this or that will, against the object as the real ideal will, which is not ourselves, and which stands to us in such a way that, *though real, it is to be realized, because it is all and the whole reality.*

A statement, no doubt, which may stagger us; but the statement, we maintain, of a simple fact of the religious consciousness. If any one likes to call it a delusion, that makes no difference; unless, as some people seem to think, you can get rid of facts by applying phrases to them. And, however surprising the fact may be to the reader, it certainly ought not to be new to him.

We find the same difficulty, that the real is to be realized, both in art and science. The self dimly feels, or fore-feels, itself as full of truth and beauty, and unconsciously sets that fullness before it as an object, a not-itself which is against itself as this or that man. And so the self goes on to realize what it obscurely foreknows as real; it realizes it, although, and because, it is aware of it as real. And in this, so far, art, philosophy, and religion are the same.

But, as we saw, they are also different. In art and science

the will of the man who realizes is not of the essence. The essence of the matter is that a certain result should be produced, that, of the unseen object which is divined to be real, a part at least should become visible, that in short, however it comes about, some element of the real should be *seen* to be realized. Here the end is the sight of the object, as such, and the will which procures that sight is not taken into account. No doubt it would be a great mistake to forget that art and science involve will, and the will of particular persons, and that it is this will which realizes the object; and that hence, since the object of science and art is at least partly identical with the object of religion, both science and art may so far be said to imply religion, since they imply the relation of the particular will to the real ideal. For suppose that the human-divine life is one process, and suppose again that art and science and religion are distinguishable elements or aspects of this one whole process. Then, if this is so, neither art nor science nor religion can exist as a thing by itself, and the two former will necessarily imply the latter. But on the other hand, though we may not divide, yet we have to distinguish; and when by an abstraction we consider one side, e. g. the side of science or that of art, by itself, and take them as mere theoretic activities, then we must say that in this character neither of them is religion; and they are not religion because the will of this or that man, over against the real ideal as will, is not an element in the scientific or artistic process as such. The real ideal of science and art is not will, and the relation of my will to it falls outside them; and we must say, and we think that the reader will agree, that, so soon as the philosopher or artist is conscious of his will in relation to the real ideal, as a will which has demands on him, he ceases to be a mere philosopher or artist as such (which after all no human being is), and becomes also religious or irreligious.[1]

To proceed, we find in the religious consciousness the

[1] [Or at least 'moral'. Here, as in the religious consciousness (on next line), I take the 'real ideal' as *perfect*, and demanding perfection on my side.]

ideal self as the complete reality; and we have, besides, its claim upon us. Both elements, and their relation, are given in one and the same consciousness. We are given as this will, which, because this will, is to realize the real ideal: the real ideal is given as the will which is wholly real, and therefore to be realized in us.

Now nothing is easier than for a one-sided reflection to rush in with a cry for clearness and consistency, and to apply its favourite ' either—or '. '*If* real, how realize? *If* realize, then not real.' We, however, must not allow ourselves to give way to the desire for drawing conclusions, but have to observe the facts; and we see that the religious consciousness refuses the dilemma. It holds to both one and the other, and to one because of the other; and pronounces such reflections irreligious.

In the moral consciousness we found two poles, myself and the ideal self. The latter claimed to be real, and to have all as its reality,[1] so far as willed; but, for the moral consciousness, it was not thus real either in the world or in us, and the evil in us and the world was *as* real. In religion we find once more two poles, myself and the ideal self. But here the latter not only claims to be, but also is, real and all reality; and yet (at this stage[2]) it is not realized either in the world or in me. It is not one pole, however, that in religion is different, but both: for morality the world and the self remained both non-moral and immoral, yet each was real; for religion the world is alienated from God, and the self is sunk in sin; and that means that, against the whole reality, they are felt or known as what is not and is contrary to the all and the only real, and yet as things that exist. In sin the self feels itself in contradiction with all that truly is. It is the unreal, that, knowing itself to be so, contradicts itself as the real; it

---

[1] [Cf. p. 313, and note.]

[2] The thoughtful reader may at once object that here we have an incomplete account of religion. That is quite true, and we purposely delay the consideration of religion as a whole. Here we are insisting on certain elements of the religious consciousness, in order to see that they are no more than elements, which call for comprehension in something higher.

is the real, which, feeling itself to be so, contradicts itself as the unreal, and in the pain of its intolerable discord can find no word so strong, no image so glaring as to portray its torment.

For it really is itself, against which, in sin, it feels itself. We can not stay to develop this doctrine, and must content ourselves with pointing out that the opposite is utterly incomprehensible. The two poles are what they are, because they are against each other in consciousness. In them the self feels itself divided against itself; and, unless they both fall within one subject, how is this possible? We have not the felt struggle of ourself against a perceived or thought external object; we have the felt struggle in us of two wills, with both of which we feel ourselves identified. And this relation of the divine and human will *in* one subject is a psychological impossibility, unless they are the wills *of* one subject. Remove that condition, and the phenomena in their specific character instantly disappear. You can not understand the recognition of and desire for the divine will; nor the consciousness of sin and rebellion, with the need for grace on the one hand and its supply on the other; you turn every fact of religion into unmeaning nonsense, and you pluck up by the root and utterly destroy all possibility of the Atonement, when you deny that the religious consciousness implies that God and man are identical in a subject.[1]

[1] On this whole matter, and not specially with reference to religion, it is worth while to consider the position of our philosophy. People find a subject and object correlated in consciousness; and, having got this *in* the mind, they at once project it outside the mind, and talk as if two independent realities knocked themselves together, and so produced the unity that apprehends them; while, all the time, to go out of that unity is for us literally to go out of our minds. And when the monstrous nature of their position dawns on some few, and they begin to see that without some higher unity this ' correlation' is pure nonsense, then answering to that felt need, they invent a third reality, which is neither subject nor object but the ' Unknowable ' or the Thing-in-itself (there is no difference). But here, since the two correlates are still left together with, and yet are *not*, the Unknowable, the question arises, How does this latter stand to them? And the result is that the Unknowable becomes the subject of predicates (see Mr. Spencer's *First Principles*), and it becomes impossible for any one who cares for consistency to go on calling it the Unknowable. So it is necessary to go

For it is the atonement, the reconciliation (call it what you please, and bring it before your mind in the way most easy to you), to which we must come, if we mean to follow the facts of the religious consciousness. Here, as everywhere, the felt contradiction implies, and is only possible through, a unity above the discord : take that away, and the discord goes. The antithesis of the sinful and divine will is implicitly their union ; and that union, in the subject, requires only to be made explicit, for the subject, by thought and will.

But for the subject it is not yet explicit ; and it is only we who reflect upon the religious consciousness that see the

a step further, and, giving up our third, which is *not* the correlates, to recognize an Identity of subject and object, still however persisting in the statement that this identity is *not* mind. But here again, as with the Unknowable, and as before with the two correlated realities, it is forgotten that, when mind is made only a part of the whole, there is a question which *must* be answered ; ' If so, how can the whole be known, and for the mind ? If about any matter we know nothing whatever, can we say anything about it ? Can we even say that it is ? And, if it is not in consciousness, how can we know it ? And if it is in and for the mind, how can it be a whole which is *not* mind, and in which the mind is only a part or element ? If the ultimate unity were not self or mind, we could not know that it was not mind : that would mean going out of our minds. And, conversely, if we know it, it can not be not mind. All in short we can know (the psychological form is another question) is the self and elements in the self. To know a not-self is to transcend and leave one's mind. If we know the whole, it can only be because the whole knows itself in us, because the whole is self or mind, which is and knows, knows and is, the identity and correlation of subject and object.'

There is nothing in the above which has not been before the world for years, and it is time that it should be admitted or refuted. I think it will not be much longer disregarded. Much against its will English thought has been forced from the correlation as far as the identity ; and, if it means to hold to the doctrine of ' relativity of knowledge ', it must go on to mind or self in some sense of the word, as this identity of inner and outer. Perhaps not that ; but if not that, then I think we must begin on a fresh basis, or else give up the attempt to have any theory of first principles. But if we do (as perhaps we may do) the latter, then let me conclude this note by observing that amongst the other doctrines which must go is the doctrine of Relativity.*

---

* [I hope that the present-day Realist will agree with the *last* paragraph of this foot-note.]

matter thus. That consciousness as such has not the insight that the divine will is the will of its own true and inmost self; I may know that, as a fact, in God there is the unity of the two natures; but for me God is (here at least) *only* not *my* self; the divine is an object between which and me there is a chasm; my inner self may desire it, but can only desire it as an other and a beyond. True that the object is already the identity of God and man, but man does not include me: that object is not in me, it is only for me; it remains an object, and I remain outside. And for the religious consciousness the problem is, How can I be reconciled with this will which is not mine?

And the answer is that in the object the reconciliation of the divine and human is real; the principle is there already; and in its reality, the reality of the reconciliation of the human as such, is ideally contained my reconciliation. Yes, mine is there if only I can take hold of it, if only I can make it my own; but how with the sin that adheres to me can this ever be? How can the human-divine ideal ever be my will?

The answer is, Your will it never can be as the will of your private self, so that your private self should become wholly good. To that self you must die, and by faith be made one with the ideal. You must resolve to give up your will, as the mere will of this or that man, and you must put your whole self, your entire will, into the will of the divine. That must be your one self, as it is your true self; that you must hold to both with thought and will, and all other you must renounce; you must both refuse to recognize it as yours, and practically with your whole self deny it. You must believe that you too really are one with the divine, and must act as if you believed it. In short, you must be justified not by works but solely by faith. This doctrine, which Protestantism, to its eternal glory,[1] has made its own and sealed with its blood, is the very centre of Christianity; and, where you have not this in one form or another, there Christianity is nothing but a name.

[1] [Yes, and has too often perverted, to its eternal disgrace.]

In mere morality this faith is impossible. There you have not a real unity of the divine and human, with which to identify yourself; and there again the self, which is outside the ideal, is not known as unreal, and can not be, since the ideal is not all reality.

But what is faith?[1] It is perhaps not an easy question to answer, but in some sort it must be answered; and to neglect it as worthless, or stand aloof from it as a mystery, are both wrong positions. It is easy to say what faith is not. It is not mere belief, the simple holding for true or fact; it is no mere theoretic act of judgement.[2] Every one knows you may have this, and yet not have faith.

Faith does imply belief, but more than this, it implies also will. If my will is not identified with that which I hold for fact, I have not faith in it. Faith is both the belief in the reality of an object, and the will that that object be real; and where either of these elements fails, there is no faith. But even this is not all. When Mr. Bain, for instance (p. 526), says, 'The infant who has found the way to the mother's breast for food, and to her side for warmth, has made progress in the power of faith', we are struck at once by an incongruity. That the child who is most forward in a matter of this sort, is most likely in after life to have what we call faith, we see no reason to believe; that he has it already, we see is an absurdity. And we found above (p. 183) that, even in 'My Station and its Duties', we could not properly speak of faith, because there was there what might be called sight.

What does this point to? Does it mean that faith implies uncertainty, or defective knowledge; and that this is the reason why, where you see, you can not have faith?

---

[1] [I am speaking here of *religious* faith. How far *all* faith is religious, and must be practical, is irrelevant. For this question see *Essays on Truth and Reality*, Chapter II.]

[2] I use belief in the ordinary sense. Of course our account of the matter is wrong if all belief is practical. This Mr. Bain (*Emotions*, ed. ii, p. 524 and foll.) tries to show; as it seems to us, at the expense of facts, and with not sufficient success to warrant our entering on the matter.

No, this we think is a mistaken view, and the facts confute it. Certainly you may have faith without feeling sure of the fact; but, generally speaking, a doubt about the fact weakens faith. Nor is it the case that theoretic certainty excludes faith.[1] If it were so, the raising of belief with doubt to belief without doubt would *ipso facto* destroy faith; and this is not so.

We can not maintain that, when mere belief is raised to speculative certainty, the necessity for faith disappears; or further, that faith is here impossible. We must try to show the cause of the error. What can be said in its favour is this, that sight does exclude faith; and hence faith is not imagined to exist in the Paradise after death, nor, I suppose, in ecstatic vision during life. This is all consistent; but what it points to is the fact that faith is incompatible, not with such and such a *degree*, but with such and such a *kind* of knowledge. Faith is incompatible with common immediate sensuous knowing or with a higher knowledge of the same simple direct nature: and, because our knowledge of the highest is, in religion, not thus immediate, therefore we are said to have *only* faith; and faith is, by a confusion, supposed to exclude, not one kind of certainty, but all kinds. Whence the above mistake, which, however, has a truth in it.

Why is it then that faith is incompatible with sensuous knowledge? It is because, in religious language, faith is a rise beyond 'this world', and a rise in which I stay here. What does this mean? Does it mean that the object must not be a part of the visible world? It means this, and more; faith implies the rise in thought, but not that only; it implies also the rise of the *will* to the object, which is not seen but thought. And this presupposes the practical separation for me of myself and the object. In the mere theoretic rise I do not think of myself, but only of the object: in faith I must also have myself before me; I must perceive the

[1] [So far as faith is *practical*, certainly not. Otherwise it *may* do so —so far at least. It depends on what kind of theoretic certainty it is, and how reached. See again *Essays on Truth and Reality*, Chapter II. See also there for the question whether we can have faith which is not practical.]

chasm between myself, as this or that unreal part of the unreal finite world, and at the same time must perceive the
ideal-real object, which is all reality, and my true reality.
And it is this presupposed consciousness of absolute separation (which, in terms of space or time, we express by 'this
world' and the 'other world') which is necessary for faith,
and which survives therein as a suppressed element. Hence,
where this is not, faith can not be.

Faith then is the recognition of my true self in the religious
object, and the identification of myself with that both by
judgement and will; the determination to negate the self
opposed to the object by making the whole self one with
what it really is. It is, in a word, of the heart.[1] It is the
belief that only the ideal is real, and the will to realize
therefore nothing but the ideal, the theoretical and practical
assertion that only as ideal is the self real.

Justification by faith means that, having thus identified
myself with the object, I feel myself in that identification
to be already one with it, and enjoy the bliss of being, all
falsehood overcome, what I truly am. By my claim to be
one with the ideal, which comprehends me too, and by
assertion of the non-reality of all that is opposed to it, the
evil in the world and the evil incarnate in me through past
bad acts, all this falls into the unreal: I being one with the
ideal, this is not mine, and so imputation of offences goes
with the change of self, and applies not now to my true
self, but to the unreal, which I repudiate and hand over to
destruction.[2]

[1] 'True faith is no mere thought or admission of the truth of a
history.' 'The true Christian is not the man who knows history.'
'Christianity should know that faith is not merely a history or a science.
To have faith is nought else than for a man to make his will one with
God's, and take up God's word and might in his will, so that these
twain, God's will and man's will, turn to one being and substance.
Thereupon, in the man, Christ, in his passion, his dying, his death, and
uprising, in his own humanity, is reckoned for righteousness, so that
the man becomes Christ, that is after the spiritual man. . . . He who
teaches and wills otherwise is yet in the whoredom of Babylon.'—
J. BÖHME.

[2] Hear again the vehement expression of mysticism. 'When reason

In one way faith is of course *only* ideal, for the bad self does not cease. Yet religion is here very different from morality. Recalling to the reader what we said as to the meaning of 'evolution' or 'progress' (p. 191), we say here that morality is an evolution or progress. The end, which is involved in these, is becoming realized *in* the evolution or progress, and therefore is not yet real ; and so in morality we have the end presented as what claims to be real, together with the process of its realization, and that means its non-reality. Here we are not what we are, and must welcome a progress ; though that means a contradiction, which again we know we are not. But for religious faith the end of the evolution is presented as that which, despite the fact of the evolution, is already evolved ; or rather which stands above the element of event, contradiction, and finitude. Despite what seems, we feel that we are more than a progress or evolution, in fact not that at all, but now fully real : and this full reality of ourselves we present to ourselves as an object, and by recognizing, both by judgement and will, in that object our real self, we anticipate, or rather rise above the sphere of, progress. Ourselves being one with that object, we say we are a whole, and harmonious now. So far as we are not so, we are mere appearance ; and by the standing will to negate that seeming self we are one with the true and real self. For this point of view and in this sphere (not outside it) imputation ceases, though the bad self is still a fact ; and in this sense faith remains only ideal.

But that it is in any other sense merely ideal, is a vulgar and gross error, which, so far as it rests on St. Paul, rests on an entire misunderstanding of him. In faith we do not rise by the intellect to an idea, and leave our will somewhere else behind us. Where there is no will to realize the object, there is no faith ; and where there are no works, there is no will. If works cease, will has ceased ; if will has ceased, faith has

tells thee, "Thou art outside God", then answer thou, "No, I am in God, I am in heaven, in it, in him, and for eternity will never leave him. The devil may keep my sins, and the world my flesh ; I live in God's will, his life shall be my life, his will my will ; I will be dead in my reason that he may live in me, and all my deeds shall be his deeds." '

ceased. Faith is not the desperate leap of a moment; in true religion there is no one washing which makes clean. In Pauline language, that ' I have died ', have in idea and by will anticipated the end, proves itself a reality only by the fact that ' I die daily ', do perpetually in my particular acts will the realization of the end which is anticipated. Nor does faith mean simply works; it means the works *of* faith ; it means that the ideal, however incompletely, is realized. But, on the other hand, because the ideal is not realized completely and truly *as* the ideal, therefore I am not justified by the works, which issue from faith, *as* works; since they remain imperfect. I am justified solely and entirely by the ideal identification; the existence of which in me is on the other hand indicated and guaranteed by works, and in its very essence implies them.

What we have now to do is to ask, What is the *object* with which the self is made one by faith ? For our answer to this question we must go to the facts of the Christian consciousness. But the reader must remember that we shall touch these facts solely so far as is necessary to bring out the connexion between religion and morality. We are to keep to a minimum, and the reader must not conclude that we repudiate whatever we say nothing about.

The object, which by faith the self appropriates, is in Christianity nothing alien from and outside the world, not an abstract divine which excludes the human; but it is the inseparable unity of human [1]* and divine. It is the ideal which, as will, affirms itself in and by will; it is will which is one with the ideal. And this whole object, while presented in a finite individual form, is not yet truly presented. It is

---

[1] By the term ' human ' we understand all rational finite mind.*
Whether that exists or not outside our planet is not a matter which concerns us, though it does touch very nearly certain forms of Christian belief.

---

* [Certainly this must *not* include only ' rational ' finite mind. It must include even *more* than what appears to us as mind. The whole of Nature must, *in some sense*, be included and itself will the Divine, e. g. ' My brother the sun '.]

known, in its truth, not until it is apprehended as an organic human-divine totality; as one body with diverse members, as one self which, in many selves, realizes, wills, and loves itself, as they do themselves in it.

And for faith this object is the real, and the only real. What seems to oppose it is, if fact, not reality: and this seeming fact has two forms: one the imperfection and evil in the heart, the inner self; and the other the imperfection and evil in the world of which my external self is a part. In both these spheres, the inner and outer, the object of religion is real; and the object has two corresponding sides, the inner and personal, and the external side; which two sides are sides of a single whole.

Faith involves the belief (1) that the course of the external world, despite appearances, is the realization of the ideal will; (2) that on the inner side the human and divine are one: or the belief (1) that the world is the realization of humanity as a divine organic whole;[1] and (2) that with that whole the inner wills of particular persons are identified. Faith must hold that, in biblical language, there is 'a kingdom of God', that there is an organism which realizes itself in its members, and also in those members, on the subjective side, wills and is conscious of itself, as they will and are conscious of themselves in it.

If the reader will refer back to 'My Station and its Duties' (p. 177), he will see that what we had there in the relative totality of the political organism, we have here once more, though with a difference. That difference is that (1) what there was finite (one amongst and against others) is here infinite (a whole in itself), and what there was in a manner visible is here invisible; (2) the relation of the particular subject to the whole was there immediate unity by unreflecting habituation and direct perception; here it involves the

---

[1] I need not say that here are very great difficulties. Apart from others, the relation of the physical world to the divine will is a well-known problem. But we have nothing to do with the (possible or impossible) solution of these questions. We have to keep to what is contained in the religious consciousness, and that we take to be as above.

thought which rises above the given, and the consciousness of a presupposed and suppressed estrangement.

Here, as in the world of my station, we have the objective side, the many affirmations of the one will, the one body, the real ideal humanity, which in all its members is the same, although in every one it is different ; and which is completely realized not in only one this or that, nor in any mere 'collective unity' of such particulars, but only in the whole as a whole. And we have the subjective personal side, where the one will of the whole is, in its unity with the conscious members, self-conscious, and wills itself as the personal identity of the universal and particular will.[1]

[1] By faith, and so far as faith holds, the ideal as the self, and the self as the ideal, is all that is real ; and so, on the external side of my works, I regard myself as, with others, the member or function of the divine whole. What falls outside, however much a fact, is still unreal. Again, on the inside, through faith I, as the mere this me, no longer am ; but only I as the self-conscious personal will of the divine, the spirit of the whole, which, as that spirit, knows itself in me. On both sides, though the form is not swallowed up nor lost, yet the mere particular content of the self has for faith disappeared.

But there is a difference on the two sides, which was also there in 'My Station', but the losing sight of which was there not likely to lead to confusion ; while here a confusion on this head may happen, and is a serious matter. To explain—on the inside the particular self knows and feels itself now immediately one with the universal, which is the will of all selves ; but on the outside, its realization in works, it is only one member of the whole, one function or set of functions which is not, and which falls outside of, other sides or sets of functions. So long as it remains on the inside, the self is not apart from other selves ; it is when it comes out to act that it is forced to distinguish itself.*

It is quite true that, when we act, on the inside also the whole will is for each person diverse ; for it is not a universal which remains inert. It is presented in a specialized form as what is a relative 'to be done' in such and such a case, which, if reflected on, is seen to be *not* other cases—but on the inner side this reflection, and hence this discrimination,* does not exist. The member feels and knows itself, not as this member distinct from that member, but (since for faith the bad self is not) immediately one with the will of the entire organism. On the outside, on the other hand, the knowledge of its distinctness is forced

* [This goes, I think, too far. What ceases is the possibility of opposition and of separation in spirit. The consciousness of oneness does not exclude *more* than this.]

Such is the object, the fore-realized divine ideal; and by faith the particular man has to make that his, to identify himself therewith, behold and feel himself therewith identified, and in his own self-consciousness have the witness of it. And this, as we explained, is done by the dying to the private self as such, by the bestowal of it on the object, and by the living in the self which is one with the divine ideal that is felt and known as the only real self, and now too as my self. To our previous remarks on this head we have nothing to add, and must proceed to discuss more closely the relation of religion to morality.[1]

These, as we saw, are to a certain extent the same; and the question at once arises, Has the divine will of the religious consciousness any other content than the moral ideal? We answer, Certainly not. Religion is practical; it means doing something which is a duty. Apart from duties, there is no duty; and as all moral duties are also religious, so all religious duties are also moral.[2]

In order to be, religion must do. Its practice is the realization of the ideal in me and in the world. Separate religion from the real world, and you will find it has nothing left it to do; it becomes a form, and so ceases. The practical content which religion carries out comes from the state, society, art, and science. But the whole of this sphere is the world of morality, and all our duties there are moral duties. And if this is so, then this religious duty may collide with that religious duty, just as one moral duty may be contrary to another; but that religion, as such, should be in collision with morality, as such, is out of the question.

upon it. There its realization is indeed the affirmation of the will of the whole, but the entire whole is not there; some of it is elsewhere, and, as a whole, it is realized only in the whole, which this or that man is not. In its works the self-conscious function finds that it is not other functions; it remains finite, and all possibility of the confounding the merely human with the divine is excluded.

[1] [Religion and Morality. Cf. *Essays on Truth and Reality* (pp. 441-2, ED.).]

[2] Religion in the sense of the cultus, &c., will be considered lower down.

So far religion and morality are the same; though, as we have seen, they are also different. The main difference is that what in morality only is to be, in religion somehow and somewhere really is, and what we are to do is done. Whether it is thought of as what is done now, or what will be done hereafter, makes in this respect no practical difference. They are different ways of looking at the same thing; and, whether present or future, the reality is equally certain. The importance for practice of this religious point of view is that what is to be done is approached, not with the knowledge of a doubtful success, but with the fore-felt certainty of already accomplished victory.

Morality, the process of realization, thus survives within religion. It is only as mere morality that it vanishes; as an element it remains and is stimulated. Not only is strength increased by assurance of success, but in addition the importance of success is magnified. The individual life for religion is one with the divine; it possesses infinite worth, a value no terms can express. And the bad gains a corresponding intensity of badness. It is infinitely evil, so that, for the religious consciousness, different amounts of badness are not measurable. All men are equally, because utterly, sinful. But this extreme of evil is therefore the more easy to subdue. It is not a reality against a mere ideal, but a mere fact which is contrary to the whole reality, an unutterable contradiction. Other incentives to good also come in. For the religious consciousness evil is an offence against what we love, and what loves us, not against something not real,[1] which no one can well love. This makes evil worse, and more painful, and increases accordingly the power of good. All external control disappears, and in its place is gratitude to that which has conquered, confidence in it, and inability to be false to it.[2]

---

[1] [But (as the foot-note says) this is not the case in *all* morality, only in abstract morality.]

[2] We had this, too, in ' My Station and its Duties '. Let me remark that, if humanity is a collection, active gratitude to it is impossible without the most childish self-delusion. Unless there is a real identity

It is the same objective will, which in 'My Station' we
see accomplished, in ideal morality know should be accomplished, and in religion by faith believe accomplished, which
reflects itself into itself on the subjective side, and thence
reasserts itself explicitly as the real identity of the human and
divine will. And so the content of religion and morality is the
same, though the spirit in which it is done is widely different.

But all this, we may be told, though true to a certain
extent, is one-sided; there is religion beyond all this. And
this objection must be attended to. We have never lost
sight of the fact it rests upon, although we may have seemed
to do so. That fact is what some would call religion proper,
the creed, the public cultus, and the sphere of private
devotion. These we must now consider, but no further than
we are obliged, i. e. so far as the question is touched, Has
religious duty another content than the moral content?

Put in this way, the question is on our view of morality
absurd. If anything ought to be done, then it must be a
moral duty; and the notion of religious duty, as such, outside of and capable of colliding with moral duty as such, is
preposterous nonsense. If it is a religious duty to be
'religious', then it is also a moral duty to be religious;
precisely as, if it is a moral duty to be moral, it is also a
religious duty to be moral.

A better way to put the question is, Does passing from
the mere moral sphere into the religious introduce a new
order of duties, to take in which morality has now to be
extended? That, however, is again an improper question,
since, if it is right to be thus 'religious', we have no business
previously to narrow morality, i. e. to exclude religiousness
from the ideal which morality is to realize. It seems quite
plain that the sphere of morality is the sphere of practice,
and the sphere of practice is the sphere of morality. There

in men, the 'Inasmuch as ye did it to the least of these' becomes an
absurdity. And I have never heard of any one who, owing a debt to
one man, thought he could pay it by giving to another man who was
like the first, no matter how like.

is no escaping this conclusion; and then, so far as religion is practical, the worlds of morality and religion must coincide.

What is really at issue is this, *Is* religion altogether practical? Is, that is to say, the theoretical element of it co-ordinate with, or subordinate to, the practical element? Does religion, like art and science, include a theoretical sphere, which in respect of its production in and by the subject is practice, but, in itself and as produced, is not so? And next, if there is such a region, how does it stand to practice? Is it subsidiary to that, or is it an end in itself, when not brought under the practical end? And then further, how in respect of such a region is morality situated?

Instead of trying to give direct answers, the best way to clear the matter will be to begin with the extreme of a one-sided view: and, first, there is an opinion which may be said simply to identify religion with orthodoxy, with the holding for true what is true. No doubt right doctrine is a very important matter, but does that make it religion? Put it to the religious consciousness, and the answer is, No. It is the belief 'with the heart' that is wanted; and where that is not, religion is not. Else even the very devils would be religious; for they, as we are told, go further even than is required of them, and add to orthodoxy the fear of God.

So, in morality, a man must know what is right; but no one is moral simply because he has that knowledge. In both cases you can not do, without knowing what you are to do; but mere knowing, apart from doing, is neither religion nor morality.

The next modification of this one-sided opinion is the view, which is all too popular, and says, 'No doubt it is true that to know is not enough; action ought to follow; but, for all that, it is religion when I say my prayers, or meditate, or go to church, and that whether it goes any further, and whether anything comes of it, or not'.

By denying such a doctrine we ought not to give offence to Christians. Whether we shall give offence or not is another matter. We are sorry if it is so; but nevertheless we deny the assertion, and we think that on our side we have the religious consciousness[1] and the New Testament. There we do not have the love of God and man put side by side, as things which exist or can exist apart, but, where the latter fails there fails, also the former, and with it, I suppose, religion. There we are told that 'pure religion' means duty to the afflicted, and the 'world', by which we are not to be spotted, is hardly all spheres outside our devotions, not every region where the authority of the clergyman ceases.

We maintain that neither church-going, meditation, nor prayer, except so far as it reacts on practice and subserves that, is religious at all. Aesthetic or speculative contemplation it may be; it may be a production of the feeling *at least in part*, which results from the satisfied religious will; but religious it is not, except so far as it means will to do: and it is not that will, except so far as it manifests itself in religious-moral acts, external or internal—acts, that is, which realize the social, ideal-social, or ideal self, or again which are means to such realization.

It is the same with morality. I may retire into my conscience, enjoy there the happiness of virtue, edify myself with, and find pleasure in, the contemplation of it in myself or others; but that by itself is surely not moral. It may be a good thing to do this, but, if so, it is a good only so far as it strengthens the will for good, and so issues in practice. If it go beyond that, it is at best harmless; but it may be, and more often is, pernicious and positively immoral. To dwell on the satisfaction which comes from right doing need not be wrong, but it is very dangerous, it is a most slippery position; for the moment it leads us to enjoyment which does not arise from function, or does not react to stimulate function, then, from that moment, it is bad and goes to corrupt.

If a man were to please himself with thoughts of virtue, and then go out, neglect the virtue, and fall into the vice,

---

[1] I am happy to say that 'religieux' has no English equivalent.*

* [This is not true except of Modern English only. And, in any case, it won't do, and was wrong and due to ignorance. However secluded the religious life, it may be practical indirectly *if* through the unity of the spiritual body it can be taken as vicarious.]

would that be morality? But if a man does the same by religion, there are people who call it 'religious'.

The true doctrine is, that devotional exercises, and sacraments, and church-goings, not only should not and ought not to go by themselves, but that by themselves they simply are not religious at all. They are the isolating a sphere of religion which, so isolated, loses the character of religion, and is often even positively sinful, a hollow mockery of the divine, which takes the enjoyment without giving the activity, and degenerates into what may be well enough as aesthetic or contemplative, but, for all that, is both irreligious and immoral. By themselves, when religiously considered, these things are not ends at all; they are so only when they are means to faith, and so to will, and so to practice in the world.

But how is it that such one-sided views, such gross mistakes, are possible? This is not very hard to understand. And in the first place

(1) Both in the moral and religious will is implied knowledge, and it obviously matters for practice what a man does know. Hence correct views are wanted; and this, which so far is true, is then twisted into making religion consist in the having right opinions, or in orthodoxy. But as we have seen, the presence of the religious object for the theoretical consciousness, in any form, is not religion.

(2) The second mistake is more common. In morality what we know we feel or see, and can not doubt. There is nothing to believe against appearances. We have a claim and the consciousness that this is satisfied or unsatisfied, but nothing beyond ourselves to hold for true; except so far as in the social object it is before our eyes. But in religion, despite of appearances, we have to believe that something is real. We must have an inward assurance that the reality is above the facts; and we must carry that out against facts in which we can not see the inward reality, and seem to see what is contrary thereto. It is by faith in our reconcilement with the invisible one reality that we are justified.

That inward assurance, the self-consciousness that we are

one with the divine, and one with others because one with the divine, naturally does not exist without expressing itself. And moreover it is right that it should express itself; because that expression reacts most powerfully upon the self-consciousness, to intensify it, and so strengthen the conviction and will in which faith consists. It is right that the certainty of identity with the divine, and with others in the divine, should be brought home by the foretasted pleasure of unalloyed union; and that in short is the rationale of the cultus. The cultus is a means to the strengthening of faith, and is an end in itself by subserving that end. As anything more and beyond it is not an end; it may be harmless, and again it may be the destruction of true religion.

And the religious community entails signs of communion; and these, as the cultus generally, entail ministers; and it is generally found more convenient to have certain persons set apart, just as again the state generally finds it convenient to support and regulate one or more religious communities.[1] These ministers, however appointed, are a means to a means to the end; and here we have the rationale of the clerical office.

You can have true religion without sacraments or public worship, and again both without clergymen; just as you can have clergymen and sacraments without true religion. And if some of the clergy think that they stand in a more intimate relation with the divine Spirit than the rest of the community do, then they both go against the first principles

---

[1] Religious communities may be called 'churches'; but churches in this sense must not be confounded with the Church proper. That is the whole body of Christ, and whether it is limited or not depends on the answer to the question whether the spirit of Christ is limited; whether it is visible or not, is answered with that answer; as also the questions whether it can be divided, re-united, and so forth. A true view of the Church is of the last importance. From that view, in our opinion, it follows that in the one Church proper there is no hierarchy, no spiritual superior, and can be none, because the spirit of Christianity excludes such things. Wherever there are ecclesiastical superiors (as it is convenient that there should be), there *ipso facto* you have a finite religious body, which, as a consequence, can not be nor represent the Church proper.

of Christianity, and moreover any one, who does not shut his eyes, can see that the facts of life confute them. What Christianity, if we mistake not, tells them is that, their gifts and functions being not those of others, they have the one spirit in another way from others ; but when they want to go from an 'other' to a 'higher', then we must tell them that there are steps wanted to reach that conclusion, and such steps as Christianity can not admit.

The sum of the matter is this. Practical faith is the end , and what helps that is good, because that is good ; and where a religious ordinance does not help that, there it is not good. And often it may do worse than not help, and then it is positively hurtful.

So with religious exercises, and what too exclusively is called personal piety. They are religious if they are the simple expression of, or helps to, religion ; and if not, then they are not religious, and perhaps even irreligious. Religion issues in the practical realizing of the reconcilement; and where there is no such realization, there is no faith, and no religion.

Neither against the clergy, nor the sacraments, nor private devotion am I saying one word ; and the reader who so understands me altogether misunderstands me. For a large number of our clergy I have a sincere personal respect, and there is scarcely any office [1] which in my eyes is higher than that of the minister. And I recognize fully the general necessity both for private devotion and public worship. It is the abuse, and the excess of them, against which we have to protest. Whatever is the expression of the religious spirit, which carries itself out in the world, is religious and good, unless it goes to excess ; and the excess is measured by the failure to strengthen, or the weakening of, the will. Just so any institution, observance, or discipline (it matters not what) which strengthens the religious will, is good, provided it does so strengthen it as a whole, and is not in other ways contrary to religion and morality. The same holds

[1] [Is there *any*? Is any one 'office' really higher than another? Or was I thinking of the self-sacrifice entailed in some modes of life?]

good in the moral sphere; there we may have ascetic exercises which strengthen the will, and are therefore, and so far as they do that, good; but not good, or even bad, when they go beyond. But as to what in detail is legitimate or not, all this is matter of particular fact, with which we have nothing to do.

To repeat, public and private exercises are religious and good as the simple voice of, or as means to the strengthening of, the religious will. That will consists in the faith that overcomes the world, by turning it into the Christian world which for faith it is. The inner sphere of religion, which brings home to itself its assurance and its bliss, is only the inner sphere, and by itself is not religion. By itself it is not even the inner, for it is so only when it is the inner of the outer; and that outer, where faith fails, is not, and with it goes the inner as such. A sensuous or semi-sensuous gloating over the pleasures of the anticipated result is, in morals as in religion, when considered in reference to the will, at least not moral, and may degenerate into a mere debauchery. Here as there it is the Hedonism which kills practice; and considered as θεωρία, it belongs to art or science, not religion at all. Furthermore sensitiveness or intensity of the religious consciousness is no more religion than that of the moral consciousness is morality; nor again is a right perception in these matters any more than a right perception. It is religion only when the divine will, of which for faith the world is the realization, reflects itself in us, and, with the personal energy of our own and its self-consciousness, carries out both its and our will into the world, which is its own and ours, and gives us, in the feeling which results from function, that inner assurance of identity which precedes and accompanies the action of our will. And thus for religion and morality the content of the will is the same, though the knowledge and the spirit are widely different.

If this is so, then our Essays have, in a way too imperfect, yet brought us to the end, where morality is removed and survives in its fulfilment. In our journey we have not seen

much, and much that we have seen was perhaps little worth
the effort, or might have been had without it. Be that as it
may, the hunt after pleasure in any shape has proved itself
a delusion, and the form of duty a snare, and the finite realization of ' my station ' was truth indeed, and a happiness that
called to us to stay, but was too narrow to satisfy wholly the
spirit's hunger; and ideal morality brought the sickening
sense of inevitable failure. Here where we are landed at last,
the process is at an end, though the best activity here first
begins. Here our morality is consummated in oneness with
God, and everywhere we find that ' immortal Love', which
builds itself for ever on contradiction, but in which the
contradiction is eternally resolved.

> Hic nullus labor est, raborque nullus;
> Hoc juvit, juvat, et diu juvabit ;
> Hoc non deficit, incipitque semper.

Note.—While these last sheets were going through the press, Mr.
Harrison's article (*Cont. Rev.*, May 1876) appeared, and touches so
nearly on much that I have said, that it seems advisable to make some
remarks upon it, taking it as it stands, and without any reference to
Comte's own views, with which I am not acquainted.

What I have to remark first is, that with the leading idea of Mr.
Harrison's creed a man may be familiar, and substantially, perhaps,
in agreement, without having come into contact, direct or indirect,
with Positivism. Whoever may claim to have originated it, it was
distinctly set forth forty years ago by Strauss, in intimate connexion
with the speculative metaphysic of the first quarter of the century.
(See an interesting article in the same number of the *C. R.*) It took
its place in German literature as a metaphysical interpretation of the
central doctrine of Christianity.

Mr. Harrison appears to believe that in his case the element of
metaphysic at least is absent. And here, I think, he makes a great
mistake. For what is implied in his *credo*? He seems to hold that
humanity is the evolution of an organic whole, while at the same time
he asserts that it is 'a collective unity', and that its evolution is 'a
collective evolution'. Here we are at once in the midst of metaphysic ;
and, so far as I understand the matter, of *bad* metaphysic. To me the
evolution of a collection * means the evolutions of the units of that

---

* [The point here is that 'evolution' and 'collection' don't har-
monize, if collection means mere 'aggregate'. Mr. Harrison would

collection, and it means no more. To Mr. Harrison it seems to mean a great deal more. He seems to believe that in his collection there is a real identity, which under changes of component parts is permanent and the *same*; an identity, further, not of mere material particles or of lorce in general, but a *human* identity. If this is his belief, what is the basis of it? What is the *ground* for his assertion that in past, present (and future?) human beings there is a real self-sameness? I find no hint of any ground in the article; and while no one, who knows what metaphysic is, can doubt that in the above assertion we have metaphysic, it is hard to stifle the doubt whether we have not also mere dogmatic metaphysic.

But I may be doing the writer a wrong. Perhaps he does not affirm that, under differences, humanity is one and the same real being. Perhaps all that he means is that the summed particular *effects* of past and present human lives are existing in, and can be recognized by, the individual. If so, then, unless we are once more to have a metaphysical doctrine of the identity of cause and effect, this commonplace mechanical view is but a small foundation for Mr. Harrison's superstructure.

Collective humanity is at any rate *organic*; and that seems to be the reason for the somewhat strange denial of a 'collective force' to the universe as a whole (p. 874). In his definition of an organism the writer seems to me to introduce the ideas of identity and teleology (877). If so, we have once more metaphysical doctrine. If not so, then (*vide* Essay V, p. 191) the evolution of humanity is a phrase which has no meaning. In the one case what becomes of the writer's position against the metaphysicians? In the other, what becomes of his religion and his rhetoric?

But, passing by this, what reason is put forward for the belief that humanity is an organism? Mr. Harrison starts from the *social* organism—a conception, by the way, not wholly unknown to the metaphysic of the beginning of this century. Let that be as it may, how are we to go from the organism of the state to the organism of humanity? Admit the metaphysical assertion, that civilization is 'the activity of a being just as real as you or 1, and far more permanent' (879)—but does history, after all, verify the belief that all or most of the perished millions who have covered this globe have entered into the main stream of civilization? Does observation of facts now show that all or most of the dwellers on this globe are organically connected? To show mere reciprocal influence is not enough; for that holds good also of mere physical phenomena. Will observation warrant more than the hope that some day, we know not when, humanity may *become* an organic whole (cf. Trendelenburg, *Naturrecht*, 610)?

After all this, it may be idle to say anything about religion; but I

probably admit that, and he uses 'collective' in a vague sense only (as others do).]

must point out that, even if humanity be more than the name of an imaginary collection, even if it really is a self-same being which evolves itself amid change of particles, and in which we are members—even then it can not be the object of modern religion. Our minds and hearts are not bounded to one among the phenomena of this one among the bodies in the universe ; and to attempt to set this finite phenomenon before us as an object of worship is an attempt to turn the history of religion backwards, and to close on us once more those Jewish fetters which Christian civilization, after so many efforts, has burst through. If humanity is adorable, it is so only because it is *not* merely the last product of terrestrial development, but because the idea of the identity of God and man is the absolute truth, because finite rational mind (wherever it exist) is not *merely* such, but, in another sense than physical or animal nature, is the self-realization of the Spirit in which all moves and lives, and so is an organic whole in that unity. Such a thesis I do not affirm, and to the enormous difficulties which beset it I am not blind. A scientific basis can be given to it, if at all, by a critical metaphysic, whose problems begin where Mr. Harrison's end, and which asks where he dogmatizes. But whether such a science is possible or impossible, after all a great religion is still a great religion ; nor is it easy to believe that it will not be so, when another of the sects which have lived and live in its life has gone the way it seems likely to go.*

---

* [The fact is, I believe, that since the revival of the study of philosophy in England some sixty years ago *no* young man who has studied philosophy has joined the Positivists. How much better it would have been if Mr. Harrison and others, while advocating Positivism, had shown some knowledge of, and sympathy with, the course of European speculation in the first quarter of the nineteenth century.]